los bros hernandez

duck feet

FANTAGRAPHICS BOOKS A Love and Rockets Collection

Love and Rockets Book 6:

Duck Feet

Fantagraphics Books
7563 Lake City Way NE
Seattle Washington 98115

Editor: Gary Groth
Art Director: Peppy White
Front cover colored by Jim Woodring
Back cover colored by Monster X

First Fantagraphics Books edition: May, 1989
Second Fantagraphics Books edition: October, 1995

ISBN: 0 930193 81 4
PRINTED IN CANADA

los bros hernandez

duck feet

FANTAGRAPHICS BOOKS A Love and Rockets Collection

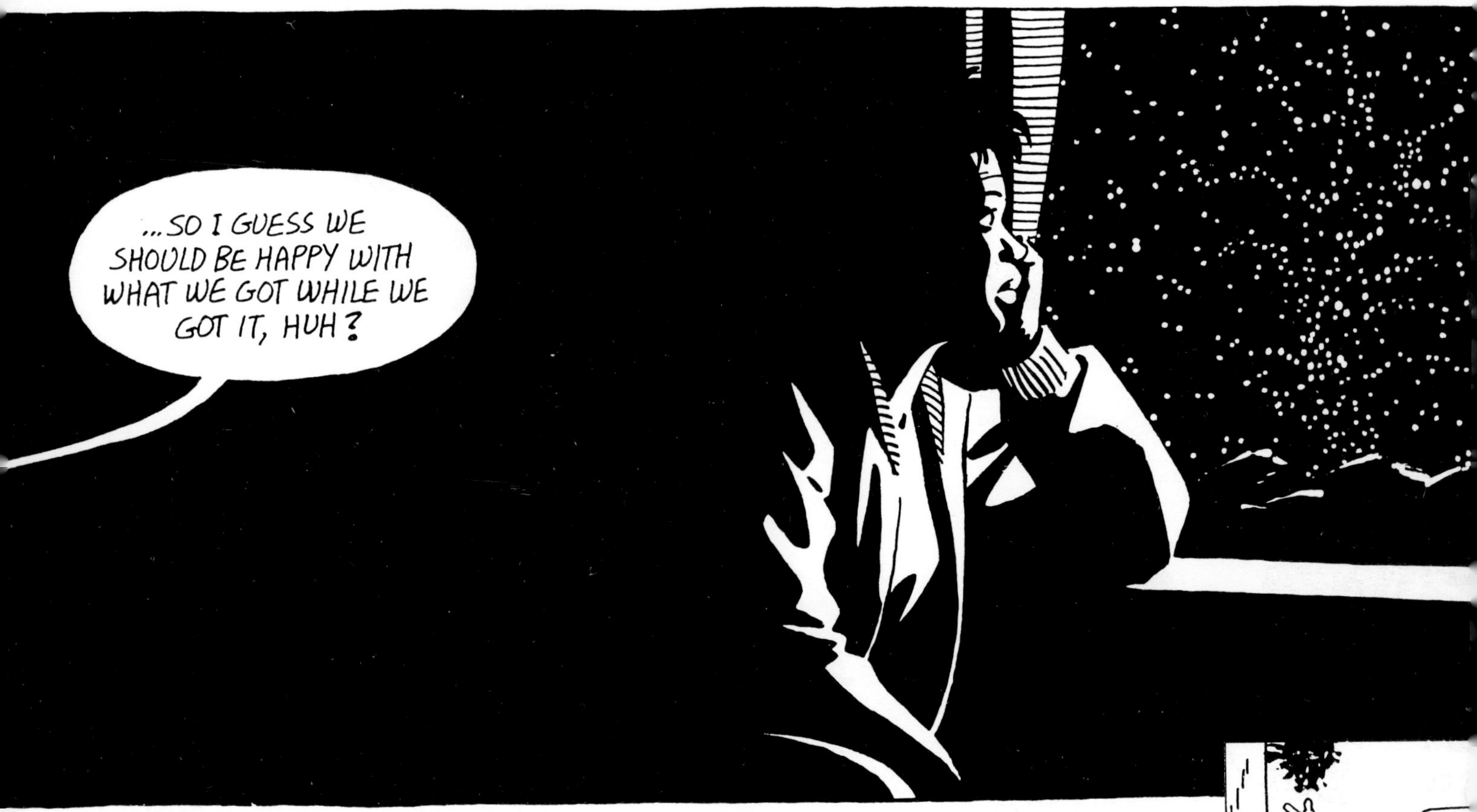
...SO I GUESS WE SHOULD BE HAPPY WITH WHAT WE GOT WHILE WE GOT IT, HUH?

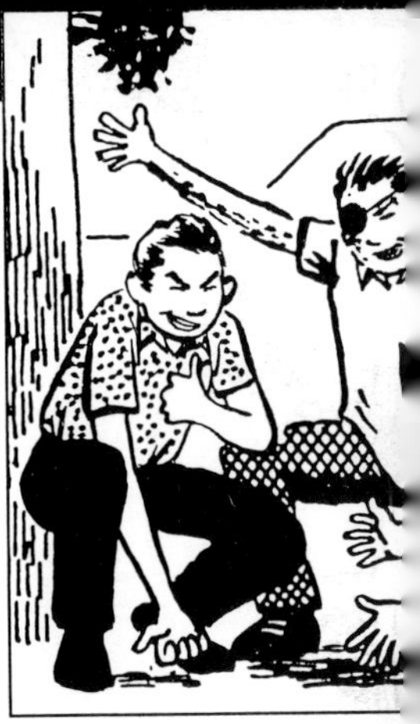

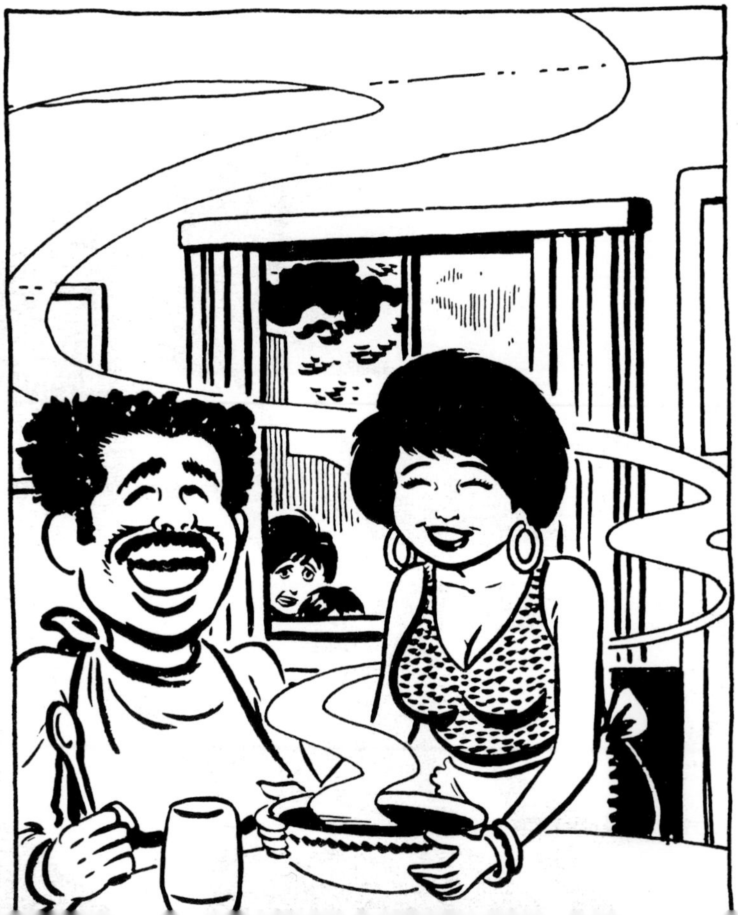

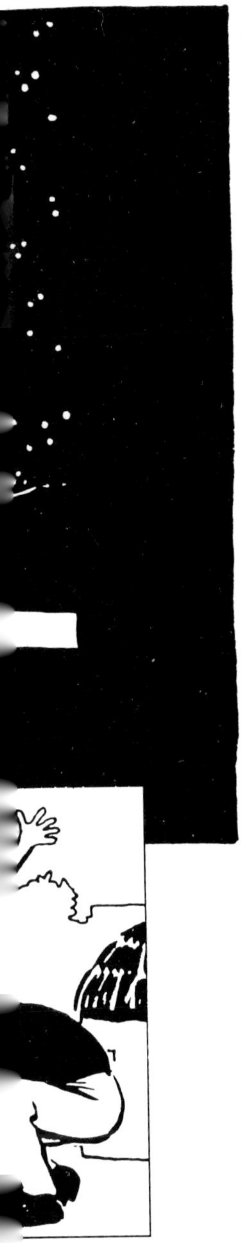

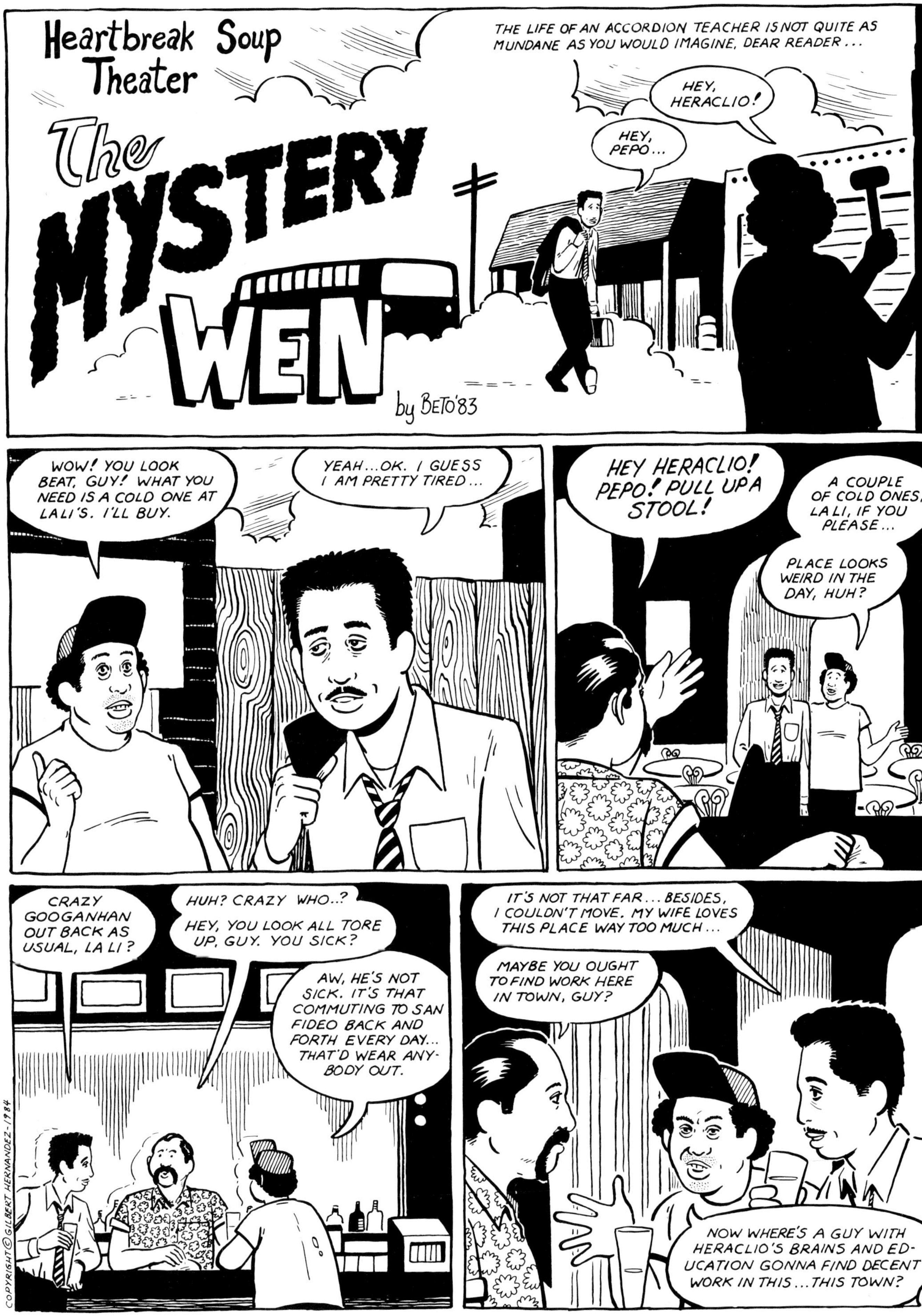
Heartbreak Soup Theater
The MYSTERY WEN
by BETO '83
THE LIFE OF AN ACCORDION TEACHER IS NOT QUITE AS MUNDANE AS YOU WOULD IMAGINE, DEAR READER . . .
HEY, HERACLIO!
HEY, PEPO . . .
WOW! YOU LOOK BEAT, GUY! WHAT YOU NEED IS A COLD ONE AT LALI'S. I'LL BUY.
YEAH...OK. I GUESS I AM PRETTY TIRED . . .
HEY HERACLIO! PEPO! PULL UP A STOOL!
A COUPLE OF COLD ONES, LALI, IF YOU PLEASE . . .
PLACE LOOKS WEIRD IN THE DAY, HUH?
CRAZY GOOGANHAN OUT BACK AS USUAL, LALI?
HUH? CRAZY WHO..?
HEY, YOU LOOK ALL TORE UP, GUY. YOU SICK?
AW, HE'S NOT SICK. IT'S THAT COMMUTING TO SAN FIDEO BACK AND FORTH EVERY DAY... THAT'D WEAR ANYBODY OUT.
IT'S NOT THAT FAR . . . BESIDES, I COULDN'T MOVE. MY WIFE LOVES THIS PLACE WAY TOO MUCH . . .
MAYBE YOU OUGHT TO FIND WORK HERE IN TOWN, GUY?
NOW WHERE'S A GUY WITH HERACLIO'S BRAINS AND EDUCATION GONNA FIND DECENT WORK IN THIS . . . THIS TOWN?
1
COPYRIGHT © GILBERT HERNANDEZ - 1984

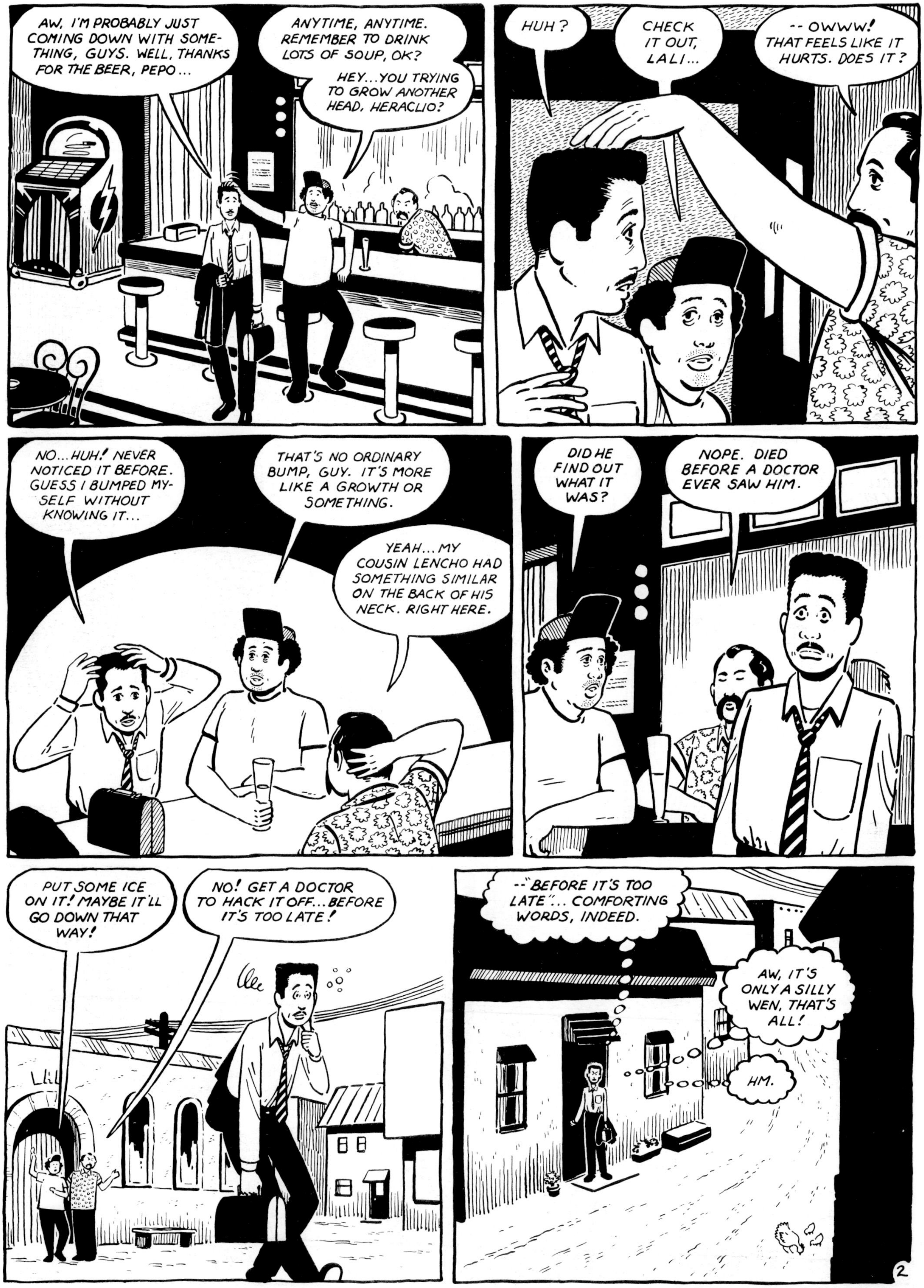
AW, I'M PROBABLY JUST COMING DOWN WITH SOMETHING, GUYS. WELL, THANKS FOR THE BEER, PEPO...
ANYTIME, ANYTIME. REMEMBER TO DRINK LOTS OF SOUP, OK?
HEY...YOU TRYING TO GROW ANOTHER HEAD, HERACLIO?
HUH?
CHECK IT OUT, LALI...
-- OWWW! THAT FEELS LIKE IT HURTS. DOES IT?
NO...HUH! NEVER NOTICED IT BEFORE. GUESS I BUMPED MYSELF WITHOUT KNOWING IT...
THAT'S NO ORDINARY BUMP, GUY. IT'S MORE LIKE A GROWTH OR SOMETHING.
YEAH...MY COUSIN LENCHO HAD SOMETHING SIMILAR ON THE BACK OF HIS NECK. RIGHT HERE.
DID HE FIND OUT WHAT IT WAS?
NOPE. DIED BEFORE A DOCTOR EVER SAW HIM.
PUT SOME ICE ON IT! MAYBE IT'LL GO DOWN THAT WAY!
NO! GET A DOCTOR TO HACK IT OFF...BEFORE IT'S TOO LATE!
--"BEFORE IT'S TOO LATE"... COMFORTING WORDS, INDEED.
AW, IT'S ONLY A SILLY WEN, THAT'S ALL!
HM.
2

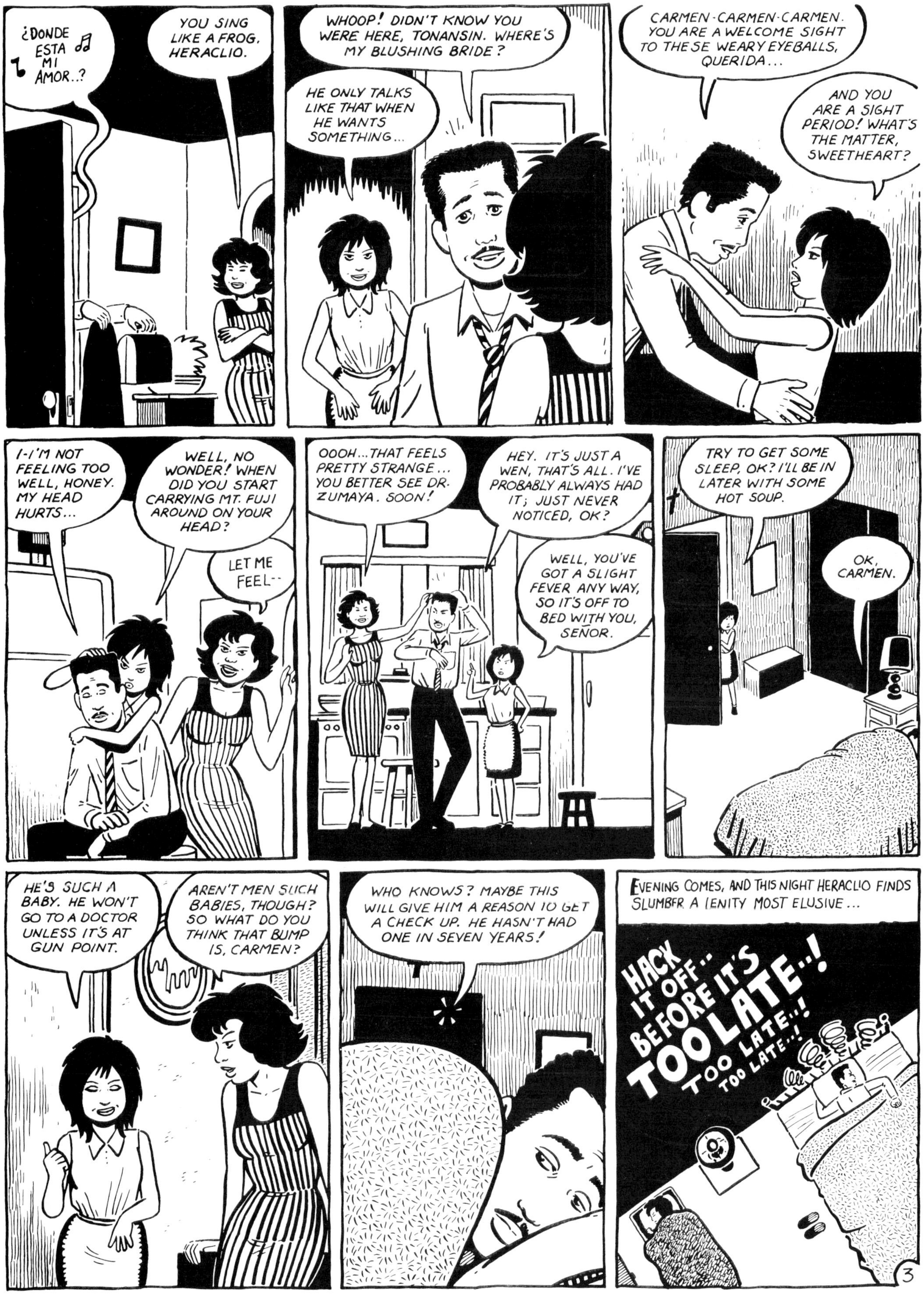
¿DONDE ESTA MI AMOR..?
YOU SING LIKE A FROG, HERACLIO.
WHOOP! DIDN'T KNOW YOU WERE HERE, TONANSIN. WHERE'S MY BLUSHING BRIDE?
HE ONLY TALKS LIKE THAT WHEN HE WANTS SOMETHING...
CARMEN-CARMEN-CARMEN. YOU ARE A WELCOME SIGHT TO THESE WEARY EYEBALLS, QUERIDA...
AND YOU ARE A SIGHT PERIOD! WHAT'S THE MATTER, SWEETHEART?
I-I'M NOT FEELING TOO WELL, HONEY. MY HEAD HURTS...
WELL, NO WONDER! WHEN DID YOU START CARRYING MT. FUJI AROUND ON YOUR HEAD?
LET ME FEEL--
OOOH... THAT FEELS PRETTY STRANGE... YOU BETTER SEE DR. ZUMAYA. SOON!
HEY. IT'S JUST A WEN, THAT'S ALL. I'VE PROBABLY ALWAYS HAD IT; JUST NEVER NOTICED, OK?
WELL, YOU'VE GOT A SLIGHT FEVER ANY WAY, SO IT'S OFF TO BED WITH YOU, SEÑOR.
TRY TO GET SOME SLEEP, OK? I'LL BE IN LATER WITH SOME HOT SOUP.
OK, CARMEN.
HE'S SUCH A BABY. HE WON'T GO TO A DOCTOR UNLESS IT'S AT GUN POINT.
AREN'T MEN SUCH BABIES, THOUGH? SO WHAT DO YOU THINK THAT BUMP IS, CARMEN?
WHO KNOWS? MAYBE THIS WILL GIVE HIM A REASON TO GET A CHECK UP. HE HASN'T HAD ONE IN SEVEN YEARS!
EVENING COMES, AND THIS NIGHT HERACLIO FINDS SLUMBER A LENITY MOST ELUSIVE...
HACK IT OFF.. BEFORE IT'S TOO LATE..! TOO LATE..! TOO LATE..!
3

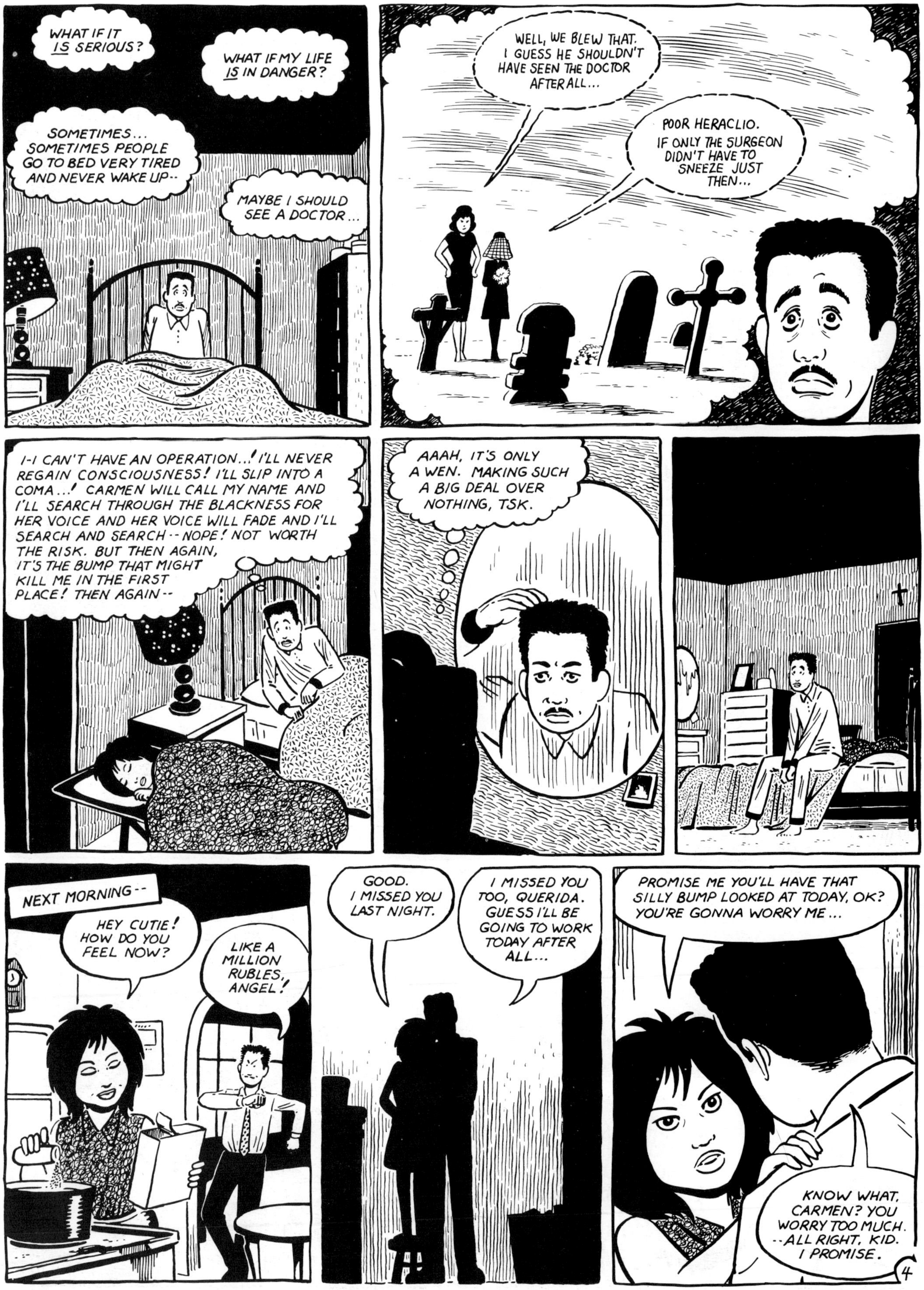

WHAT IF IT IS SERIOUS?
WHAT IF MY LIFE IS IN DANGER?
SOMETIMES... SOMETIMES PEOPLE GO TO BED VERY TIRED AND NEVER WAKE UP--
MAYBE I SHOULD SEE A DOCTOR...
WELL, WE BLEW THAT. I GUESS HE SHOULDN'T HAVE SEEN THE DOCTOR AFTER ALL...
POOR HERACLIO. IF ONLY THE SURGEON DIDN'T HAVE TO SNEEZE JUST THEN...
I-I CAN'T HAVE AN OPERATION...! I'LL NEVER REGAIN CONSCIOUSNESS! I'LL SLIP INTO A COMA...! CARMEN WILL CALL MY NAME AND I'LL SEARCH THROUGH THE BLACKNESS FOR HER VOICE AND HER VOICE WILL FADE AND I'LL SEARCH AND SEARCH--NOPE! NOT WORTH THE RISK. BUT THEN AGAIN, IT'S THE BUMP THAT MIGHT KILL ME IN THE FIRST PLACE! THEN AGAIN--
AAAH, IT'S ONLY A WEN. MAKING SUCH A BIG DEAL OVER NOTHING, TSK.
NEXT MORNING--
HEY CUTIE! HOW DO YOU FEEL NOW?
LIKE A MILLION RUBLES, ANGEL!
GOOD. I MISSED YOU LAST NIGHT.
I MISSED YOU TOO, QUERIDA. GUESS I'LL BE GOING TO WORK TODAY AFTER ALL...
PROMISE ME YOU'LL HAVE THAT SILLY BUMP LOOKED AT TODAY, OK? YOU'RE GONNA WORRY ME...
KNOW WHAT, CARMEN? YOU WORRY TOO MUCH. --ALL RIGHT, KID. I PROMISE.

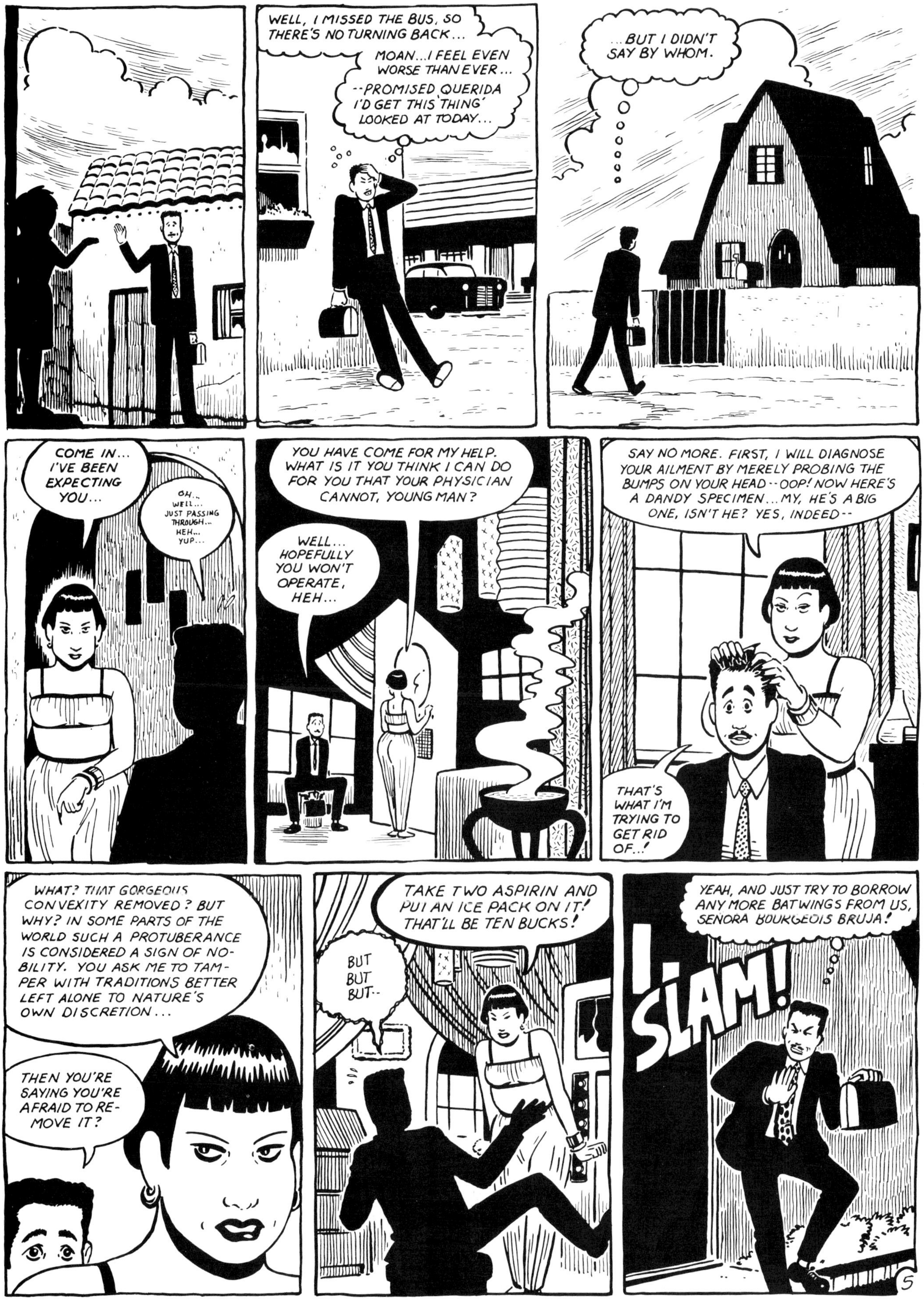
WELL, I MISSED THE BUS, SO THERE'S NO TURNING BACK...
MOAN...I FEEL EVEN WORSE THAN EVER...
--PROMISED QUERIDA I'D GET THIS 'THING' LOOKED AT TODAY...
...BUT I DIDN'T SAY BY WHOM.
COME IN... I'VE BEEN EXPECTING YOU...
OH... WELL... JUST PASSING THROUGH... HEH... YUP...
YOU HAVE COME FOR MY HELP. WHAT IS IT YOU THINK I CAN DO FOR YOU THAT YOUR PHYSICIAN CANNOT, YOUNG MAN?
WELL... HOPEFULLY YOU WON'T OPERATE, HEH...
SAY NO MORE. FIRST, I WILL DIAGNOSE YOUR AILMENT BY MERELY PROBING THE BUMPS ON YOUR HEAD--OOP! NOW HERE'S A DANDY SPECIMEN...MY, HE'S A BIG ONE, ISN'T HE? YES, INDEED--
THAT'S WHAT I'M TRYING TO GET RID OF..!
WHAT? THAT GORGEOUS CONVEXITY REMOVED? BUT WHY? IN SOME PARTS OF THE WORLD SUCH A PROTUBERANCE IS CONSIDERED A SIGN OF NOBILITY. YOU ASK ME TO TAMPER WITH TRADITIONS BETTER LEFT ALONE TO NATURE'S OWN DISCRETION...
THEN YOU'RE SAYING YOU'RE AFRAID TO REMOVE IT?
TAKE TWO ASPIRIN AND PUT AN ICE PACK ON IT! THAT'LL BE TEN BUCKS!
BUT BUT BUT--
YEAH, AND JUST TRY TO BORROW ANY MORE BATWINGS FROM US, SEÑORA BOURGEOIS BRUJA!
SLAM!
5

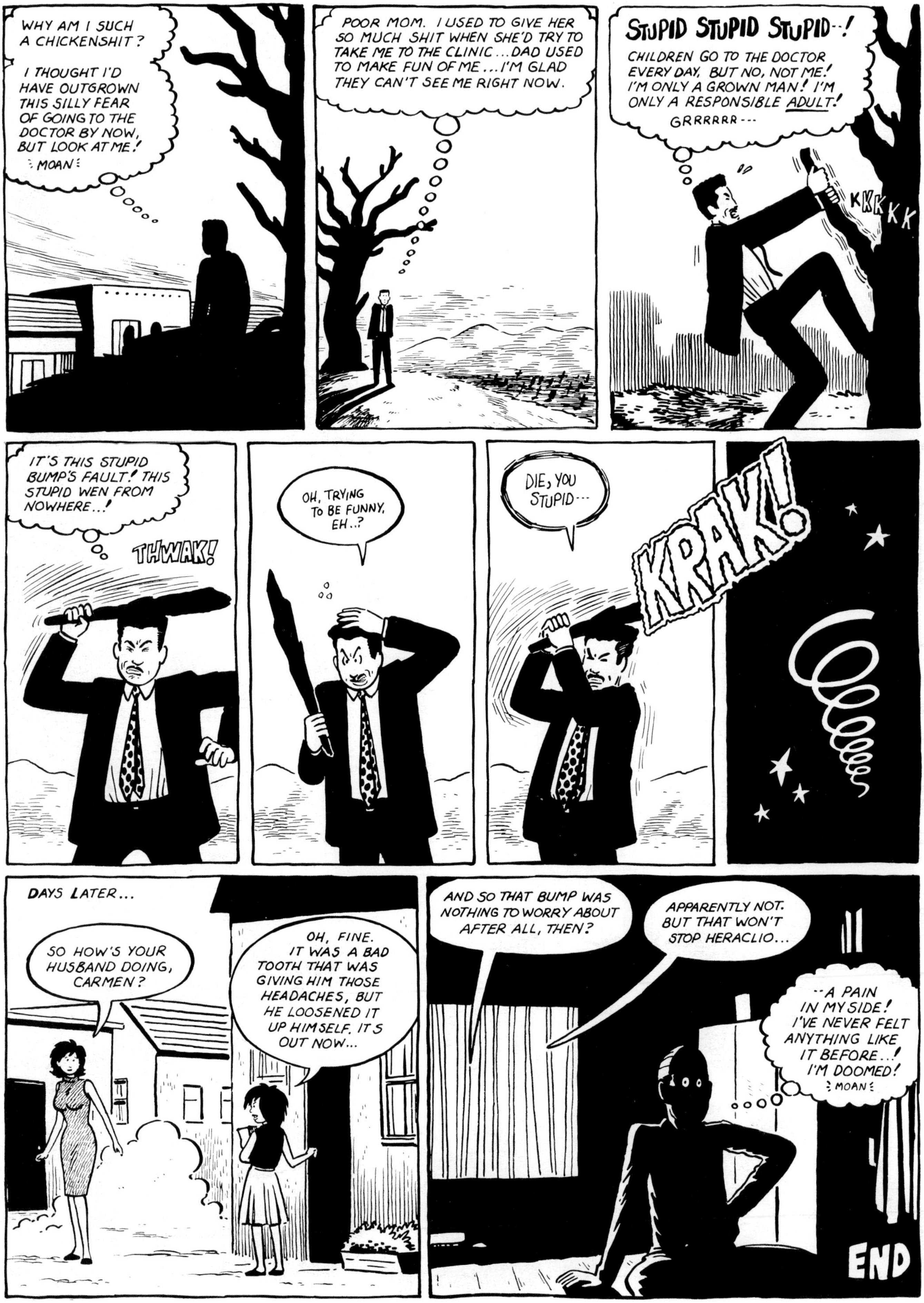

WHY AM I SUCH A CHICKENSHIT? I THOUGHT I'D HAVE OUTGROWN THIS SILLY FEAR OF GOING TO THE DOCTOR BY NOW, BUT LOOK AT ME! MOAN
POOR MOM. I USED TO GIVE HER SO MUCH SHIT WHEN SHE'D TRY TO TAKE ME TO THE CLINIC... DAD USED TO MAKE FUN OF ME... I'M GLAD THEY CAN'T SEE ME RIGHT NOW.
STUPID STUPID STUPID--!
CHILDREN GO TO THE DOCTOR EVERY DAY, BUT NO, NOT ME! I'M ONLY A GROWN MAN! I'M ONLY A RESPONSIBLE ADULT! GRRRRRR---
KKKKK
IT'S THIS STUPID BUMP'S FAULT! THIS STUPID WEN FROM NOWHERE...!
THWAK!
OH, TRYING TO BE FUNNY, EH..?
DIE, YOU STUPID---
KRAK!
DAYS LATER...
SO HOW'S YOUR HUSBAND DOING, CARMEN?
OH, FINE. IT WAS A BAD TOOTH THAT WAS GIVING HIM THOSE HEADACHES, BUT HE LOOSENED IT UP HIMSELF. IT'S OUT NOW...
AND SO THAT BUMP WAS NOTHING TO WORRY ABOUT AFTER ALL, THEN?
APPARENTLY NOT. BUT THAT WON'T STOP HERACLIO...
--A PAIN IN MY SIDE! I'VE NEVER FELT ANYTHING LIKE IT BEFORE..! I'M DOOMED! MOAN
END

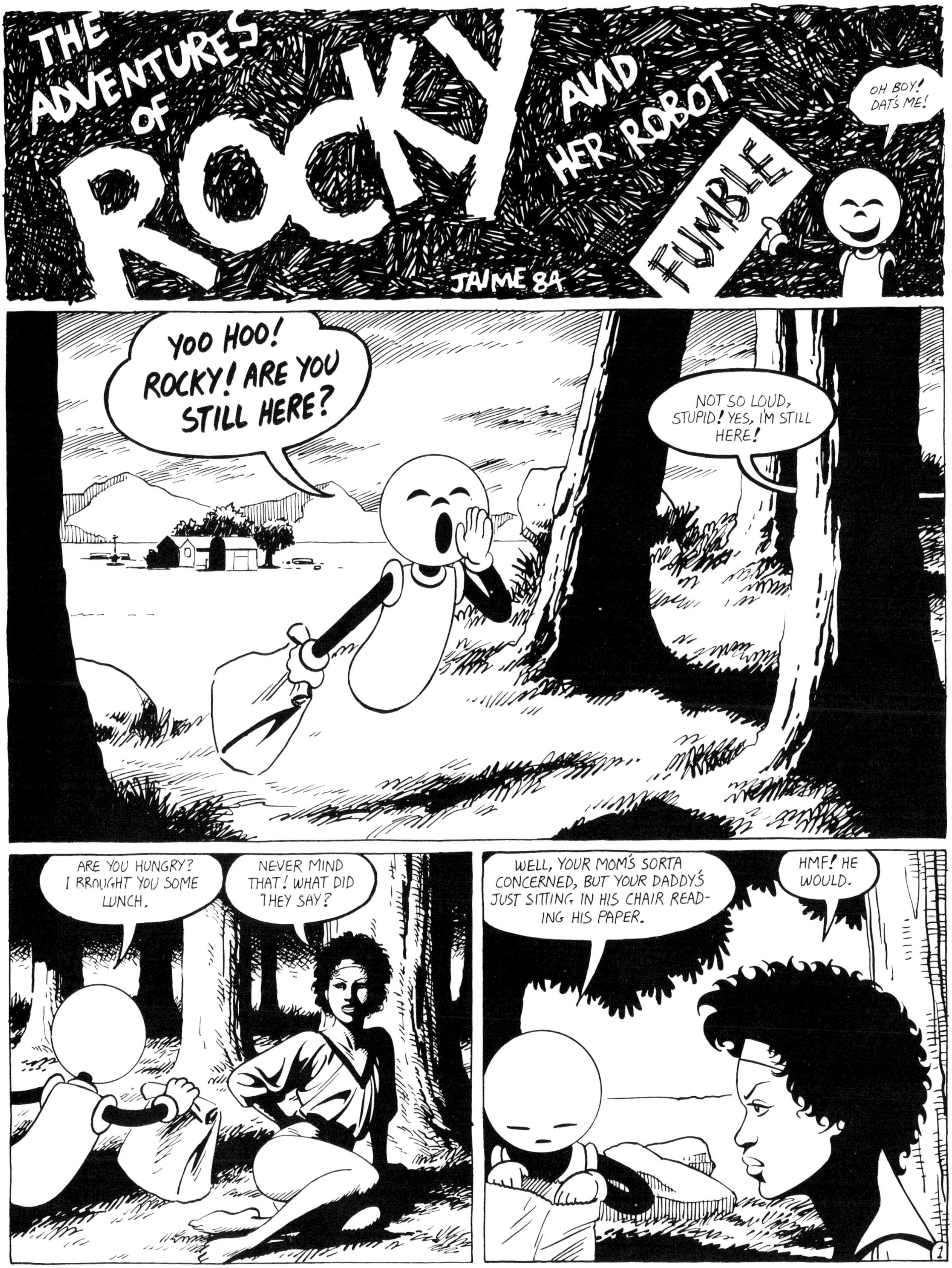
THE ADVENTURES OF ROCKY AND HER ROBOT FUMBLE
OH BOY! DAT'S ME!
JAIME 84
YOO HOO! ROCKY! ARE YOU STILL HERE?
NOT SO LOUD, STUPID! YES, I'M STILL HERE!
ARE YOU HUNGRY? I BROUGHT YOU SOME LUNCH.
NEVER MIND THAT! WHAT DID THEY SAY?
WELL, YOUR MOM'S SORTA CONCERNED, BUT YOUR DADDY'S JUST SITTING IN HIS CHAIR READ-ING HIS PAPER.
HMF! HE WOULD.
1

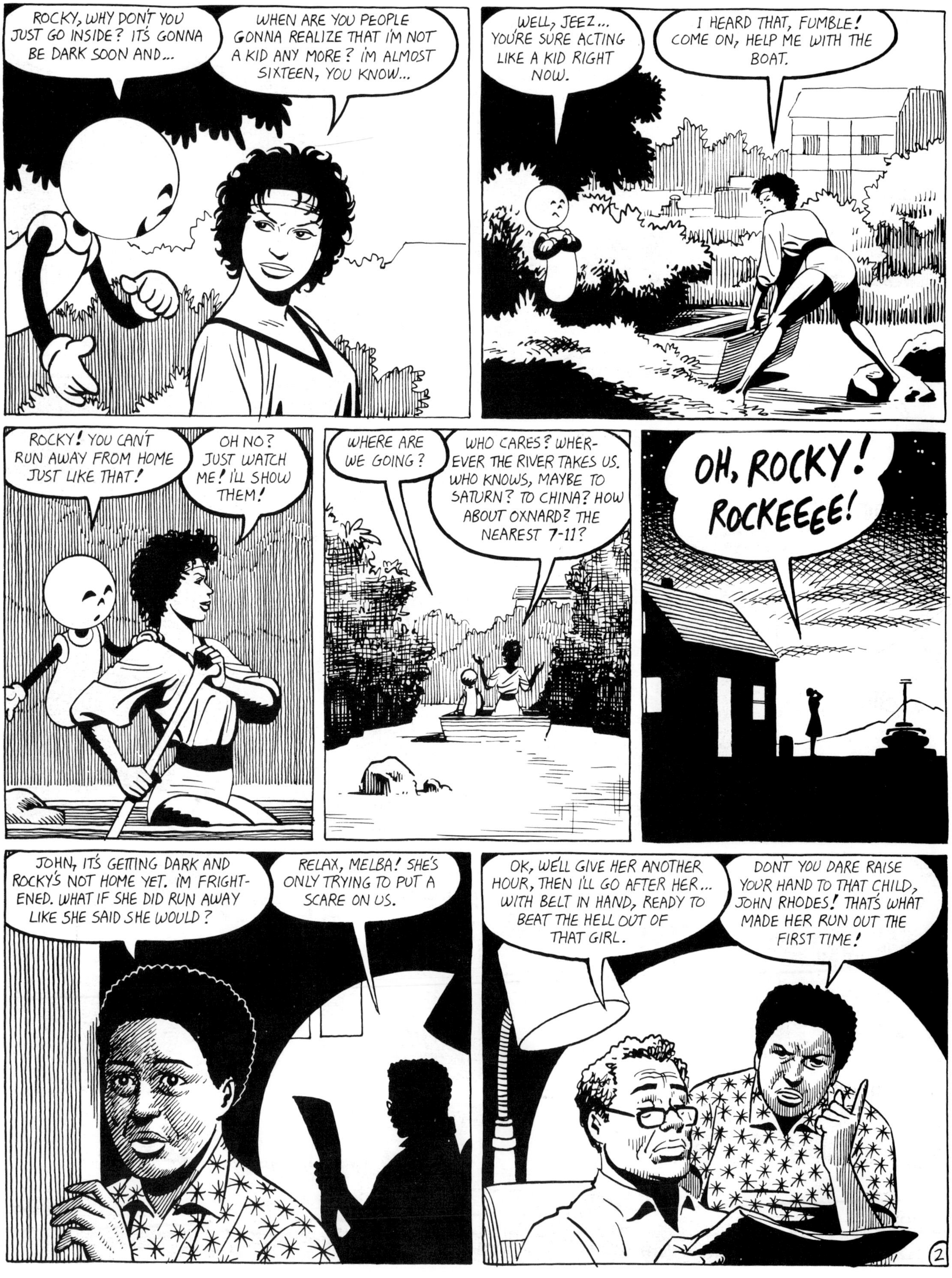
ROCKY, WHY DON'T YOU JUST GO INSIDE? IT'S GONNA BE DARK SOON AND...
WHEN ARE YOU PEOPLE GONNA REALIZE THAT I'M NOT A KID ANY MORE? I'M ALMOST SIXTEEN, YOU KNOW...
WELL, JEEZ... YOU'RE SURE ACTING LIKE A KID RIGHT NOW.
I HEARD THAT, FUMBLE! COME ON, HELP ME WITH THE BOAT.
ROCKY! YOU CAN'T RUN AWAY FROM HOME JUST LIKE THAT!
OH NO? JUST WATCH ME! I'LL SHOW THEM!
WHERE ARE WE GOING?
WHO CARES? WHEREVER THE RIVER TAKES US. WHO KNOWS, MAYBE TO SATURN? TO CHINA? HOW ABOUT OXNARD? THE NEAREST 7-11?
OH, ROCKY! ROCKEEEEE!
JOHN, IT'S GETTING DARK AND ROCKY'S NOT HOME YET. I'M FRIGHTENED. WHAT IF SHE DID RUN AWAY LIKE SHE SAID SHE WOULD?
RELAX, MELBA! SHE'S ONLY TRYING TO PUT A SCARE ON US.
OK, WE'LL GIVE HER ANOTHER HOUR, THEN I'LL GO AFTER HER... WITH BELT IN HAND, READY TO BEAT THE HELL OUT OF THAT GIRL.
DON'T YOU DARE RAISE YOUR HAND TO THAT CHILD, JOHN RHODES! THAT'S WHAT MADE HER RUN OUT THE FIRST TIME!
2

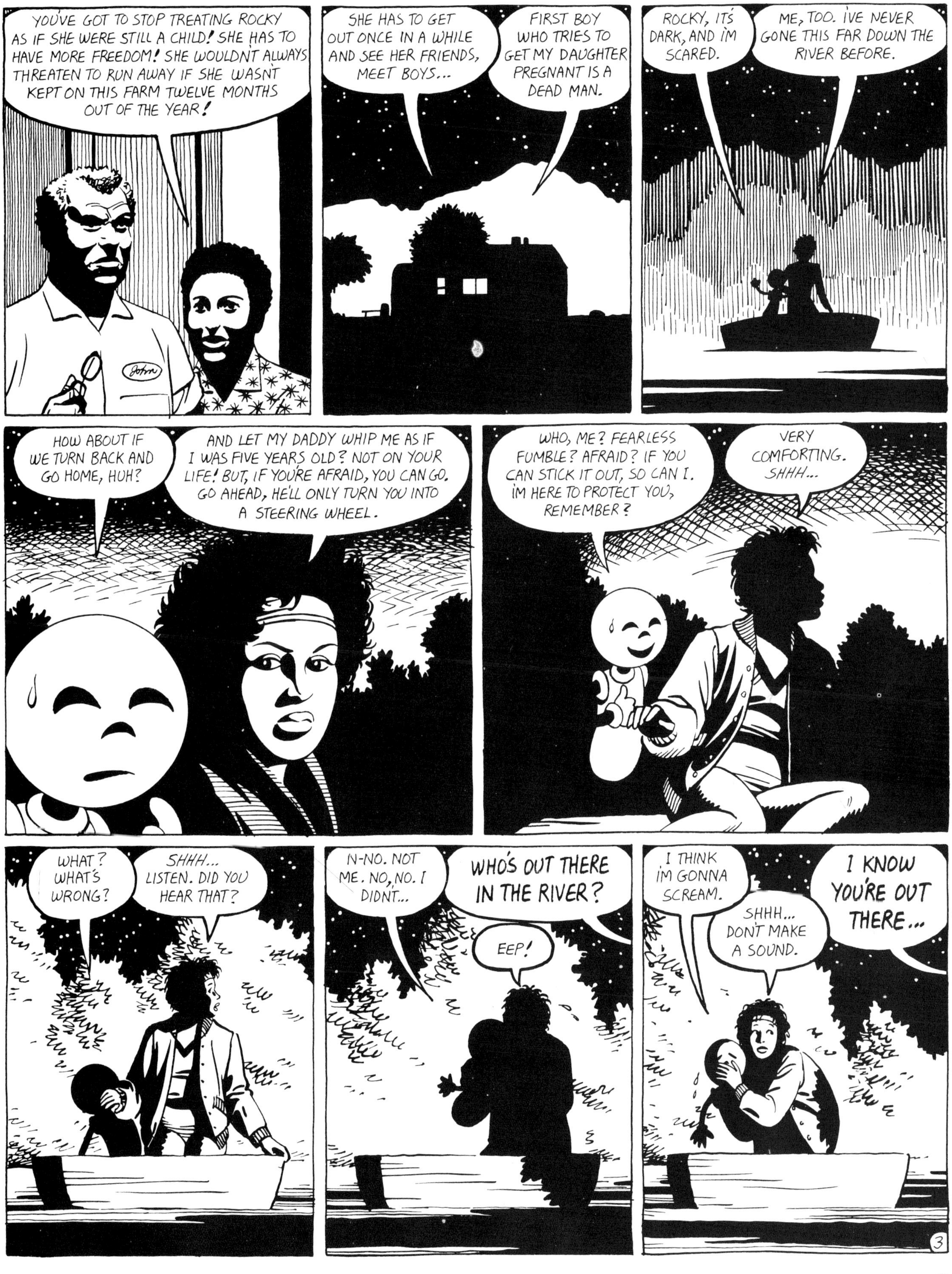

YOU'VE GOT TO STOP TREATING ROCKY AS IF SHE WERE STILL A CHILD! SHE HAS TO HAVE MORE FREEDOM! SHE WOULDN'T ALWAYS THREATEN TO RUN AWAY IF SHE WASN'T KEPT ON THIS FARM TWELVE MONTHS OUT OF THE YEAR!
John
SHE HAS TO GET OUT ONCE IN A WHILE AND SEE HER FRIENDS, MEET BOYS...
FIRST BOY WHO TRIES TO GET MY DAUGHTER PREGNANT IS A DEAD MAN.
ROCKY, IT'S DARK, AND I'M SCARED.
ME, TOO. I'VE NEVER GONE THIS FAR DOWN THE RIVER BEFORE.
HOW ABOUT IF WE TURN BACK AND GO HOME, HUH?
AND LET MY DADDY WHIP ME AS IF I WAS FIVE YEARS OLD? NOT ON YOUR LIFE! BUT, IF YOU'RE AFRAID, YOU CAN GO. GO AHEAD, HE'LL ONLY TURN YOU INTO A STEERING WHEEL.
WHO, ME? FEARLESS FUMBLE? AFRAID? IF YOU CAN STICK IT OUT, SO CAN I. I'M HERE TO PROTECT YOU, REMEMBER?
VERY COMFORTING. SHHH...
WHAT? WHAT'S WRONG?
SHHH... LISTEN. DID YOU HEAR THAT?
N-NO. NOT ME. NO, NO. I DIDN'T...
WHO'S OUT THERE IN THE RIVER?
EEP!
I THINK I'M GONNA SCREAM.
SHHH... DON'T MAKE A SOUND.
I KNOW YOU'RE OUT THERE...
3

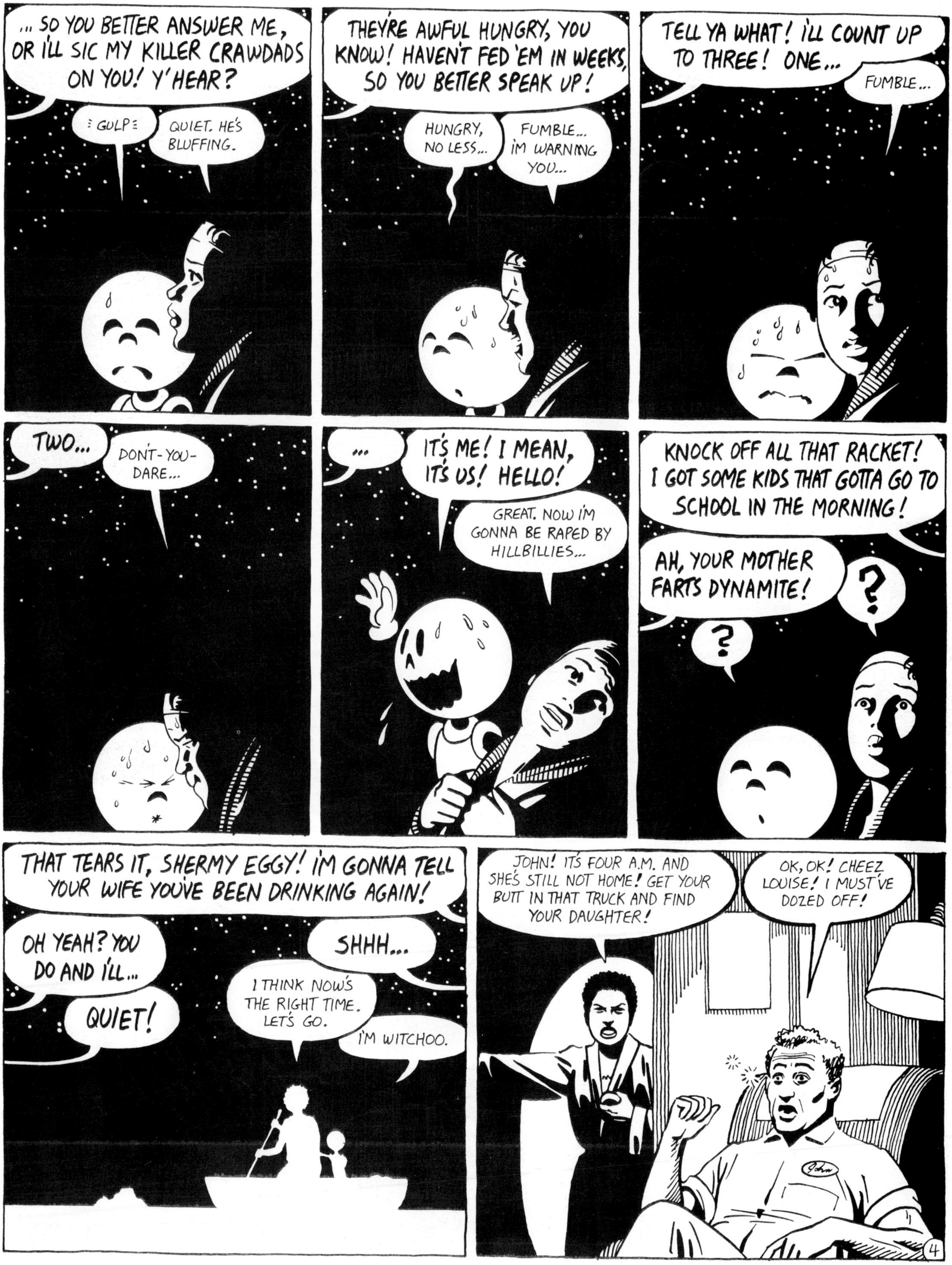
... SO YOU BETTER ANSWER ME, OR I'LL SIC MY KILLER CRAWDADS ON YOU! Y'HEAR?
GULP
QUIET. HE'S BLUFFING.
THEY'RE AWFUL HUNGRY, YOU KNOW! HAVEN'T FED 'EM IN WEEKS, SO YOU BETTER SPEAK UP!
HUNGRY, NO LESS...
FUMBLE... I'M WARNING YOU...
TELL YA WHAT! I'LL COUNT UP TO THREE! ONE...
FUMBLE...
TWO...
DON'T-YOU-DARE...
...
IT'S ME! I MEAN, IT'S US! HELLO!
GREAT. NOW I'M GONNA BE RAPED BY HILLBILLIES...
KNOCK OFF ALL THAT RACKET! I GOT SOME KIDS THAT GOTTA GO TO SCHOOL IN THE MORNING!
AH, YOUR MOTHER FARTS DYNAMITE!
?
?
THAT TEARS IT, SHERMY EGGY! I'M GONNA TELL YOUR WIFE YOU'VE BEEN DRINKING AGAIN!
OH YEAH? YOU DO AND I'LL...
QUIET!
SHHH...
I THINK NOW'S THE RIGHT TIME. LET'S GO.
I'M WITCHOO.
JOHN! IT'S FOUR A.M. AND SHE'S STILL NOT HOME! GET YOUR BUTT IN THAT TRUCK AND FIND YOUR DAUGHTER!
OK, OK! CHEEZ LOUISE! I MUST'VE DOZED OFF!
4

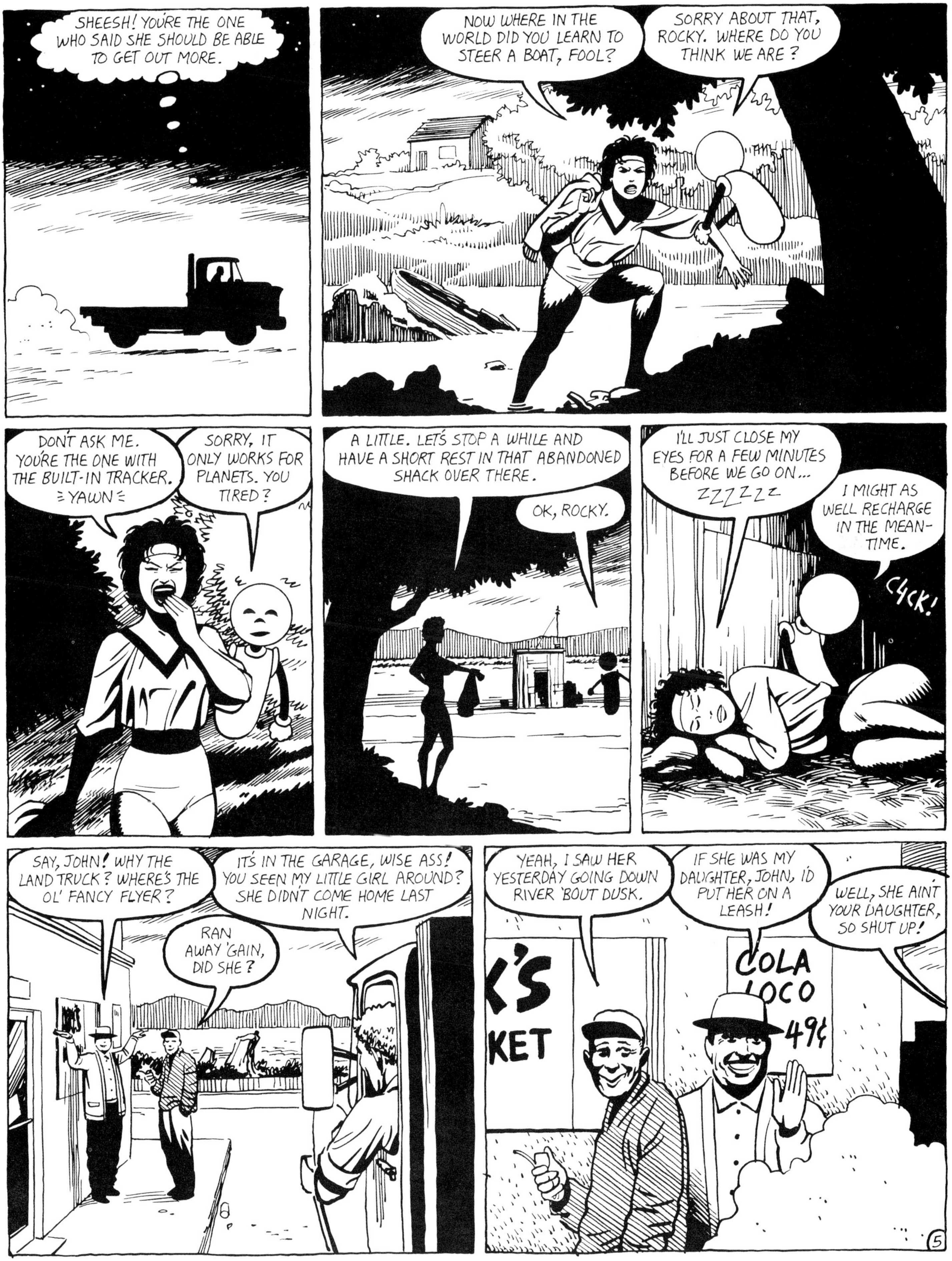
SHEESH! YOU'RE THE ONE WHO SAID SHE SHOULD BE ABLE TO GET OUT MORE.
NOW WHERE IN THE WORLD DID YOU LEARN TO STEER A BOAT, FOOL?
SORRY ABOUT THAT, ROCKY. WHERE DO YOU THINK WE ARE?
DON'T ASK ME. YOU'RE THE ONE WITH THE BUILT-IN TRACKER. YAWN
SORRY, IT ONLY WORKS FOR PLANETS. YOU TIRED?
A LITTLE. LET'S STOP A WHILE AND HAVE A SHORT REST IN THAT ABANDONED SHACK OVER THERE.
OK, ROCKY.
I'LL JUST CLOSE MY EYES FOR A FEW MINUTES BEFORE WE GO ON... ZZZZZZ
I MIGHT AS WELL RECHARGE IN THE MEAN-TIME.
C4CK!
SAY, JOHN! WHY THE LAND TRUCK? WHERE'S THE OL' FANCY FLYER?
IT'S IN THE GARAGE, WISE ASS! YOU SEEN MY LITTLE GIRL AROUND? SHE DIDN'T COME HOME LAST NIGHT.
RAN AWAY 'GAIN, DID SHE?
YEAH, I SAW HER YESTERDAY GOING DOWN RIVER 'BOUT DUSK.
IF SHE WAS MY DAUGHTER, JOHN, I'D PUT HER ON A LEASH!
WELL, SHE AIN'T YOUR DAUGHTER, SO SHUT UP!
K'S
KET
COLA LOCO
49¢
5

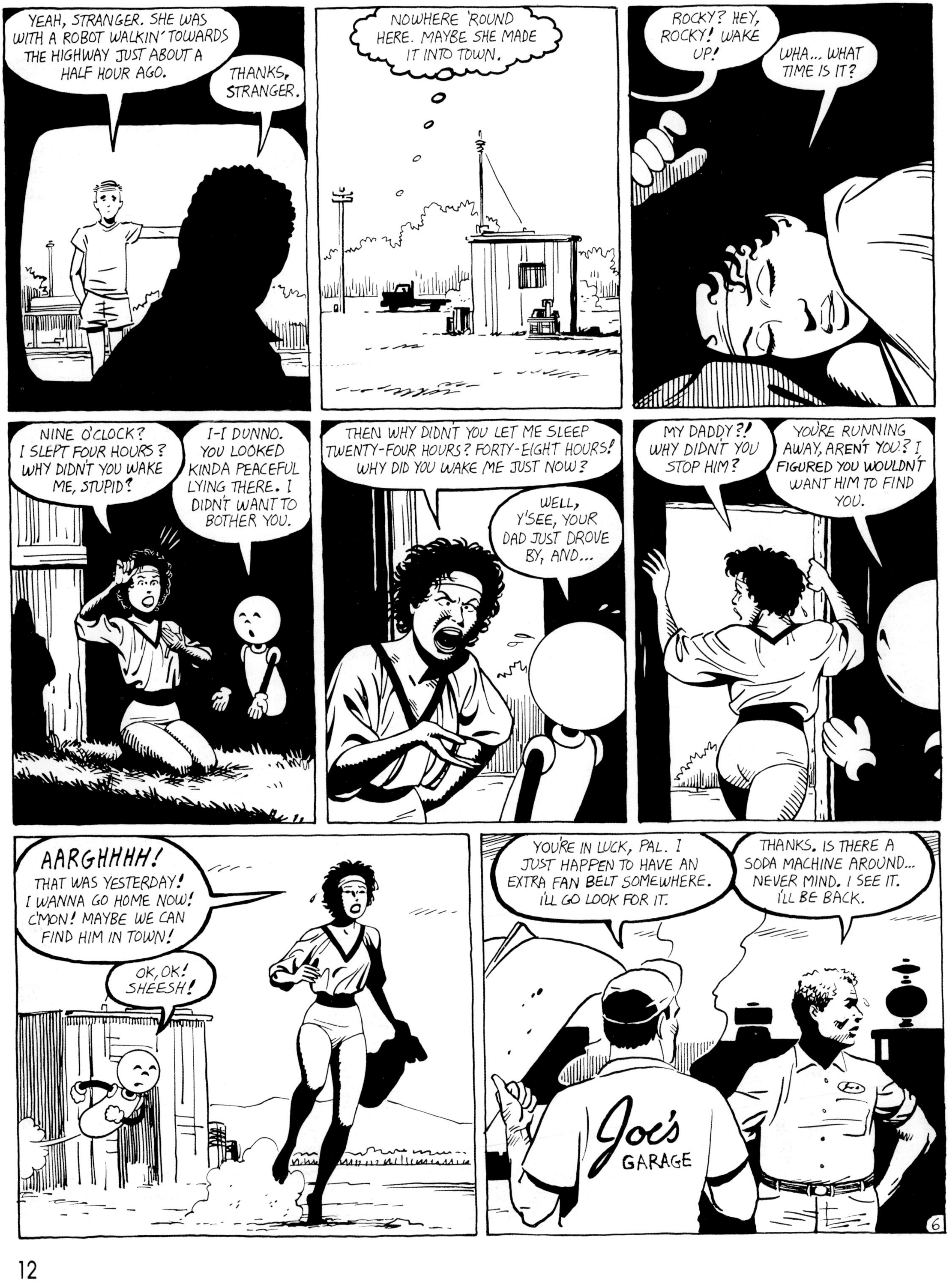
YEAH, STRANGER. SHE WAS WITH A ROBOT WALKIN' TOWARDS THE HIGHWAY JUST ABOUT A HALF HOUR AGO.
THANKS, STRANGER.
NOWHERE 'ROUND HERE. MAYBE SHE MADE IT INTO TOWN.
ROCKY? HEY, ROCKY! WAKE UP!
WHA... WHAT TIME IS IT?
NINE O'CLOCK? I SLEPT FOUR HOURS? WHY DIDN'T YOU WAKE ME, STUPID?
I-I DUNNO. YOU LOOKED KINDA PEACEFUL LYING THERE. I DIDN'T WANT TO BOTHER YOU.
THEN WHY DIDN'T YOU LET ME SLEEP TWENTY-FOUR HOURS? FORTY-EIGHT HOURS! WHY DID YOU WAKE ME JUST NOW?
WELL, Y'SEE, YOUR DAD JUST DROVE BY, AND...
MY DADDY?! WHY DIDN'T YOU STOP HIM?
YOU'RE RUNNING AWAY, AREN'T YOU? I FIGURED YOU WOULDN'T WANT HIM TO FIND YOU.
AARGHHHH! THAT WAS YESTERDAY! I WANNA GO HOME NOW! C'MON! MAYBE WE CAN FIND HIM IN TOWN!
OK, OK! SHEESH!
YOU'RE IN LUCK, PAL. I JUST HAPPEN TO HAVE AN EXTRA FAN BELT SOMEWHERE. I'LL GO LOOK FOR IT.
THANKS. IS THERE A SODA MACHINE AROUND... NEVER MIND. I SEE IT. I'LL BE BACK.
Joe's GARAGE
6

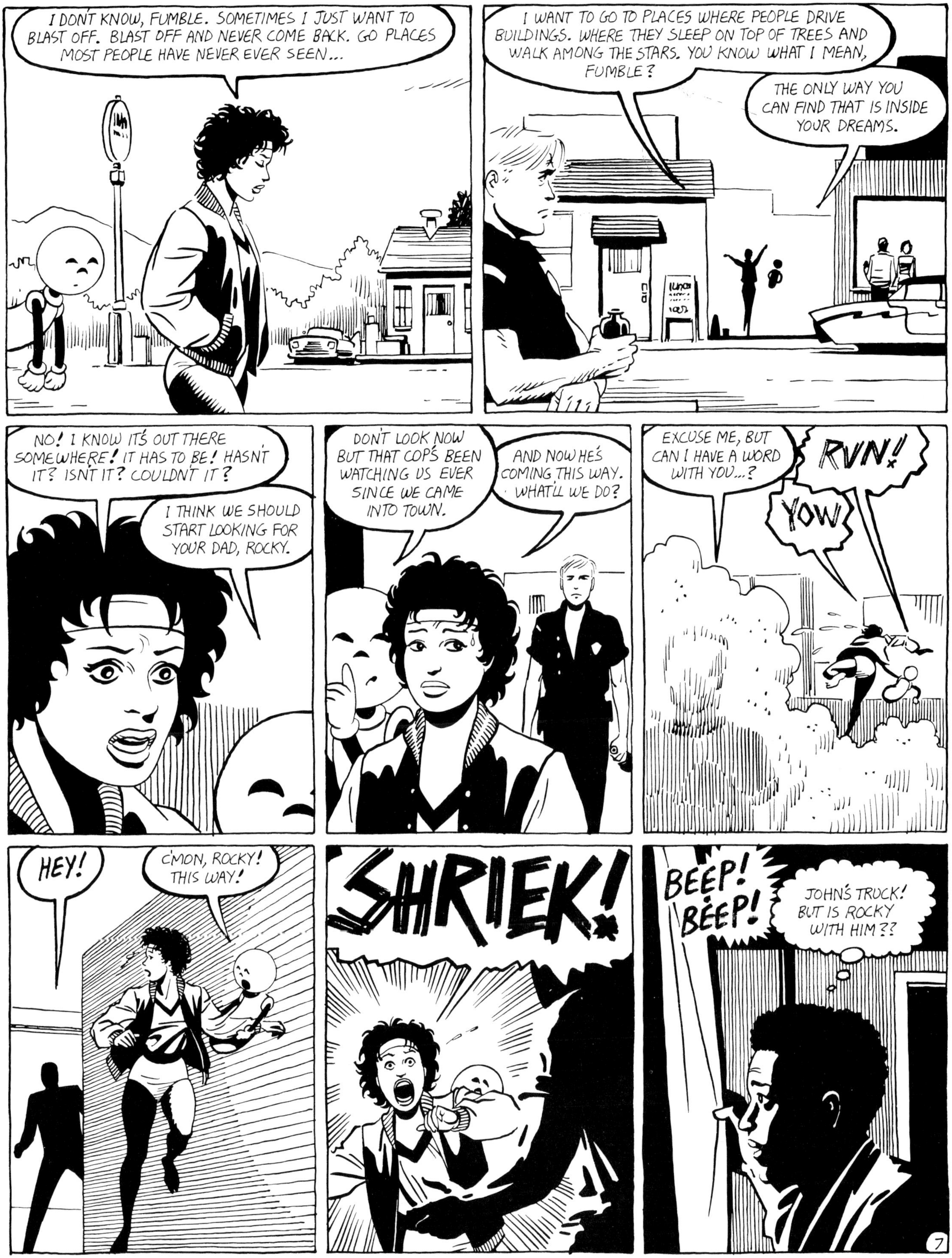

I DON'T KNOW, FUMBLE. SOMETIMES I JUST WANT TO BLAST OFF. BLAST OFF AND NEVER COME BACK. GO PLACES MOST PEOPLE HAVE NEVER EVER SEEN...
I WANT TO GO TO PLACES WHERE PEOPLE DRIVE BUILDINGS. WHERE THEY SLEEP ON TOP OF TREES AND WALK AMONG THE STARS. YOU KNOW WHAT I MEAN, FUMBLE?
THE ONLY WAY YOU CAN FIND THAT IS INSIDE YOUR DREAMS.
NO! I KNOW IT'S OUT THERE SOMEWHERE! IT HAS TO BE! HASN'T IT? ISN'T IT? COULDN'T IT?
I THINK WE SHOULD START LOOKING FOR YOUR DAD, ROCKY.
DON'T LOOK NOW BUT THAT COP'S BEEN WATCHING US EVER SINCE WE CAME INTO TOWN.
AND NOW HE'S COMING THIS WAY. WHAT'LL WE DO?
EXCUSE ME, BUT CAN I HAVE A WORD WITH YOU...?
RUN!
YOW
HEY!
C'MON, ROCKY! THIS WAY!
SHRIEK!
BEEP! BEEP!
JOHN'S TRUCK! BUT IS ROCKY WITH HIM??
7

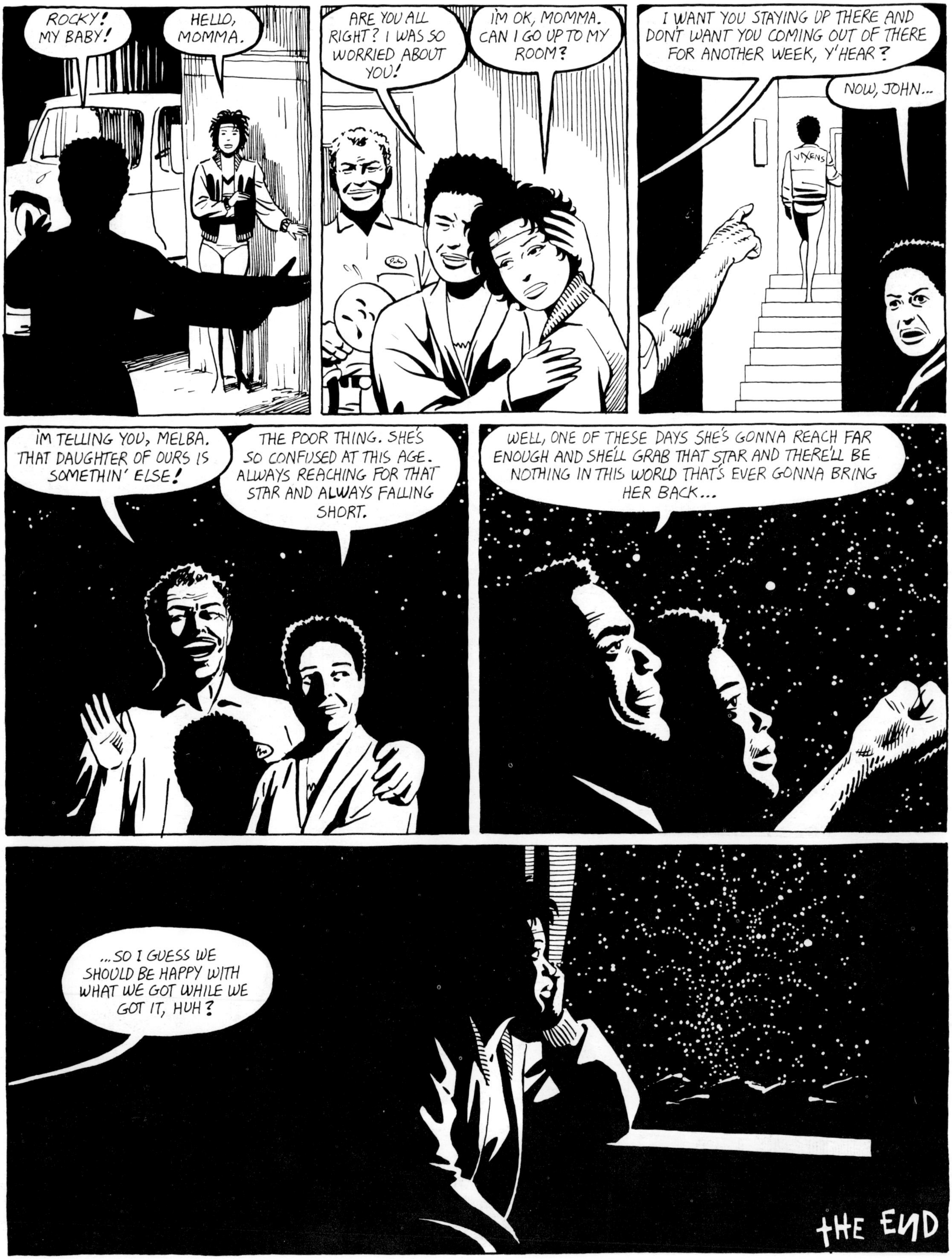
ROCKY! MY BABY!
HELLO, MOMMA.
ARE YOU ALL RIGHT? I WAS SO WORRIED ABOUT YOU!
I'M OK, MOMMA. CAN I GO UP TO MY ROOM?
I WANT YOU STAYING UP THERE AND DON'T WANT YOU COMING OUT OF THERE FOR ANOTHER WEEK, Y'HEAR?
NOW, JOHN...
VIXENS
I'M TELLING YOU, MELBA. THAT DAUGHTER OF OURS IS SOMETHIN' ELSE!
THE POOR THING. SHE'S SO CONFUSED AT THIS AGE. ALWAYS REACHING FOR THAT STAR AND ALWAYS FALLING SHORT.
WELL, ONE OF THESE DAYS SHE'S GONNA REACH FAR ENOUGH AND SHE'LL GRAB THAT STAR AND THERE'LL BE NOTHING IN THIS WORLD THAT'S EVER GONNA BRING HER BACK...
...SO I GUESS WE SHOULD BE HAPPY WITH WHAT WE GOT WHILE WE GOT IT, HUH?
THE END

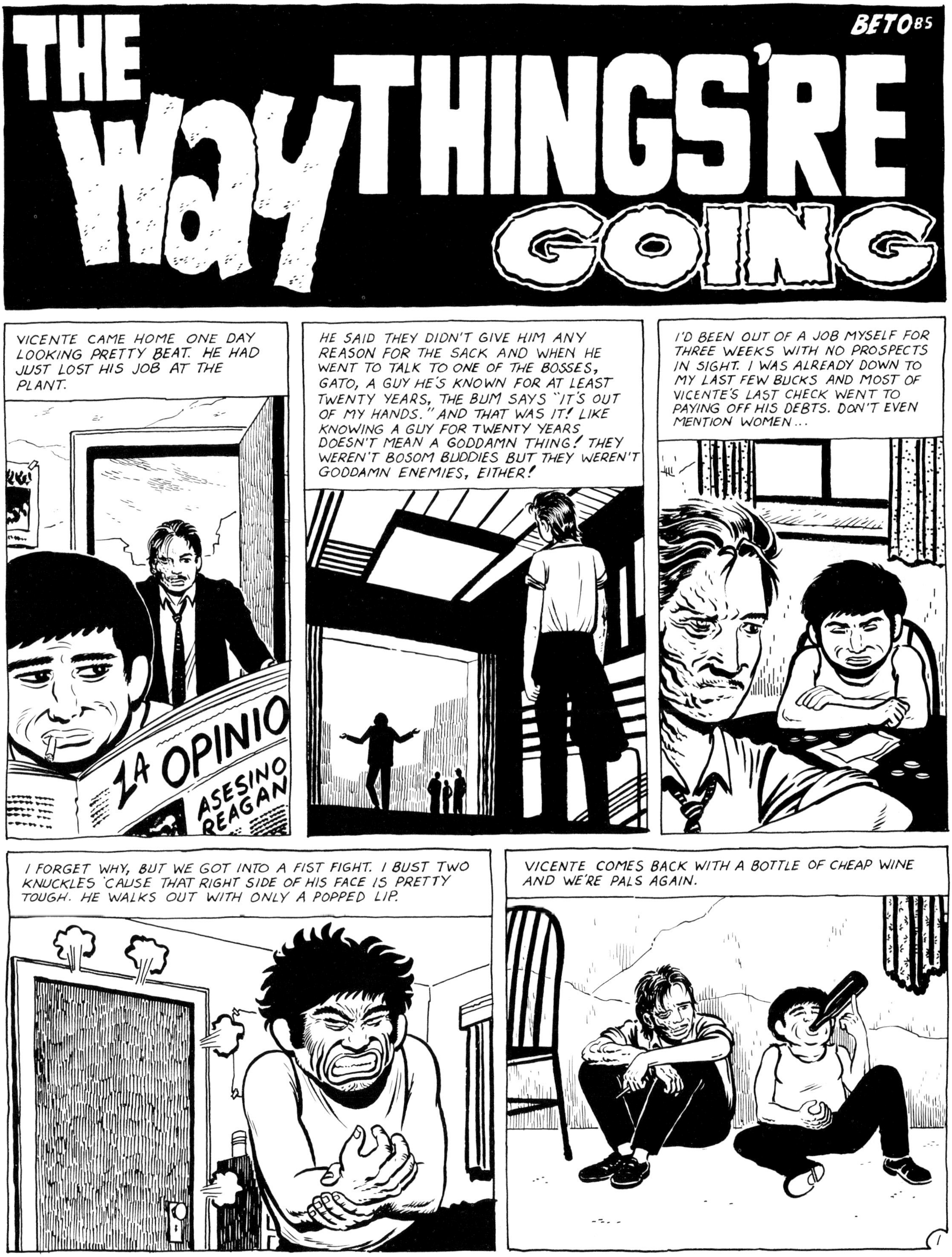
THE WAY THINGS'RE GOING
BETO 85
VICENTE CAME HOME ONE DAY LOOKING PRETTY BEAT. HE HAD JUST LOST HIS JOB AT THE PLANT.
LA OPINIO
ASESINO REAGAN
HE SAID THEY DIDN'T GIVE HIM ANY REASON FOR THE SACK AND WHEN HE WENT TO TALK TO ONE OF THE BOSSES, GATO, A GUY HE'S KNOWN FOR AT LEAST TWENTY YEARS, THE BUM SAYS "IT'S OUT OF MY HANDS." AND THAT WAS IT! LIKE KNOWING A GUY FOR TWENTY YEARS DOESN'T MEAN A GODDAMN THING! THEY WEREN'T BOSOM BUDDIES BUT THEY WEREN'T GODDAMN ENEMIES, EITHER!
I'D BEEN OUT OF A JOB MYSELF FOR THREE WEEKS WITH NO PROSPECTS IN SIGHT. I WAS ALREADY DOWN TO MY LAST FEW BUCKS AND MOST OF VICENTE'S LAST CHECK WENT TO PAYING OFF HIS DEBTS. DON'T EVEN MENTION WOMEN...
I FORGET WHY, BUT WE GOT INTO A FIST FIGHT. I BUST TWO KNUCKLES 'CAUSE THAT RIGHT SIDE OF HIS FACE IS PRETTY TOUGH. HE WALKS OUT WITH ONLY A POPPED LIP.
VICENTE COMES BACK WITH A BOTTLE OF CHEAP WINE AND WE'RE PALS AGAIN.
1

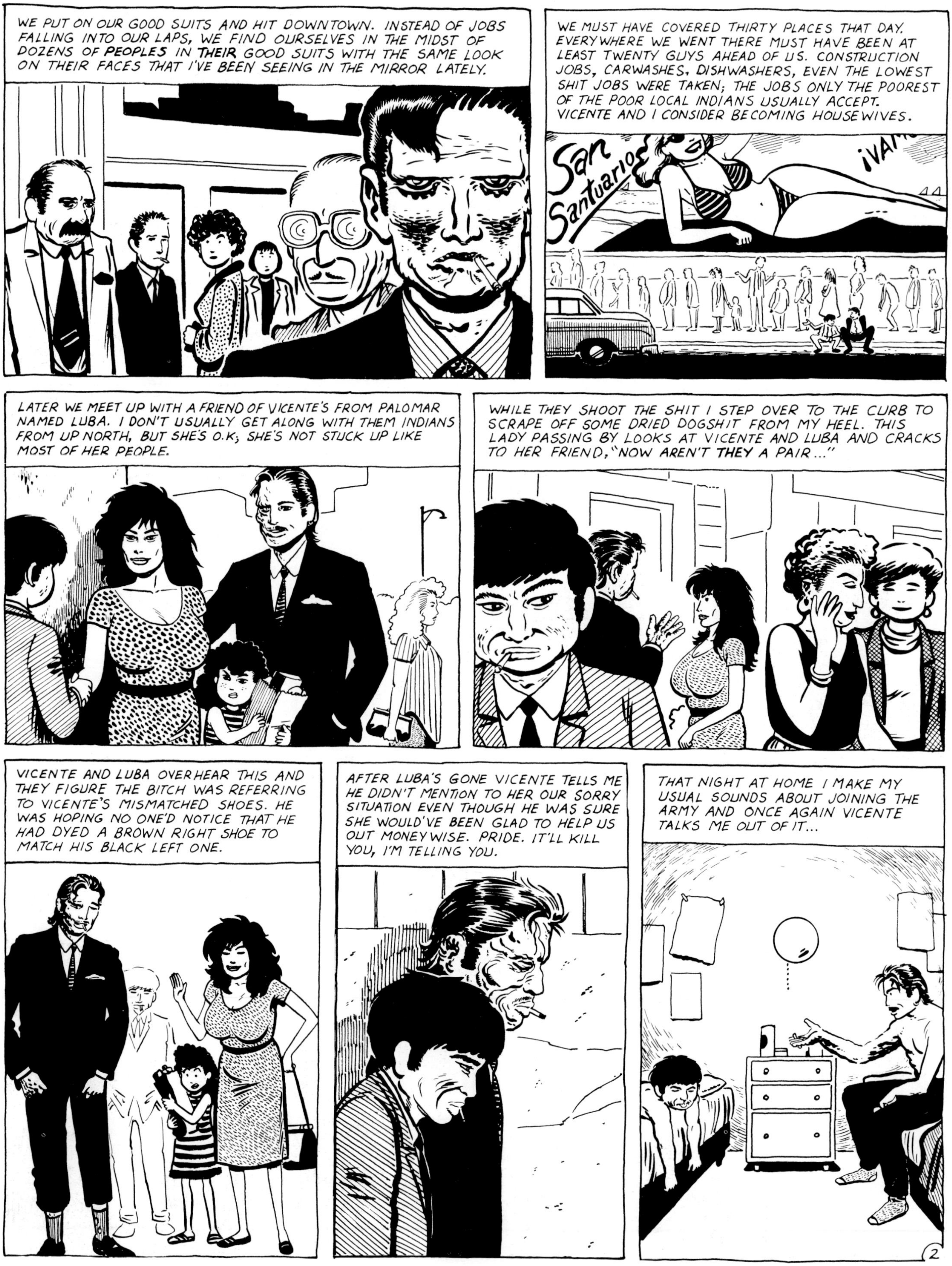
WE PUT ON OUR GOOD SUITS AND HIT DOWNTOWN. INSTEAD OF JOBS FALLING INTO OUR LAPS, WE FIND OURSELVES IN THE MIDST OF DOZENS OF PEOPLES IN THEIR GOOD SUITS WITH THE SAME LOOK ON THEIR FACES THAT I'VE BEEN SEEING IN THE MIRROR LATELY.
WE MUST HAVE COVERED THIRTY PLACES THAT DAY. EVERYWHERE WE WENT THERE MUST HAVE BEEN AT LEAST TWENTY GUYS AHEAD OF US. CONSTRUCTION JOBS, CARWASHES, DISHWASHERS, EVEN THE LOWEST SHIT JOBS WERE TAKEN; THE JOBS ONLY THE POOREST OF THE POOR LOCAL INDIANS USUALLY ACCEPT. VICENTE AND I CONSIDER BECOMING HOUSEWIVES.
San Santuario
LATER WE MEET UP WITH A FRIEND OF VICENTE'S FROM PALOMAR NAMED LUBA. I DON'T USUALLY GET ALONG WITH THEM INDIANS FROM UP NORTH, BUT SHE'S O.K; SHE'S NOT STUCK UP LIKE MOST OF HER PEOPLE.
WHILE THEY SHOOT THE SHIT I STEP OVER TO THE CURB TO SCRAPE OFF SOME DRIED DOGSHIT FROM MY HEEL. THIS LADY PASSING BY LOOKS AT VICENTE AND LUBA AND CRACKS TO HER FRIEND, "NOW AREN'T THEY A PAIR..."
VICENTE AND LUBA OVERHEAR THIS AND THEY FIGURE THE BITCH WAS REFERRING TO VICENTE'S MISMATCHED SHOES. HE WAS HOPING NO ONE'D NOTICE THAT HE HAD DYED A BROWN RIGHT SHOE TO MATCH HIS BLACK LEFT ONE.
AFTER LUBA'S GONE VICENTE TELLS ME HE DIDN'T MENTION TO HER OUR SORRY SITUATION EVEN THOUGH HE WAS SURE SHE WOULD'VE BEEN GLAD TO HELP US OUT MONEYWISE. PRIDE. IT'LL KILL YOU, I'M TELLING YOU.
THAT NIGHT AT HOME I MAKE MY USUAL SOUNDS ABOUT JOINING THE ARMY AND ONCE AGAIN VICENTE TALKS ME OUT OF IT...
2

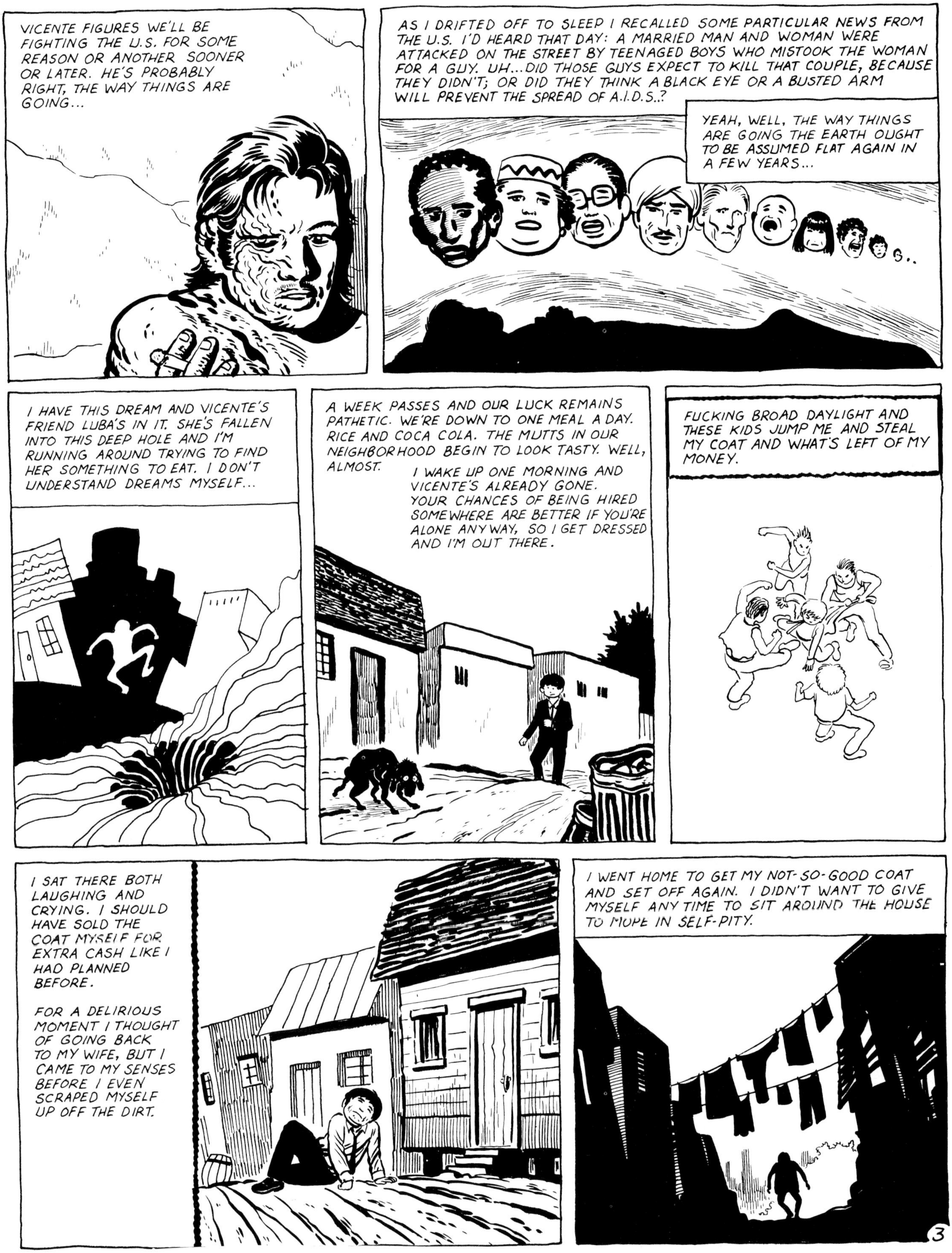
VICENTE FIGURES WE'LL BE FIGHTING THE U.S. FOR SOME REASON OR ANOTHER SOONER OR LATER. HE'S PROBABLY RIGHT, THE WAY THINGS ARE GOING...
AS I DRIFTED OFF TO SLEEP I RECALLED SOME PARTICULAR NEWS FROM THE U.S. I'D HEARD THAT DAY: A MARRIED MAN AND WOMAN WERE ATTACKED ON THE STREET BY TEENAGED BOYS WHO MISTOOK THE WOMAN FOR A GUY. UH...DID THOSE GUYS EXPECT TO KILL THAT COUPLE, BECAUSE THEY DIDN'T; OR DID THEY THINK A BLACK EYE OR A BUSTED ARM WILL PREVENT THE SPREAD OF A.I.D.S..?
YEAH, WELL, THE WAY THINGS ARE GOING THE EARTH OUGHT TO BE ASSUMED FLAT AGAIN IN A FEW YEARS...
I HAVE THIS DREAM AND VICENTE'S FRIEND LUBA'S IN IT. SHE'S FALLEN INTO THIS DEEP HOLE AND I'M RUNNING AROUND TRYING TO FIND HER SOMETHING TO EAT. I DON'T UNDERSTAND DREAMS MYSELF...
A WEEK PASSES AND OUR LUCK REMAINS PATHETIC. WE'RE DOWN TO ONE MEAL A DAY. RICE AND COCA COLA. THE MUTTS IN OUR NEIGHBORHOOD BEGIN TO LOOK TASTY. WELL, ALMOST.
I WAKE UP ONE MORNING AND VICENTE'S ALREADY GONE. YOUR CHANCES OF BEING HIRED SOMEWHERE ARE BETTER IF YOU'RE ALONE ANYWAY, SO I GET DRESSED AND I'M OUT THERE.
FUCKING BROAD DAYLIGHT AND THESE KIDS JUMP ME AND STEAL MY COAT AND WHAT'S LEFT OF MY MONEY.
I SAT THERE BOTH LAUGHING AND CRYING. I SHOULD HAVE SOLD THE COAT MYSELF FOR EXTRA CASH LIKE I HAD PLANNED BEFORE.
FOR A DELIRIOUS MOMENT I THOUGHT OF GOING BACK TO MY WIFE, BUT I CAME TO MY SENSES BEFORE I EVEN SCRAPED MYSELF UP OFF THE DIRT.
I WENT HOME TO GET MY NOT-SO-GOOD COAT AND SET OFF AGAIN. I DIDN'T WANT TO GIVE MYSELF ANY TIME TO SIT AROUND THE HOUSE TO MOPE IN SELF-PITY.
3

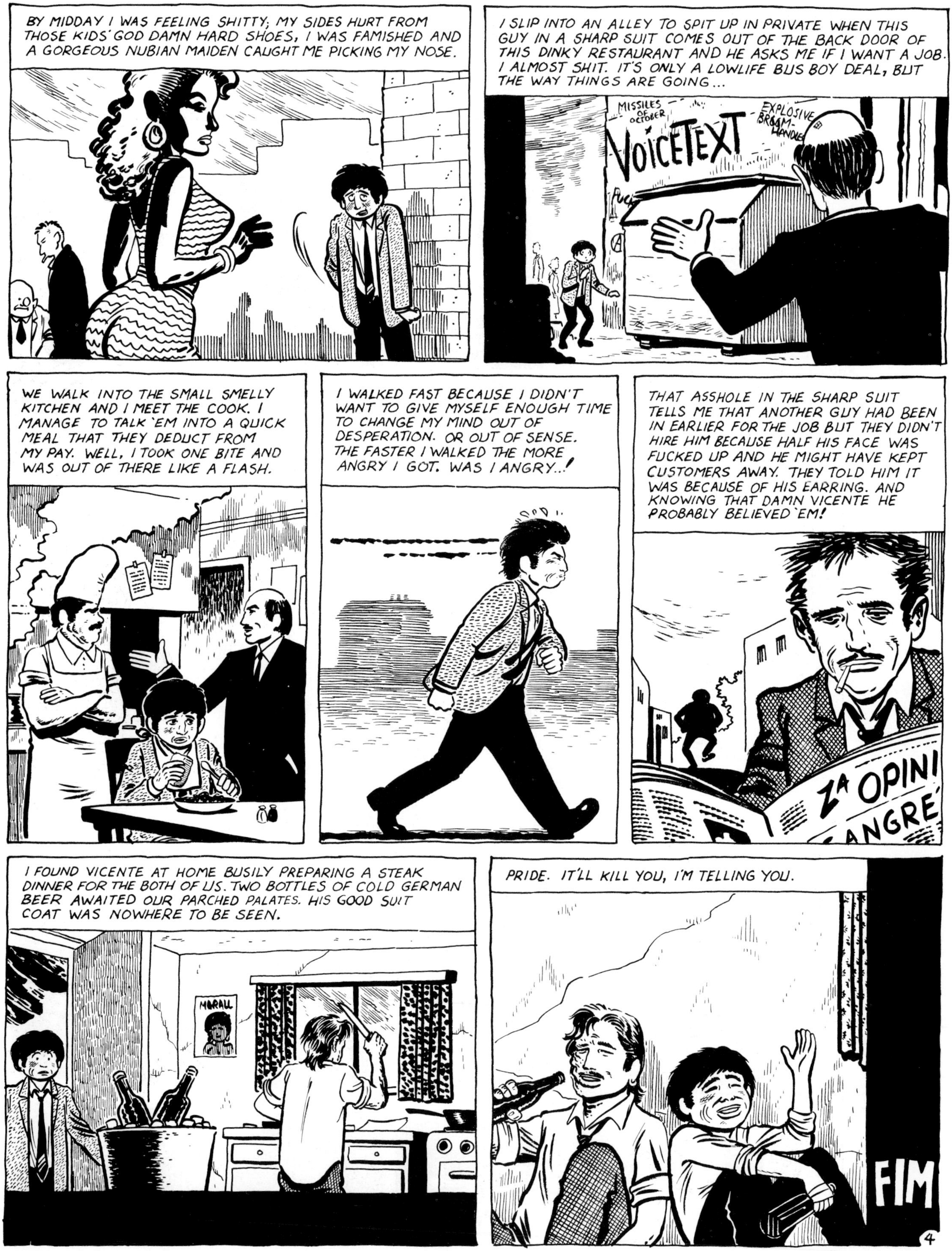
BY MIDDAY I WAS FEELING SHITTY; MY SIDES HURT FROM THOSE KIDS' GOD DAMN HARD SHOES, I WAS FAMISHED AND A GORGEOUS NUBIAN MAIDEN CAUGHT ME PICKING MY NOSE.
I SLIP INTO AN ALLEY TO SPIT UP IN PRIVATE WHEN THIS GUY IN A SHARP SUIT COMES OUT OF THE BACK DOOR OF THIS DINKY RESTAURANT AND HE ASKS ME IF I WANT A JOB. I ALMOST SHIT. IT'S ONLY A LOWLIFE BUS BOY DEAL, BUT THE WAY THINGS ARE GOING...
MISSILES OF OCTOBER
EXPLOSIVE BROOM-HANDLE
VOICETEXT
WE WALK INTO THE SMALL SMELLY KITCHEN AND I MEET THE COOK. I MANAGE TO TALK 'EM INTO A QUICK MEAL THAT THEY DEDUCT FROM MY PAY. WELL, I TOOK ONE BITE AND WAS OUT OF THERE LIKE A FLASH.
I WALKED FAST BECAUSE I DIDN'T WANT TO GIVE MYSELF ENOUGH TIME TO CHANGE MY MIND OUT OF DESPERATION. OR OUT OF SENSE. THE FASTER I WALKED THE MORE ANGRY I GOT. WAS I ANGRY...!
THAT ASSHOLE IN THE SHARP SUIT TELLS ME THAT ANOTHER GUY HAD BEEN IN EARLIER FOR THE JOB BUT THEY DIDN'T HIRE HIM BECAUSE HALF HIS FACE WAS FUCKED UP AND HE MIGHT HAVE KEPT CUSTOMERS AWAY. THEY TOLD HIM IT WAS BECAUSE OF HIS EARRING. AND KNOWING THAT DAMN VICENTE HE PROBABLY BELIEVED 'EM!
I FOUND VICENTE AT HOME BUSILY PREPARING A STEAK DINNER FOR THE BOTH OF US. TWO BOTTLES OF COLD GERMAN BEER AWAITED OUR PARCHED PALATES. HIS GOOD SUIT COAT WAS NOWHERE TO BE SEEN.
PRIDE. IT'LL KILL YOU, I'M TELLING YOU.
FIM
4

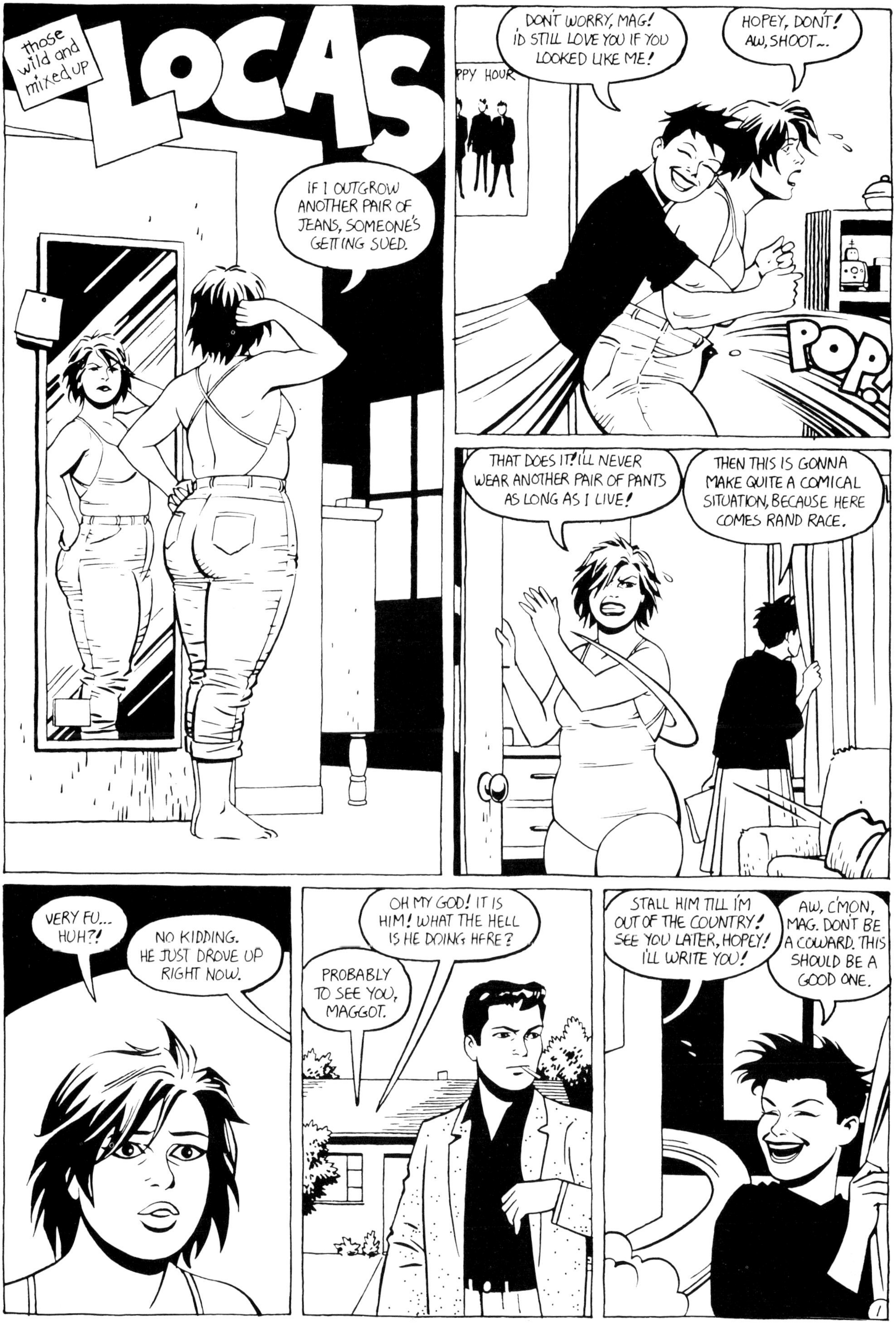
those wild and mixed up
LOCAS
IF I OUTGROW ANOTHER PAIR OF JEANS, SOMEONE'S GETTING SUED.
DON'T WORRY, MAG! I'D STILL LOVE YOU IF YOU LOOKED LIKE ME!
HOPEY, DON'T! AW, SHOOT...
PPY HOUR
POP!
THAT DOES IT! I'LL NEVER WEAR ANOTHER PAIR OF PANTS AS LONG AS I LIVE!
THEN THIS IS GONNA MAKE QUITE A COMICAL SITUATION, BECAUSE HERE COMES RAND RACE.
VERY FU... HUH?!
NO KIDDING. HE JUST DROVE UP RIGHT NOW.
OH MY GOD! IT IS HIM! WHAT THE HELL IS HE DOING HERE?
PROBABLY TO SEE YOU, MAGGOT.
STALL HIM TILL I'M OUT OF THE COUNTRY! SEE YOU LATER, HOPEY! I'LL WRITE YOU!
AW, C'MON, MAG. DON'T BE A COWARD. THIS SHOULD BE A GOOD ONE.

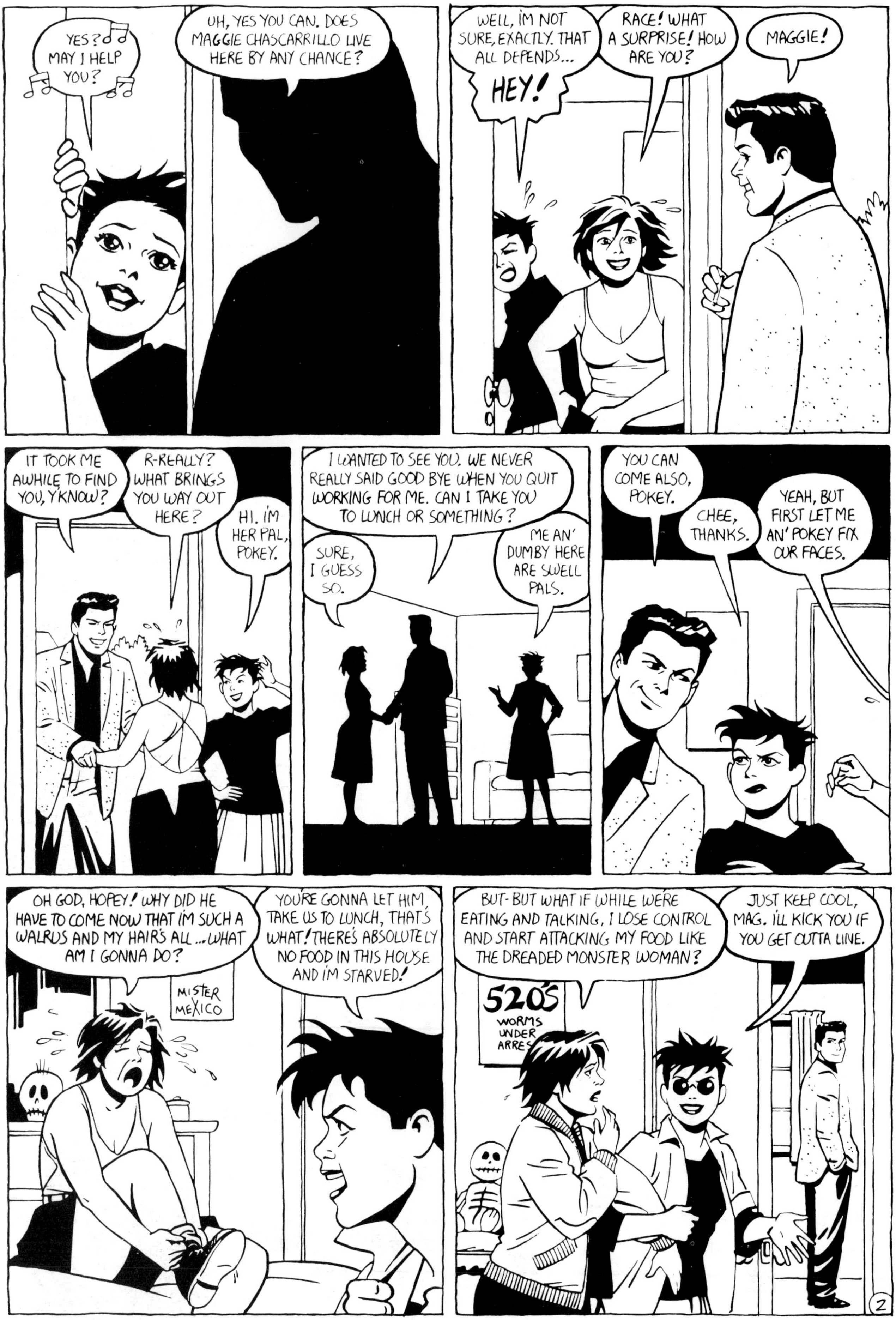
YES? MAY I HELP YOU?
UH, YES YOU CAN. DOES MAGGIE CHASCARRILLO LIVE HERE BY ANY CHANCE?
WELL, I'M NOT SURE, EXACTLY. THAT ALL DEPENDS...
HEY!
RACE! WHAT A SURPRISE! HOW ARE YOU?
MAGGIE!
IT TOOK ME AWHILE TO FIND YOU, Y'KNOW?
R-REALLY? WHAT BRINGS YOU WAY OUT HERE?
HI. I'M HER PAL, POKEY.
I WANTED TO SEE YOU. WE NEVER REALLY SAID GOOD BYE WHEN YOU QUIT WORKING FOR ME. CAN I TAKE YOU TO LUNCH OR SOMETHING?
SURE, I GUESS SO.
ME AN' DUMBY HERE ARE SWELL PALS.
YOU CAN COME ALSO, POKEY.
CHEE, THANKS.
YEAH, BUT FIRST LET ME AN' POKEY FIX OUR FACES.
OH GOD, HOPEY! WHY DID HE HAVE TO COME NOW THAT I'M SUCH A WALRUS AND MY HAIR'S ALL...WHAT AM I GONNA DO?
MISTER MEXICO
YOU'RE GONNA LET HIM TAKE US TO LUNCH, THAT'S WHAT! THERE'S ABSOLUTELY NO FOOD IN THIS HOUSE AND I'M STARVED!
BUT-BUT WHAT IF WHILE WE'RE EATING AND TALKING, I LOSE CONTROL AND START ATTACKING MY FOOD LIKE THE DREADED MONSTER WOMAN?
520'S
WORMS UNDER ARRES
JUST KEEP COOL, MAG. I'LL KICK YOU IF YOU GET OUTTA LINE.
2

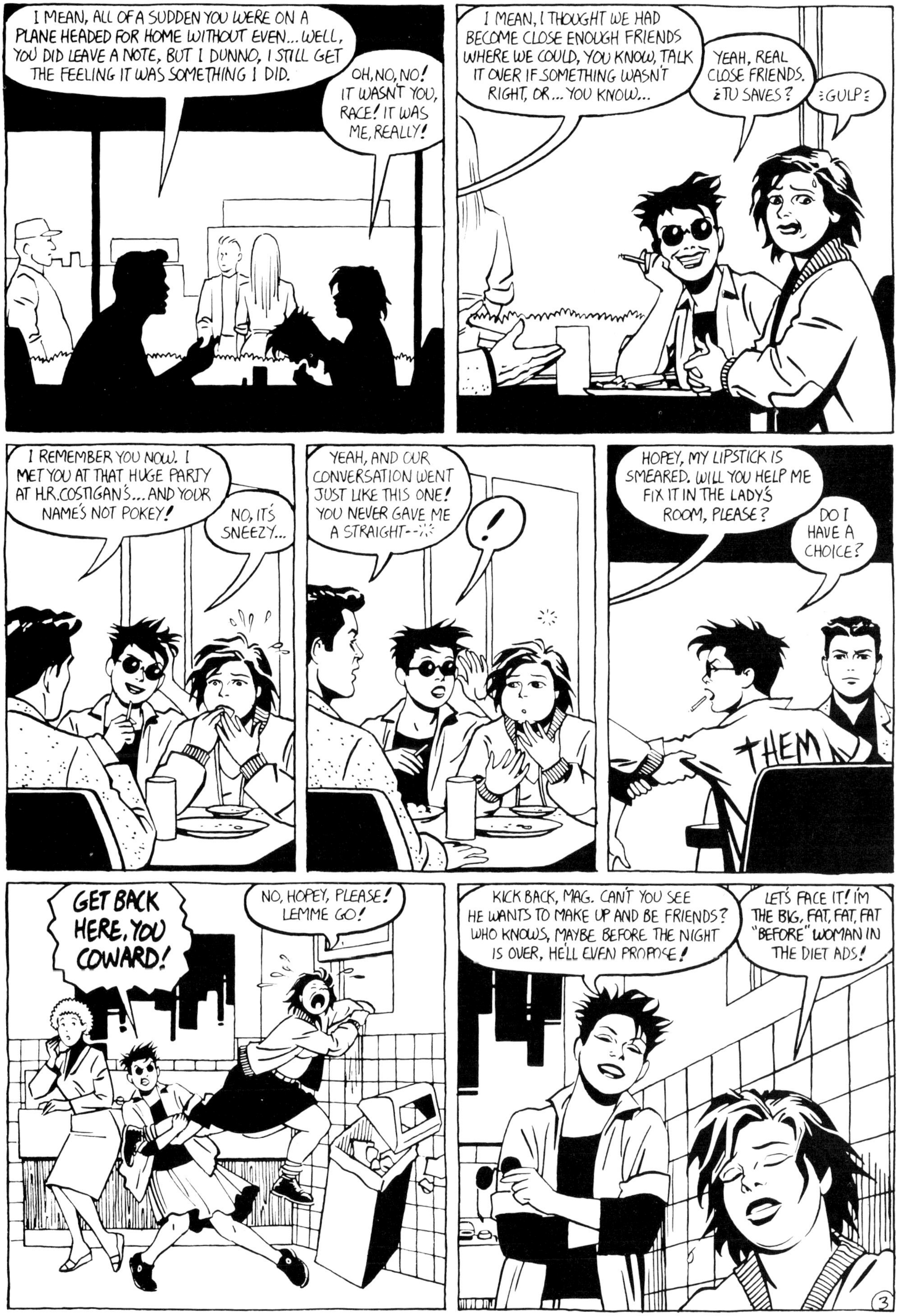
I MEAN, ALL OF A SUDDEN YOU WERE ON A PLANE HEADED FOR HOME WITHOUT EVEN... WELL, YOU DID LEAVE A NOTE, BUT I DUNNO, I STILL GET THE FEELING IT WAS SOMETHING I DID.
OH, NO, NO! IT WASN'T YOU, RACE! IT WAS ME, REALLY!
I MEAN, I THOUGHT WE HAD BECOME CLOSE ENOUGH FRIENDS WHERE WE COULD, YOU KNOW, TALK IT OVER IF SOMETHING WASN'T RIGHT, OR... YOU KNOW...
YEAH, REAL CLOSE FRIENDS. ¿TU SAVES?
GULP
I REMEMBER YOU NOW. I MET YOU AT THAT HUGE PARTY AT H.R. COSTIGAN'S... AND YOUR NAME'S NOT POKEY!
NO, IT'S SNEEZY...
YEAH, AND OUR CONVERSATION WENT JUST LIKE THIS ONE! YOU NEVER GAVE ME A STRAIGHT--
!
HOPEY, MY LIPSTICK IS SMEARED. WILL YOU HELP ME FIX IT IN THE LADY'S ROOM, PLEASE?
DO I HAVE A CHOICE?
THEM
GET BACK HERE, YOU COWARD!
NO, HOPEY, PLEASE! LEMME GO!
KICK BACK, MAG. CAN'T YOU SEE HE WANTS TO MAKE UP AND BE FRIENDS? WHO KNOWS, MAYBE BEFORE THE NIGHT IS OVER, HE'LL EVEN PROPOSE!
LET'S FACE IT! I'M THE BIG, FAT, FAT, FAT "BEFORE" WOMAN IN THE DIET ADS!
3

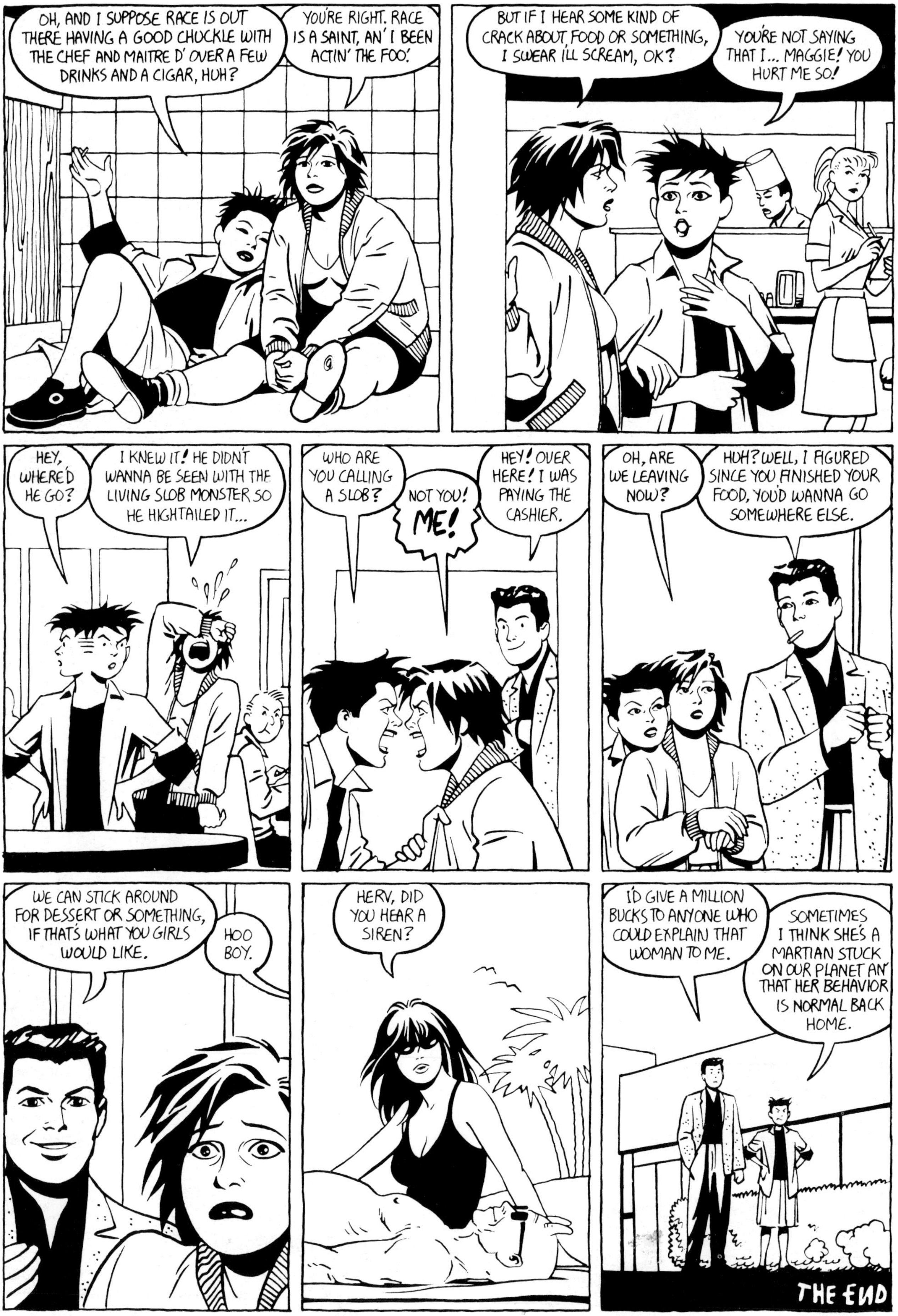

OH, AND I SUPPOSE RACE IS OUT THERE HAVING A GOOD CHUCKLE WITH THE CHEF AND MAITRE D' OVER A FEW DRINKS AND A CIGAR, HUH?
YOU'RE RIGHT. RACE IS A SAINT, AN' I BEEN ACTIN' THE FOO'.
BUT IF I HEAR SOME KIND OF CRACK ABOUT FOOD OR SOMETHING, I SWEAR I'LL SCREAM, OK?
YOU'RE NOT SAYING THAT I... MAGGIE! YOU HURT ME SO!
HEY, WHERE'D HE GO?
I KNEW IT! HE DIDN'T WANNA BE SEEN WITH THE LIVING SLOB MONSTER SO HE HIGHTAILED IT...
WHO ARE YOU CALLING A SLOB?
NOT YOU! ME!
HEY! OVER HERE! I WAS PAYING THE CASHIER.
OH, ARE WE LEAVING NOW?
HUH? WELL, I FIGURED SINCE YOU FINISHED YOUR FOOD, YOU'D WANNA GO SOMEWHERE ELSE.
WE CAN STICK AROUND FOR DESSERT OR SOMETHING, IF THAT'S WHAT YOU GIRLS WOULD LIKE.
HOO BOY.
HERV, DID YOU HEAR A SIREN?
I'D GIVE A MILLION BUCKS TO ANYONE WHO COULD EXPLAIN THAT WOMAN TO ME.
SOMETIMES I THINK SHE'S A MARTIAN STUCK ON OUR PLANET AN' THAT HER BEHAVIOR IS NORMAL BACK HOME.
THE END

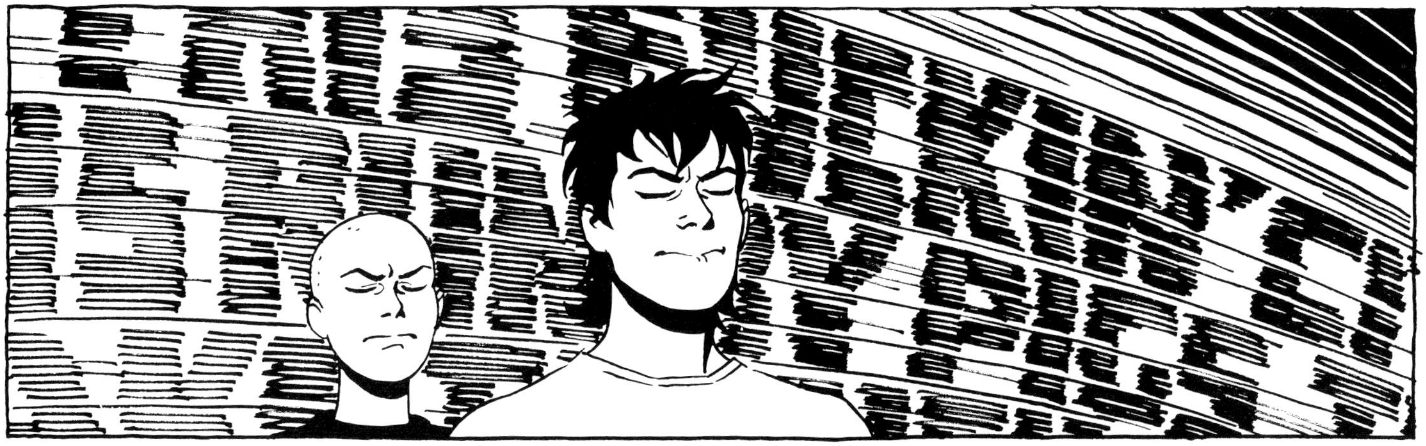

LOCAS vs LOCOS

BIG DADDY 86

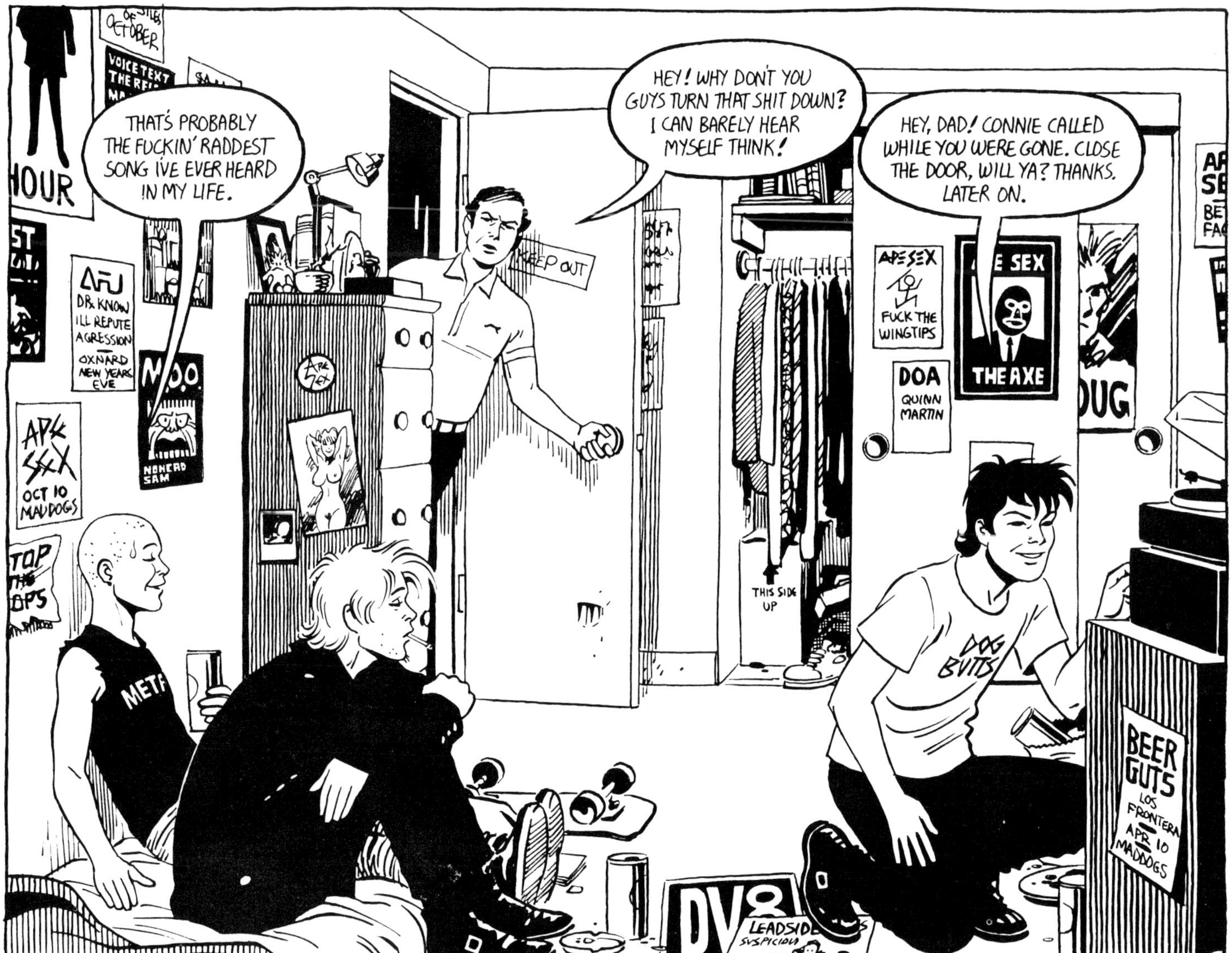
THAT'S PROBABLY THE FUCKIN' RADDEST SONG I'VE EVER HEARD IN MY LIFE.
HEY! WHY DON'T YOU GUYS TURN THAT SHIT DOWN? I CAN BARELY HEAR MYSELF THINK!
HEY, DAD! CONNIE CALLED WHILE YOU WERE GONE. CLOSE THE DOOR, WILL YA? THANKS. LATER ON.
HOUR
AFJ DR. KNOW ILL REPUTE AGRESSION OXNARD NEW YEARS EVE
APE SEX OCT 10 MADDOGS
KEEP OUT
APE SEX FUCK THE WINGTIPS
DOA QUINN MARTIN
THE AXE
THIS SIDE UP
DOG GUTS
BEER GUTS LOS FRONTERA APR 10 MADDOGS
DV8
LEADSIDE
SUSPICION

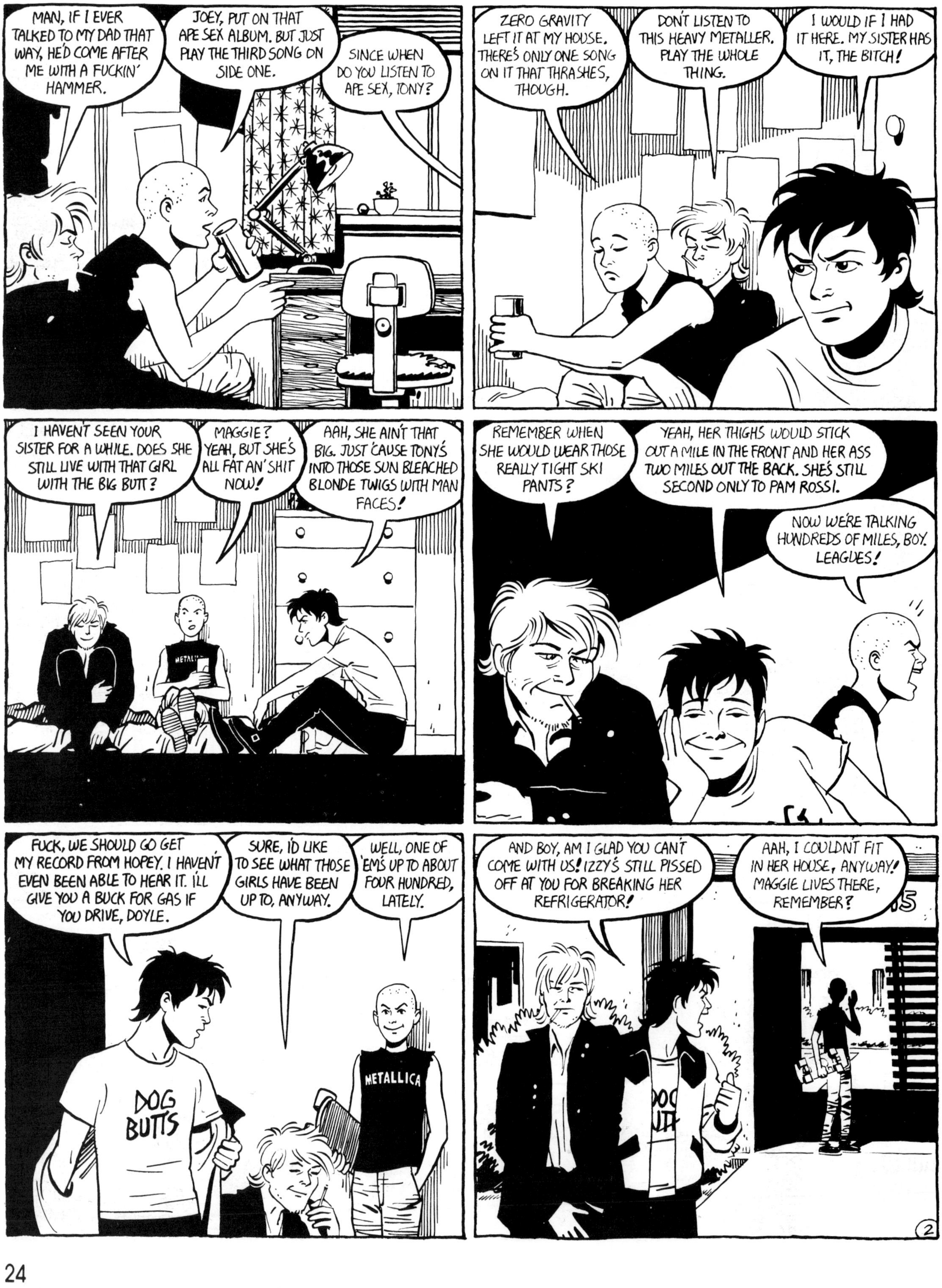
MAN, IF I EVER TALKED TO MY DAD THAT WAY, HE'D COME AFTER ME WITH A FUCKIN' HAMMER.
JOEY, PUT ON THAT APE SEX ALBUM. BUT JUST PLAY THE THIRD SONG ON SIDE ONE.
SINCE WHEN DO YOU LISTEN TO APE SEX, TONY?
ZERO GRAVITY LEFT IT AT MY HOUSE. THERE'S ONLY ONE SONG ON IT THAT THRASHES, THOUGH.
DON'T LISTEN TO THIS HEAVY METALLER. PLAY THE WHOLE THING.
I WOULD IF I HAD IT HERE. MY SISTER HAS IT, THE BITCH!
I HAVEN'T SEEN YOUR SISTER FOR A WHILE. DOES SHE STILL LIVE WITH THAT GIRL WITH THE BIG BUTT?
MAGGIE? YEAH, BUT SHE'S ALL FAT AN' SHIT NOW!
AAH, SHE AIN'T THAT BIG. JUST 'CAUSE TONY'S INTO THOSE SUN BLEACHED BLONDE TWIGS WITH MAN FACES!
METALLICA
REMEMBER WHEN SHE WOULD WEAR THOSE REALLY TIGHT SKI PANTS?
YEAH, HER THIGHS WOULD STICK OUT A MILE IN THE FRONT AND HER ASS TWO MILES OUT THE BACK. SHE'S STILL SECOND ONLY TO PAM ROSSI.
NOW WE'RE TALKING HUNDREDS OF MILES, BOY. LEAGUES!
FUCK, WE SHOULD GO GET MY RECORD FROM HOPEY. I HAVEN'T EVEN BEEN ABLE TO HEAR IT. I'LL GIVE YOU A BUCK FOR GAS IF YOU DRIVE, DOYLE.
SURE, I'D LIKE TO SEE WHAT THOSE GIRLS HAVE BEEN UP TO, ANYWAY.
WELL, ONE OF 'EM'S UP TO ABOUT FOUR HUNDRED, LATELY.
DOG BUTTS
METALLICA
AND BOY, AM I GLAD YOU CAN'T COME WITH US! IZZY'S STILL PISSED OFF AT YOU FOR BREAKING HER REFRIGERATOR!
AAH, I COULDN'T FIT IN HER HOUSE, ANYWAY! MAGGIE LIVES THERE, REMEMBER?
2

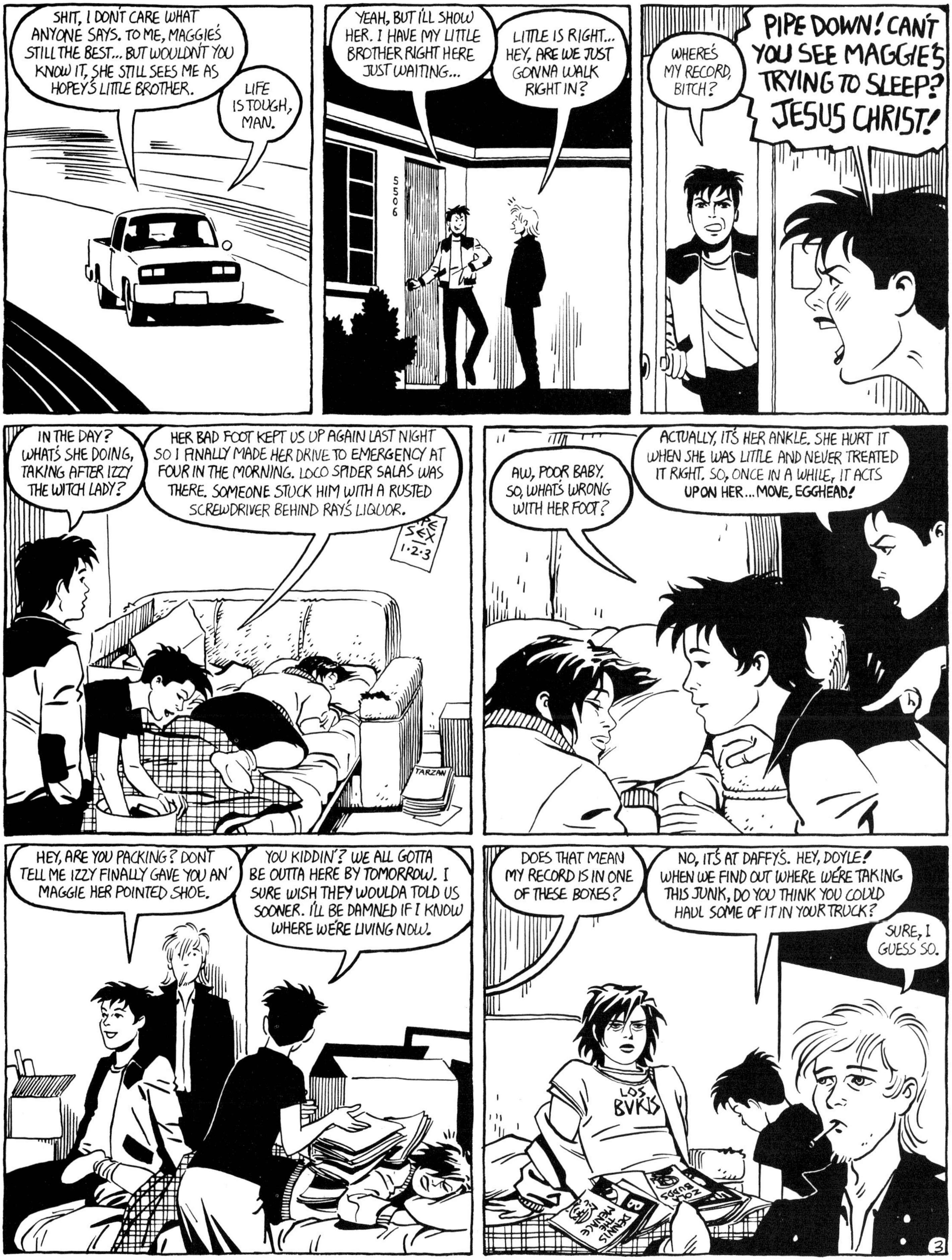
SHIT, I DON'T CARE WHAT ANYONE SAYS. TO ME, MAGGIE'S STILL THE BEST... BUT WOULDN'T YOU KNOW IT, SHE STILL SEES ME AS HOPEY'S LITTLE BROTHER.
LIFE IS TOUGH, MAN.
YEAH, BUT I'LL SHOW HER. I HAVE MY LITTLE BROTHER RIGHT HERE JUST WAITING...
LITTLE IS RIGHT... HEY, ARE WE JUST GONNA WALK RIGHT IN?
5506
WHERE'S MY RECORD, BITCH?
PIPE DOWN! CAN'T YOU SEE MAGGIE'S TRYING TO SLEEP? JESUS CHRIST!
IN THE DAY? WHAT'S SHE DOING, TAKING AFTER IZZY THE WITCH LADY?
HER BAD FOOT KEPT US UP AGAIN LAST NIGHT SO I FINALLY MADE HER DRIVE TO EMERGENCY AT FOUR IN THE MORNING. LOCO SPIDER SALAS WAS THERE. SOMEONE STUCK HIM WITH A RUSTED SCREWDRIVER BEHIND RAY'S LIQUOR.
SEX
1·2·3
TARZAN
AW, POOR BABY. SO, WHAT'S WRONG WITH HER FOOT?
ACTUALLY, IT'S HER ANKLE. SHE HURT IT WHEN SHE WAS LITTLE AND NEVER TREATED IT RIGHT. SO, ONCE IN A WHILE, IT ACTS UP ON HER... MOVE, EGGHEAD!
HEY, ARE YOU PACKING? DON'T TELL ME IZZY FINALLY GAVE YOU AN' MAGGIE HER POINTED SHOE.
YOU KIDDIN'? WE ALL GOTTA BE OUTTA HERE BY TOMORROW. I SURE WISH THEY WOULDA TOLD US SOONER. I'LL BE DAMNED IF I KNOW WHERE WE'RE LIVING NOW.
DOES THAT MEAN MY RECORD IS IN ONE OF THESE BOXES?
NO, IT'S AT DAFFY'S. HEY, DOYLE! WHEN WE FIND OUT WHERE WE'RE TAKING THIS JUNK, DO YOU THINK YOU COULD HAUL SOME OF IT IN YOUR TRUCK?
SURE, I GUESS SO.
LOS BVKIS
DENNIS THE MENACE
ZOO BUDDS
3

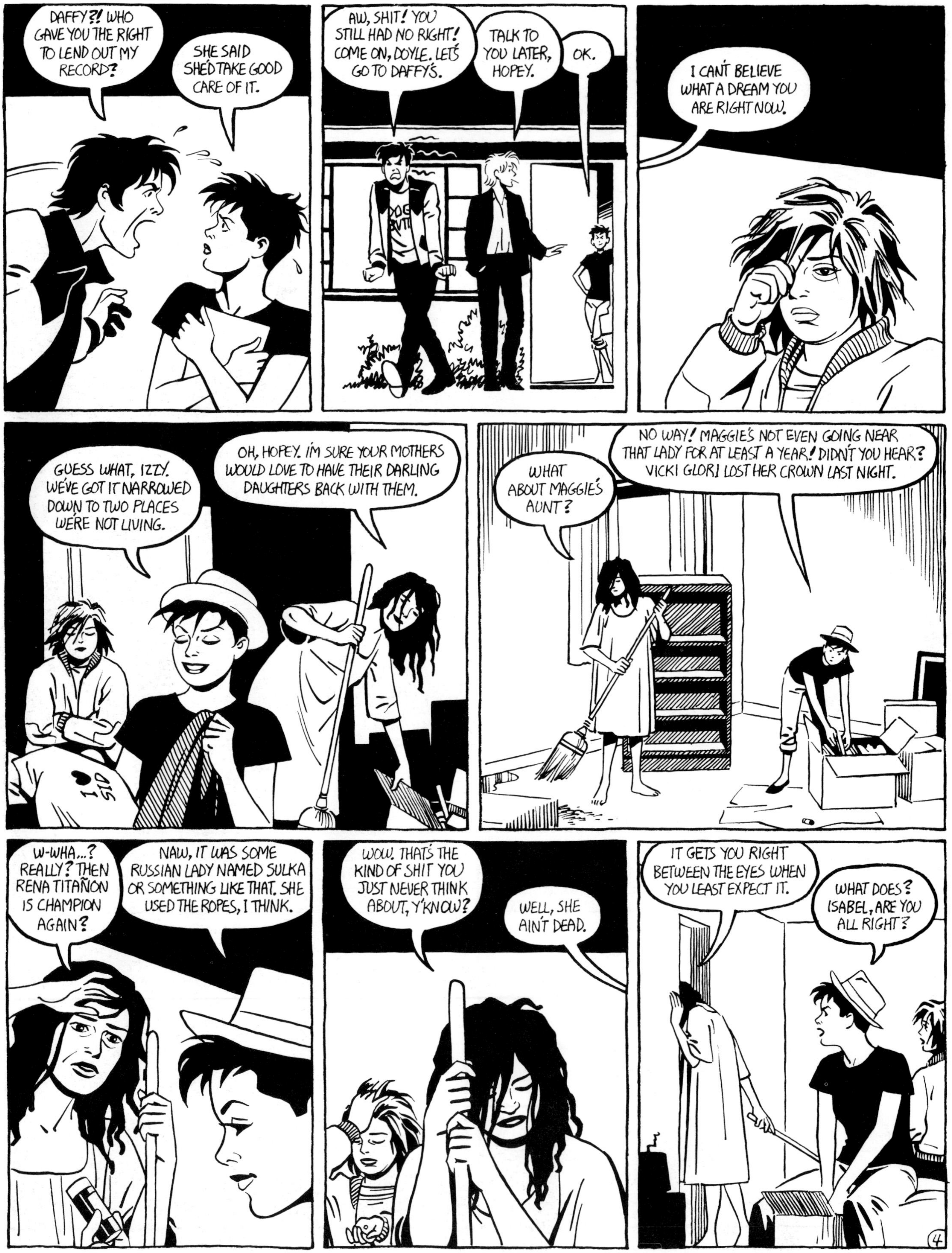
DAFFY?! WHO GAVE YOU THE RIGHT TO LEND OUT MY RECORD?
SHE SAID SHE'D TAKE GOOD CARE OF IT.
AW, SHIT! YOU STILL HAD NO RIGHT! COME ON, DOYLE. LET'S GO TO DAFFY'S.
TALK TO YOU LATER, HOPEY.
OK.
I CAN'T BELIEVE WHAT A DREAM YOU ARE RIGHT NOW.
GUESS WHAT, IZZY. WE'VE GOT IT NARROWED DOWN TO TWO PLACES WE'RE NOT LIVING.
OH, HOPEY. I'M SURE YOUR MOTHERS WOULD LOVE TO HAVE THEIR DARLING DAUGHTERS BACK WITH THEM.
WHAT ABOUT MAGGIE'S AUNT?
NO WAY! MAGGIE'S NOT EVEN GOING NEAR THAT LADY FOR AT LEAST A YEAR! DIDN'T YOU HEAR? VICKI GLORI LOST HER CROWN LAST NIGHT.
W-WHA...? REALLY? THEN RENA TITAÑON IS CHAMPION AGAIN?
NAW, IT WAS SOME RUSSIAN LADY NAMED SULKA OR SOMETHING LIKE THAT. SHE USED THE ROPES, I THINK.
WOW. THAT'S THE KIND OF SHIT YOU JUST NEVER THINK ABOUT, Y'KNOW?
WELL, SHE AIN'T DEAD.
IT GETS YOU RIGHT BETWEEN THE EYES WHEN YOU LEAST EXPECT IT.
WHAT DOES? ISABEL, ARE YOU ALL RIGHT?
4

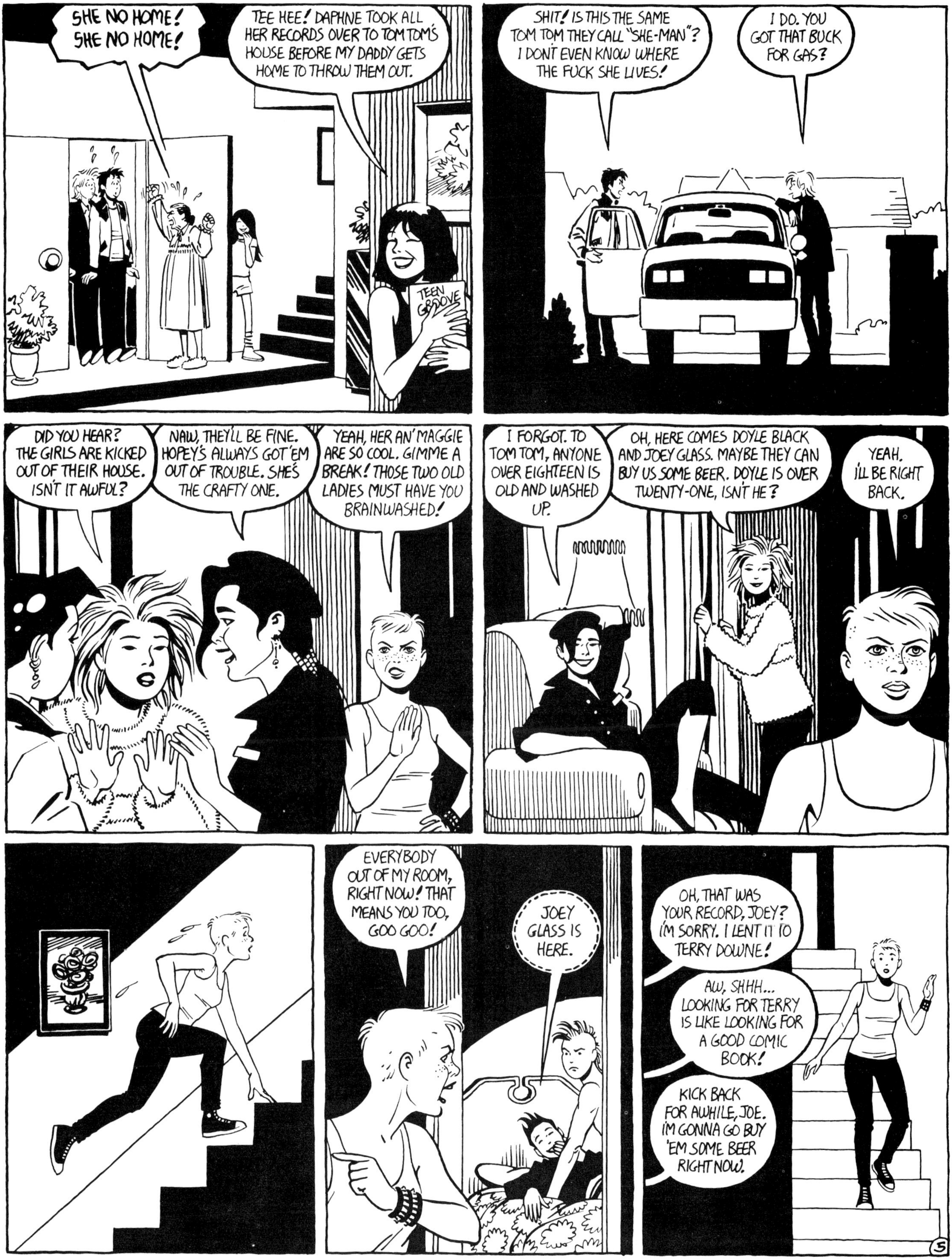
SHE NO HOME! SHE NO HOME!
TEE HEE! DAPHNE TOOK ALL HER RECORDS OVER TO TOM TOM'S HOUSE BEFORE MY DADDY GETS HOME TO THROW THEM OUT.
TEEN GROOVE
SHIT! IS THIS THE SAME TOM TOM THEY CALL "SHE-MAN"? I DON'T EVEN KNOW WHERE THE FUCK SHE LIVES!
I DO. YOU GOT THAT BUCK FOR GAS?
DID YOU HEAR? THE GIRLS ARE KICKED OUT OF THEIR HOUSE. ISN'T IT AWFUL?
NAW, THEY'LL BE FINE. HOPEY'S ALWAYS GOT 'EM OUT OF TROUBLE. SHE'S THE CRAFTY ONE.
YEAH, HER AN' MAGGIE ARE SO COOL. GIMME A BREAK! THOSE TWO OLD LADIES MUST HAVE YOU BRAINWASHED!
I FORGOT. TO TOM TOM, ANYONE OVER EIGHTEEN IS OLD AND WASHED UP.
OH, HERE COMES DOYLE BLACK AND JOEY GLASS. MAYBE THEY CAN BUY US SOME BEER. DOYLE IS OVER TWENTY-ONE, ISN'T HE?
YEAH. I'LL BE RIGHT BACK.
EVERYBODY OUT OF MY ROOM, RIGHT NOW! THAT MEANS YOU TOO, GOO GOO!
JOEY GLASS IS HERE.
OH, THAT WAS YOUR RECORD, JOEY? I'M SORRY. I LENT IT TO TERRY DOWNE!
AW, SHHH... LOOKING FOR TERRY IS LIKE LOOKING FOR A GOOD COMIC BOOK!
KICK BACK FOR AWHILE, JOE. I'M GONNA GO BUY 'EM SOME BEER RIGHT NOW.
5

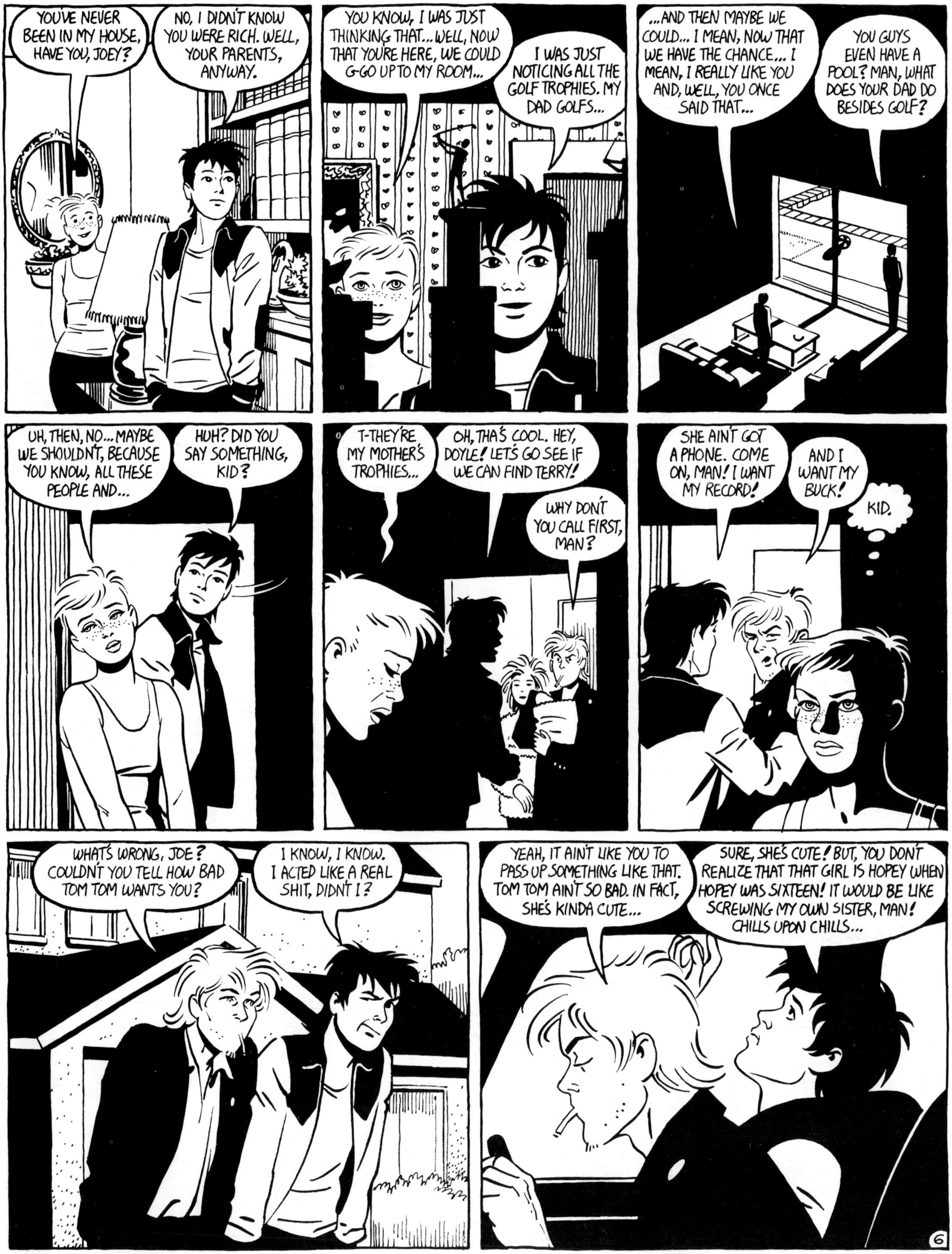
YOU'VE NEVER BEEN IN MY HOUSE, HAVE YOU, JOEY?
NO, I DIDN'T KNOW YOU WERE RICH. WELL, YOUR PARENTS, ANYWAY.
YOU KNOW, I WAS JUST THINKING THAT... WELL, NOW THAT YOU'RE HERE, WE COULD G-GO UP TO MY ROOM...
I WAS JUST NOTICING ALL THE GOLF TROPHIES. MY DAD GOLFS...
...AND THEN MAYBE WE COULD... I MEAN, NOW THAT WE HAVE THE CHANCE... I MEAN, I REALLY LIKE YOU AND, WELL, YOU ONCE SAID THAT...
YOU GUYS EVEN HAVE A POOL? MAN, WHAT DOES YOUR DAD DO BESIDES GOLF?
UH, THEN, NO... MAYBE WE SHOULDN'T, BECAUSE YOU KNOW, ALL THESE PEOPLE AND...
HUH? DID YOU SAY SOMETHING, KID?
T-THEY'RE MY MOTHER'S TROPHIES...
OH, THA'S COOL. HEY, DOYLE! LET'S GO SEE IF WE CAN FIND TERRY!
WHY DON'T YOU CALL FIRST, MAN?
SHE AIN'T GOT A PHONE. COME ON, MAN! I WANT MY RECORD!
AND I WANT MY BUCK!
KID.
WHAT'S WRONG, JOE? COULDN'T YOU TELL HOW BAD TOM TOM WANTS YOU?
I KNOW, I KNOW. I ACTED LIKE A REAL SHIT, DIDN'T I?
YEAH, IT AIN'T LIKE YOU TO PASS UP SOMETHING LIKE THAT. TOM TOM AIN'T SO BAD. IN FACT, SHE'S KINDA CUTE...
SURE, SHE'S CUTE! BUT, YOU DON'T REALIZE THAT THAT GIRL IS HOPEY WHEN HOPEY WAS SIXTEEN! IT WOULD BE LIKE SCREWING MY OWN SISTER, MAN! CHILLS UPON CHILLS...
6

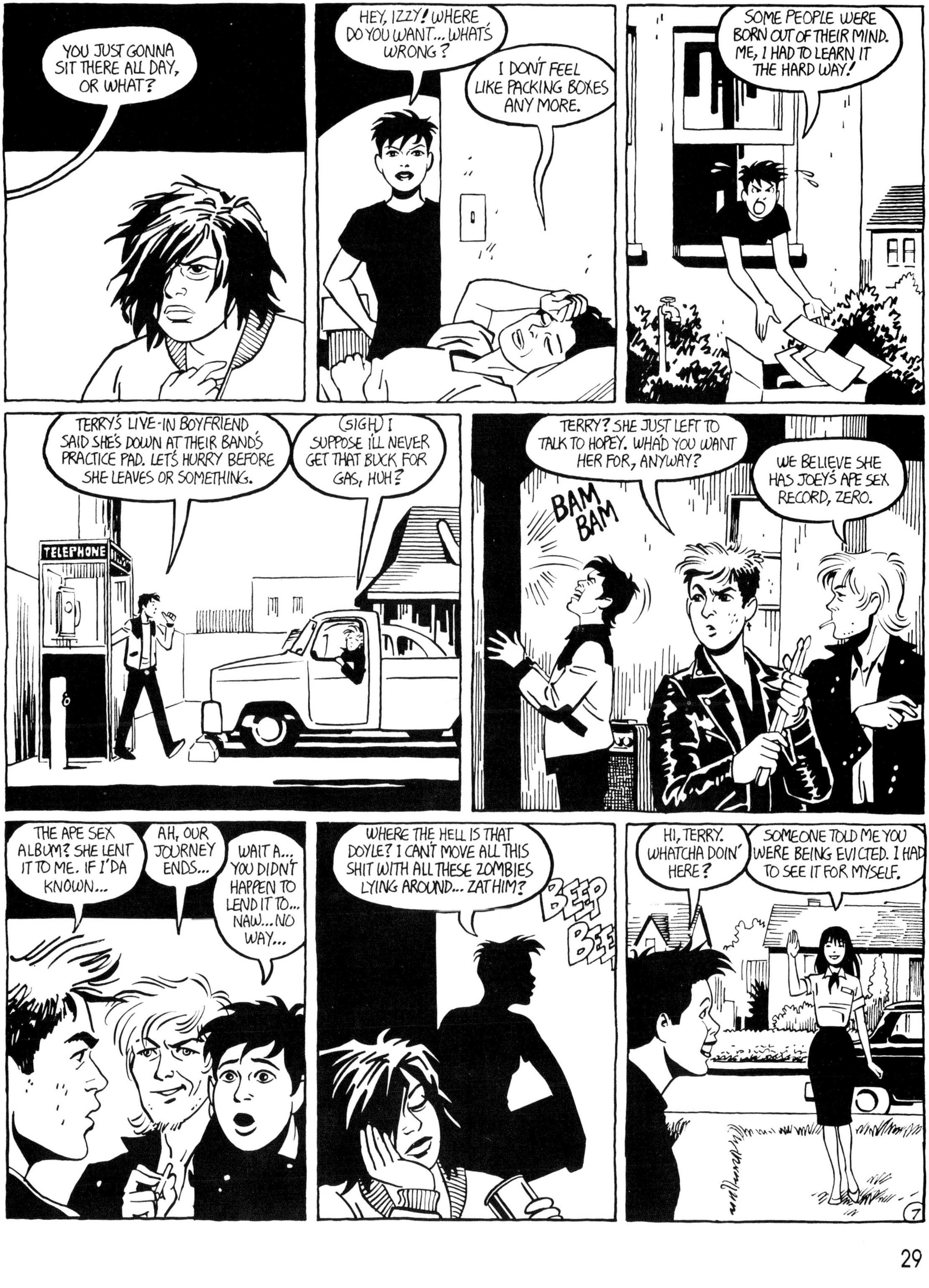
YOU JUST GONNA SIT THERE ALL DAY, OR WHAT?
HEY, IZZY! WHERE DO YOU WANT... WHAT'S WRONG?
I DON'T FEEL LIKE PACKING BOXES ANY MORE.
SOME PEOPLE WERE BORN OUT OF THEIR MIND. ME, I HAD TO LEARN IT THE HARD WAY!
TERRY'S LIVE-IN BOYFRIEND SAID SHE'S DOWN AT THEIR BAND'S PRACTICE PAD. LET'S HURRY BEFORE SHE LEAVES OR SOMETHING.
TELEPHONE
(SIGH) I SUPPOSE I'LL NEVER GET THAT BUCK FOR GAS, HUH?
TERRY? SHE JUST LEFT TO TALK TO HOPEY. WHAD'YOU WANT HER FOR, ANYWAY?
BAM BAM
WE BELIEVE SHE HAS JOEY'S APE SEX RECORD, ZERO.
THE APE SEX ALBUM? SHE LENT IT TO ME. IF I'DA KNOWN...
AH, OUR JOURNEY ENDS...
WAIT A... YOU DIDN'T HAPPEN TO LEND IT TO... NAW... NO WAY...
WHERE THE HELL IS THAT DOYLE? I CAN'T MOVE ALL THIS SHIT WITH ALL THESE ZOMBIES LYING AROUND... ZAT HIM?
BEEP BEE
HI, TERRY. WHATCHA DOIN' HERE?
SOMEONE TOLD ME YOU WERE BEING EVICTED. I HAD TO SEE IT FOR MYSELF.
7

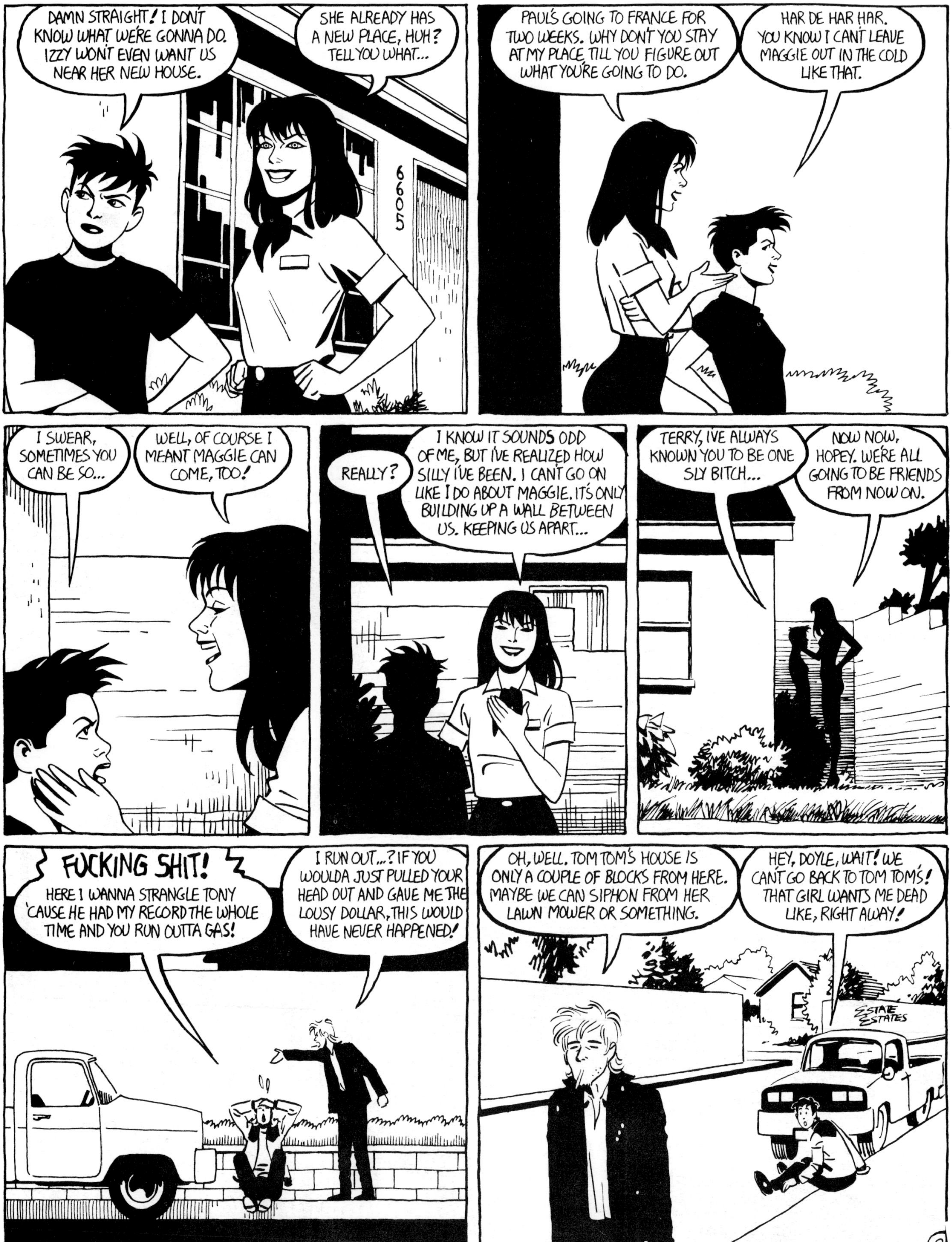
DAMN STRAIGHT! I DON'T KNOW WHAT WE'RE GONNA DO. IZZY WON'T EVEN WANT US NEAR HER NEW HOUSE.
SHE ALREADY HAS A NEW PLACE, HUH? TELL YOU WHAT...
6605
PAUL'S GOING TO FRANCE FOR TWO WEEKS. WHY DON'T YOU STAY AT MY PLACE TILL YOU FIGURE OUT WHAT YOU'RE GOING TO DO.
HAR DE HAR HAR. YOU KNOW I CAN'T LEAVE MAGGIE OUT IN THE COLD LIKE THAT.
I SWEAR, SOMETIMES YOU CAN BE SO...
WELL, OF COURSE I MEANT MAGGIE CAN COME, TOO!
REALLY?
I KNOW IT SOUNDS ODD OF ME, BUT I'VE REALIZED HOW SILLY I'VE BEEN. I CAN'T GO ON LIKE I DO ABOUT MAGGIE. IT'S ONLY BUILDING UP A WALL BETWEEN US. KEEPING US APART...
TERRY, I'VE ALWAYS KNOWN YOU TO BE ONE SLY BITCH...
NOW NOW, HOPEY. WE'RE ALL GOING TO BE FRIENDS FROM NOW ON.
FUCKING SHIT!
HERE I WANNA STRANGLE TONY 'CAUSE HE HAD MY RECORD THE WHOLE TIME AND YOU RUN OUTTA GAS!
I RUN OUT...? IF YOU WOULDA JUST PULLED YOUR HEAD OUT AND GAVE ME THE LOUSY DOLLAR, THIS WOULD HAVE NEVER HAPPENED!
OH, WELL. TOM TOM'S HOUSE IS ONLY A COUPLE OF BLOCKS FROM HERE. MAYBE WE CAN SIPHON FROM HER LAWN MOWER OR SOMETHING.
HEY, DOYLE, WAIT! WE CAN'T GO BACK TO TOM TOM'S! THAT GIRL WANTS ME DEAD LIKE, RIGHT AWAY!
ESTATE ESTATES
8

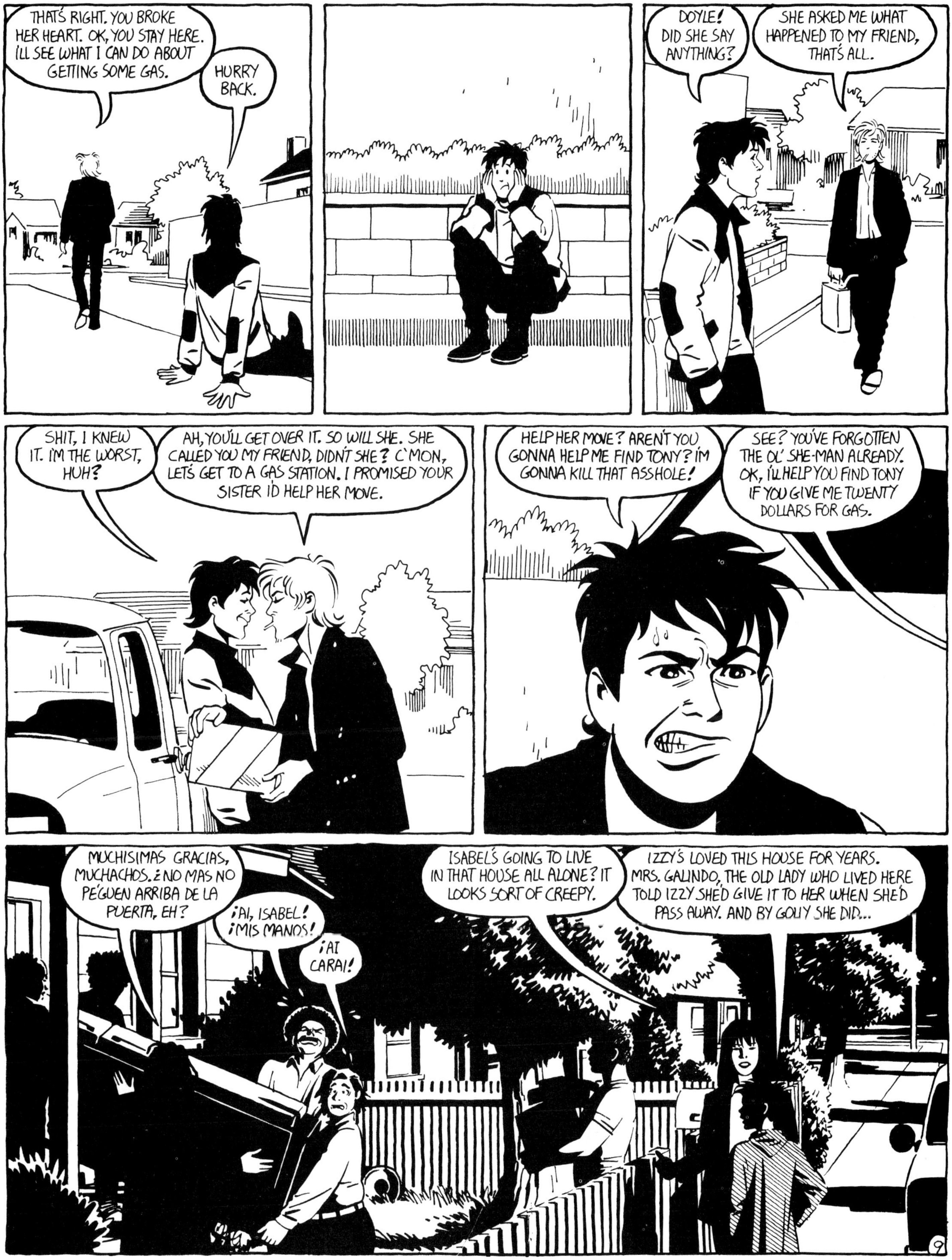
THAT'S RIGHT. YOU BROKE HER HEART. OK, YOU STAY HERE. I'LL SEE WHAT I CAN DO ABOUT GETTING SOME GAS.
HURRY BACK.
DOYLE! DID SHE SAY ANYTHING?
SHE ASKED ME WHAT HAPPENED TO MY FRIEND, THAT'S ALL.
SHIT, I KNEW IT. I'M THE WORST, HUH?
AH, YOU'LL GET OVER IT. SO WILL SHE. SHE CALLED YOU MY FRIEND, DIDN'T SHE? C'MON, LET'S GET TO A GAS STATION. I PROMISED YOUR SISTER I'D HELP HER MOVE.
HELP HER MOVE? AREN'T YOU GONNA HELP ME FIND TONY? I'M GONNA KILL THAT ASSHOLE!
SEE? YOU'VE FORGOTTEN THE OL' SHE-MAN ALREADY. OK, I'LL HELP YOU FIND TONY IF YOU GIVE ME TWENTY DOLLARS FOR GAS.
MUCHISIMAS GRACIAS, MUCHACHOS. ¿NO MAS NO PE'GUEN ARRIBA DE LA PUERTA, EH?
¡AI, ISABEL! ¡MIS MANOS!
¡AI CARAI!
ISABEL'S GOING TO LIVE IN THAT HOUSE ALL ALONE? IT LOOKS SORT OF CREEPY.
IZZY'S LOVED THIS HOUSE FOR YEARS. MRS. GALINDO, THE OLD LADY WHO LIVED HERE TOLD IZZY SHE'D GIVE IT TO HER WHEN SHE'D PASS AWAY. AND BY GOLLY SHE DID...
9

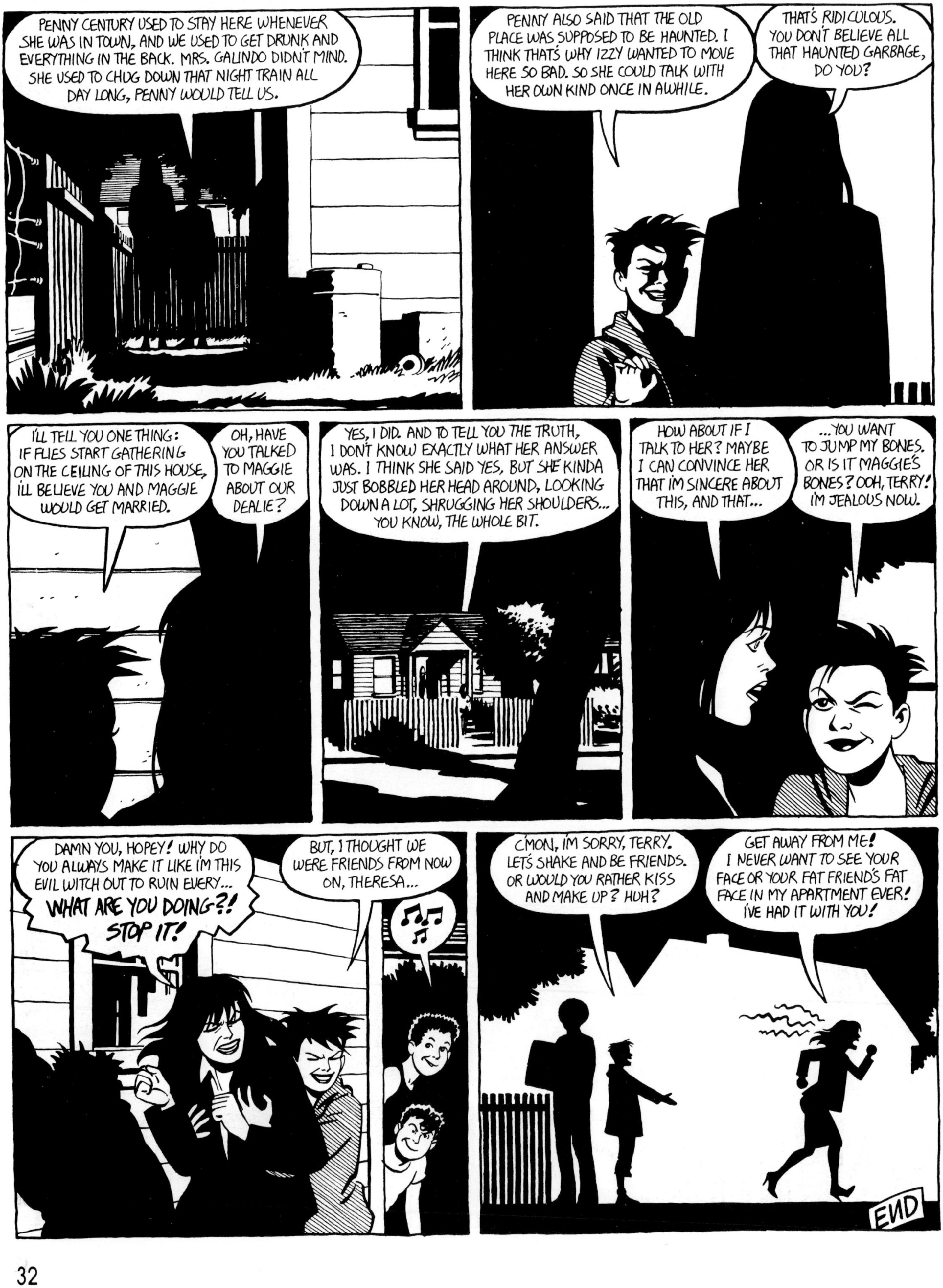
PENNY CENTURY USED TO STAY HERE WHENEVER SHE WAS IN TOWN, AND WE USED TO GET DRUNK AND EVERYTHING IN THE BACK. MRS. GALINDO DIDN'T MIND. SHE USED TO CHUG DOWN THAT NIGHT TRAIN ALL DAY LONG, PENNY WOULD TELL US.
PENNY ALSO SAID THAT THE OLD PLACE WAS SUPPOSED TO BE HAUNTED. I THINK THAT'S WHY IZZY WANTED TO MOVE HERE SO BAD. SO SHE COULD TALK WITH HER OWN KIND ONCE IN AWHILE.
THAT'S RIDICULOUS. YOU DON'T BELIEVE ALL THAT HAUNTED GARBAGE, DO YOU?
I'LL TELL YOU ONE THING: IF FLIES START GATHERING ON THE CEILING OF THIS HOUSE, I'LL BELIEVE YOU AND MAGGIE WOULD GET MARRIED.
OH, HAVE YOU TALKED TO MAGGIE ABOUT OUR DEALIE?
YES, I DID. AND TO TELL YOU THE TRUTH, I DON'T KNOW EXACTLY WHAT HER ANSWER WAS. I THINK SHE SAID YES, BUT SHE KINDA JUST BOBBLED HER HEAD AROUND, LOOKING DOWN A LOT, SHRUGGING HER SHOULDERS... YOU KNOW, THE WHOLE BIT.
HOW ABOUT IF I TALK TO HER? MAYBE I CAN CONVINCE HER THAT I'M SINCERE ABOUT THIS, AND THAT...
...YOU WANT TO JUMP MY BONES. OR IS IT MAGGIE'S BONES? OOH, TERRY! I'M JEALOUS NOW.
DAMN YOU, HOPEY! WHY DO YOU ALWAYS MAKE IT LIKE I'M THIS EVIL WITCH OUT TO RUIN EVERY... WHAT ARE YOU DOING?! STOP IT!
BUT, I THOUGHT WE WERE FRIENDS FROM NOW ON, THERESA...
C'MON, I'M SORRY, TERRY. LET'S SHAKE AND BE FRIENDS. OR WOULD YOU RATHER KISS AND MAKE UP? HUH?
GET AWAY FROM ME! I NEVER WANT TO SEE YOUR FACE OR YOUR FAT FRIEND'S FAT FACE IN MY APARTMENT EVER! I'VE HAD IT WITH YOU!
END

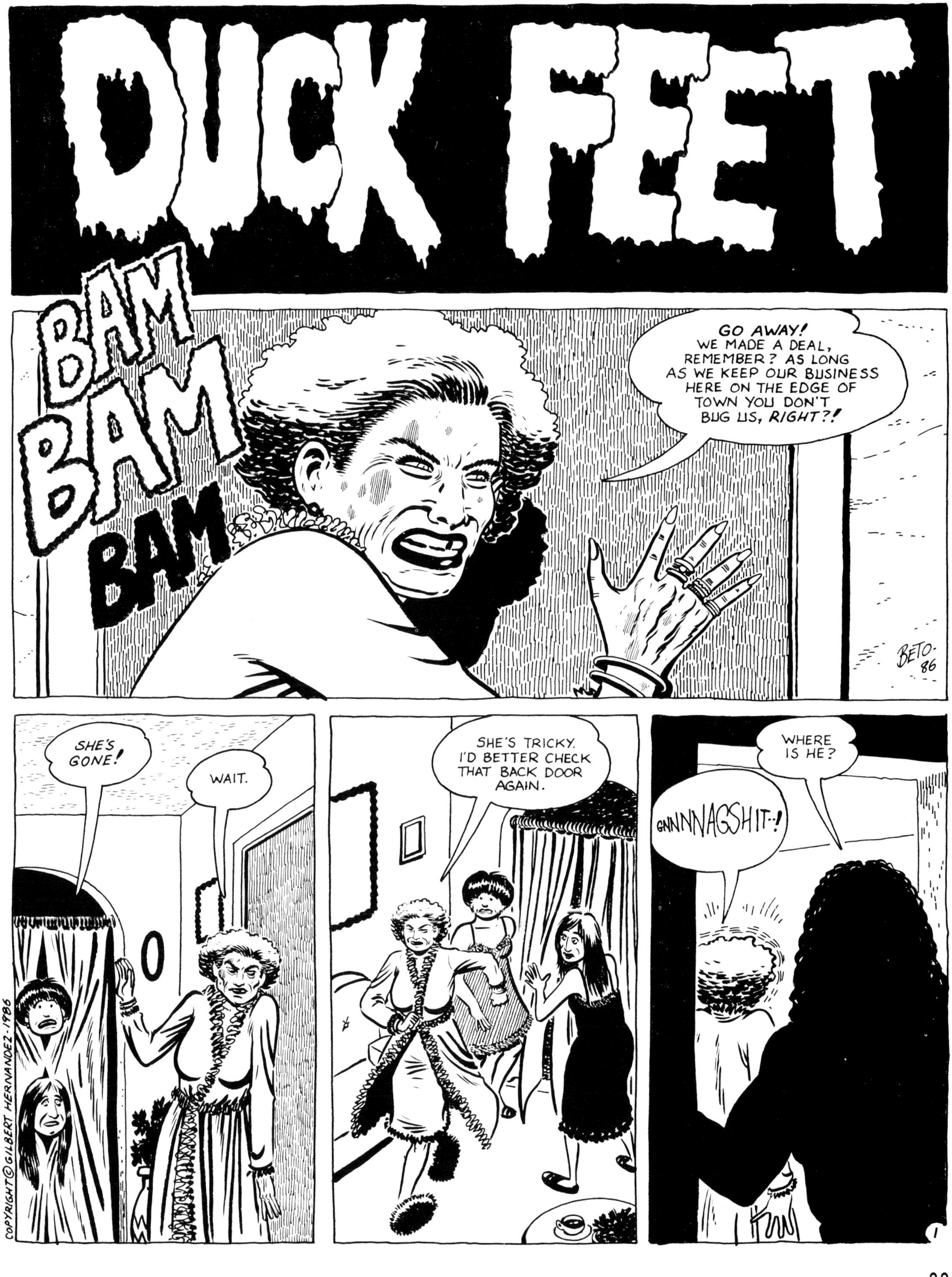
DUCK FEET
BAM BAM BAM
GO AWAY! WE MADE A DEAL, REMEMBER? AS LONG AS WE KEEP OUR BUSINESS HERE ON THE EDGE OF TOWN YOU DON'T BUG US, RIGHT?!
BETO 86
SHE'S GONE!
WAIT.
COPYRIGHT © GILBERT HERNANDEZ 1986
SHE'S TRICKY. I'D BETTER CHECK THAT BACK DOOR AGAIN.
WHERE IS HE?
GNNNNAGSHIT--!
1

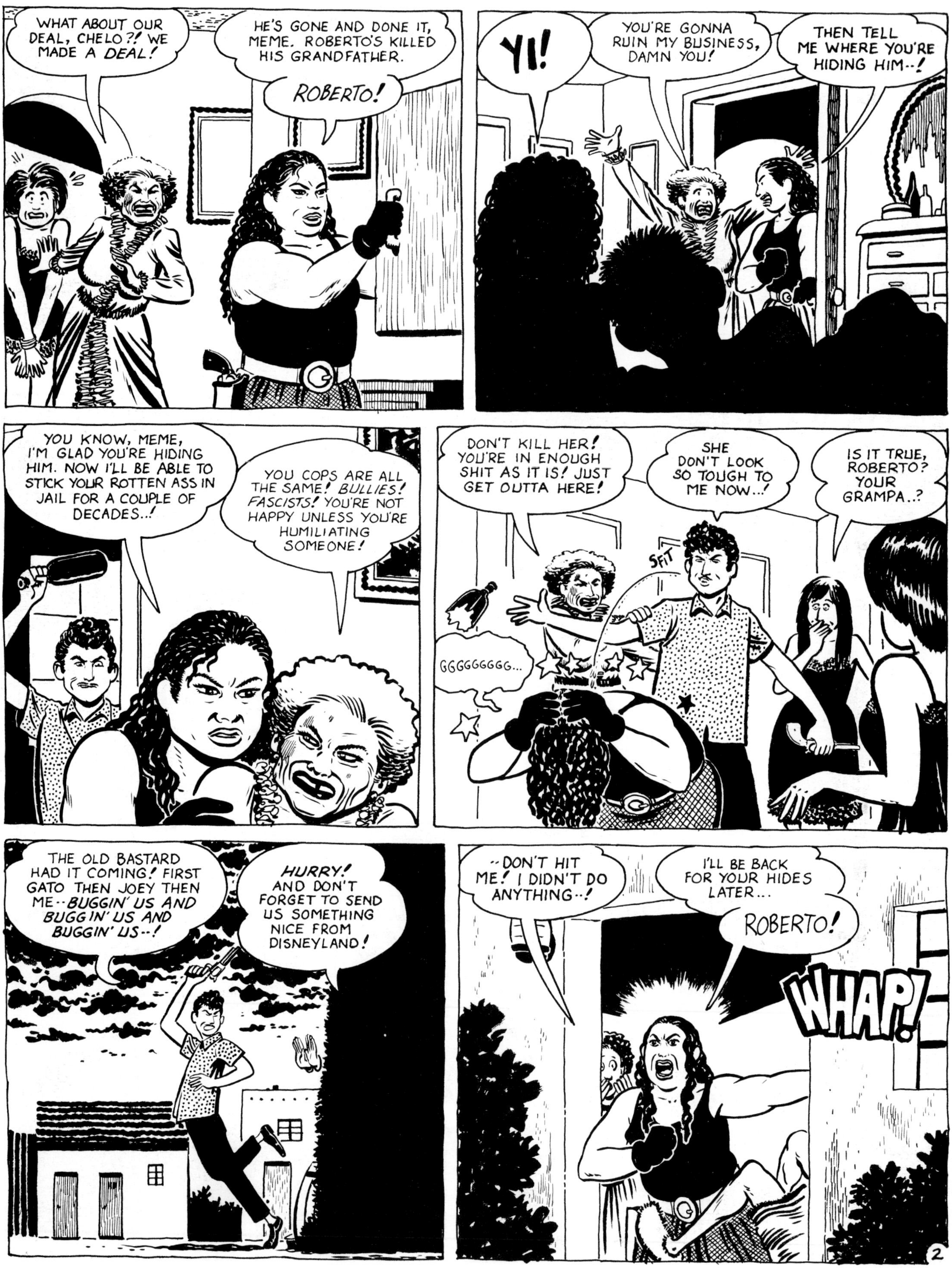
WHAT ABOUT OUR DEAL, CHELO?! WE MADE A DEAL!
HE'S GONE AND DONE IT, MEME. ROBERTO'S KILLED HIS GRANDFATHER.
ROBERTO!
YI!
YOU'RE GONNA RUIN MY BUSINESS, DAMN YOU!
THEN TELL ME WHERE YOU'RE HIDING HIM--!
YOU KNOW, MEME, I'M GLAD YOU'RE HIDING HIM. NOW I'LL BE ABLE TO STICK YOUR ROTTEN ASS IN JAIL FOR A COUPLE OF DECADES..!
YOU COPS ARE ALL THE SAME! BULLIES! FASCISTS! YOU'RE NOT HAPPY UNLESS YOU'RE HUMILIATING SOMEONE!
DON'T KILL HER! YOU'RE IN ENOUGH SHIT AS IT IS! JUST GET OUTTA HERE!
SHE DON'T LOOK SO TOUGH TO ME NOW...!
IS IT TRUE, ROBERTO? YOUR GRAMPA..?
SFIT
GGGGGGGGG...
THE OLD BASTARD HAD IT COMING! FIRST GATO THEN JOEY THEN ME--BUGGIN' US AND BUGGIN' US AND BUGGIN' US--!
HURRY! AND DON'T FORGET TO SEND US SOMETHING NICE FROM DISNEYLAND!
--DON'T HIT ME! I DIDN'T DO ANYTHING--!
I'LL BE BACK FOR YOUR HIDES LATER...
ROBERTO!
WHAP!
2

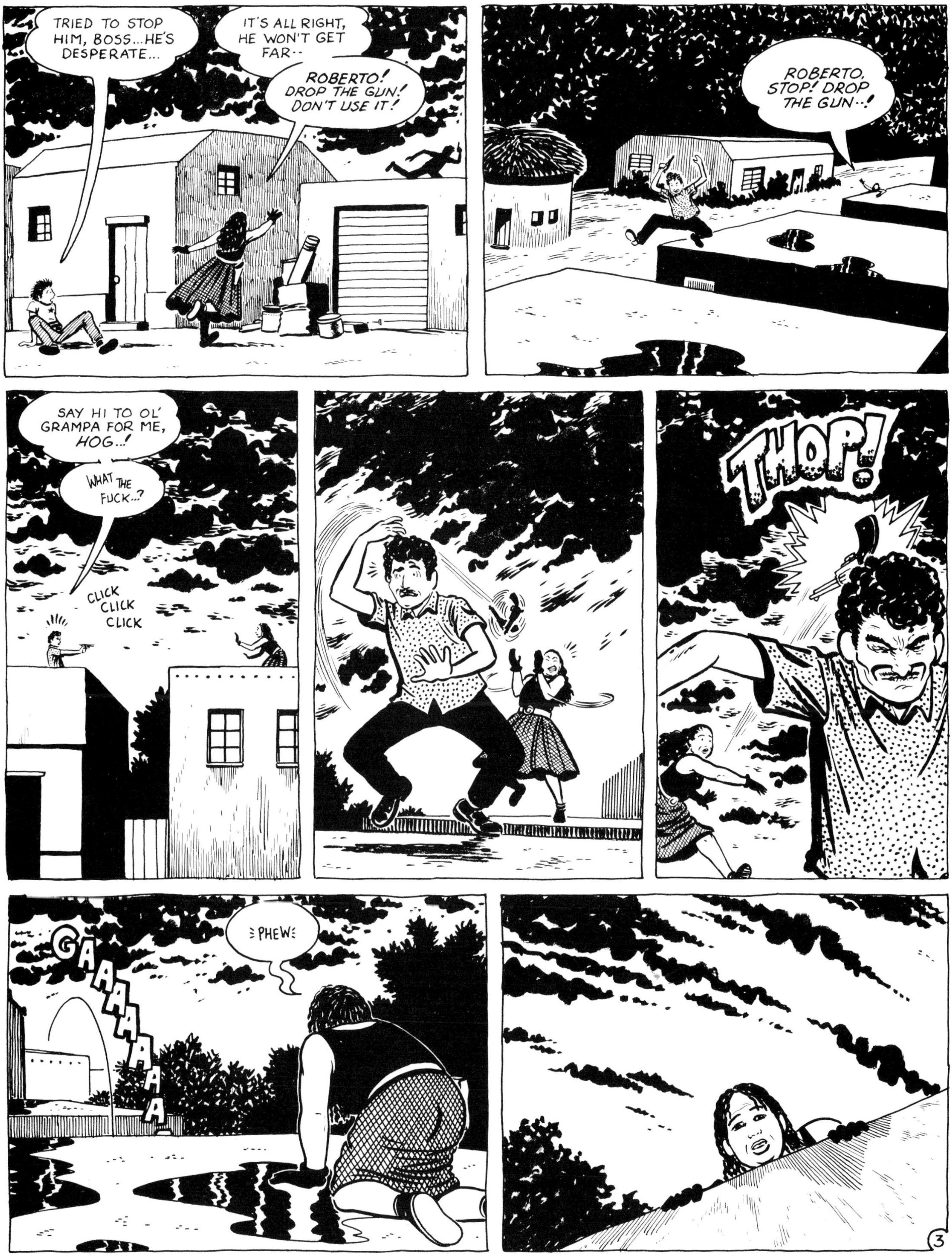
TRIED TO STOP HIM, BOSS...HE'S DESPERATE...
IT'S ALL RIGHT, HE WON'T GET FAR--
ROBERTO! DROP THE GUN! DON'T USE IT!
ROBERTO. STOP! DROP THE GUN--!
SAY HI TO OL' GRAMPA FOR ME, HOG...!
WHAT THE FUCK...?
CLICK CLICK CLICK
THOP!
GAAAAAAAAA
PHEW
3

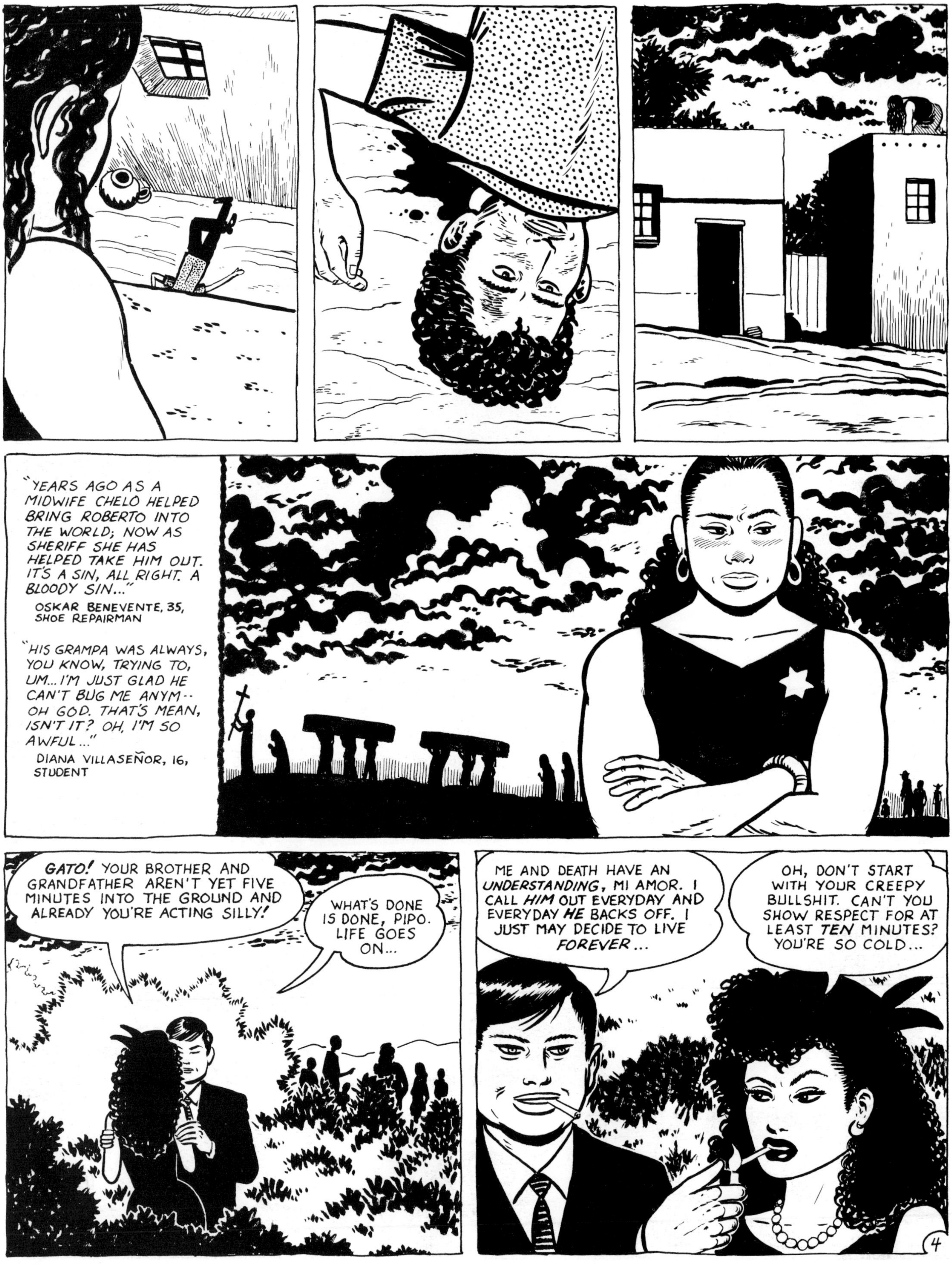
"YEARS AGO AS A MIDWIFE CHELO HELPED BRING ROBERTO INTO THE WORLD; NOW AS SHERIFF SHE HAS HELPED TAKE HIM OUT. IT'S A SIN, ALL RIGHT. A BLOODY SIN..."
OSKAR BENEVENTE, 35, SHOE REPAIRMAN
"HIS GRAMPA WAS ALWAYS, YOU KNOW, TRYING TO, UM... I'M JUST GLAD HE CAN'T BUG ME ANYM-- OH GOD. THAT'S MEAN, ISN'T IT? OH, I'M SO AWFUL..."
DIANA VILLASEÑOR, 16, STUDENT
GATO! YOUR BROTHER AND GRANDFATHER AREN'T YET FIVE MINUTES INTO THE GROUND AND ALREADY YOU'RE ACTING SILLY!
WHAT'S DONE IS DONE, PIPO. LIFE GOES ON...
ME AND DEATH HAVE AN UNDERSTANDING, MI AMOR. I CALL HIM OUT EVERYDAY AND EVERYDAY HE BACKS OFF. I JUST MAY DECIDE TO LIVE FOREVER...
OH, DON'T START WITH YOUR CREEPY BULLSHIT. CAN'T YOU SHOW RESPECT FOR AT LEAST TEN MINUTES? YOU'RE SO COLD...
4

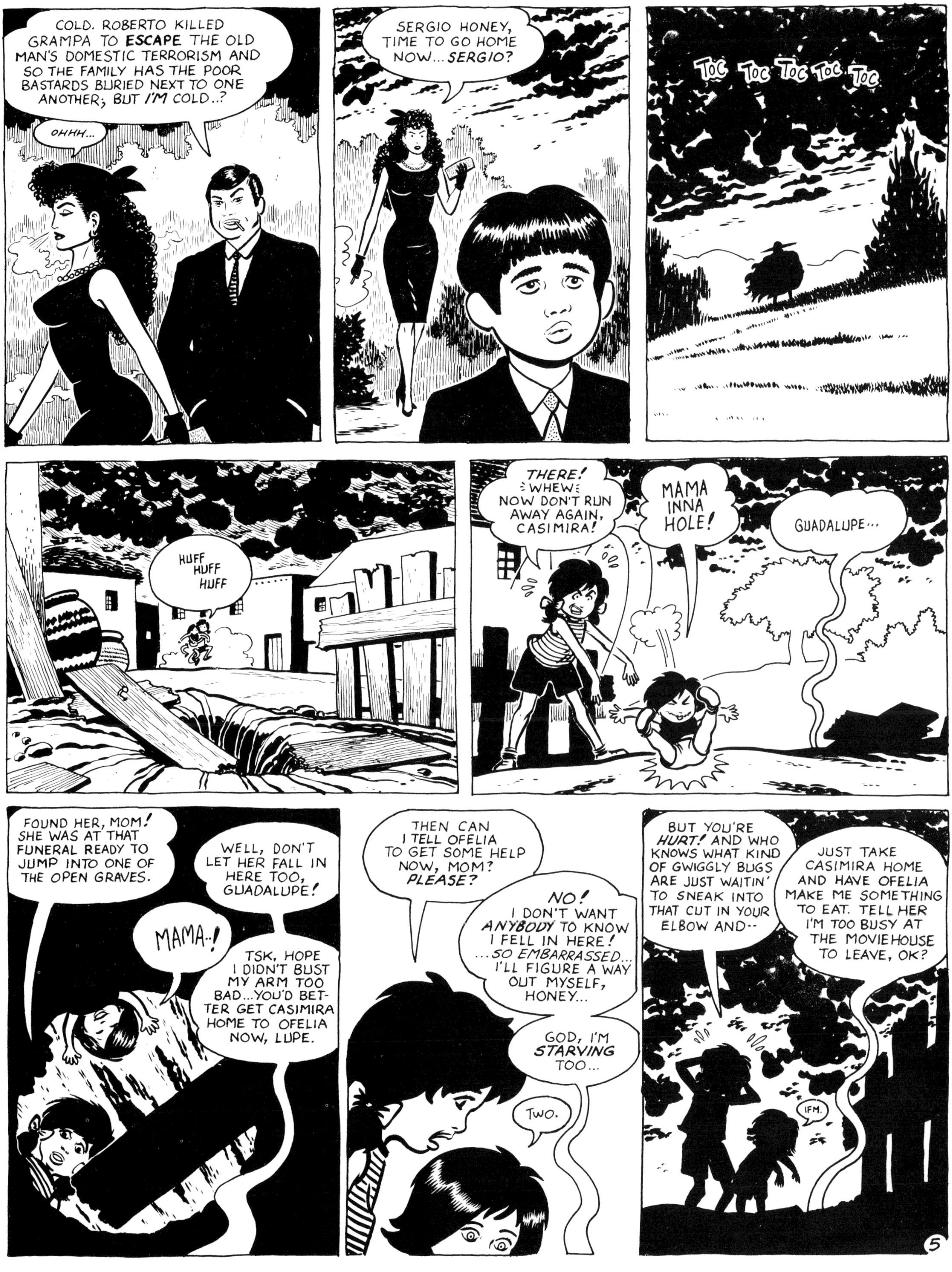
COLD. ROBERTO KILLED GRAMPA TO ESCAPE THE OLD MAN'S DOMESTIC TERRORISM AND SO THE FAMILY HAS THE POOR BASTARDS BURIED NEXT TO ONE ANOTHER; BUT I'M COLD..?
OHHH...
SERGIO HONEY, TIME TO GO HOME NOW... SERGIO?
TOC TOC TOC TOC TOC
HUFF HUFF HUFF
THERE! WHEW NOW DON'T RUN AWAY AGAIN, CASIMIRA!
MAMA INNA HOLE!
GUADALUPE...
FOUND HER, MOM! SHE WAS AT THAT FUNERAL READY TO JUMP INTO ONE OF THE OPEN GRAVES.
WELL, DON'T LET HER FALL IN HERE TOO, GUADALUPE!
MAMA..!
TSK, HOPE I DIDN'T BUST MY ARM TOO BAD... YOU'D BETTER GET CASIMIRA HOME TO OFELIA NOW, LUPE.
THEN CAN I TELL OFELIA TO GET SOME HELP NOW, MOM? PLEASE?
NO! I DON'T WANT ANYBODY TO KNOW I FELL IN HERE! ...SO EMBARRASSED... I'LL FIGURE A WAY OUT MYSELF, HONEY...
GOD, I'M STARVING TOO...
TWO.
BUT YOU'RE HURT! AND WHO KNOWS WHAT KIND OF GWIGGLY BUGS ARE JUST WAITIN' TO SNEAK INTO THAT CUT IN YOUR ELBOW AND--
JUST TAKE CASIMIRA HOME AND HAVE OFELIA MAKE ME SOMETHING TO EAT. TELL HER I'M TOO BUSY AT THE MOVIEHOUSE TO LEAVE, OK?
IFM.
5

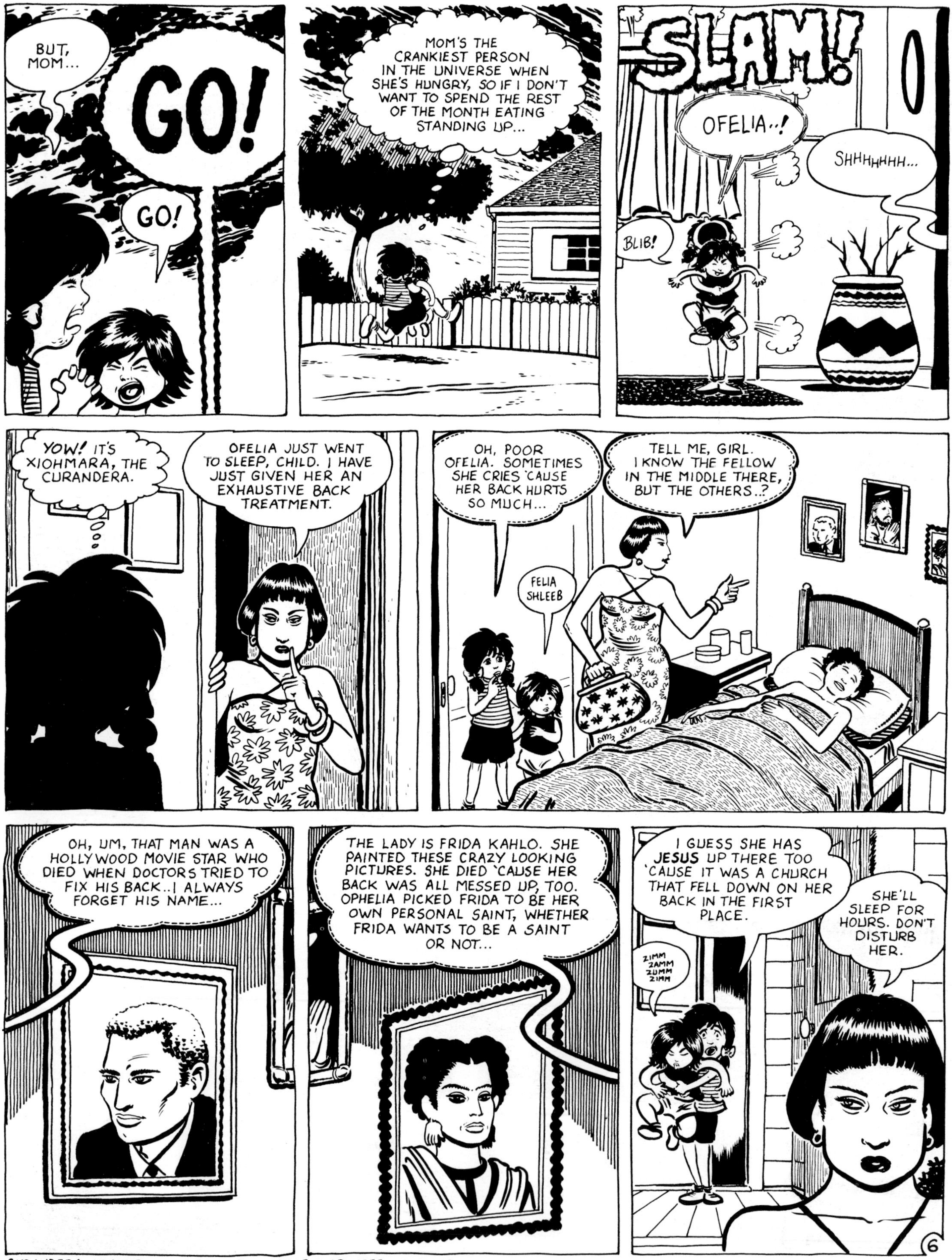
BUT, MOM...
GO!
GO!
MOM'S THE CRANKIEST PERSON IN THE UNIVERSE WHEN SHE'S HUNGRY, SO IF I DON'T WANT TO SPEND THE REST OF THE MONTH EATING STANDING UP...
SLAM!
OFELIA..!
SHHHHHHH...
BLIB!
YOW! IT'S XIOHMARA, THE CURANDERA.
OFELIA JUST WENT TO SLEEP, CHILD. I HAVE JUST GIVEN HER AN EXHAUSTIVE BACK TREATMENT.
OH, POOR OFELIA. SOMETIMES SHE CRIES 'CAUSE HER BACK HURTS SO MUCH...
FELIA SHLEEB
TELL ME, GIRL. I KNOW THE FELLOW IN THE MIDDLE THERE, BUT THE OTHERS..?
OH, UM, THAT MAN WAS A HOLLYWOOD MOVIE STAR WHO DIED WHEN DOCTORS TRIED TO FIX HIS BACK..I ALWAYS FORGET HIS NAME...
THE LADY IS FRIDA KAHLO. SHE PAINTED THESE CRAZY LOOKING PICTURES. SHE DIED 'CAUSE HER BACK WAS ALL MESSED UP, TOO. OPHELIA PICKED FRIDA TO BE HER OWN PERSONAL SAINT, WHETHER FRIDA WANTS TO BE A SAINT OR NOT...
I GUESS SHE HAS JESUS UP THERE TOO 'CAUSE IT WAS A CHURCH THAT FELL DOWN ON HER BACK IN THE FIRST PLACE.
ZIMM ZAMM ZUMM ZIMM
SHE'LL SLEEP FOR HOURS. DON'T DISTURB HER.
6

·CURANDERA - HEALER, WITCH DOCTOR ·MOVIE STAR - JEFF CHANDLER

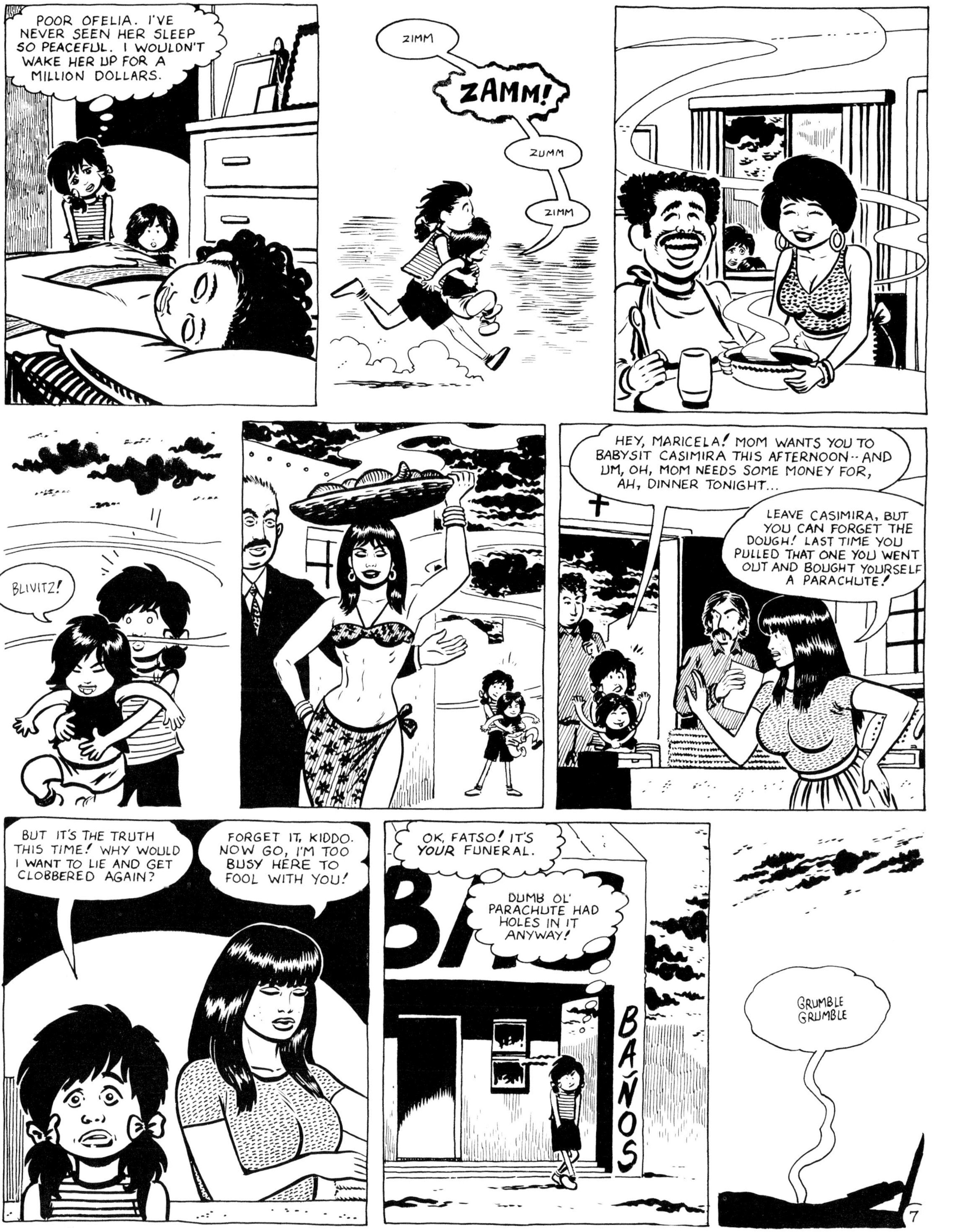
POOR OFELIA. I'VE NEVER SEEN HER SLEEP SO PEACEFUL. I WOULDN'T WAKE HER UP FOR A MILLION DOLLARS.
ZIMM
ZAMM!
ZUMM
ZIMM
BLIVITZ!
HEY, MARICELA! MOM WANTS YOU TO BABYSIT CASIMIRA THIS AFTERNOON-- AND UM, OH, MOM NEEDS SOME MONEY FOR, AH, DINNER TONIGHT...
LEAVE CASIMIRA, BUT YOU CAN FORGET THE DOUGH! LAST TIME YOU PULLED THAT ONE YOU WENT OUT AND BOUGHT YOURSELF A PARACHUTE!
BUT IT'S THE TRUTH THIS TIME! WHY WOULD I WANT TO LIE AND GET CLOBBERED AGAIN?
FORGET IT, KIDDO. NOW GO, I'M TOO BUSY HERE TO FOOL WITH YOU!
OK, FATSO! IT'S YOUR FUNERAL.
DUMB OL' PARACHUTE HAD HOLES IN IT ANYWAY!
BAÑOS
GRUMBLE GRUMBLE
7

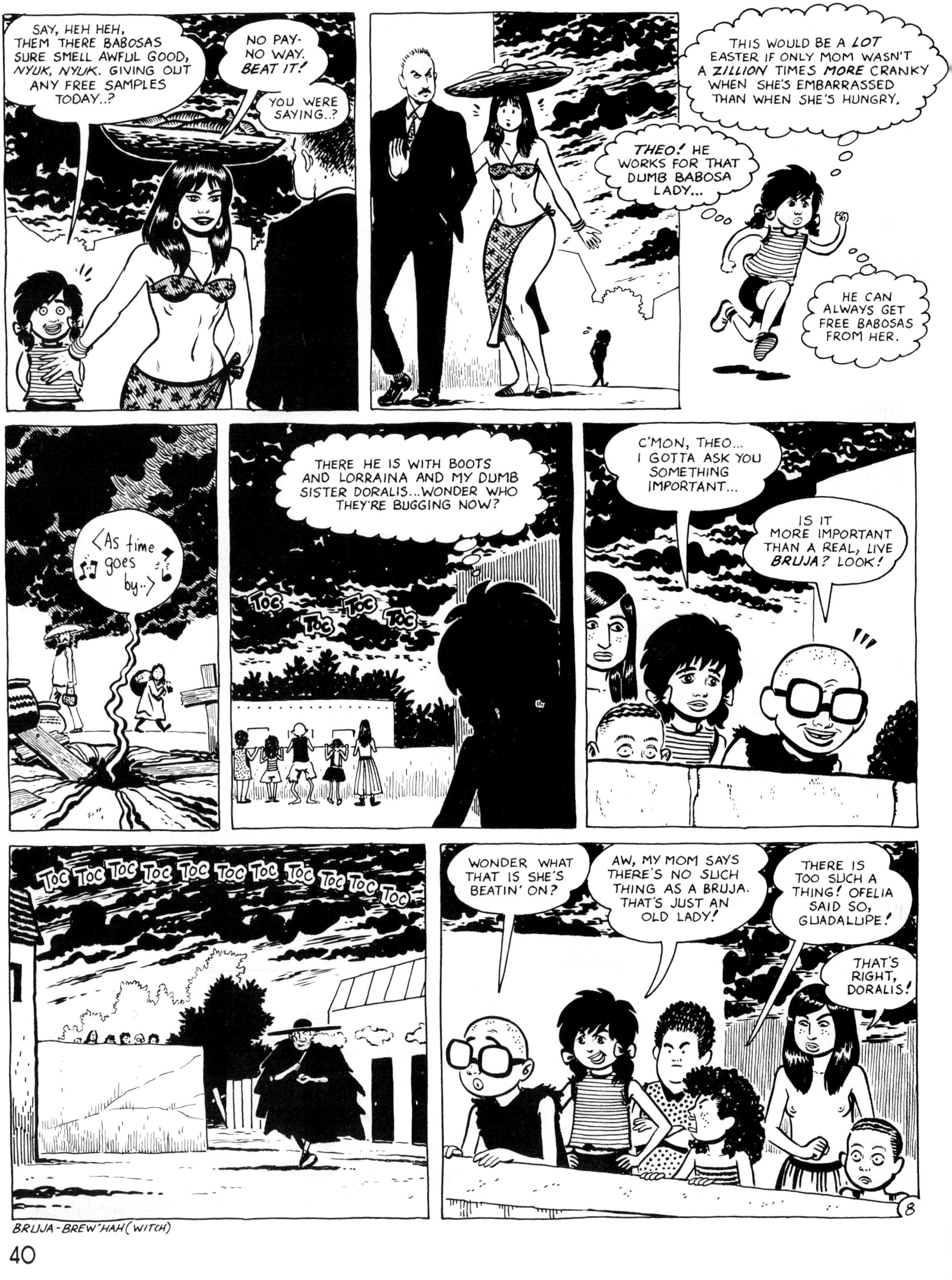

SAY, HEH HEH, THEM THERE BABOSAS SURE SMELL AWFUL GOOD, *NYUK, NYUK*. GIVING OUT ANY FREE SAMPLES TODAY..?
NO PAY- NO WAY. *BEAT IT!*
YOU WERE SAYING..?
THIS WOULD BE A *LOT* EASTER IF ONLY MOM WASN'T A *ZILLION* TIMES *MORE* CRANKY WHEN SHE'S EMBARRASSED THAN WHEN SHE'S HUNGRY.
THEO! HE WORKS FOR THAT DUMB BABOSA LADY...
HE CAN ALWAYS GET FREE BABOSAS FROM HER.
<As time goes by..>
THERE HE IS WITH BOOTS AND LORRAINA AND MY DUMB SISTER DORALIS...WONDER WHO THEY'RE BUGGING NOW?
TOC TOC TOC TOC
C'MON, THEO... I GOTTA ASK YOU SOMETHING IMPORTANT...
IS IT MORE IMPORTANT THAN A REAL, LIVE *BRUJA*? LOOK!
TOC TOC TOC TOC TOC TOC TOC TOC TOC TOC TOC
WONDER WHAT THAT IS SHE'S BEATIN' ON?
AW, MY MOM SAYS THERE'S NO SUCH THING AS A BRUJA. THAT'S JUST AN OLD LADY!
THERE IS TOO SUCH A THING! OFELIA SAID SO, GUADALUPE!
THAT'S RIGHT, DORALIS!
8
BRUJA-BREW'HAH (WITCH)

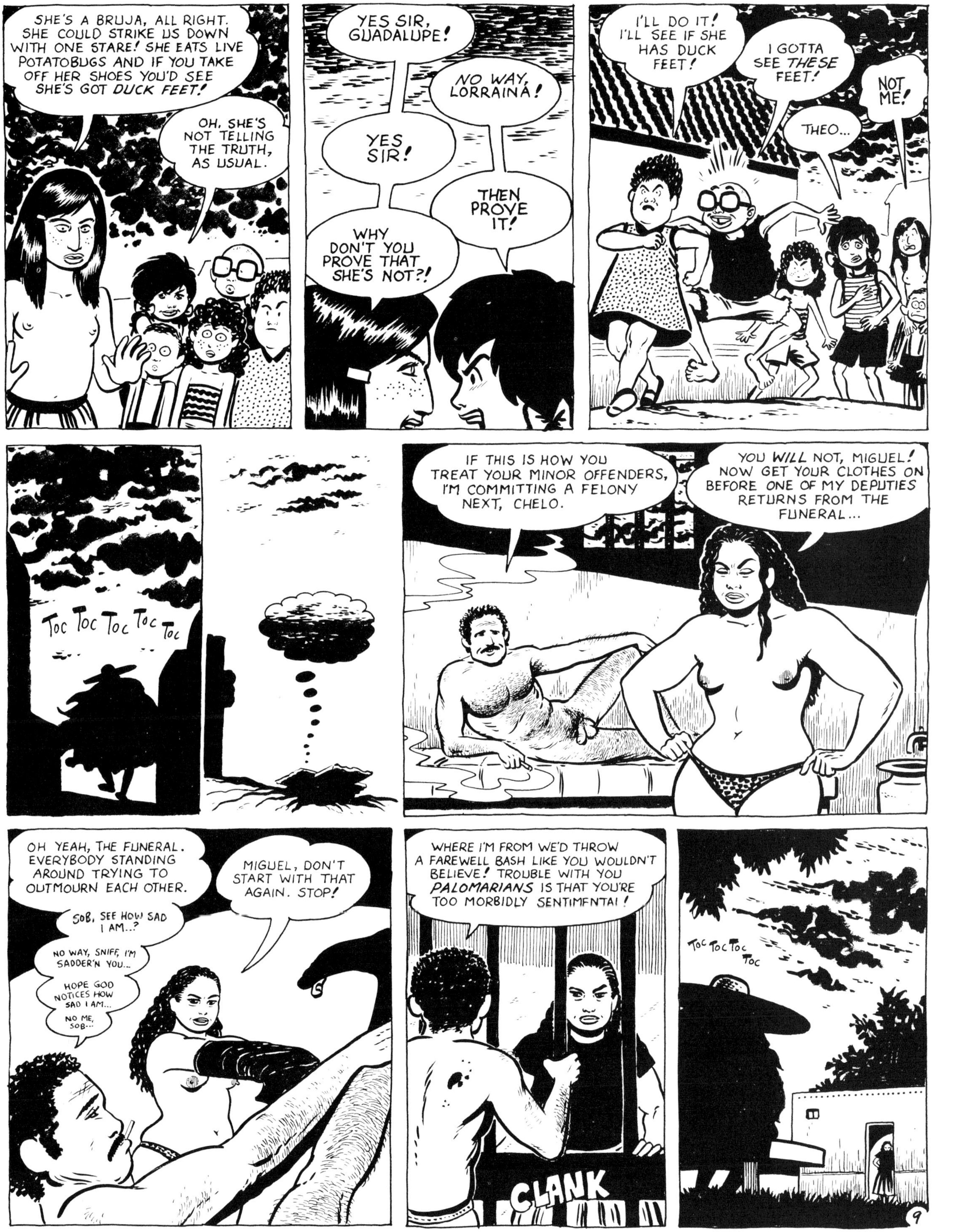

SHE'S A BRUJA, ALL RIGHT. SHE COULD STRIKE US DOWN WITH ONE STARE! SHE EATS LIVE POTATOBUGS AND IF YOU TAKE OFF HER SHOES YOU'D SEE SHE'S GOT *DUCK FEET!*
OH, SHE'S NOT TELLING THE TRUTH, AS USUAL.
YES SIR, GUADALUPE!
NO WAY, LORRAINA!
YES SIR!
THEN PROVE IT!
WHY DON'T YOU PROVE THAT SHE'S NOT?!
I'LL DO IT! I'LL SEE IF SHE HAS DUCK FEET!
I GOTTA SEE *THESE* FEET!
NOT ME!
THEO...
Toc Toc Toc Toc Toc
IF THIS IS HOW YOU TREAT YOUR MINOR OFFENDERS, I'M COMMITTING A FELONY NEXT, CHELO.
YOU *WILL* NOT, MIGUEL! NOW GET YOUR CLOTHES ON BEFORE ONE OF MY DEPUTIES RETURNS FROM THE FUNERAL...
OH YEAH, THE FUNERAL. EVERYBODY STANDING AROUND TRYING TO OUTMOURN EACH OTHER.
SOB, SEE HOW SAD I AM..?
NO WAY, SNIFF, I'M SADDER'N YOU...
HOPE GOD NOTICES HOW SAD I AM...
NO ME, SOB...
MIGUEL, DON'T START WITH THAT AGAIN. STOP!
WHERE I'M FROM WE'D THROW A FAREWELL BASH LIKE YOU WOULDN'T BELIEVE! TROUBLE WITH YOU *PALOMARIANS* IS THAT YOU'RE TOO MORBIDLY SENTIMENTAL!
CLANK
Toc Toc Toc Toc
9

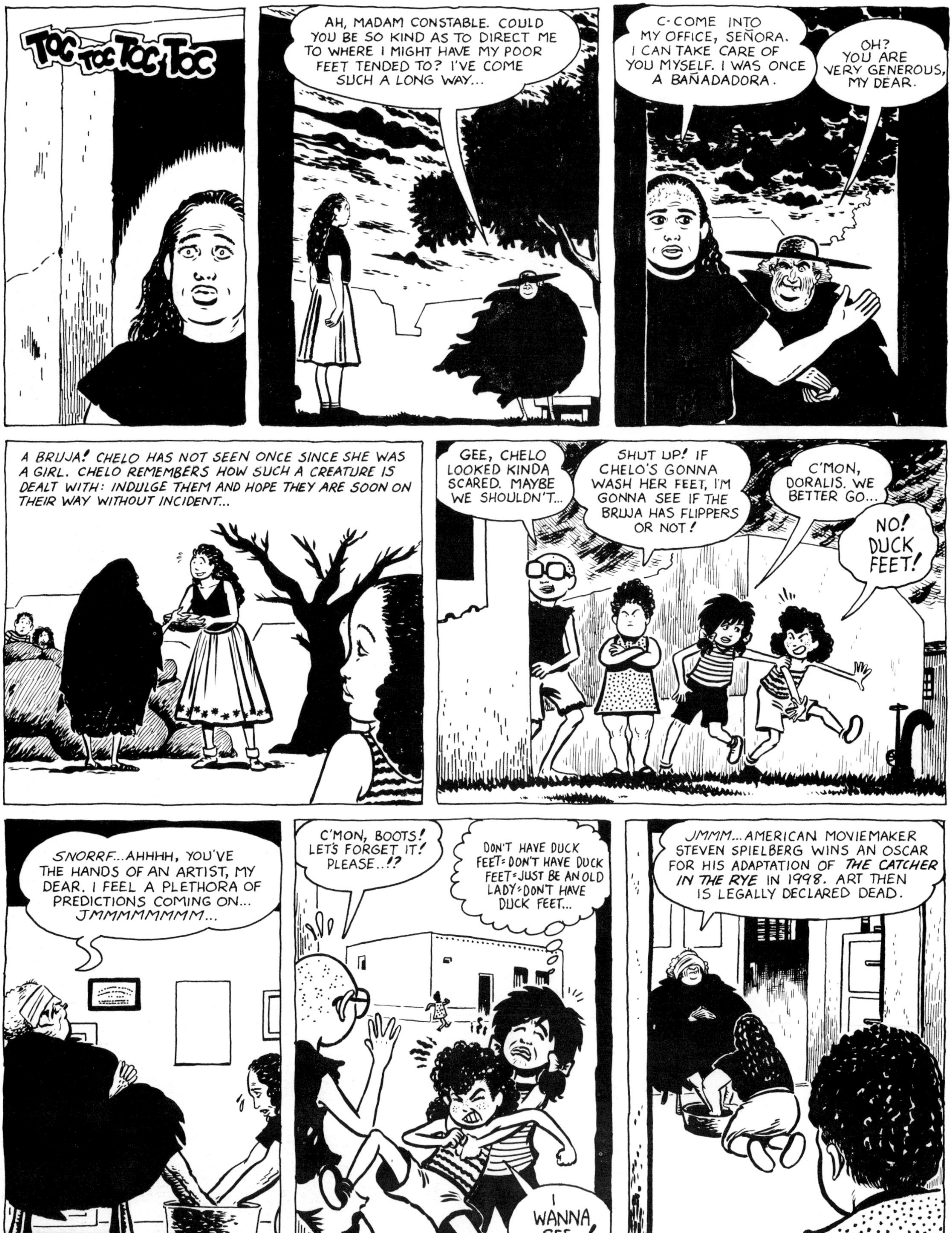
TOC TOC TOC TOC
AH, MADAM CONSTABLE. COULD YOU BE SO KIND AS TO DIRECT ME TO WHERE I MIGHT HAVE MY POOR FEET TENDED TO? I'VE COME SUCH A LONG WAY...
C-COME INTO MY OFFICE, SEÑORA. I CAN TAKE CARE OF YOU MYSELF. I WAS ONCE A BAÑADADORA.
OH? YOU ARE VERY GENEROUS, MY DEAR.
A BRUJA! CHELO HAS NOT SEEN ONCE SINCE SHE WAS A GIRL. CHELO REMEMBERS HOW SUCH A CREATURE IS DEALT WITH: INDULGE THEM AND HOPE THEY ARE SOON ON THEIR WAY WITHOUT INCIDENT...
GEE, CHELO LOOKED KINDA SCARED. MAYBE WE SHOULDN'T...
SHUT UP! IF CHELO'S GONNA WASH HER FEET, I'M GONNA SEE IF THE BRUJA HAS FLIPPERS OR NOT!
C'MON, DORALIS. WE BETTER GO...
NO! DUCK FEET!
SNORRF...AHHHH, YOU'VE THE HANDS OF AN ARTIST, MY DEAR. I FEEL A PLETHORA OF PREDICTIONS COMING ON... JMMMMMMMM...
C'MON, BOOTS! LET'S FORGET IT! PLEASE..!?
DON'T HAVE DUCK FEET=DON'T HAVE DUCK FEET=JUST BE AN OLD LADY=DON'T HAVE DUCK FEET...
I WANNA SEE--!
JMMM...AMERICAN MOVIEMAKER STEVEN SPIELBERG WINS AN OSCAR FOR HIS ADAPTATION OF THE CATCHER IN THE RYE IN 1998. ART THEN IS LEGALLY DECLARED DEAD.
10

BAÑADADORA/BAÑADORA- BATH GIUER

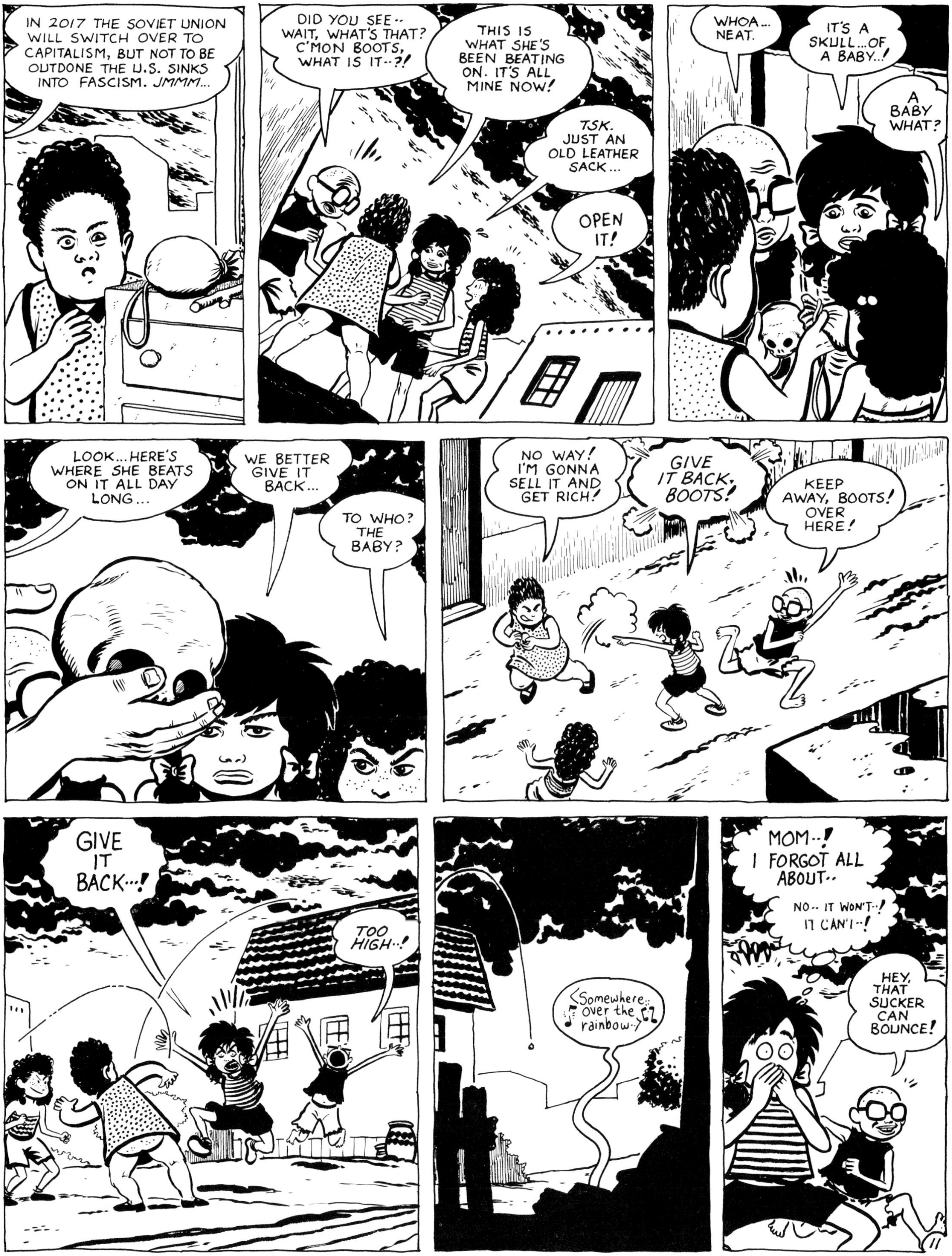
IN 2017 THE SOVIET UNION WILL SWITCH OVER TO CAPITALISM, BUT NOT TO BE OUTDONE THE U.S. SINKS INTO FASCISM. JMMM...
DID YOU SEE-- WAIT, WHAT'S THAT? C'MON BOOTS, WHAT IS IT--?!
THIS IS WHAT SHE'S BEEN BEATING ON. IT'S ALL MINE NOW!
TSK. JUST AN OLD LEATHER SACK...
OPEN IT!
WHOA... NEAT.
IT'S A SKULL...OF A BABY..!
A BABY WHAT?
LOOK...HERE'S WHERE SHE BEATS ON IT ALL DAY LONG...
WE BETTER GIVE IT BACK...
TO WHO? THE BABY?
NO WAY! I'M GONNA SELL IT AND GET RICH!
GIVE IT BACK, BOOTS!
KEEP AWAY, BOOTS! OVER HERE!
GIVE IT BACK--!
TOO HIGH--!
Somewhere over the rainbow--
MOM--! I FORGOT ALL ABOUT--
NO-- IT WON'T--! IT CAN'T--!
HEY, THAT SUCKER CAN BOUNCE!

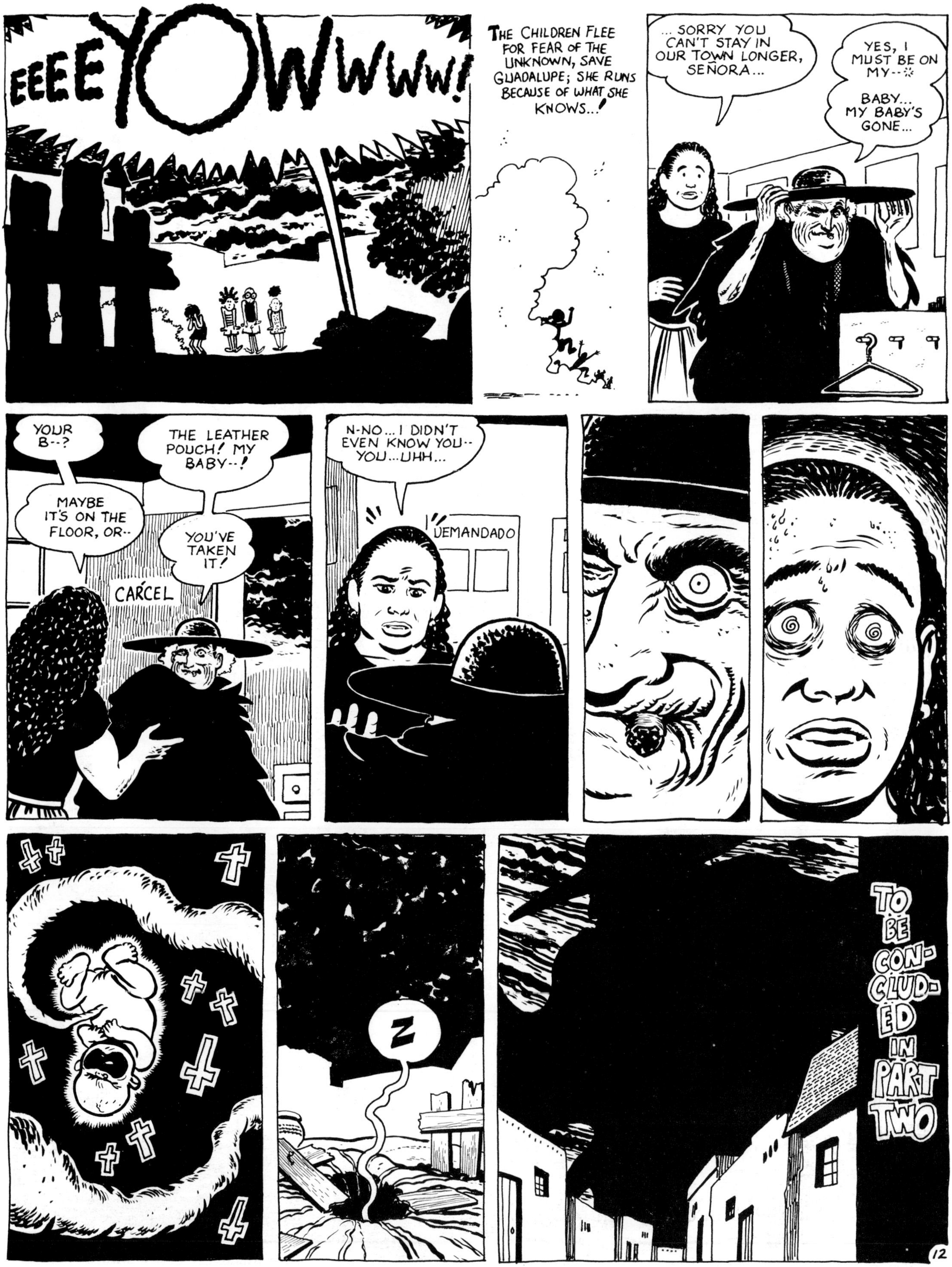
EEEEYOWWWW!
THE CHILDREN FLEE FOR FEAR OF THE UNKNOWN, SAVE GUADALUPE; SHE RUNS BECAUSE OF WHAT SHE KNOWS..!
... SORRY YOU CAN'T STAY IN OUR TOWN LONGER, SEÑORA...
YES, I MUST BE ON MY--
BABY... MY BABY'S GONE...
YOUR B--?
MAYBE IT'S ON THE FLOOR, OR--
THE LEATHER POUCH! MY BABY--!
YOU'VE TAKEN IT!
CARCEL
N-NO... I DIDN'T EVEN KNOW YOU-- YOU... UHH...
DEMANDADO
Z
TO BE CON-CLUD-ED IN PART TWO
12

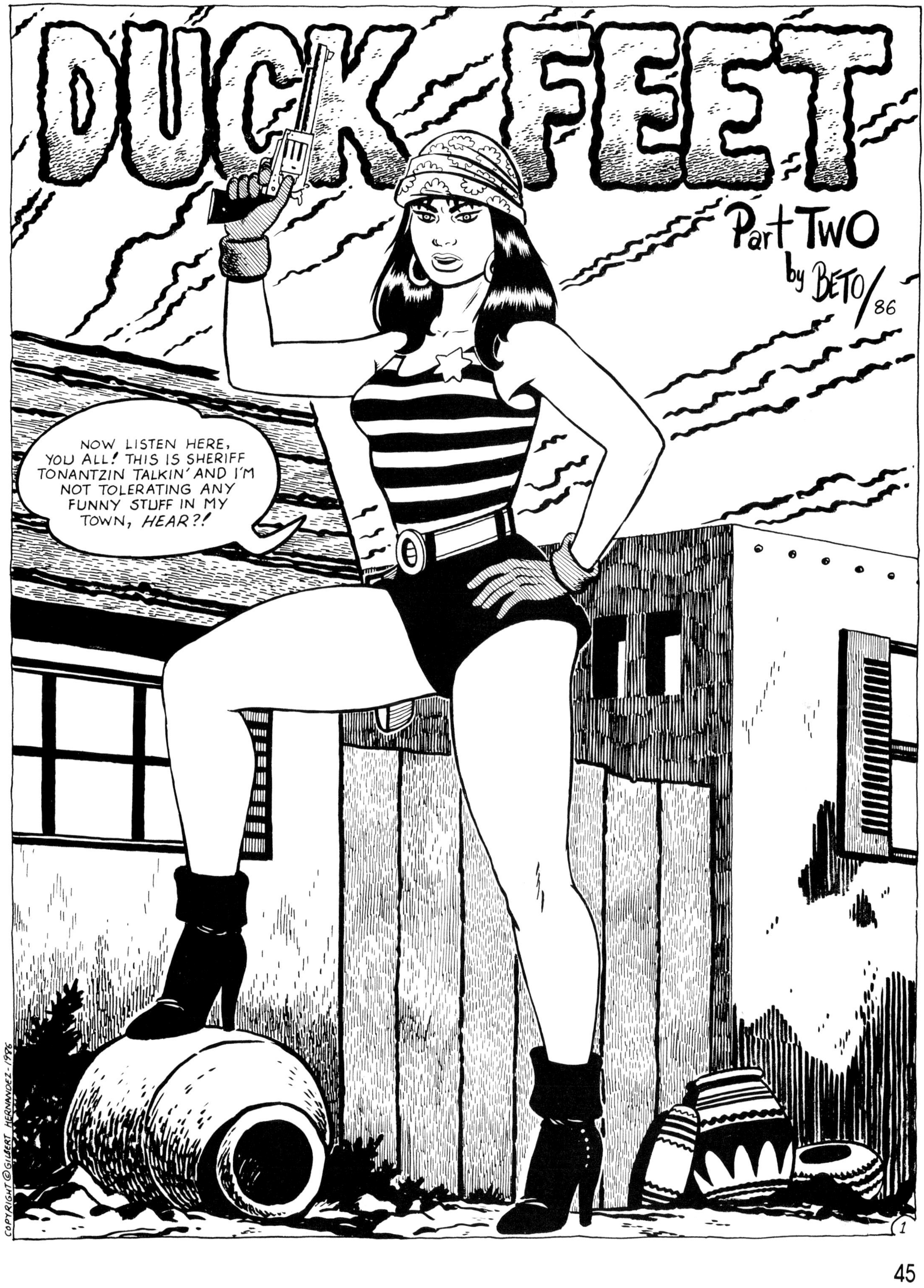
DUCK FEET
Part TWO
by BETO/86
NOW LISTEN HERE, YOU ALL! THIS IS SHERIFF TONANTZIN TALKIN' AND I'M NOT TOLERATING ANY FUNNY STUFF IN MY TOWN, HEAR?!
COPYRIGHT © GILBERT HERNANDEZ-1986
1

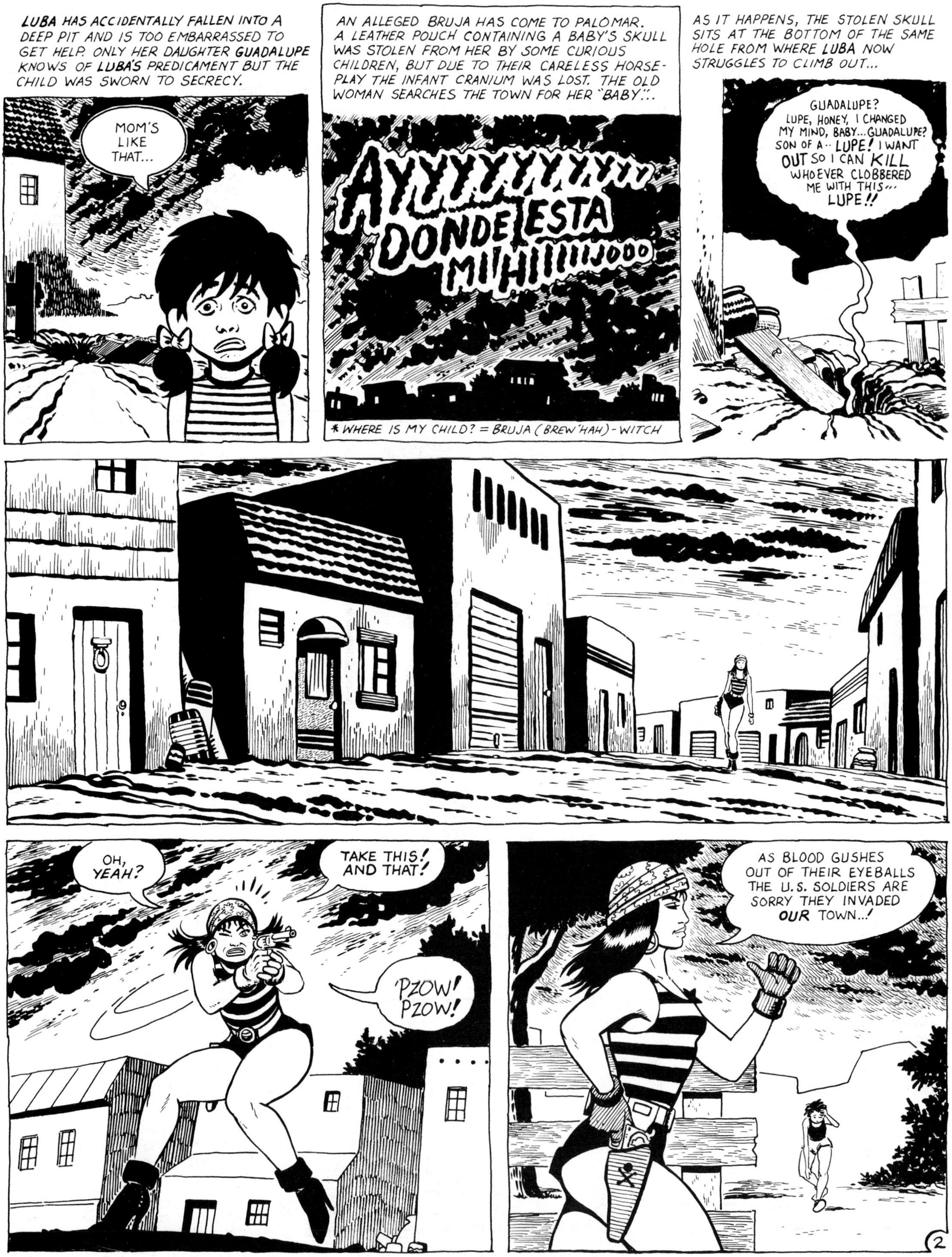
LUBA HAS ACCIDENTALLY FALLEN INTO A DEEP PIT AND IS TOO EMBARRASSED TO GET HELP. ONLY HER DAUGHTER GUADALUPE KNOWS OF LUBA'S PREDICAMENT BUT THE CHILD WAS SWORN TO SECRECY.
MOM'S LIKE THAT...
AN ALLEGED BRUJA HAS COME TO PALOMAR. A LEATHER POUCH CONTAINING A BABY'S SKULL WAS STOLEN FROM HER BY SOME CURIOUS CHILDREN, BUT DUE TO THEIR CARELESS HORSE-PLAY THE INFANT CRANIUM WAS LOST. THE OLD WOMAN SEARCHES THE TOWN FOR HER "BABY"...
AYYYYYYYYYY DONDE ESTA MI HIIIIIIJOOO
* WHERE IS MY CHILD? = BRUJA (BREW'HAH) - WITCH
AS IT HAPPENS, THE STOLEN SKULL SITS AT THE BOTTOM OF THE SAME HOLE FROM WHERE LUBA NOW STRUGGLES TO CLIMB OUT...
GUADALUPE? LUPE, HONEY, I CHANGED MY MIND, BABY...GUADALUPE? SON OF A.. LUPE! I WANT OUT SO I CAN KILL WHOEVER CLOBBERED ME WITH THIS... LUPE!!
OH, YEAH?
TAKE THIS! AND THAT!
PZOW! PZOW!
AS BLOOD GUSHES OUT OF THEIR EYEBALLS THE U.S. SOLDIERS ARE SORRY THEY INVADED OUR TOWN...!
2

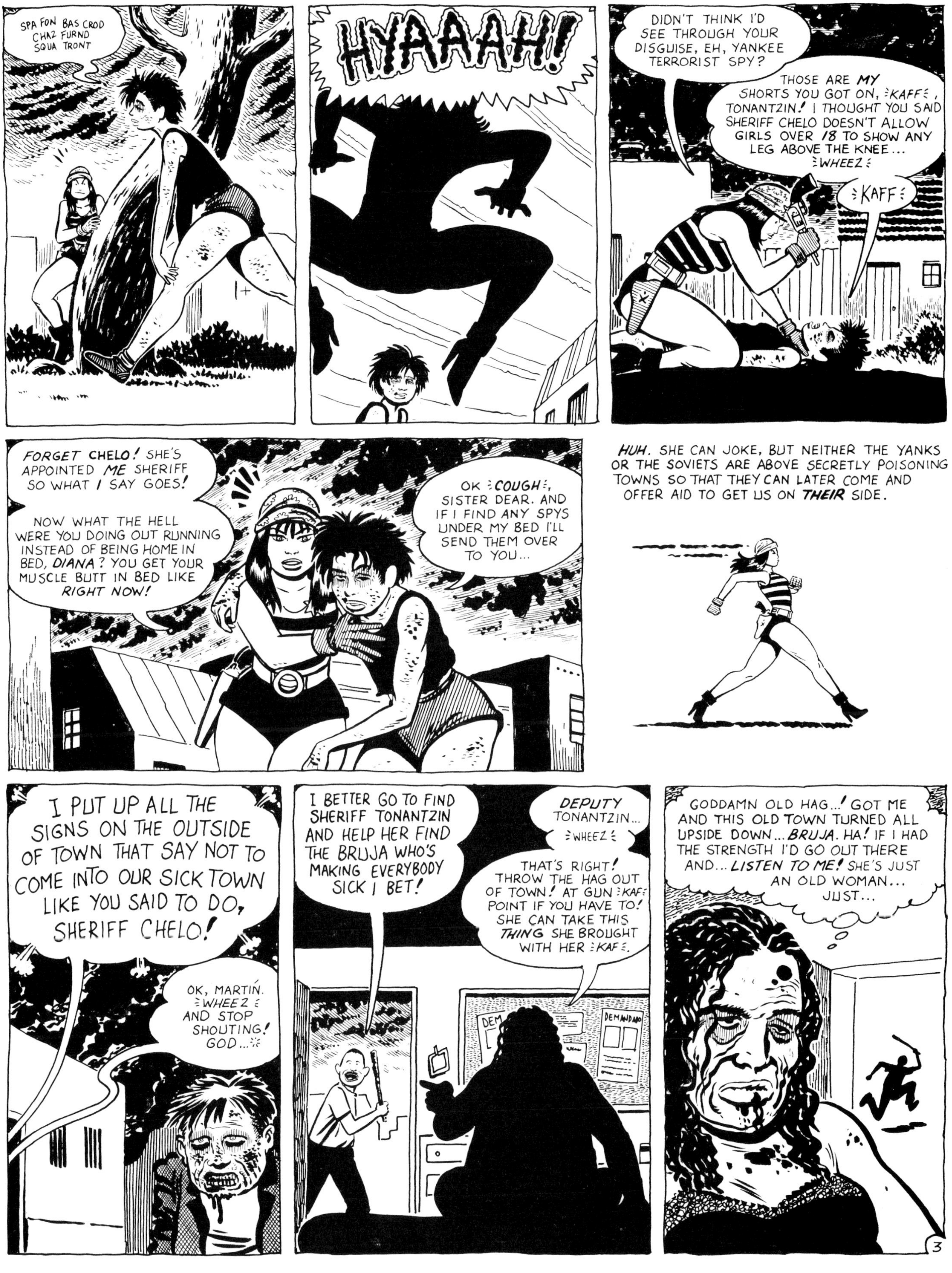

SPA FON BAS CROD CHAZ FURND SQUA TRONT
HYAAAH!
DIDN'T THINK I'D SEE THROUGH YOUR DISGUISE, EH, YANKEE TERRORIST SPY?
THOSE ARE MY SHORTS YOU GOT ON, KAFF, TONANTZIN! I THOUGHT YOU SAID SHERIFF CHELO DOESN'T ALLOW GIRLS OVER 18 TO SHOW ANY LEG ABOVE THE KNEE... WHEEZ
KAFF
FORGET CHELO! SHE'S APPOINTED ME SHERIFF SO WHAT I SAY GOES!
NOW WHAT THE HELL WERE YOU DOING OUT RUNNING INSTEAD OF BEING HOME IN BED, DIANA? YOU GET YOUR MUSCLE BUTT IN BED LIKE RIGHT NOW!
OK COUGH, SISTER DEAR. AND IF I FIND ANY SPYS UNDER MY BED I'LL SEND THEM OVER TO YOU...
HUH. SHE CAN JOKE, BUT NEITHER THE YANKS OR THE SOVIETS ARE ABOVE SECRETLY POISONING TOWNS SO THAT THEY CAN LATER COME AND OFFER AID TO GET US ON THEIR SIDE.
I PUT UP ALL THE SIGNS ON THE OUTSIDE OF TOWN THAT SAY NOT TO COME INTO OUR SICK TOWN LIKE YOU SAID TO DO, SHERIFF CHELO!
OK, MARTÍN. WHEEZ AND STOP SHOUTING! GOD...
I BETTER GO TO FIND SHERIFF TONANTZIN AND HELP HER FIND THE BRUJA WHO'S MAKING EVERYBODY SICK I BET!
DEPUTY TONANTZIN... WHEEZ
THAT'S RIGHT! THROW THE HAG OUT OF TOWN! AT GUN KAF POINT IF YOU HAVE TO! SHE CAN TAKE THIS THING SHE BROUGHT WITH HER KAF.
DEM
DEMANDMO
GODDAMN OLD HAG...! GOT ME AND THIS OLD TOWN TURNED ALL UPSIDE DOWN... BRUJA. HA! IF I HAD THE STRENGTH I'D GO OUT THERE AND... LISTEN TO ME! SHE'S JUST AN OLD WOMAN... JUST...
3

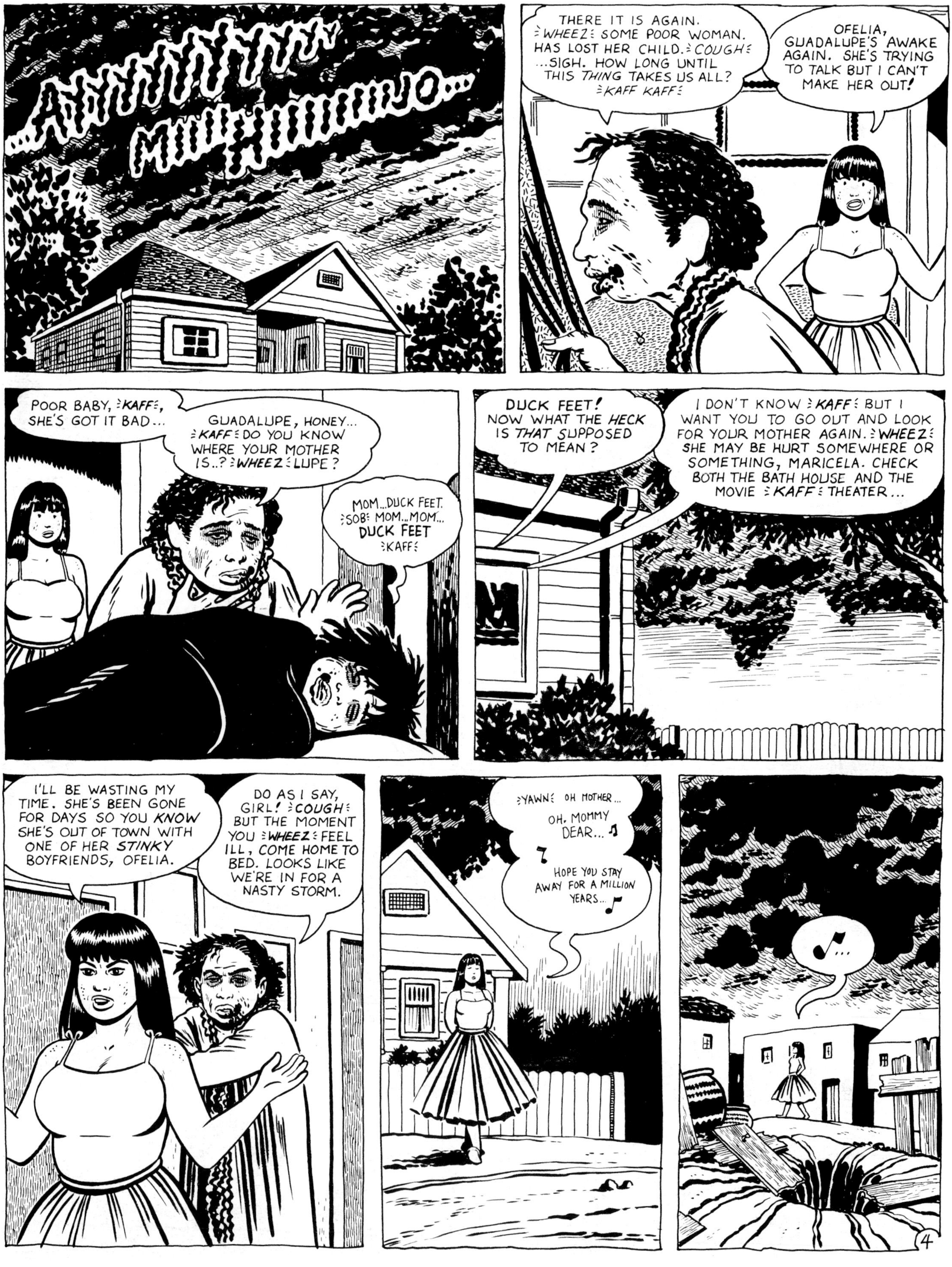
...AYYYYYYYYY MIIIIHIIIIIJO...
THERE IT IS AGAIN. ⋮WHEEZ⋮ SOME POOR WOMAN. HAS LOST HER CHILD. ⋮COUGH⋮ ...SIGH. HOW LONG UNTIL THIS THING TAKES US ALL? ⋮KAFF KAFF⋮
OFELIA, GUADALUPE'S AWAKE AGAIN. SHE'S TRYING TO TALK BUT I CAN'T MAKE HER OUT!
POOR BABY, ⋮KAFF⋮, SHE'S GOT IT BAD...
GUADALUPE, HONEY... ⋮KAFF⋮ DO YOU KNOW WHERE YOUR MOTHER IS..? ⋮WHEEZ⋮ LUPE?
MOM...DUCK FEET. ⋮SOB⋮ MOM...MOM... DUCK FEET ⋮KAFF⋮
DUCK FEET! NOW WHAT THE HECK IS THAT SUPPOSED TO MEAN?
I DON'T KNOW ⋮KAFF⋮ BUT I WANT YOU TO GO OUT AND LOOK FOR YOUR MOTHER AGAIN. ⋮WHEEZ⋮ SHE MAY BE HURT SOMEWHERE OR SOMETHING, MARICELA. CHECK BOTH THE BATH HOUSE AND THE MOVIE ⋮KAFF⋮ THEATER...
I'LL BE WASTING MY TIME. SHE'S BEEN GONE FOR DAYS SO YOU KNOW SHE'S OUT OF TOWN WITH ONE OF HER STINKY BOYFRIENDS, OFELIA.
DO AS I SAY, GIRL! ⋮COUGH⋮ BUT THE MOMENT YOU ⋮WHEEZ⋮ FEEL ILL, COME HOME TO BED. LOOKS LIKE WE'RE IN FOR A NASTY STORM.
⋮YAWN⋮ OH MOTHER... OH, MOMMY DEAR... ♪
HOPE YOU STAY AWAY FOR A MILLION YEARS... ♪
♪...
4

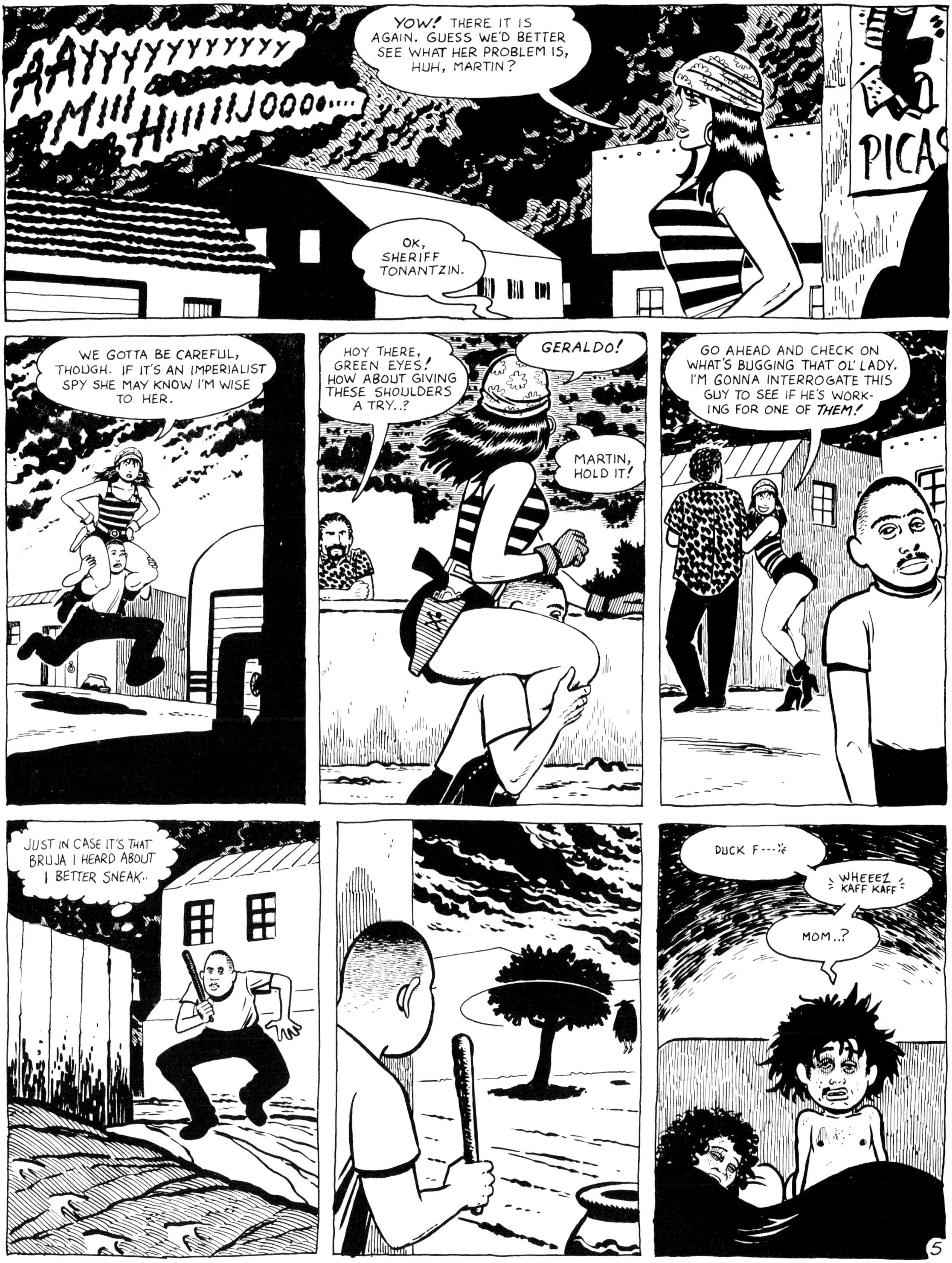
AAYYYYYYYYYYY MIII HIIIIIJOOOo....
YOW! THERE IT IS AGAIN. GUESS WE'D BETTER SEE WHAT HER PROBLEM IS, HUH, MARTIN?
PICAS
OK, SHERIFF TONANTZIN.
WE GOTTA BE CAREFUL, THOUGH. IF IT'S AN IMPERIALIST SPY SHE MAY KNOW I'M WISE TO HER.
HOY THERE, GREEN EYES! HOW ABOUT GIVING THESE SHOULDERS A TRY..?
GERALDO!
MARTIN, HOLD IT!
GO AHEAD AND CHECK ON WHAT'S BUGGING THAT OL' LADY. I'M GONNA INTERROGATE THIS GUY TO SEE IF HE'S WORKING FOR ONE OF THEM!
JUST IN CASE IT'S THAT BRUJA I HEARD ABOUT I BETTER SNEAK..
DUCK F---
WHEEEZ KAFF KAFF
MOM..?
5

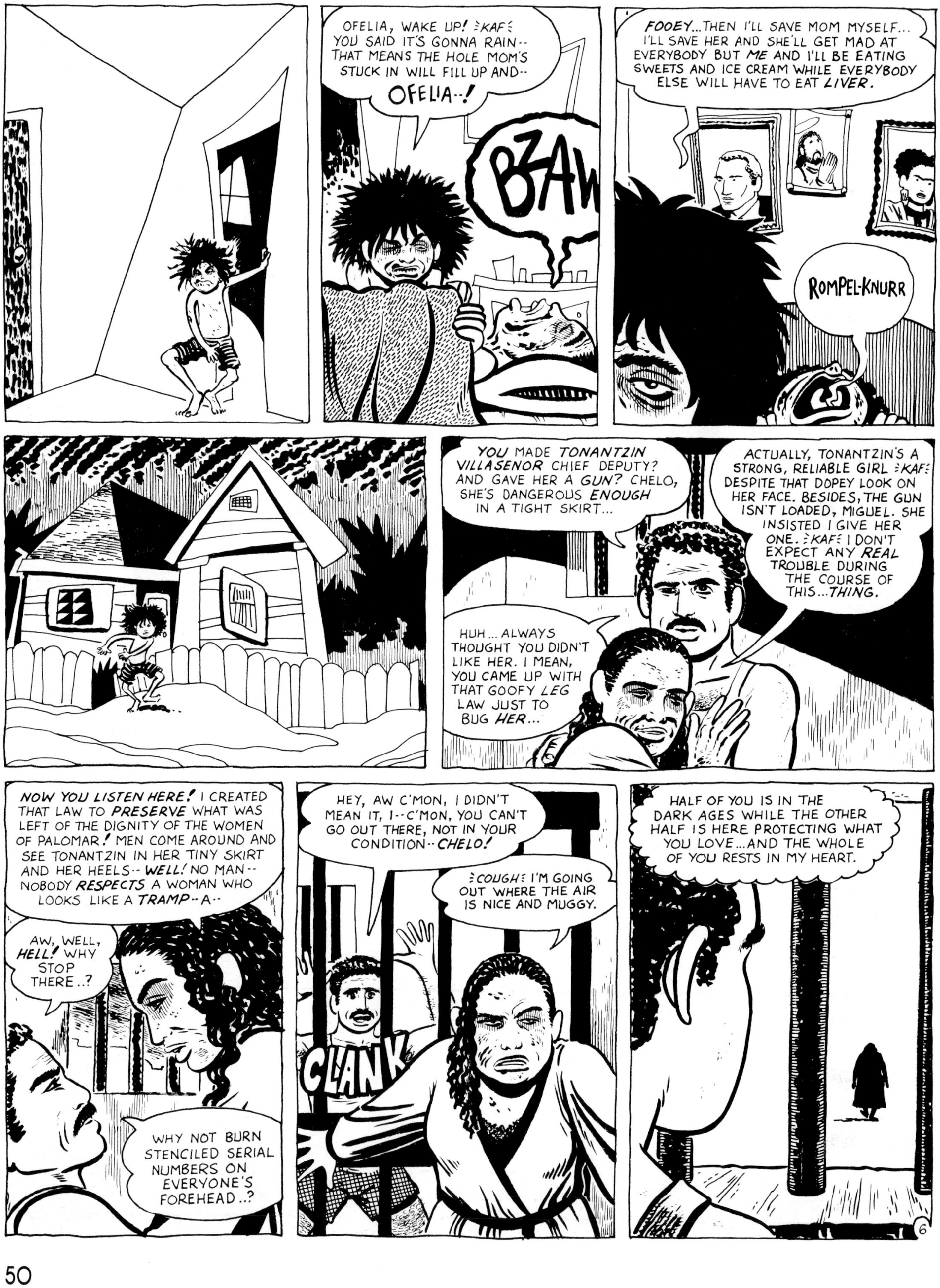
OFELIA, WAKE UP! ⁝KAF⁝ YOU SAID IT'S GONNA RAIN-- THAT MEANS THE HOLE MOM'S STUCK IN WILL FILL UP AND--
OFELIA--!
BZAW
FOOEY... THEN I'LL SAVE MOM MYSELF... I'LL SAVE HER AND SHE'LL GET MAD AT EVERYBODY BUT ME AND I'LL BE EATING SWEETS AND ICE CREAM WHILE EVERYBODY ELSE WILL HAVE TO EAT LIVER.
ROMPEL-KNURR
YOU MADE TONANTZIN VILLASENOR CHIEF DEPUTY? AND GAVE HER A GUN? CHELO, SHE'S DANGEROUS ENOUGH IN A TIGHT SKIRT...
ACTUALLY, TONANTZIN'S A STRONG, RELIABLE GIRL ⁝KAF⁝ DESPITE THAT DOPEY LOOK ON HER FACE. BESIDES, THE GUN ISN'T LOADED, MIGUEL. SHE INSISTED I GIVE HER ONE. ⁝KAF⁝ I DON'T EXPECT ANY REAL TROUBLE DURING THE COURSE OF THIS... THING.
HUH... ALWAYS THOUGHT YOU DIDN'T LIKE HER. I MEAN, YOU CAME UP WITH THAT GOOFY LEG LAW JUST TO BUG HER...
NOW YOU LISTEN HERE! I CREATED THAT LAW TO PRESERVE WHAT WAS LEFT OF THE DIGNITY OF THE WOMEN OF PALOMAR! MEN COME AROUND AND SEE TONANTZIN IN HER TINY SKIRT AND HER HEELS-- WELL! NO MAN-- NOBODY RESPECTS A WOMAN WHO LOOKS LIKE A TRAMP-- A--
AW, WELL, HELL! WHY STOP THERE..?
WHY NOT BURN STENCILED SERIAL NUMBERS ON EVERYONE'S FOREHEAD..?
HEY, AW C'MON, I DIDN'T MEAN IT, I--C'MON, YOU CAN'T GO OUT THERE, NOT IN YOUR CONDITION-- CHELO!
⁝COUGH⁝ I'M GOING OUT WHERE THE AIR IS NICE AND MUGGY.
CLANK
HALF OF YOU IS IN THE DARK AGES WHILE THE OTHER HALF IS HERE PROTECTING WHAT YOU LOVE... AND THE WHOLE OF YOU RESTS IN MY HEART.
6

ER, GERALDO, DIDN'T YOU SEE THE WARNING SIGNS OUTSIDE OF TOWN?

DON'T CHANGE THE SUBJECT! YOUR SHERIFF WHAT'S-ER-NAME MURDERED MY COUSIN ROBERTO ALL THE SAME! HE DIED LIKE A COMMON--LIKE A DOG IN THE STREET, LIKE-- HIS HEAD WAS TURNED COMPLETELY BACKWARDS! I WOULDN'T CALL THAT CRIB DEATH...!

YOU FORGET ROBERTO KILLED HIS GRAMPA IN THE FIRST PLACE, GERALDO...

AAAH, YOU KNOW WHAT KIND OF SWINE THE OLD MAN WAS! TREATED EVERYONE LIKE DIRT, LIKE-- HE CAME CLOSE TO MOLESTING YOUR LITTLE SISTER DIANA A FEW TIMES, AS I RECALL...

CHELO DIDN'T MEAN TO KILL YOUR COUSIN. SHE HIT HIM AND HE FELL...

OH SURE, THAT'S WHAT SHE TOLD EVERY-BODY. BUT I'VE BEEN IN AND OUT OF JAIL ALL MY LIFE AND I KNOW WHAT SHIT COPS PULL WHEN THEY THINK NOBODY IS LOOKING. COPS. PIMPS. THE POPE. THEY'RE ALL OF THE SAME BREED. TERRORISTS. KEEPING THE PEOPLE IN LINE WITH FEAR...

THAT'S CRAZY TALK! MAYBE I OUGHT TO SIT YOU IN A CELL FOR A FEW DAYS TO COOL YOU OFF!

HEH. I AM GOING TO JAIL REAL SOON. BUSTED A BOTTLE ACROSS SOME STUPID COP'S FACE AFTER HE POPPED ME FOR COKE. JUMPED BAIL.

THEY'LL FIND ME, NO PROBLEM.

AH, BUT ALL THIS SHIT ABOUT COPS AND STUFF IS OLD NEWS. `BUT THAT'S THE WAY IT IS, THE WAY IT'S ALWAYS BEEN, SO FORGET IT' THEY TELL YOU. YEAH, WELL, TELL THAT TO A BLACK KID IN SOUTH AFRICA...

HEY, WAIT! AREN'T WE STILL GONNA--AW, FORGET IT. GO TO HELL!

GOD, HOW'D A GUY WHO'D BEEN SO GOOD IN THE SACK TURN OUT TO BE SUCH A LOON? CRAZY PEOPLE GIVE ME THE SHIVERS...

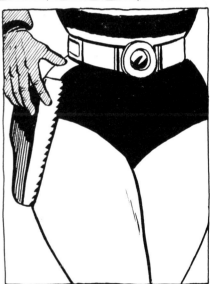

MY--MY GUN! GERALDO! DID YOU SEE WHERE I--I--

GERALDO--?

7

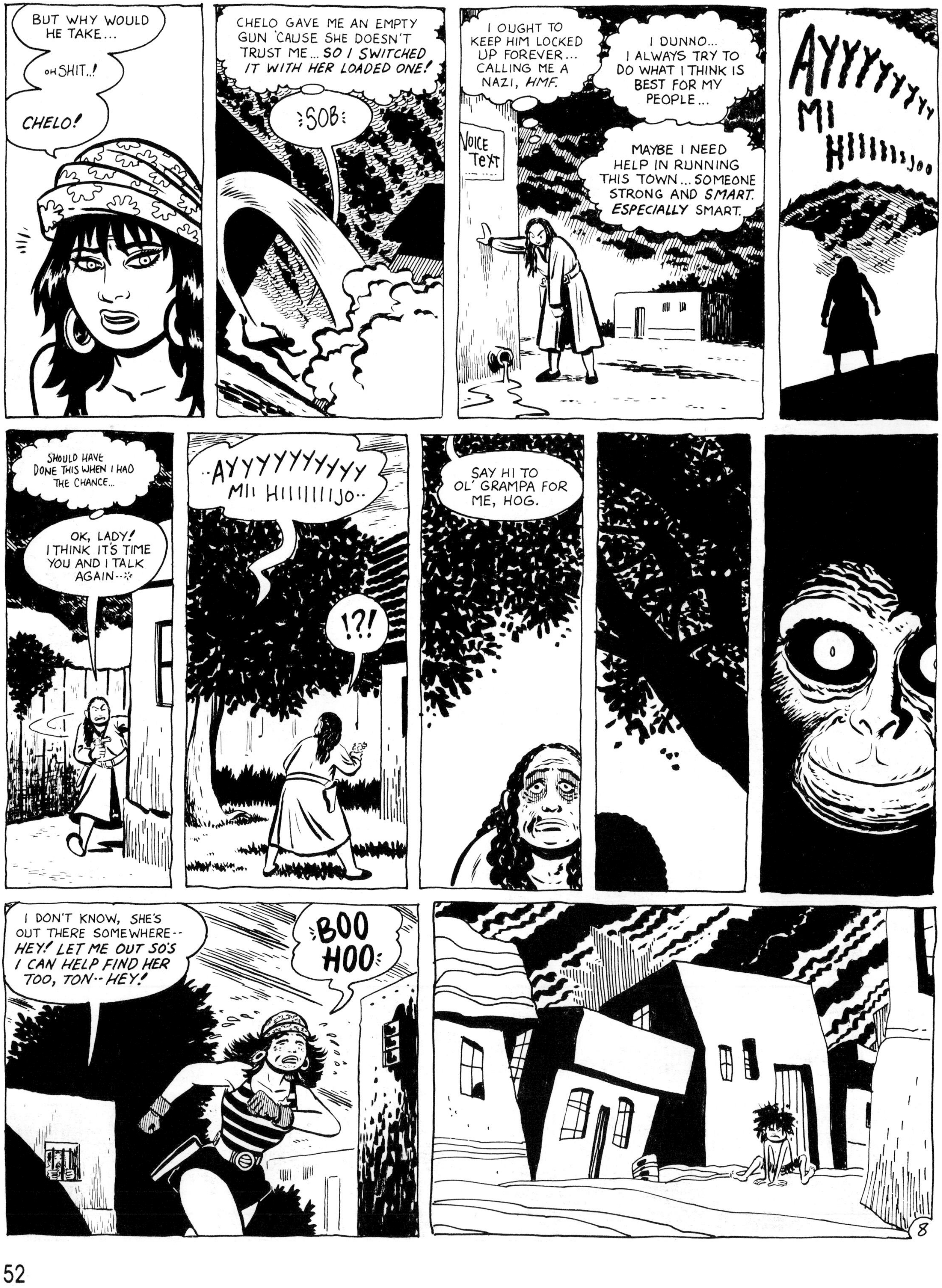

BUT WHY WOULD HE TAKE...
OH SHIT..!
CHELO!
CHELO GAVE ME AN EMPTY GUN 'CAUSE SHE DOESN'T TRUST ME... SO I SWITCHED IT WITH HER LOADED ONE!
SOB
I OUGHT TO KEEP HIM LOCKED UP FOREVER... CALLING ME A NAZI, HMF.
I DUNNO... I ALWAYS TRY TO DO WHAT I THINK IS BEST FOR MY PEOPLE...
MAYBE I NEED HELP IN RUNNING THIS TOWN... SOMEONE STRONG AND SMART. ESPECIALLY SMART.
VOICE TEXT
AYYYYYYYYY MI HIIIIIIJOO
SHOULD HAVE DONE THIS WHEN I HAD THE CHANCE...
OK, LADY! I THINK IT'S TIME YOU AND I TALK AGAIN...
..AYYYYYYYYYY MII HIIIIIIIJO..
!?!
SAY HI TO OL' GRAMPA FOR ME, HOG.
I DON'T KNOW, SHE'S OUT THERE SOMEWHERE-- HEY! LET ME OUT SO'S I CAN HELP FIND HER TOO, TON-- HEY!
BOO HOO
8

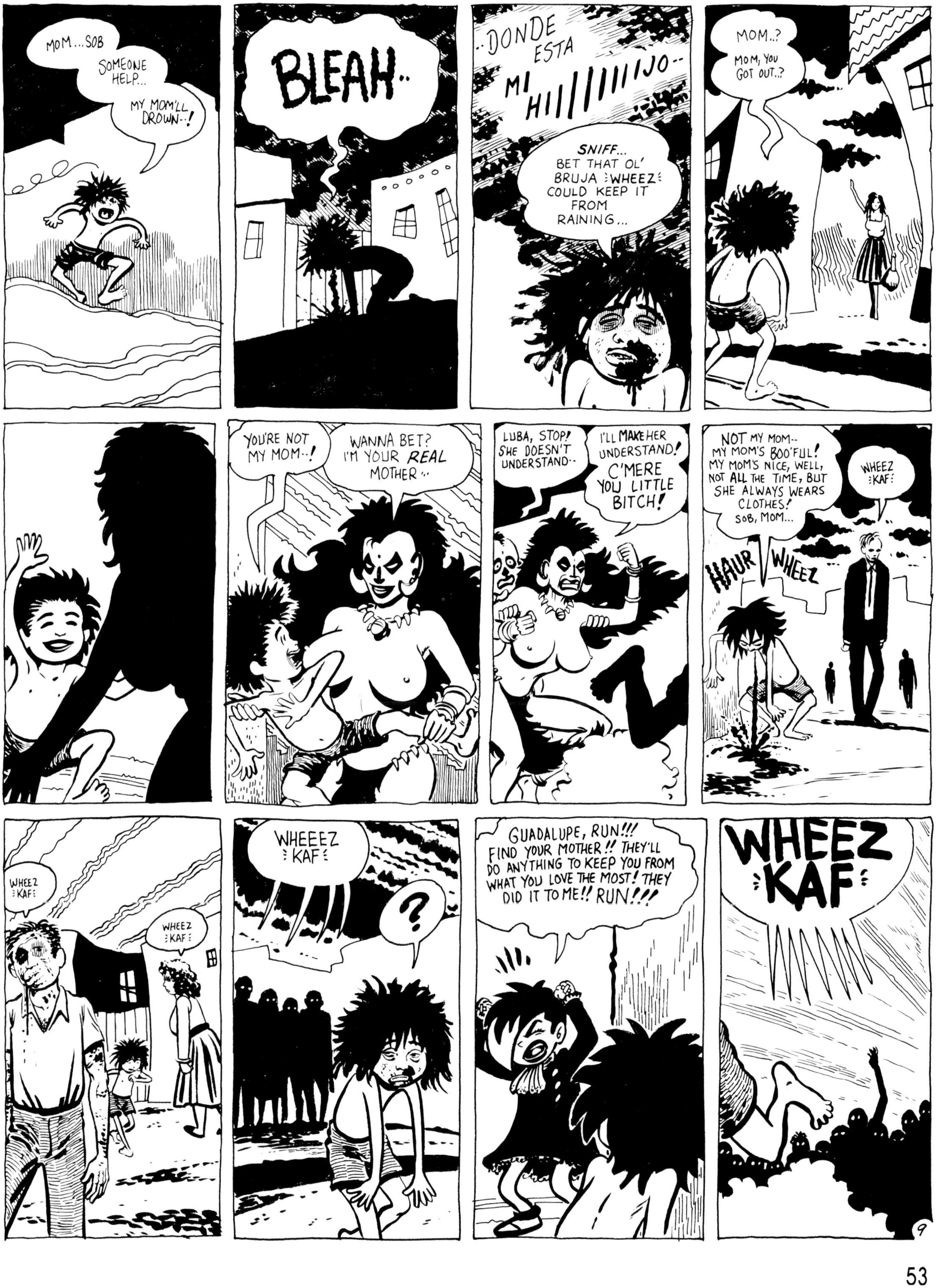
MOM... SOB
SOMEONE HELP...
MY MOM'LL DROWN..!
BLEAH..
..DONDE ESTA MI HI//////JO..
SNIFF... BET THAT OL' BRUJA WHEEZ COULD KEEP IT FROM RAINING...
MOM..?
MOM, YOU GOT OUT..?
YOU'RE NOT MY MOM..!
WANNA BET? I'M YOUR REAL MOTHER..
LUBA, STOP! SHE DOESN'T UNDERSTAND..
I'LL MAKE HER UNDERSTAND!
C'MERE YOU LITTLE BITCH!
NOT MY MOM.. MY MOM'S BOO'FUL! MY MOM'S NICE, WELL, NOT ALL THE TIME, BUT SHE ALWAYS WEARS CLOTHES! SOB, MOM...
WHEEZ KAF
HAUR
WHEEZ
WHEEZ KAF
WHEEZ KAF
WHEEEZ KAF
?
GUADALUPE, RUN!!! FIND YOUR MOTHER!! THEY'LL DO ANYTHING TO KEEP YOU FROM WHAT YOU LOVE THE MOST! THEY DID IT TO ME!! RUN!!!
WHEEZ KAF
9

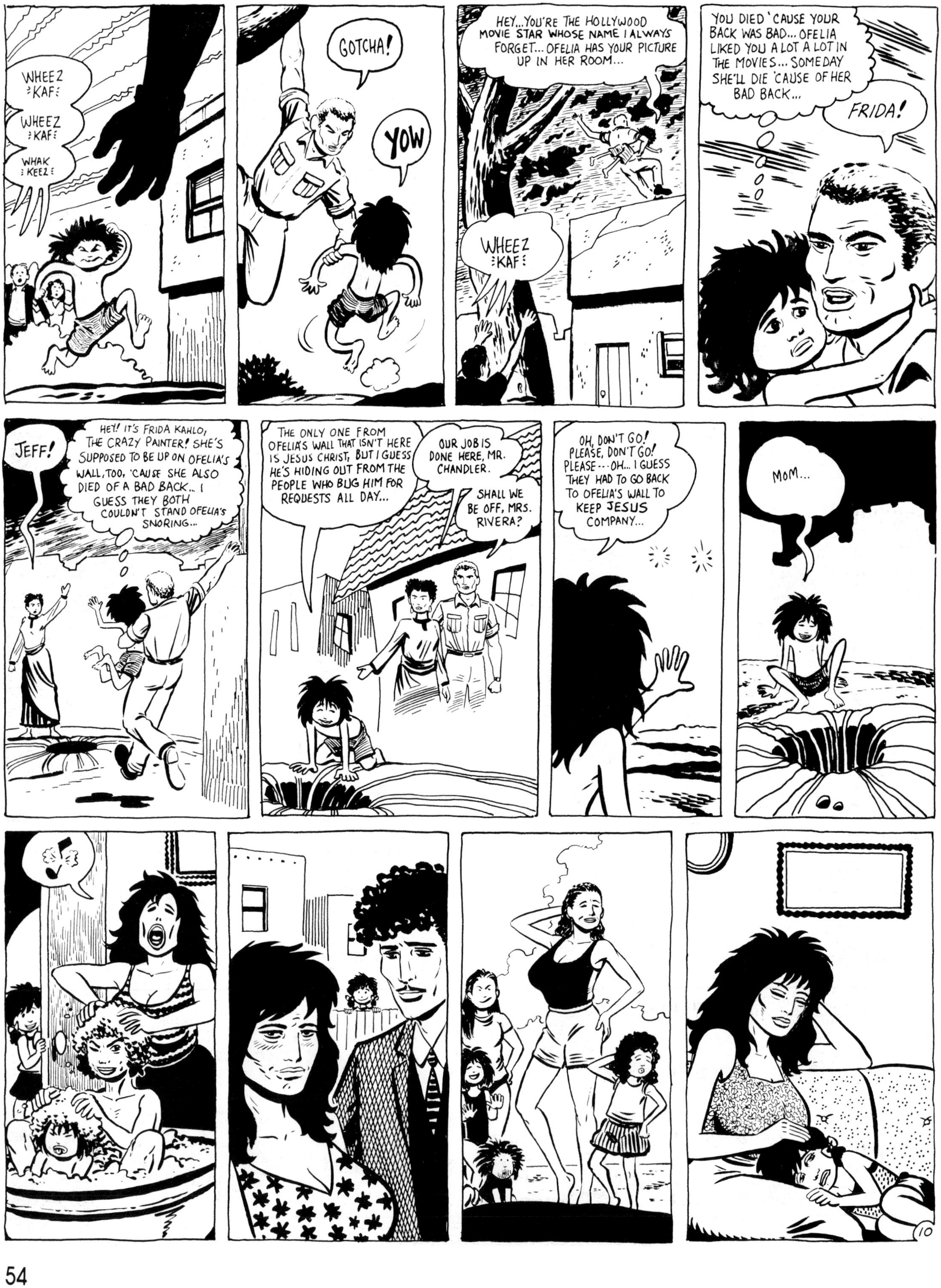
WHEEZ KAF
WHEEZ KAF
WHAK KEEZ
GOTCHA!
YOW
HEY... YOU'RE THE HOLLYWOOD MOVIE STAR WHOSE NAME I ALWAYS FORGET... OFELIA HAS YOUR PICTURE UP IN HER ROOM...
WHEEZ KAF
YOU DIED 'CAUSE YOUR BACK WAS BAD... OFELIA LIKED YOU A LOT A LOT IN THE MOVIES... SOMEDAY SHE'LL DIE 'CAUSE OF HER BAD BACK...
FRIDA!
JEFF!
HEY! IT'S FRIDA KAHLO, THE CRAZY PAINTER! SHE'S SUPPOSED TO BE UP ON OFELIA'S WALL, TOO, 'CAUSE SHE ALSO DIED OF A BAD BACK... I GUESS THEY BOTH COULDN'T STAND OFELIA'S SNORING...
THE ONLY ONE FROM OFELIA'S WALL THAT ISN'T HERE IS JESUS CHRIST, BUT I GUESS HE'S HIDING OUT FROM THE PEOPLE WHO BUG HIM FOR REQUESTS ALL DAY...
OUR JOB IS DONE HERE, MR. CHANDLER.
SHALL WE BE OFF, MRS. RIVERA?
OH, DON'T GO! PLEASE, DON'T GO! PLEASE... OH... I GUESS THEY HAD TO GO BACK TO OFELIA'S WALL TO KEEP JESUS COMPANY...
MOM...
10

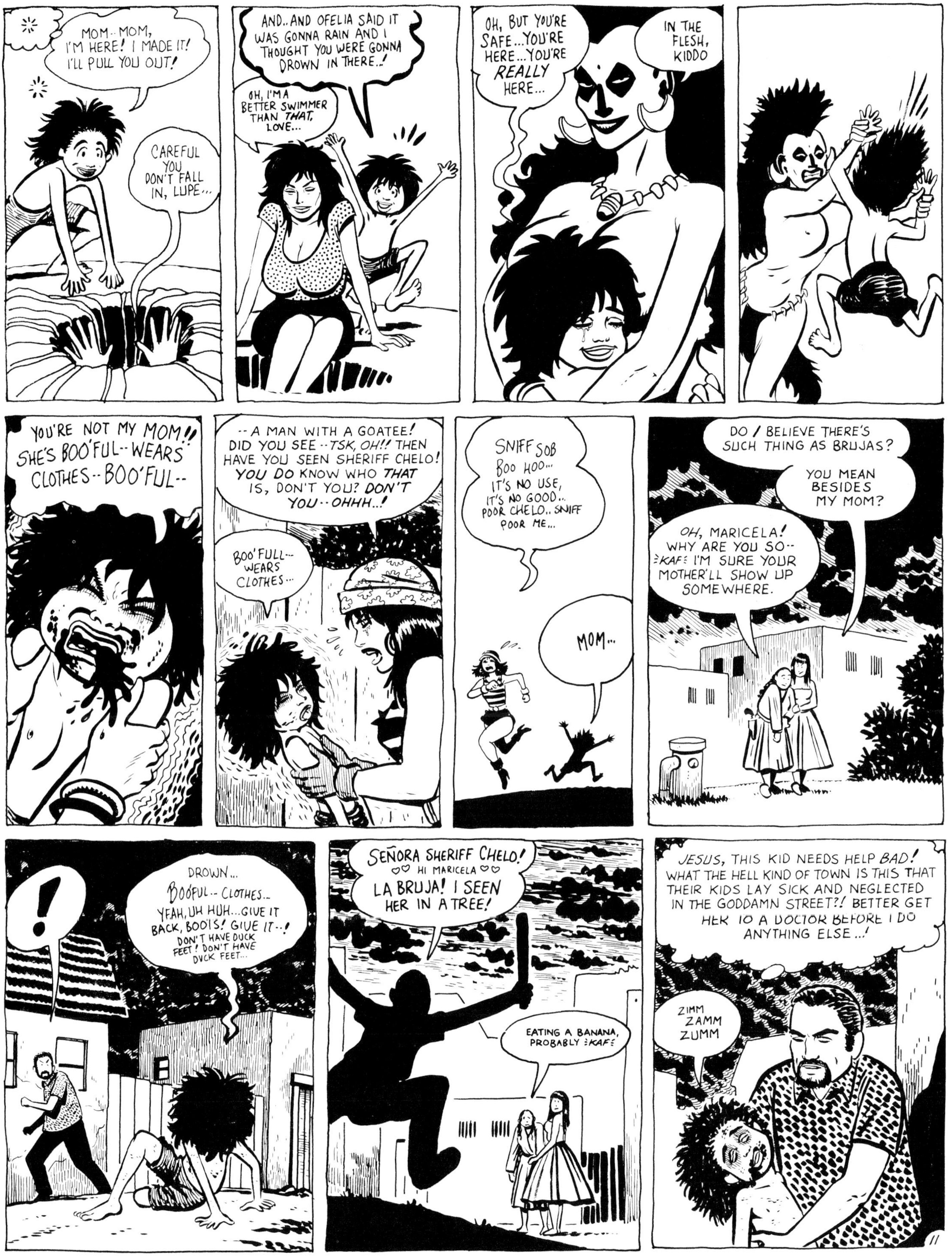
MOM.. MOM, I'M HERE! I MADE IT! I'LL PULL YOU OUT!
CAREFUL YOU DON'T FALL IN, LUPE...
AND.. AND OFELIA SAID IT WAS GONNA RAIN AND I THOUGHT YOU WERE GONNA DROWN IN THERE..!
OH, I'M A BETTER SWIMMER THAN THAT, LOVE...
OH, BUT YOU'RE SAFE... YOU'RE HERE... YOU'RE REALLY HERE...
IN THE FLESH, KIDDO
YOU'RE NOT MY MOM!! SHE'S BOO'FUL-- WEARS CLOTHES-- BOO'FUL--
--A MAN WITH A GOATEE! DID YOU SEE --TSK, OH!! THEN HAVE YOU SEEN SHERIFF CHELO! YOU DO KNOW WHO THAT IS, DON'T YOU? DON'T YOU-- OHHH..!
BOO'FULL-- WEARS CLOTHES...
SNIFF SOB BOO HOO... IT'S NO USE, IT'S NO GOOD... POOR CHELO.. SNIFF POOR ME...
MOM...
DO I BELIEVE THERE'S SUCH THING AS BRUJAS?
YOU MEAN BESIDES MY MOM?
OH, MARICELA! WHY ARE YOU SO-- KAF I'M SURE YOUR MOTHER'LL SHOW UP SOMEWHERE.
!
DROWN... BOOFUL-- CLOTHES... YEAH, UH HUH... GIVE IT BACK, BOO'S! GIVE IT--! DON'T HAVE DUCK FEET! DON'T HAVE DUCK FEET...
SEÑORA SHERIFF CHELO! HI MARICELA LA BRUJA! I SEEN HER IN A TREE!
EATING A BANANA, PROBABLY KAF
JESUS, THIS KID NEEDS HELP BAD! WHAT THE HELL KIND OF TOWN IS THIS THAT THEIR KIDS LAY SICK AND NEGLECTED IN THE GODDAMN STREET?! BETTER GET HER TO A DOCTOR BEFORE I DO ANYTHING ELSE...!
ZIMM ZAMM ZUMM
11

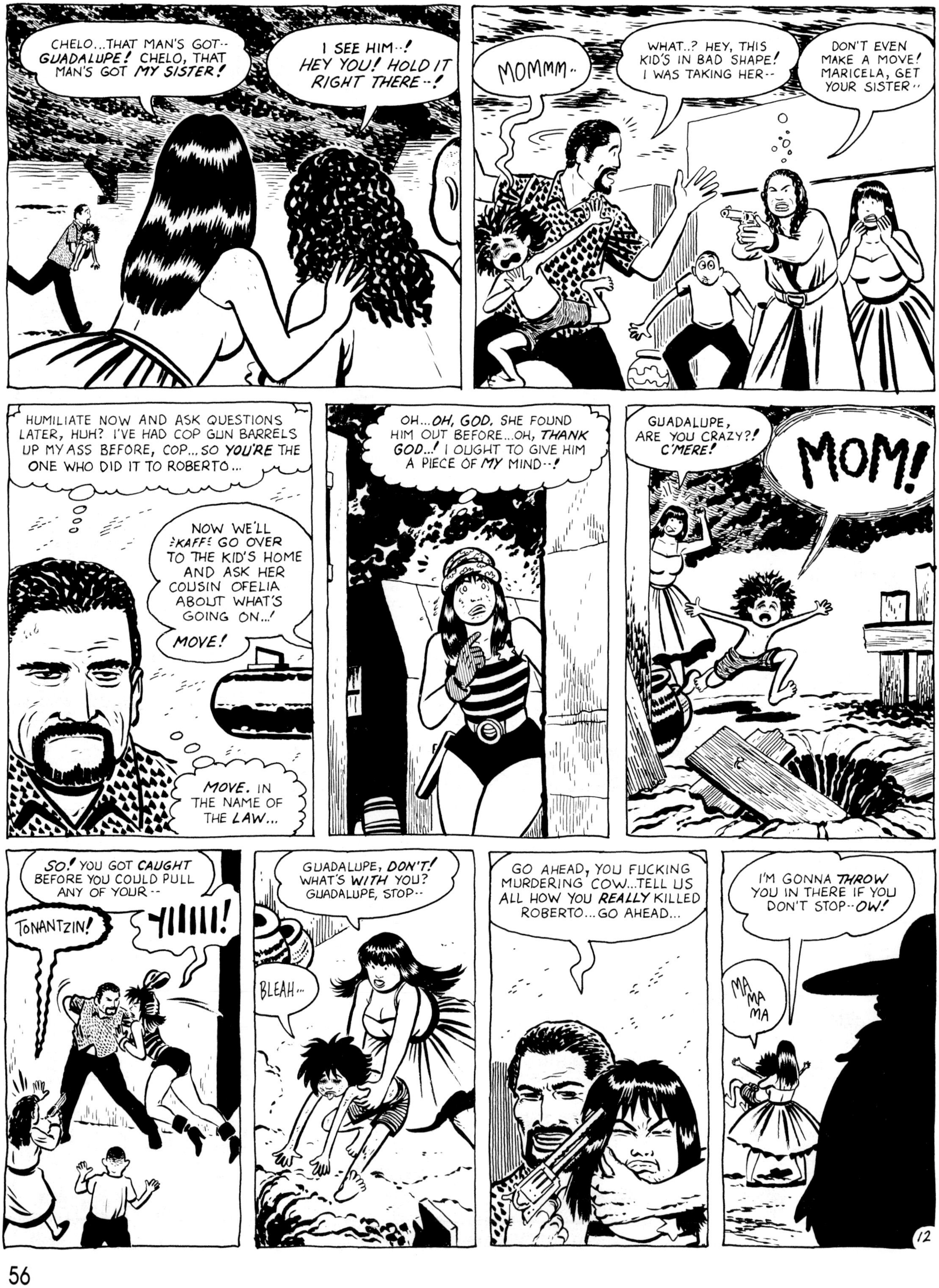
CHELO...THAT MAN'S GOT-- GUADALUPE! CHELO, THAT MAN'S GOT MY SISTER!
I SEE HIM--! HEY YOU! HOLD IT RIGHT THERE--!
MOMMM..
WHAT..? HEY, THIS KID'S IN BAD SHAPE! I WAS TAKING HER--
DON'T EVEN MAKE A MOVE! MARICELA, GET YOUR SISTER..
HUMILIATE NOW AND ASK QUESTIONS LATER, HUH? I'VE HAD COP GUN BARRELS UP MY ASS BEFORE, COP...SO YOU'RE THE ONE WHO DID IT TO ROBERTO...
NOW WE'LL KAFF GO OVER TO THE KID'S HOME AND ASK HER COUSIN OFELIA ABOUT WHAT'S GOING ON..!
MOVE!
MOVE. IN THE NAME OF THE LAW...
OH...OH, GOD, SHE FOUND HIM OUT BEFORE...OH, THANK GOD..! I OUGHT TO GIVE HIM A PIECE OF MY MIND--!
GUADALUPE, ARE YOU CRAZY?! C'MERE!
MOM!
SO! YOU GOT CAUGHT BEFORE YOU COULD PULL ANY OF YOUR--
TONANTZIN!
YIIIII!
GUADALUPE, DON'T! WHAT'S WITH YOU? GUADALUPE, STOP--
BLEAH...
GO AHEAD, YOU FUCKING MURDERING COW...TELL US ALL HOW YOU REALLY KILLED ROBERTO...GO AHEAD...
I'M GONNA THROW YOU IN THERE IF YOU DON'T STOP--OW!
MA MA MA
12

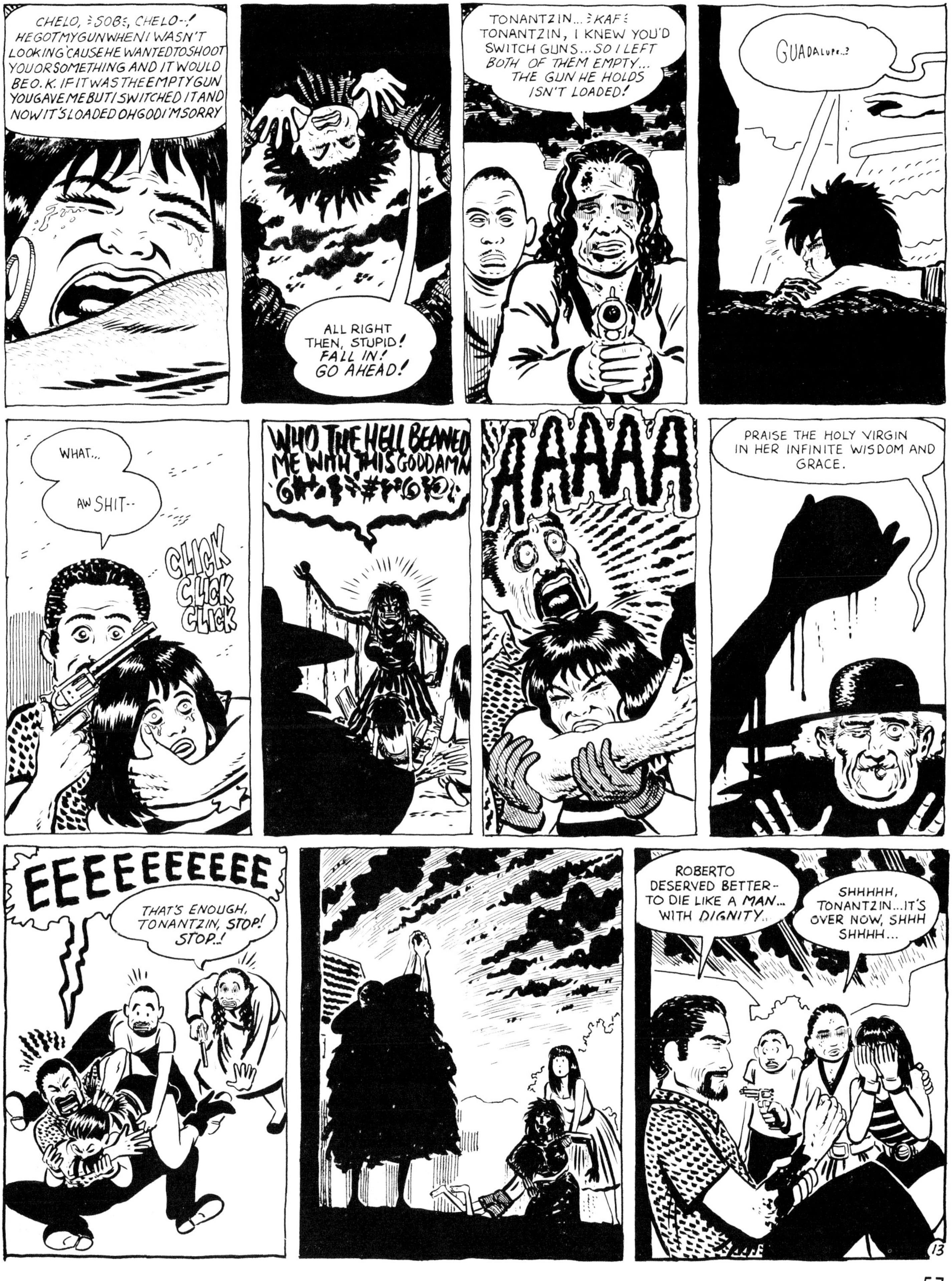
CHELO, SOB, CHELO--! HEGOTMYGUNWHENIWASN'T LOOKING'CAUSEHEWANTEDTOSHOOT YOUORSOMETHING AND IT WOULD BEO.K. IFITWASTHEEMPTYGUN YOUGAVEMEBUTISWITCHEDITAND NOWIT'SLOADEDOHGODI'MSORRY
ALL RIGHT THEN, STUPID! FALL IN! GO AHEAD!
TONANTZIN... KAF TONANTZIN, I KNEW YOU'D SWITCH GUNS... SO I LEFT BOTH OF THEM EMPTY... THE GUN HE HOLDS ISN'T LOADED!
GUADALUPE..?
WHAT...
AW SHIT--
CLICK CLICK CLICK
WHO THE HELL BEANED ME WITH THIS GODDAMN
AAAAA
PRAISE THE HOLY VIRGIN IN HER INFINITE WISDOM AND GRACE.
EEEEEEEEEE
THAT'S ENOUGH, TONANTZIN, STOP! STOP..!
ROBERTO DESERVED BETTER-- TO DIE LIKE A MAN... WITH DIGNITY...
SHHHHH, TONANTZIN... IT'S OVER NOW, SHHH SHHHH...
13

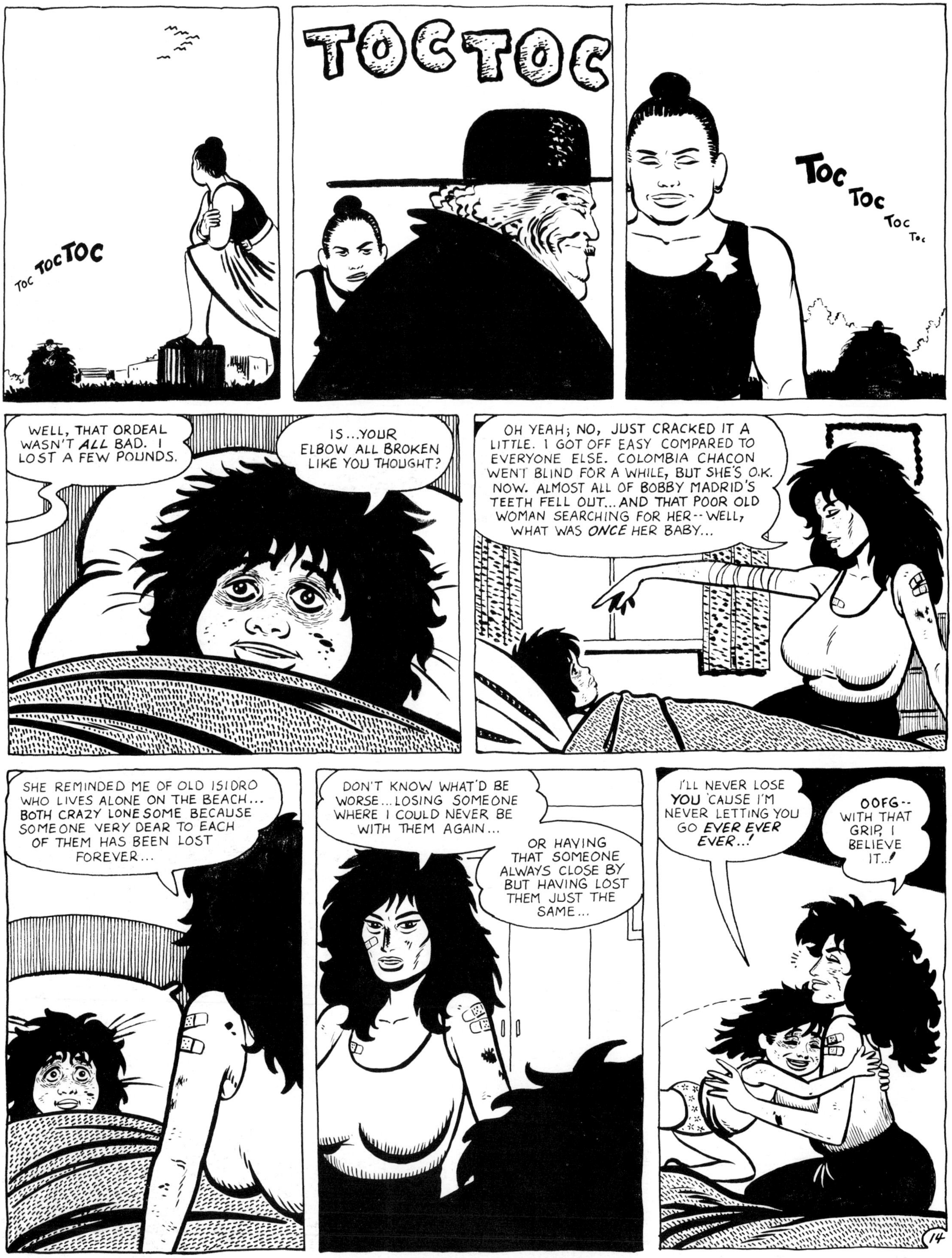
TOC TOC TOC
TOC TOC
TOC TOC TOC TOC
WELL, THAT ORDEAL WASN'T ALL BAD. I LOST A FEW POUNDS.
IS...YOUR ELBOW ALL BROKEN LIKE YOU THOUGHT?
OH YEAH; NO, JUST CRACKED IT A LITTLE. I GOT OFF EASY COMPARED TO EVERYONE ELSE. COLOMBIA CHACON WENT BLIND FOR A WHILE, BUT SHE'S O.K. NOW. ALMOST ALL OF BOBBY MADRID'S TEETH FELL OUT...AND THAT POOR OLD WOMAN SEARCHING FOR HER-- WELL, WHAT WAS ONCE HER BABY...
SHE REMINDED ME OF OLD ISIDRO WHO LIVES ALONE ON THE BEACH... BOTH CRAZY LONESOME BECAUSE SOMEONE VERY DEAR TO EACH OF THEM HAS BEEN LOST FOREVER...
DON'T KNOW WHAT'D BE WORSE...LOSING SOMEONE WHERE I COULD NEVER BE WITH THEM AGAIN...
OR HAVING THAT SOMEONE ALWAYS CLOSE BY BUT HAVING LOST THEM JUST THE SAME...
I'LL NEVER LOSE YOU 'CAUSE I'M NEVER LETTING YOU GO EVER EVER EVER..!
OOFG-- WITH THAT GRIP, I BELIEVE IT..!
14

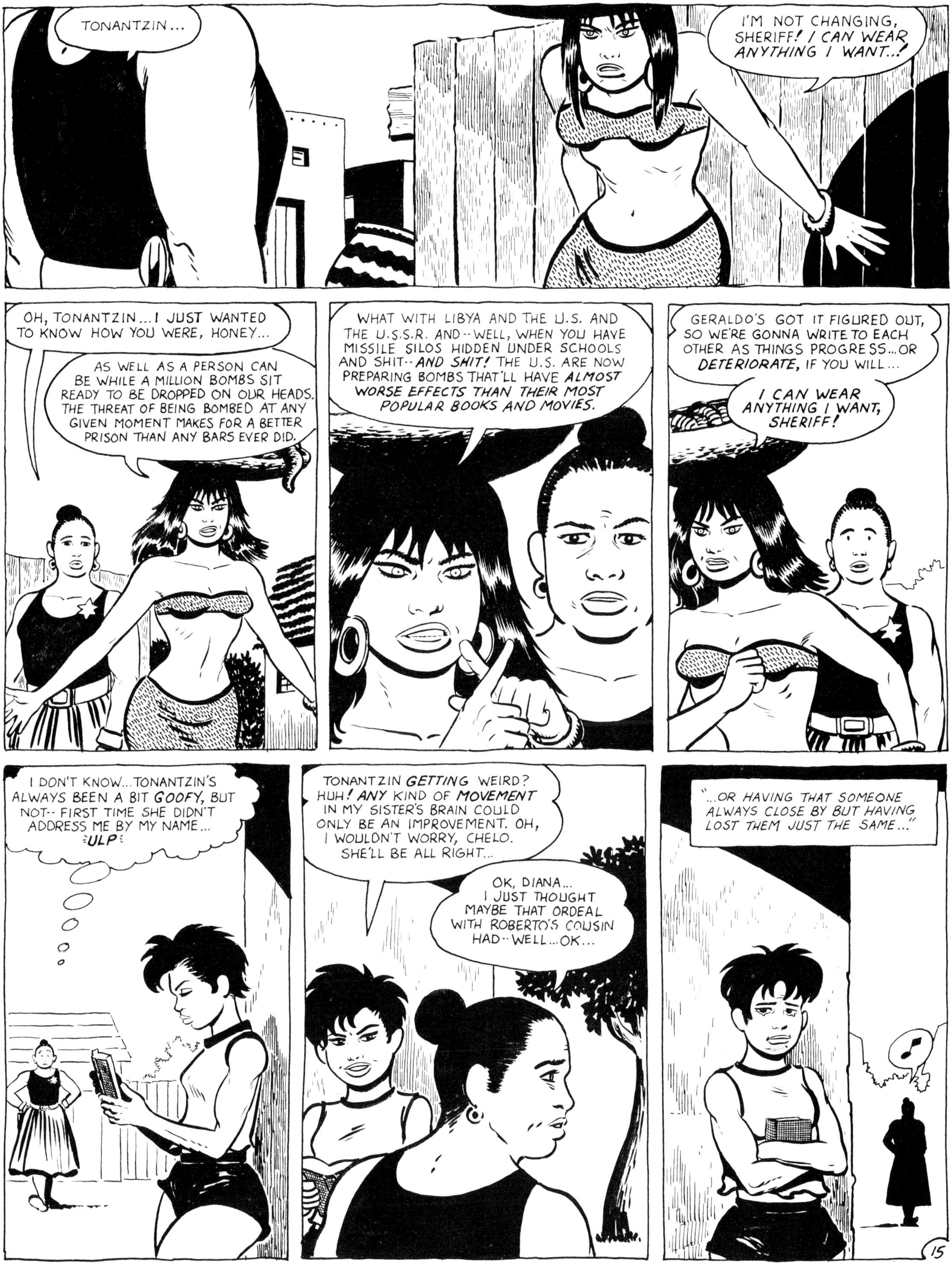
TONANTZIN...
I'M NOT CHANGING, SHERIFF! I CAN WEAR ANYTHING I WANT..!
OH, TONANTZIN... I JUST WANTED TO KNOW HOW YOU WERE, HONEY...
AS WELL AS A PERSON CAN BE WHILE A MILLION BOMBS SIT READY TO BE DROPPED ON OUR HEADS. THE THREAT OF BEING BOMBED AT ANY GIVEN MOMENT MAKES FOR A BETTER PRISON THAN ANY BARS EVER DID.
WHAT WITH LIBYA AND THE U.S. AND THE U.S.S.R. AND--WELL, WHEN YOU HAVE MISSILE SILOS HIDDEN UNDER SCHOOLS AND SHIT--AND SHIT! THE U.S. ARE NOW PREPARING BOMBS THAT'LL HAVE ALMOST WORSE EFFECTS THAN THEIR MOST POPULAR BOOKS AND MOVIES.
GERALDO'S GOT IT FIGURED OUT, SO WE'RE GONNA WRITE TO EACH OTHER AS THINGS PROGRESS...OR DETERIORATE, IF YOU WILL...
I CAN WEAR ANYTHING I WANT, SHERIFF!
I DON'T KNOW...TONANTZIN'S ALWAYS BEEN A BIT GOOFY, BUT NOT--FIRST TIME SHE DIDN'T ADDRESS ME BY MY NAME... ULP
TONANTZIN GETTING WEIRD? HUH! ANY KIND OF MOVEMENT IN MY SISTER'S BRAIN COULD ONLY BE AN IMPROVEMENT. OH, I WOULDN'T WORRY, CHELO. SHE'LL BE ALL RIGHT...
OK, DIANA... I JUST THOUGHT MAYBE THAT ORDEAL WITH ROBERTO'S COUSIN HAD--WELL...OK...
"...OR HAVING THAT SOMEONE ALWAYS CLOSE BY BUT HAVING LOST THEM JUST THE SAME..."
15

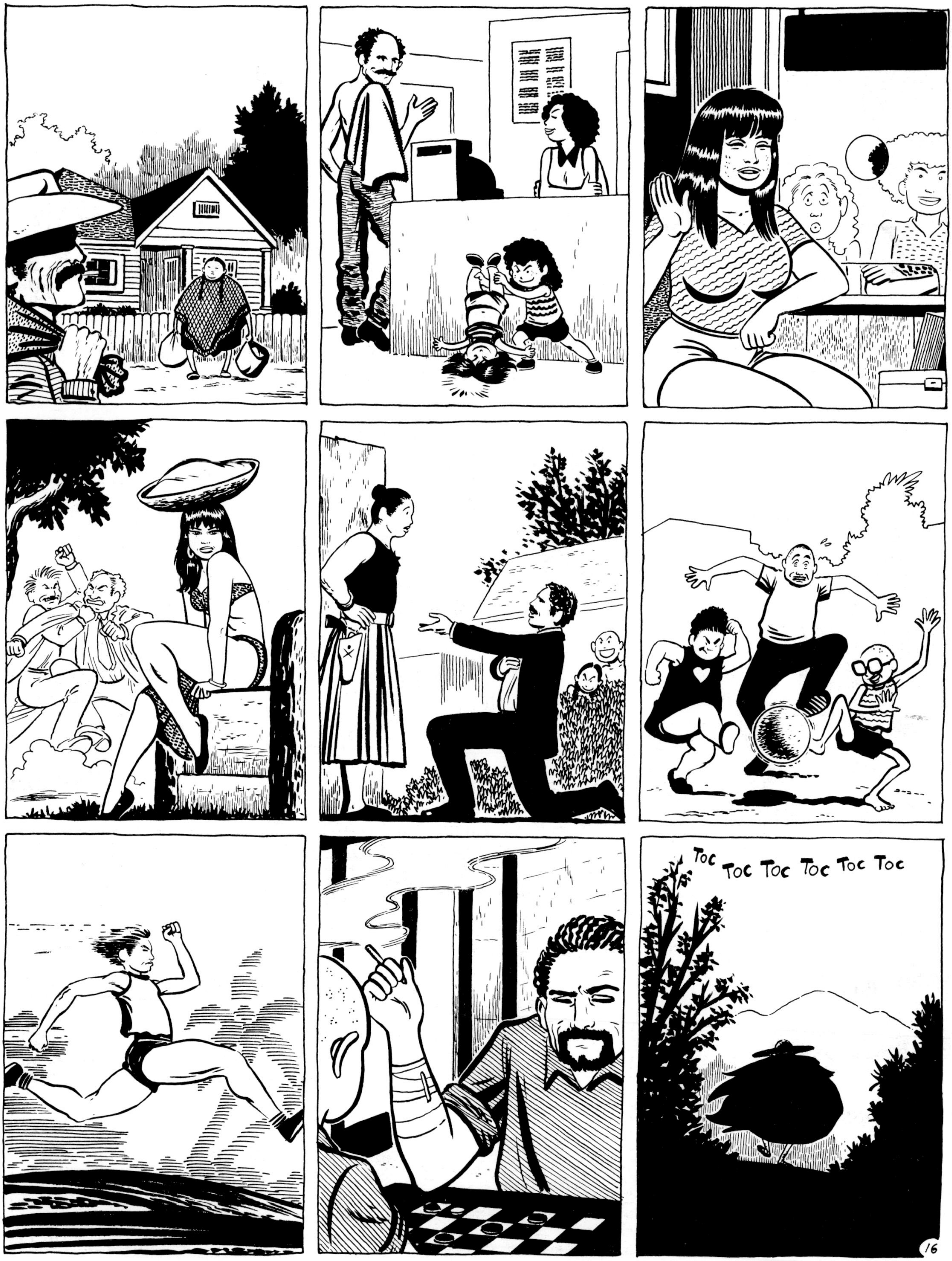
Toc Toc Toc Toc Toc Toc
16

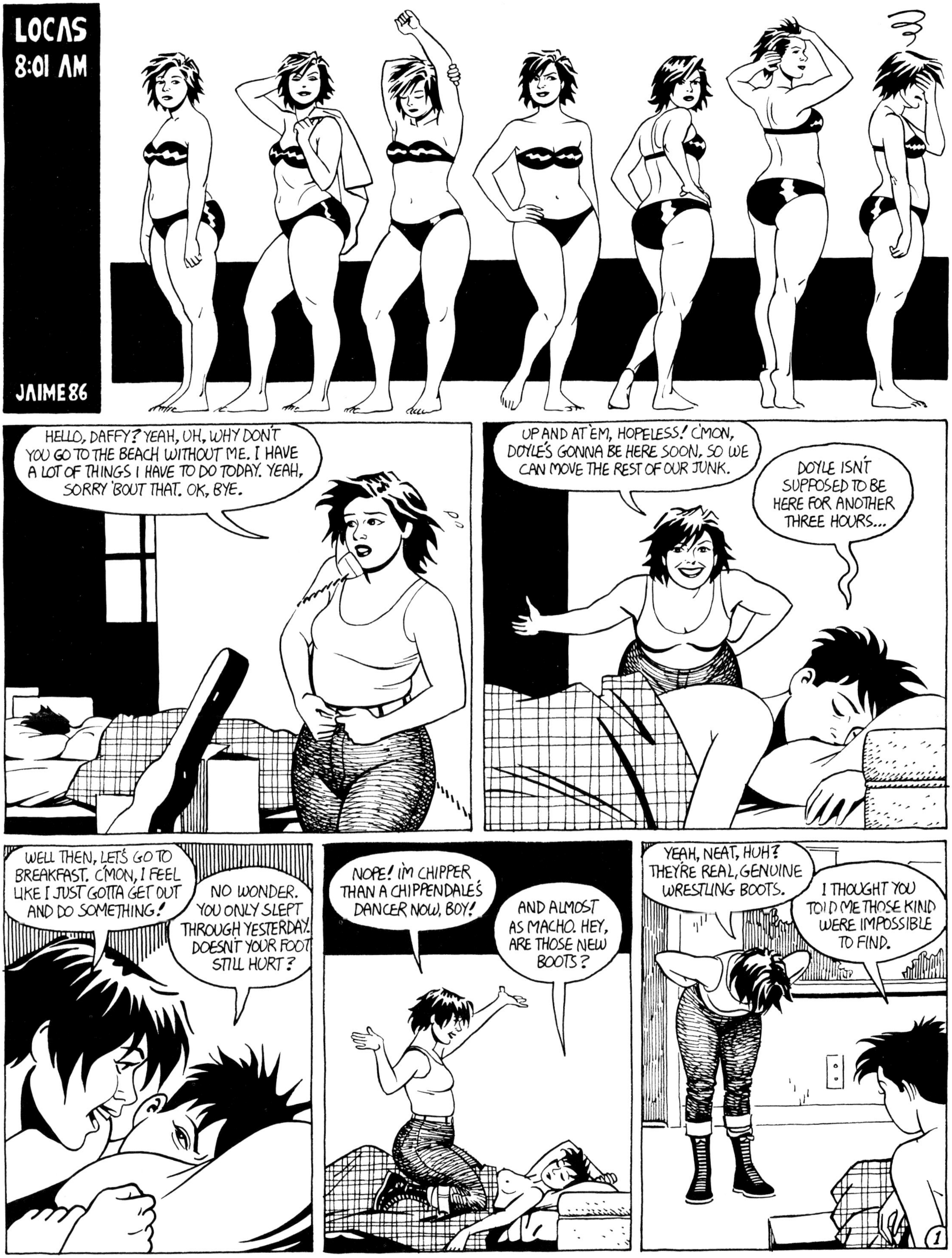
LOCAS
8:01 AM
JAIME 86
HELLO, DAFFY? YEAH, UH, WHY DON'T YOU GO TO THE BEACH WITHOUT ME. I HAVE A LOT OF THINGS I HAVE TO DO TODAY. YEAH, SORRY 'BOUT THAT. OK, BYE.
UP AND AT 'EM, HOPELESS! C'MON, DOYLE'S GONNA BE HERE SOON, SO WE CAN MOVE THE REST OF OUR JUNK.
DOYLE ISN'T SUPPOSED TO BE HERE FOR ANOTHER THREE HOURS...
WELL THEN, LET'S GO TO BREAKFAST. C'MON, I FEEL LIKE I JUST GOTTA GET OUT AND DO SOMETHING!
NO WONDER. YOU ONLY SLEPT THROUGH YESTERDAY. DOESN'T YOUR FOOT STILL HURT?
NOPE! I'M CHIPPER THAN A CHIPPENDALE'S DANCER NOW, BOY!
AND ALMOST AS MACHO. HEY, ARE THOSE NEW BOOTS?
YEAH, NEAT, HUH? THEY'RE REAL, GENUINE WRESTLING BOOTS.
I THOUGHT YOU TOLD ME THOSE KIND WERE IMPOSSIBLE TO FIND.
1

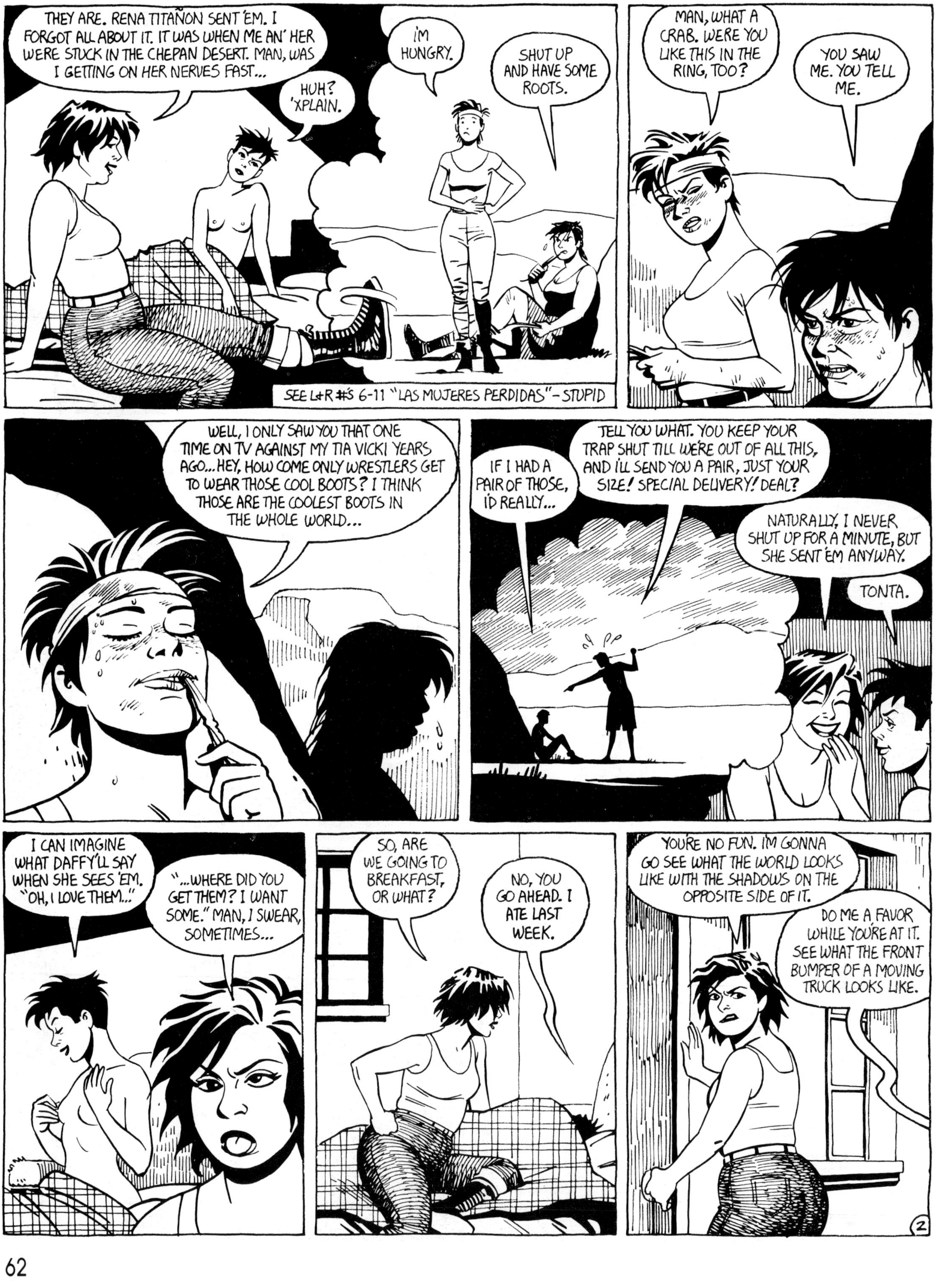
THEY ARE. RENA TITAÑON SENT 'EM. I FORGOT ALL ABOUT IT. IT WAS WHEN ME AN' HER WERE STUCK IN THE CHEPAN DESERT. MAN, WAS I GETTING ON HER NERVES FAST...
HUH? 'XPLAIN.
I'M HUNGRY.
SHUT UP AND HAVE SOME ROOTS.
SEE L&R #'S 6-11 "LAS MUJERES PERDIDAS"–STUPID
MAN, WHAT A CRAB. WERE YOU LIKE THIS IN THE RING, TOO?
YOU SAW ME. YOU TELL ME.
WELL, I ONLY SAW YOU THAT ONE TIME ON TV AGAINST MY TIA VICKI YEARS AGO... HEY, HOW COME ONLY WRESTLERS GET TO WEAR THOSE COOL BOOTS? I THINK THOSE ARE THE COOLEST BOOTS IN THE WHOLE WORLD...
IF I HAD A PAIR OF THOSE, I'D REALLY...
TELL YOU WHAT. YOU KEEP YOUR TRAP SHUT TILL WE'RE OUT OF ALL THIS, AND I'LL SEND YOU A PAIR, JUST YOUR SIZE! SPECIAL DELIVERY! DEAL?
NATURALLY, I NEVER SHUT UP FOR A MINUTE, BUT SHE SENT 'EM ANYWAY.
TONTA.
I CAN IMAGINE WHAT DAFFY'LL SAY WHEN SHE SEES 'EM. "OH, I LOVE THEM..."
"...WHERE DID YOU GET THEM? I WANT SOME." MAN, I SWEAR, SOMETIMES...
SO, ARE WE GOING TO BREAKFAST, OR WHAT?
NO, YOU GO AHEAD. I ATE LAST WEEK.
YOU'RE NO FUN. I'M GONNA GO SEE WHAT THE WORLD LOOKS LIKE WITH THE SHADOWS ON THE OPPOSITE SIDE OF IT.
DO ME A FAVOR WHILE YOU'RE AT IT. SEE WHAT THE FRONT BUMPER OF A MOVING TRUCK LOOKS LIKE.
2

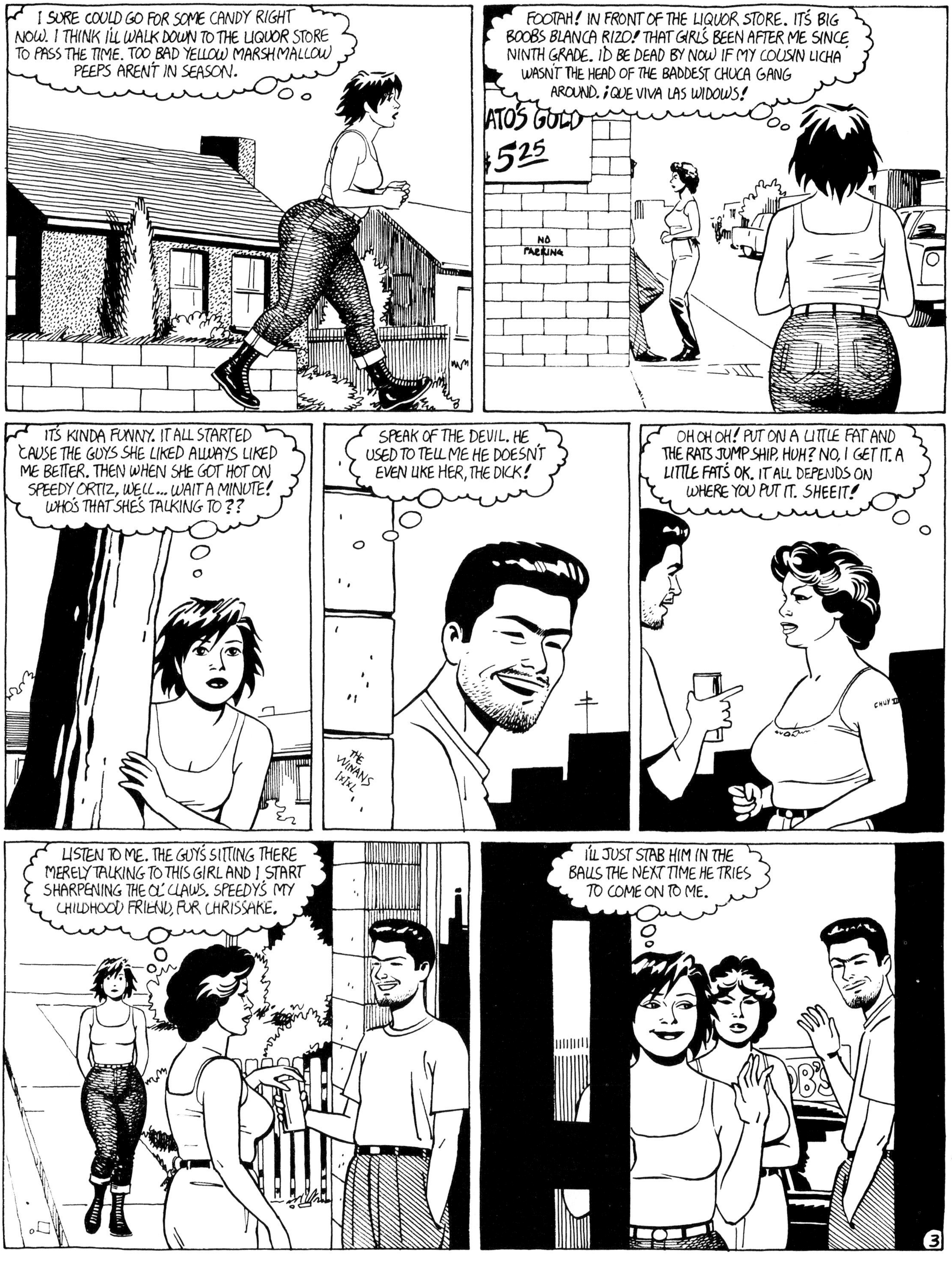
I SURE COULD GO FOR SOME CANDY RIGHT NOW. I THINK I'LL WALK DOWN TO THE LIQUOR STORE TO PASS THE TIME. TOO BAD YELLOW MARSHMALLOW PEEPS AREN'T IN SEASON.
FOOTAH! IN FRONT OF THE LIQUOR STORE. IT'S BIG BOOBS BLANCA RIZO! THAT GIRL'S BEEN AFTER ME SINCE NINTH GRADE. I'D BE DEAD BY NOW IF MY COUSIN LICHA WASN'T THE HEAD OF THE BADDEST CHUCA GANG AROUND. ¡QUE VIVA LAS WIDOWS!
ATO'S GOLD
$5.25
NO PARKING
IT'S KINDA FUNNY. IT ALL STARTED 'CAUSE THE GUYS SHE LIKED ALWAYS LIKED ME BETTER. THEN WHEN SHE GOT HOT ON SPEEDY ORTIZ, WELL... WAIT A MINUTE! WHO'S THAT SHE'S TALKING TO??
SPEAK OF THE DEVIL. HE USED TO TELL ME HE DOESN'T EVEN LIKE HER, THE DICK!
THE WINANS
OH OH OH! PUT ON A LITTLE FAT AND THE RATS JUMP SHIP, HUH? NO, I GET IT. A LITTLE FAT'S OK. IT ALL DEPENDS ON WHERE YOU PUT IT. SHEEIT!
CHUY
LISTEN TO ME. THE GUY'S SITTING THERE MERELY TALKING TO THIS GIRL AND I START SHARPENING THE OL' CLAWS. SPEEDY'S MY CHILDHOOD FRIEND, FOR CHRISSAKE.
I'LL JUST STAB HIM IN THE BALLS THE NEXT TIME HE TRIES TO COME ON TO ME.
3

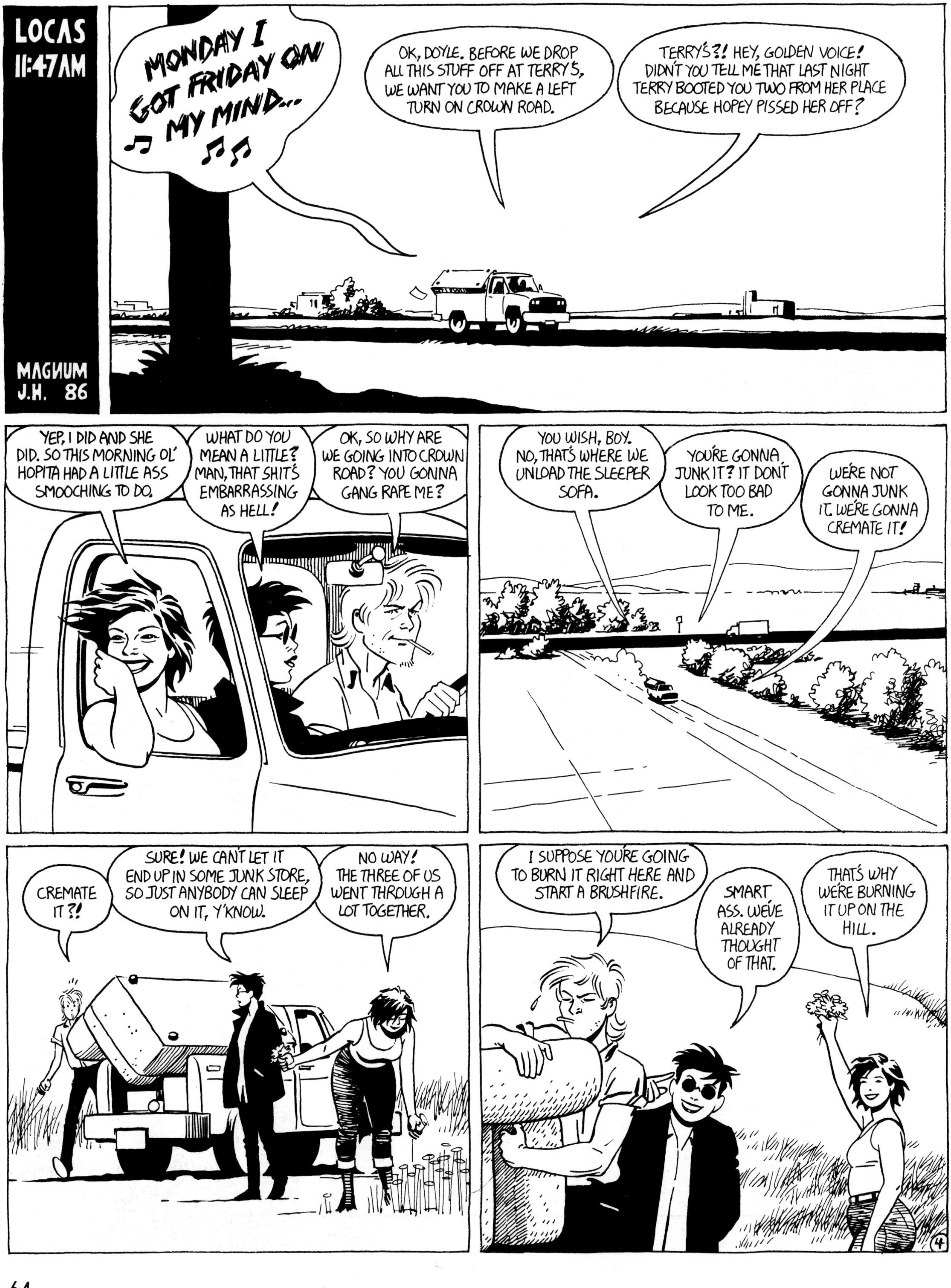
LOCAS
11:47AM
MAGNUM
J.H. 86
MONDAY I GOT FRIDAY ON MY MIND...
OK, DOYLE. BEFORE WE DROP ALL THIS STUFF OFF AT TERRY'S, WE WANT YOU TO MAKE A LEFT TURN ON CROWN ROAD.
TERRY'S?! HEY, GOLDEN VOICE! DIDN'T YOU TELL ME THAT LAST NIGHT TERRY BOOTED YOU TWO FROM HER PLACE BECAUSE HOPEY PISSED HER OFF?
YEP, I DID AND SHE DID. SO THIS MORNING OL' HOPITA HAD A LITTLE ASS SMOOCHING TO DO.
WHAT DO YOU MEAN A LITTLE? MAN, THAT SHIT'S EMBARRASSING AS HELL!
OK, SO WHY ARE WE GOING INTO CROWN ROAD? YOU GONNA GANG RAPE ME?
YOU WISH, BOY. NO, THAT'S WHERE WE UNLOAD THE SLEEPER SOFA.
YOU'RE GONNA JUNK IT? IT DON'T LOOK TOO BAD TO ME.
WE'RE NOT GONNA JUNK IT. WE'RE GONNA CREMATE IT!
CREMATE IT?!
SURE! WE CAN'T LET IT END UP IN SOME JUNK STORE, SO JUST ANYBODY CAN SLEEP ON IT, Y'KNOW.
NO WAY! THE THREE OF US WENT THROUGH A LOT TOGETHER.
I SUPPOSE YOU'RE GOING TO BURN IT RIGHT HERE AND START A BRUSHFIRE.
SMART ASS. WE'VE ALREADY THOUGHT OF THAT.
THAT'S WHY WE'RE BURNING IT UP ON THE HILL.
4

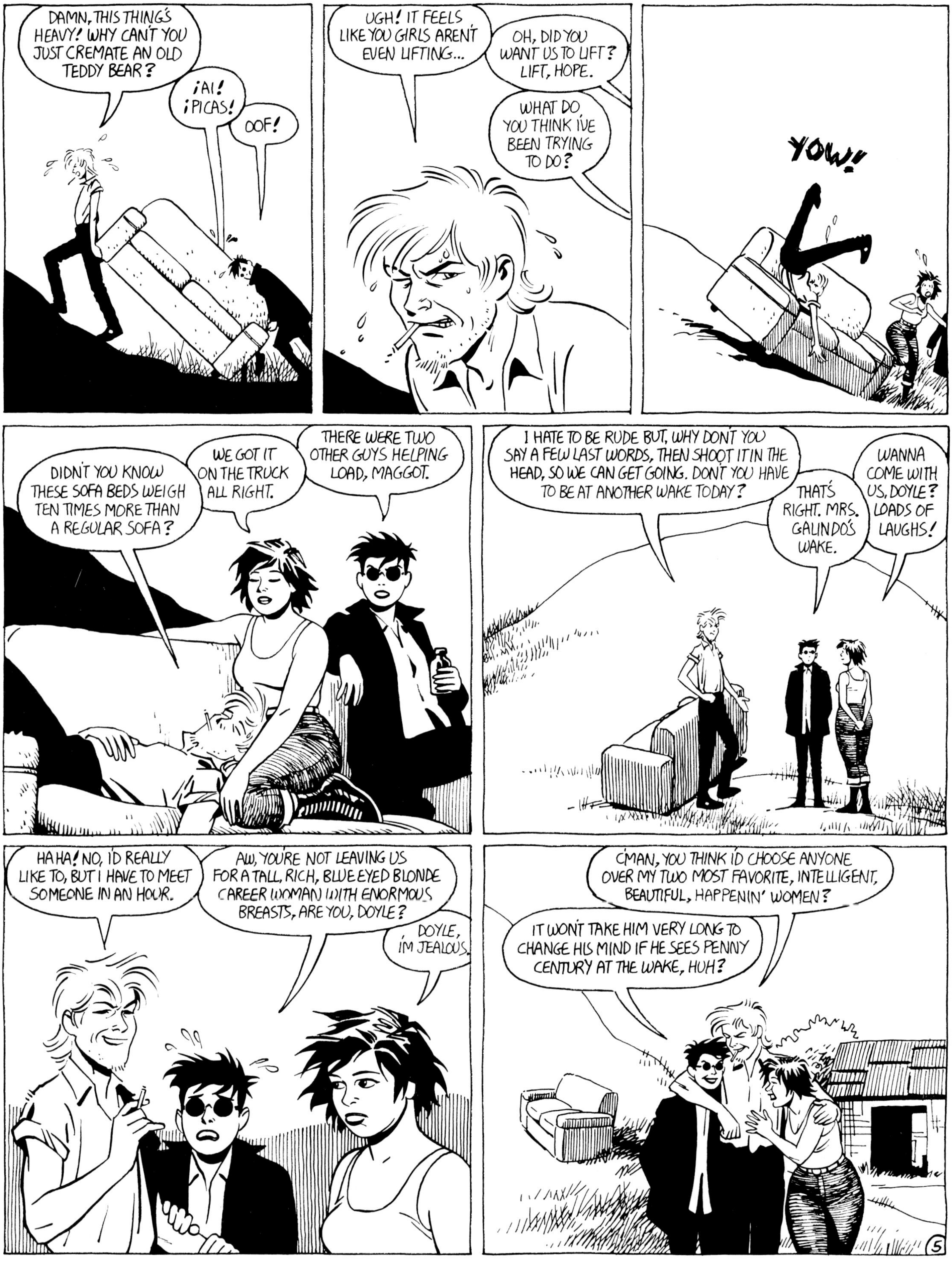
DAMN, THIS THING'S HEAVY! WHY CAN'T YOU JUST CREMATE AN OLD TEDDY BEAR?
¡AI! ¡PICAS!
OOF!
UGH! IT FEELS LIKE YOU GIRLS AREN'T EVEN LIFTING...
OH, DID YOU WANT US TO LIFT? LIFT, HOPE.
WHAT DO YOU THINK I'VE BEEN TRYING TO DO?
YOW!
DIDN'T YOU KNOW THESE SOFA BEDS WEIGH TEN TIMES MORE THAN A REGULAR SOFA?
WE GOT IT ON THE TRUCK ALL RIGHT.
THERE WERE TWO OTHER GUYS HELPING LOAD, MAGGOT.
I HATE TO BE RUDE BUT, WHY DON'T YOU SAY A FEW LAST WORDS, THEN SHOOT IT IN THE HEAD, SO WE CAN GET GOING. DON'T YOU HAVE TO BE AT ANOTHER WAKE TODAY?
THAT'S RIGHT. MRS. GALINDO'S WAKE.
WANNA COME WITH US, DOYLE? LOADS OF LAUGHS!
HA HA! NO, I'D REALLY LIKE TO, BUT I HAVE TO MEET SOMEONE IN AN HOUR.
AW, YOU'RE NOT LEAVING US FOR A TALL, RICH, BLUE EYED BLONDE CAREER WOMAN WITH ENORMOUS BREASTS, ARE YOU, DOYLE?
DOYLE, I'M JEALOUS.
C'MAN, YOU THINK I'D CHOOSE ANYONE OVER MY TWO MOST FAVORITE, INTELLIGENT, BEAUTIFUL, HAPPENIN' WOMEN?
IT WON'T TAKE HIM VERY LONG TO CHANGE HIS MIND IF HE SEES PENNY CENTURY AT THE WAKE, HUH?
5

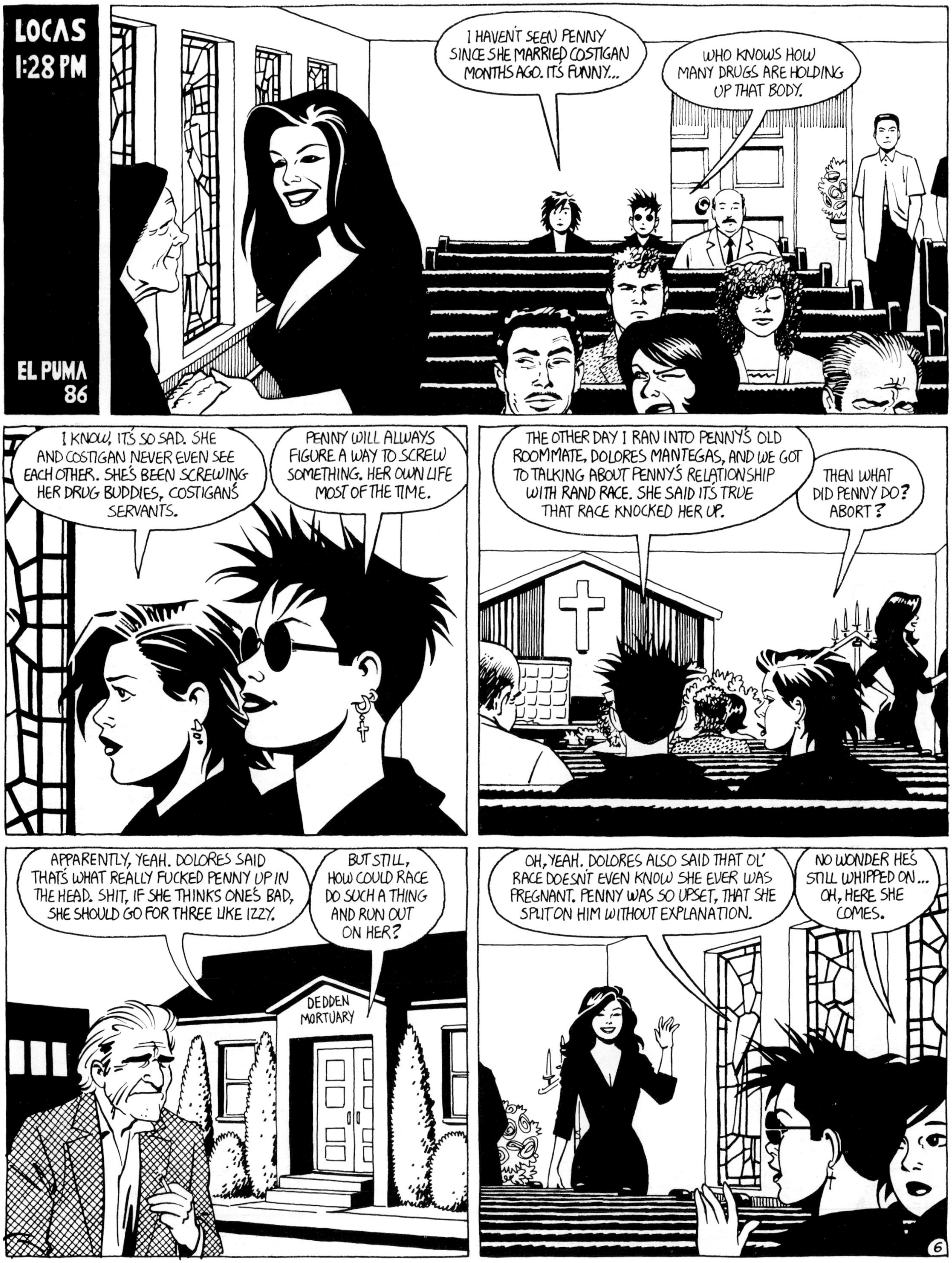
LOCAS
1:28 PM
EL PUMA
86
I HAVEN'T SEEN PENNY SINCE SHE MARRIED COSTIGAN MONTHS AGO. IT'S FUNNY...
WHO KNOWS HOW MANY DRUGS ARE HOLDING UP THAT BODY.
I KNOW, IT'S SO SAD. SHE AND COSTIGAN NEVER EVEN SEE EACH OTHER. SHE'S BEEN SCREWING HER DRUG BUDDIES, COSTIGAN'S SERVANTS.
PENNY WILL ALWAYS FIGURE A WAY TO SCREW SOMETHING. HER OWN LIFE MOST OF THE TIME.
THE OTHER DAY I RAN INTO PENNY'S OLD ROOMMATE, DOLORES MANTEGAS, AND WE GOT TO TALKING ABOUT PENNY'S RELATIONSHIP WITH RAND RACE. SHE SAID IT'S TRUE THAT RACE KNOCKED HER UP.
THEN WHAT DID PENNY DO? ABORT?
APPARENTLY, YEAH. DOLORES SAID THAT'S WHAT REALLY FUCKED PENNY UP IN THE HEAD. SHIT, IF SHE THINKS ONE'S BAD, SHE SHOULD GO FOR THREE LIKE IZZY.
BUT STILL, HOW COULD RACE DO SUCH A THING AND RUN OUT ON HER?
DEDDEN MORTUARY
OH, YEAH. DOLORES ALSO SAID THAT OL' RACE DOESN'T EVEN KNOW SHE EVER WAS PREGNANT. PENNY WAS SO UPSET, THAT SHE SPLIT ON HIM WITHOUT EXPLANATION.
NO WONDER HE'S STILL WHIPPED ON... OH, HERE SHE COMES.
6

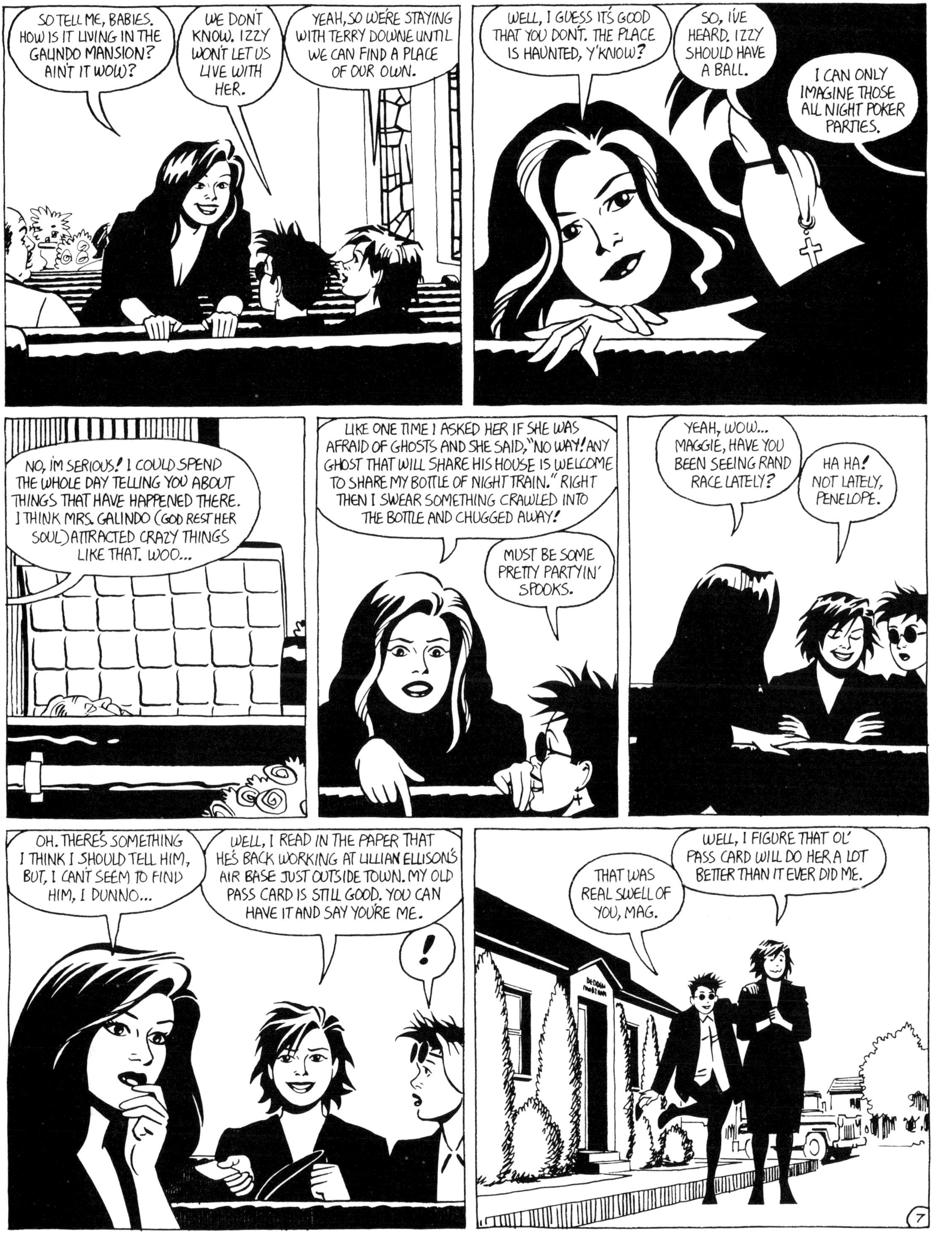

SO TELL ME, BABIES. HOW IS IT LIVING IN THE GALINDO MANSION? AIN'T IT WOW?
WE DON'T KNOW. IZZY WON'T LET US LIVE WITH HER.
YEAH, SO WE'RE STAYING WITH TERRY DOWNE UNTIL WE CAN FIND A PLACE OF OUR OWN.
WELL, I GUESS IT'S GOOD THAT YOU DON'T. THE PLACE IS HAUNTED, Y'KNOW?
SO, I'VE HEARD. IZZY SHOULD HAVE A BALL.
I CAN ONLY IMAGINE THOSE ALL NIGHT POKER PARTIES.
NO, I'M SERIOUS! I COULD SPEND THE WHOLE DAY TELLING YOU ABOUT THINGS THAT HAVE HAPPENED THERE. I THINK MRS. GALINDO (GOD REST HER SOUL) ATTRACTED CRAZY THINGS LIKE THAT. WOO...
LIKE ONE TIME I ASKED HER IF SHE WAS AFRAID OF GHOSTS AND SHE SAID, "NO WAY! ANY GHOST THAT WILL SHARE HIS HOUSE IS WELCOME TO SHARE MY BOTTLE OF NIGHT TRAIN." RIGHT THEN I SWEAR SOMETHING CRAWLED INTO THE BOTTLE AND CHUGGED AWAY!
MUST BE SOME PRETTY PARTYIN' SPOOKS.
YEAH, WOW... MAGGIE, HAVE YOU BEEN SEEING RAND RACE LATELY?
HA HA! NOT LATELY, PENELOPE.
OH. THERE'S SOMETHING I THINK I SHOULD TELL HIM, BUT, I CAN'T SEEM TO FIND HIM, I DUNNO...
WELL, I READ IN THE PAPER THAT HE'S BACK WORKING AT LILLIAN ELLISON'S AIR BASE JUST OUTSIDE TOWN. MY OLD PASS CARD IS STILL GOOD. YOU CAN HAVE IT AND SAY YOU'RE ME.
!
THAT WAS REAL SWELL OF YOU, MAG.
WELL, I FIGURE THAT OL' PASS CARD WILL DO HER A LOT BETTER THAN IT EVER DID ME.
7

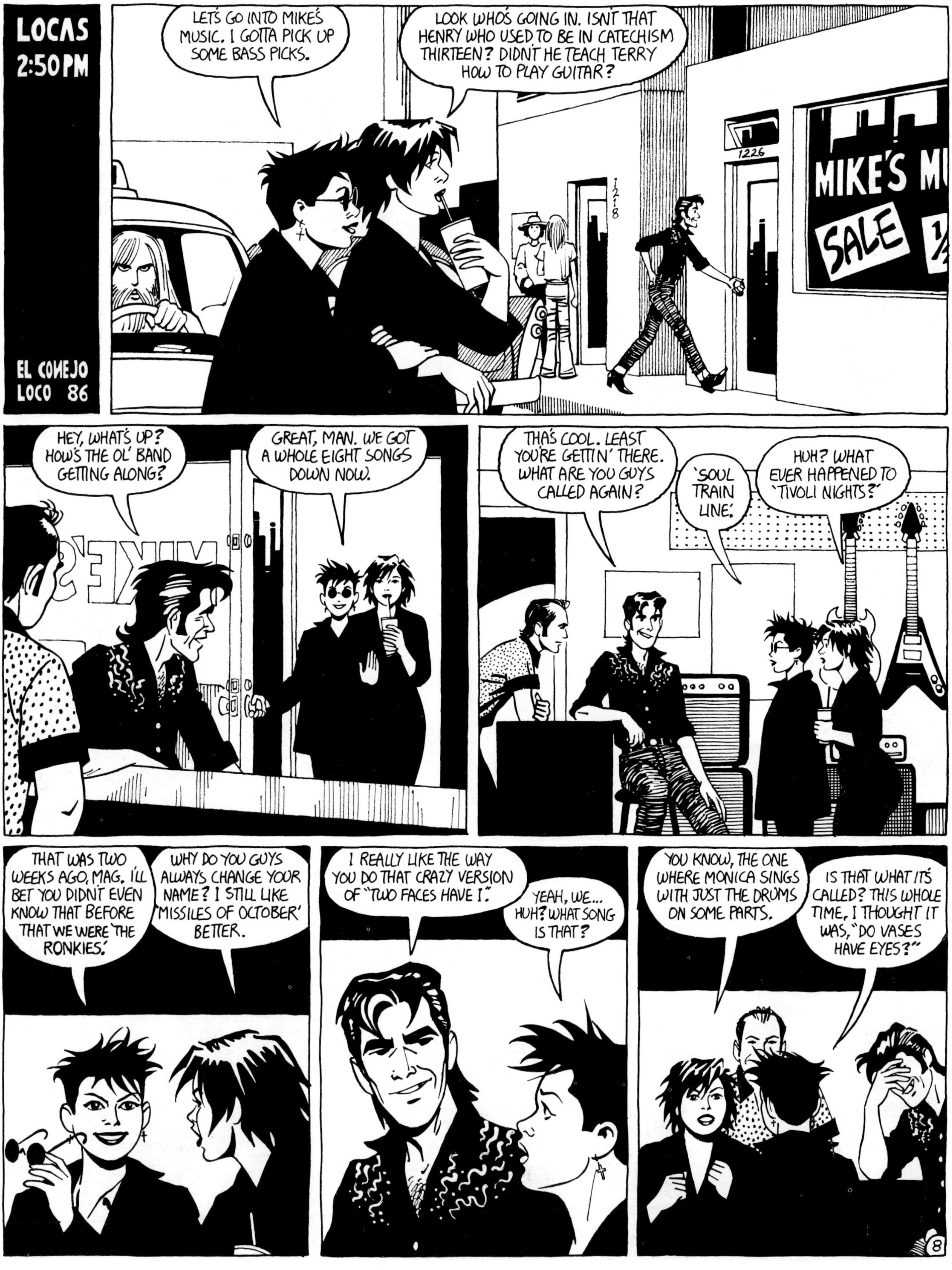
LOCAS
2:50PM
EL CONEJO LOCO 86
LET'S GO INTO MIKE'S MUSIC. I GOTTA PICK UP SOME BASS PICKS.
LOOK WHO'S GOING IN. ISN'T THAT HENRY WHO USED TO BE IN CATECHISM THIRTEEN? DIDN'T HE TEACH TERRY HOW TO PLAY GUITAR?
1218
1226
MIKE'S MU
SALE
HEY, WHAT'S UP? HOW'S THE OL' BAND GETTING ALONG?
GREAT, MAN. WE GOT A WHOLE EIGHT SONGS DOWN NOW.
THA'S COOL. LEAST YOU'RE GETTIN' THERE. WHAT ARE YOU GUYS CALLED AGAIN?
'SOUL TRAIN LINE.'
HUH? WHAT EVER HAPPENED TO 'TIVOLI NIGHTS?'
THAT WAS TWO WEEKS AGO, MAG. I'LL BET YOU DIDN'T EVEN KNOW THAT BEFORE THAT WE WERE 'THE RONKIES.'
WHY DO YOU GUYS ALWAYS CHANGE YOUR NAME? I STILL LIKE 'MISSILES OF OCTOBER' BETTER.
I REALLY LIKE THE WAY YOU DO THAT CRAZY VERSION OF "TWO FACES HAVE I."
YEAH, WE... HUH? WHAT SONG IS THAT?
YOU KNOW, THE ONE WHERE MONICA SINGS WITH JUST THE DRUMS ON SOME PARTS.
IS THAT WHAT IT'S CALLED? THIS WHOLE TIME, I THOUGHT IT WAS, "DO VASES HAVE EYES?"
8

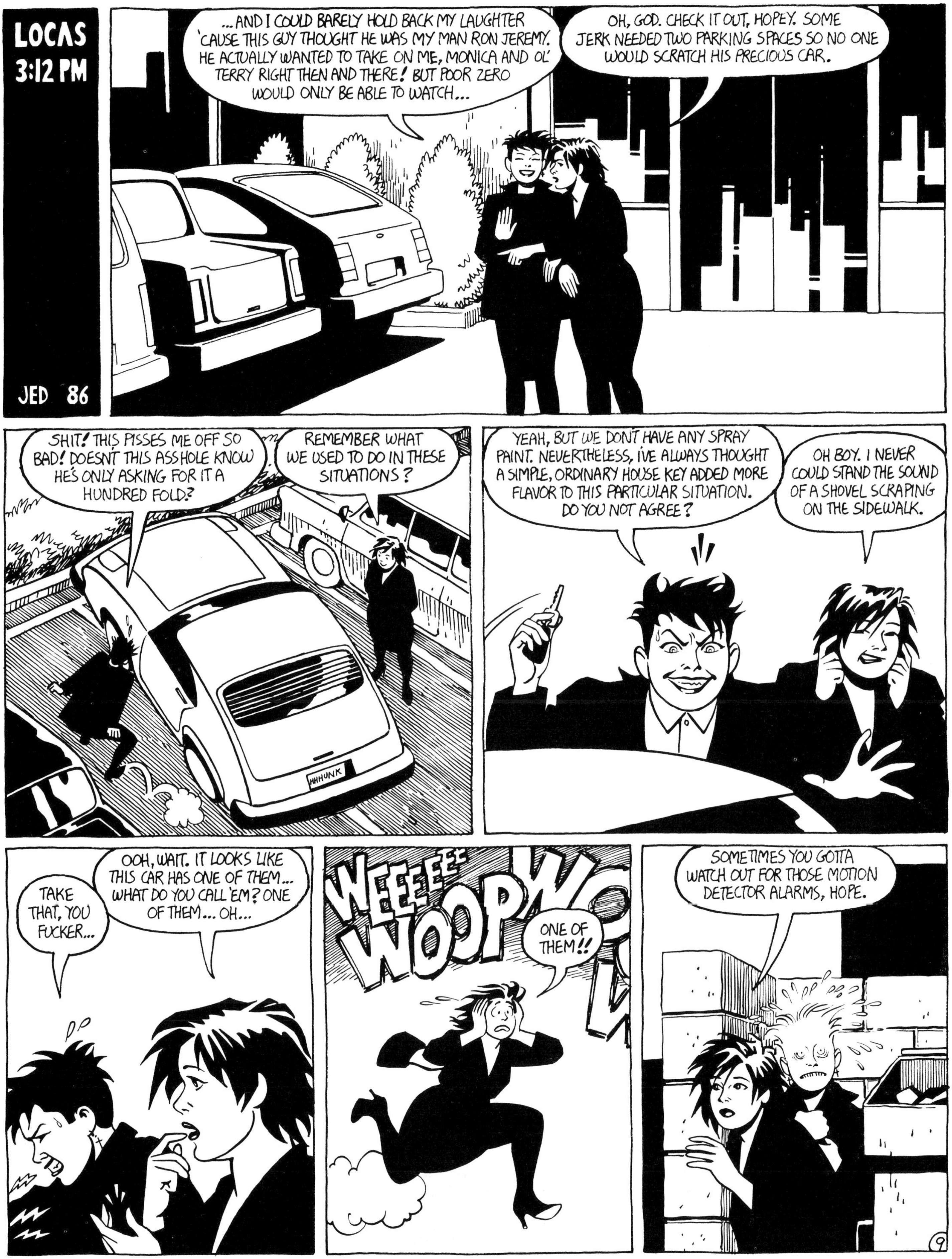
LOCAS
3:12 PM
JED 86
...AND I COULD BARELY HOLD BACK MY LAUGHTER 'CAUSE THIS GUY THOUGHT HE WAS MY MAN RON JEREMY. HE ACTUALLY WANTED TO TAKE ON ME, MONICA AND OL' TERRY RIGHT THEN AND THERE! BUT POOR ZERO WOULD ONLY BE ABLE TO WATCH...
OH, GOD. CHECK IT OUT, HOPEY. SOME JERK NEEDED TWO PARKING SPACES SO NO ONE WOULD SCRATCH HIS PRECIOUS CAR.
SHIT! THIS PISSES ME OFF SO BAD! DOESN'T THIS ASSHOLE KNOW HE'S ONLY ASKING FOR IT A HUNDRED FOLD?
REMEMBER WHAT WE USED TO DO IN THESE SITUATIONS?
HHHUNK
YEAH, BUT WE DON'T HAVE ANY SPRAY PAINT. NEVERTHELESS, I'VE ALWAYS THOUGHT A SIMPLE, ORDINARY HOUSE KEY ADDED MORE FLAVOR TO THIS PARTICULAR SITUATION. DO YOU NOT AGREE?
OH BOY. I NEVER COULD STAND THE SOUND OF A SHOVEL SCRAPING ON THE SIDEWALK.
TAKE THAT, YOU FUCKER...
OOH, WAIT. IT LOOKS LIKE THIS CAR HAS ONE OF THEM... WHAT DO YOU CALL 'EM? ONE OF THEM... OH...
WEEEEEE-WOOP WOOP
ONE OF THEM!!
SOMETIMES YOU GOTTA WATCH OUT FOR THOSE MOTION DETECTOR ALARMS, HOPE.
9

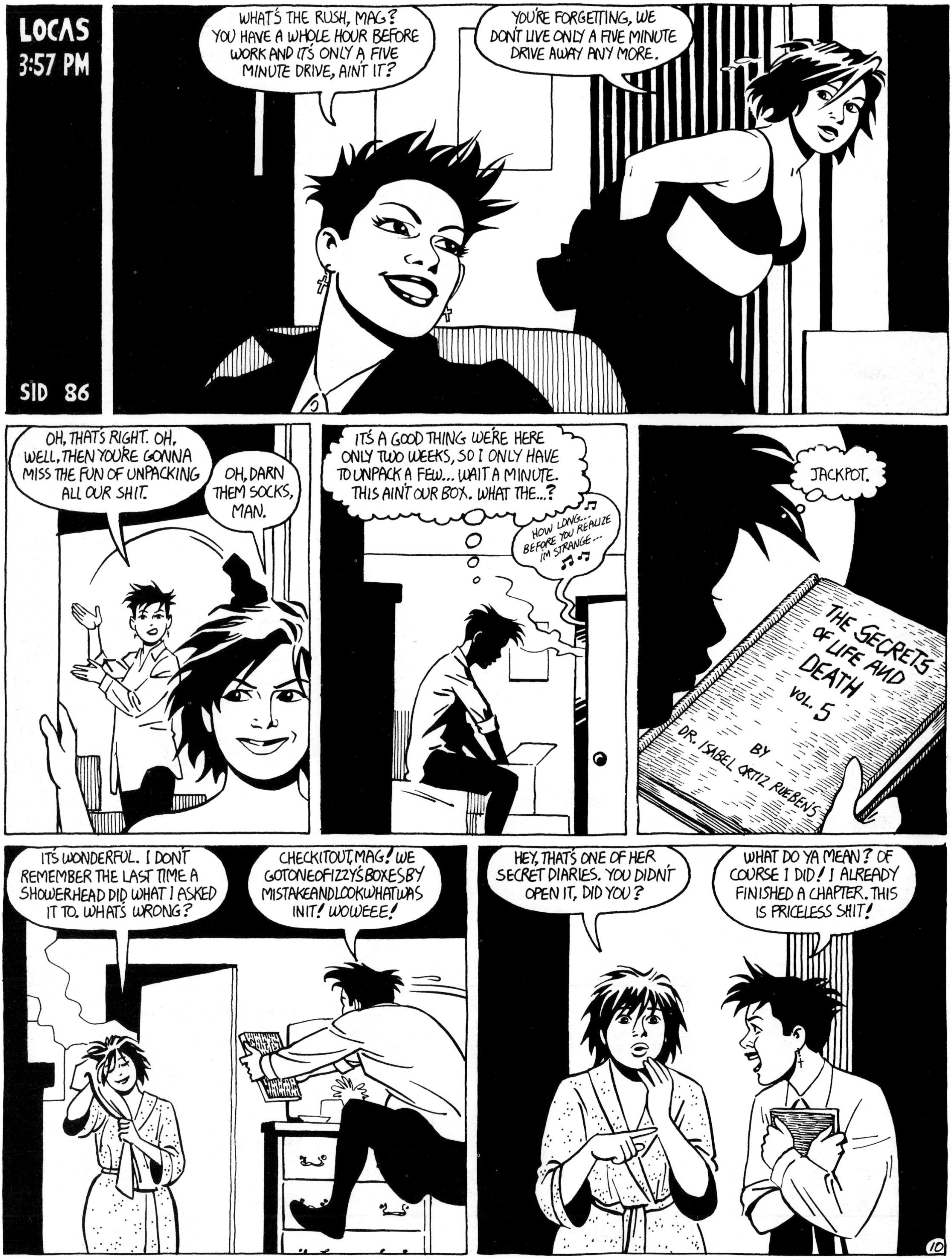
LOCAS
3:57 PM
SID 86
WHAT'S THE RUSH, MAG? YOU HAVE A WHOLE HOUR BEFORE WORK AND IT'S ONLY A FIVE MINUTE DRIVE, AIN'T IT?
YOU'RE FORGETTING, WE DON'T LIVE ONLY A FIVE MINUTE DRIVE AWAY ANY MORE.
OH, THAT'S RIGHT. OH, WELL, THEN YOU'RE GONNA MISS THE FUN OF UNPACKING ALL OUR SHIT.
OH, DARN THEM SOCKS, MAN.
IT'S A GOOD THING WE'RE HERE ONLY TWO WEEKS, SO I ONLY HAVE TO UNPACK A FEW... WAIT A MINUTE. THIS AIN'T OUR BOX. WHAT THE...?
HOW LONG... BEFORE YOU REALIZE I'M STRANGE...
JACKPOT.
THE SECRETS OF LIFE AND DEATH VOL. 5 BY DR. ISABEL ORTIZ RUEBENS
IT'S WONDERFUL. I DON'T REMEMBER THE LAST TIME A SHOWERHEAD DID WHAT I ASKED IT TO. WHAT'S WRONG?
CHECKITOUT, MAG! WE GOTONEOFIZZY'S BOXES BY MISTAKEANDLOOKWHATWAS INIT! WOWEEE!
HEY, THAT'S ONE OF HER SECRET DIARIES. YOU DIDN'T OPEN IT, DID YOU?
WHAT DO YA MEAN? OF COURSE I DID! I ALREADY FINISHED A CHAPTER. THIS IS PRICELESS SHIT!
10

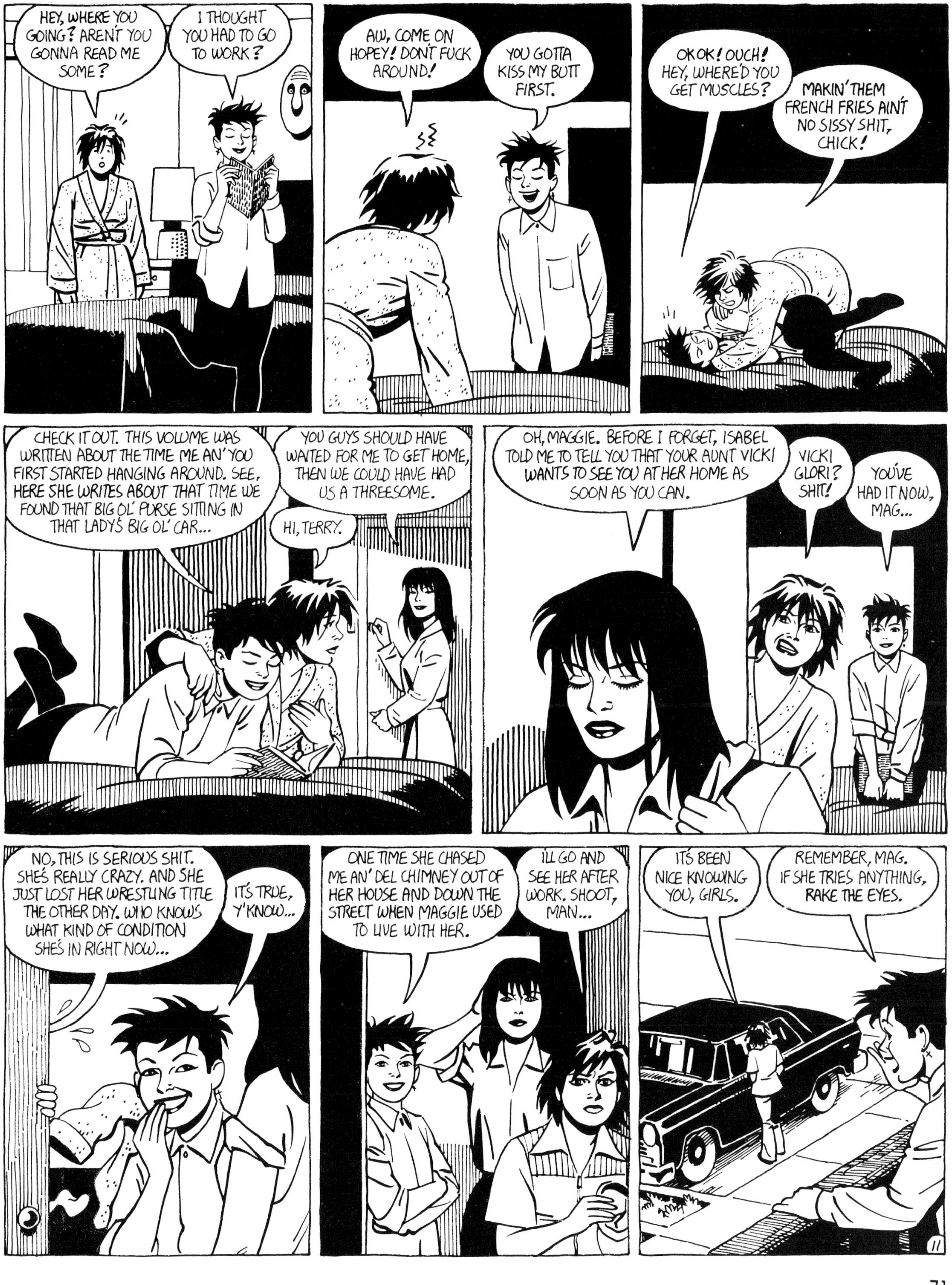
HEY, WHERE YOU GOING? AREN'T YOU GONNA READ ME SOME?
I THOUGHT YOU HAD TO GO TO WORK?
AW, COME ON HOPEY! DON'T FUCK AROUND!
YOU GOTTA KISS MY BUTT FIRST.
OK OK! OUCH! HEY, WHERE'D YOU GET MUSCLES?
MAKIN' THEM FRENCH FRIES AIN'T NO SISSY SHIT, CHICK!
CHECK IT OUT. THIS VOLUME WAS WRITTEN ABOUT THE TIME ME AN' YOU FIRST STARTED HANGING AROUND. SEE, HERE SHE WRITES ABOUT THAT TIME WE FOUND THAT BIG OL' PURSE SITTING IN THAT LADY'S BIG OL' CAR...
YOU GUYS SHOULD HAVE WAITED FOR ME TO GET HOME, THEN WE COULD HAVE HAD US A THREESOME.
HI, TERRY.
OH, MAGGIE. BEFORE I FORGET, ISABEL TOLD ME TO TELL YOU THAT YOUR AUNT VICKI WANTS TO SEE YOU AT HER HOME AS SOON AS YOU CAN.
VICKI GLORI? SHIT!
YOU'VE HAD IT NOW, MAG...
NO, THIS IS SERIOUS SHIT. SHE'S REALLY CRAZY. AND SHE JUST LOST HER WRESTLING TITLE THE OTHER DAY. WHO KNOWS WHAT KIND OF CONDITION SHE'S IN RIGHT NOW...
IT'S TRUE, Y'KNOW...
ONE TIME SHE CHASED ME AN' DEL CHIMNEY OUT OF HER HOUSE AND DOWN THE STREET WHEN MAGGIE USED TO LIVE WITH HER.
I'LL GO AND SEE HER AFTER WORK. SHOOT, MAN...
IT'S BEEN NICE KNOWING YOU, GIRLS.
REMEMBER, MAG. IF SHE TRIES ANYTHING, RAKE THE EYES.
11

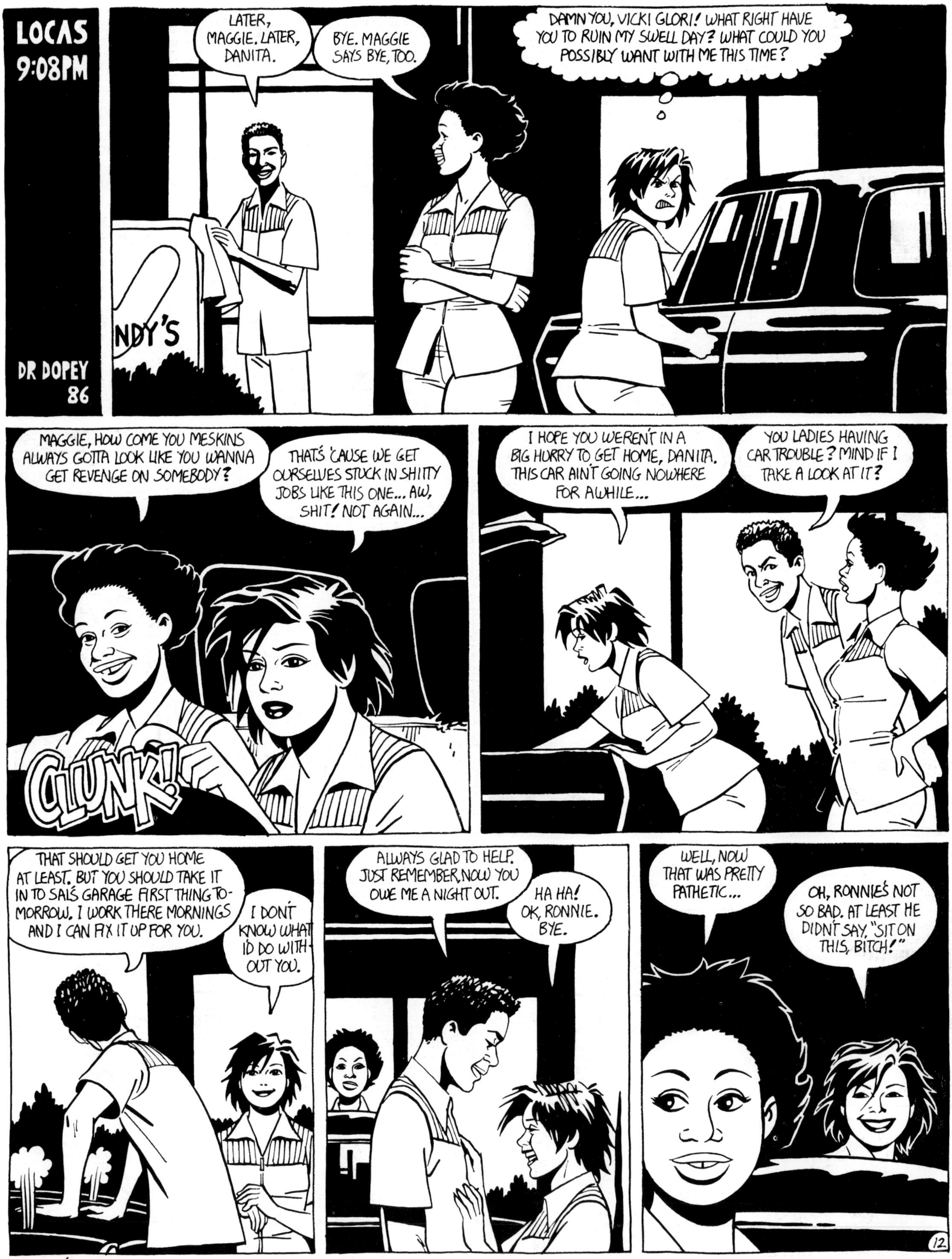
LOCAS
9:08PM
DR DOPEY
86
LATER, MAGGIE. LATER, DANITA.
BYE. MAGGIE SAYS BYE, TOO.
NDY'S
DAMN YOU, VICKI GLORI! WHAT RIGHT HAVE YOU TO RUIN MY SWELL DAY? WHAT COULD YOU POSSIBLY WANT WITH ME THIS TIME?
MAGGIE, HOW COME YOU MESKINS ALWAYS GOTTA LOOK LIKE YOU WANNA GET REVENGE ON SOMEBODY?
THAT'S 'CAUSE WE GET OURSELVES STUCK IN SHITTY JOBS LIKE THIS ONE... AW, SHIT! NOT AGAIN...
CLUNK!
I HOPE YOU WEREN'T IN A BIG HURRY TO GET HOME, DANITA. THIS CAR AIN'T GOING NOWHERE FOR AWHILE...
YOU LADIES HAVING CAR TROUBLE? MIND IF I TAKE A LOOK AT IT?
THAT SHOULD GET YOU HOME AT LEAST. BUT YOU SHOULD TAKE IT IN TO SAL'S GARAGE FIRST THING TOMORROW. I WORK THERE MORNINGS AND I CAN FIX IT UP FOR YOU.
I DON'T KNOW WHAT I'D DO WITHOUT YOU.
ALWAYS GLAD TO HELP. JUST REMEMBER, NOW YOU OWE ME A NIGHT OUT.
HA HA! OK, RONNIE. BYE.
WELL, NOW THAT WAS PRETTY PATHETIC...
OH, RONNIE'S NOT SO BAD. AT LEAST HE DIDN'T SAY, "SIT ON THIS, BITCH!"
12

MESKIN/MEXICAN

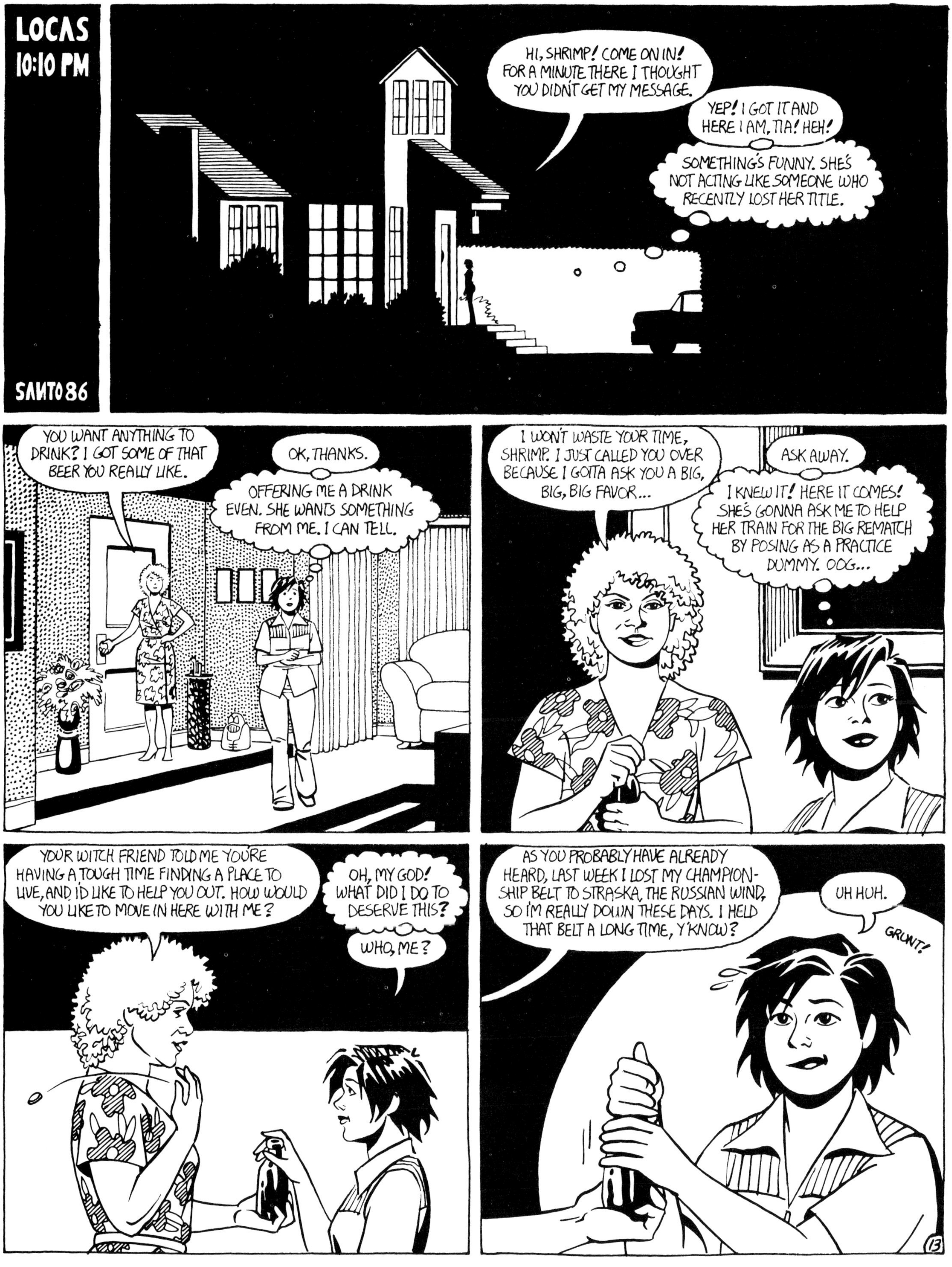

LOCAS
10:10 PM
SANTO 86
HI, SHRIMP! COME ON IN! FOR A MINUTE THERE I THOUGHT YOU DIDN'T GET MY MESSAGE.
YEP! I GOT IT AND HERE I AM, TIA! HEH!
SOMETHING'S FUNNY. SHE'S NOT ACTING LIKE SOMEONE WHO RECENTLY LOST HER TITLE.
YOU WANT ANYTHING TO DRINK? I GOT SOME OF THAT BEER YOU REALLY LIKE.
OK, THANKS.
OFFERING ME A DRINK EVEN. SHE WANTS SOMETHING FROM ME. I CAN TELL.
I WON'T WASTE YOUR TIME, SHRIMP. I JUST CALLED YOU OVER BECAUSE I GOTTA ASK YOU A BIG, BIG, BIG FAVOR...
ASK AWAY.
I KNEW IT! HERE IT COMES! SHE'S GONNA ASK ME TO HELP HER TRAIN FOR THE BIG REMATCH BY POSING AS A PRACTICE DUMMY. OOG...
YOUR WITCH FRIEND TOLD ME YOU'RE HAVING A TOUGH TIME FINDING A PLACE TO LIVE, AND I'D LIKE TO HELP YOU OUT. HOW WOULD YOU LIKE TO MOVE IN HERE WITH ME?
OH, MY GOD! WHAT DID I DO TO DESERVE THIS?
WHO, ME?
AS YOU PROBABLY HAVE ALREADY HEARD, LAST WEEK I LOST MY CHAMPIONSHIP BELT TO STRASKA, THE RUSSIAN WIND, SO I'M REALLY DOWN THESE DAYS. I HELD THAT BELT A LONG TIME, Y'KNOW?
UH HUH.
GRUNT!
13

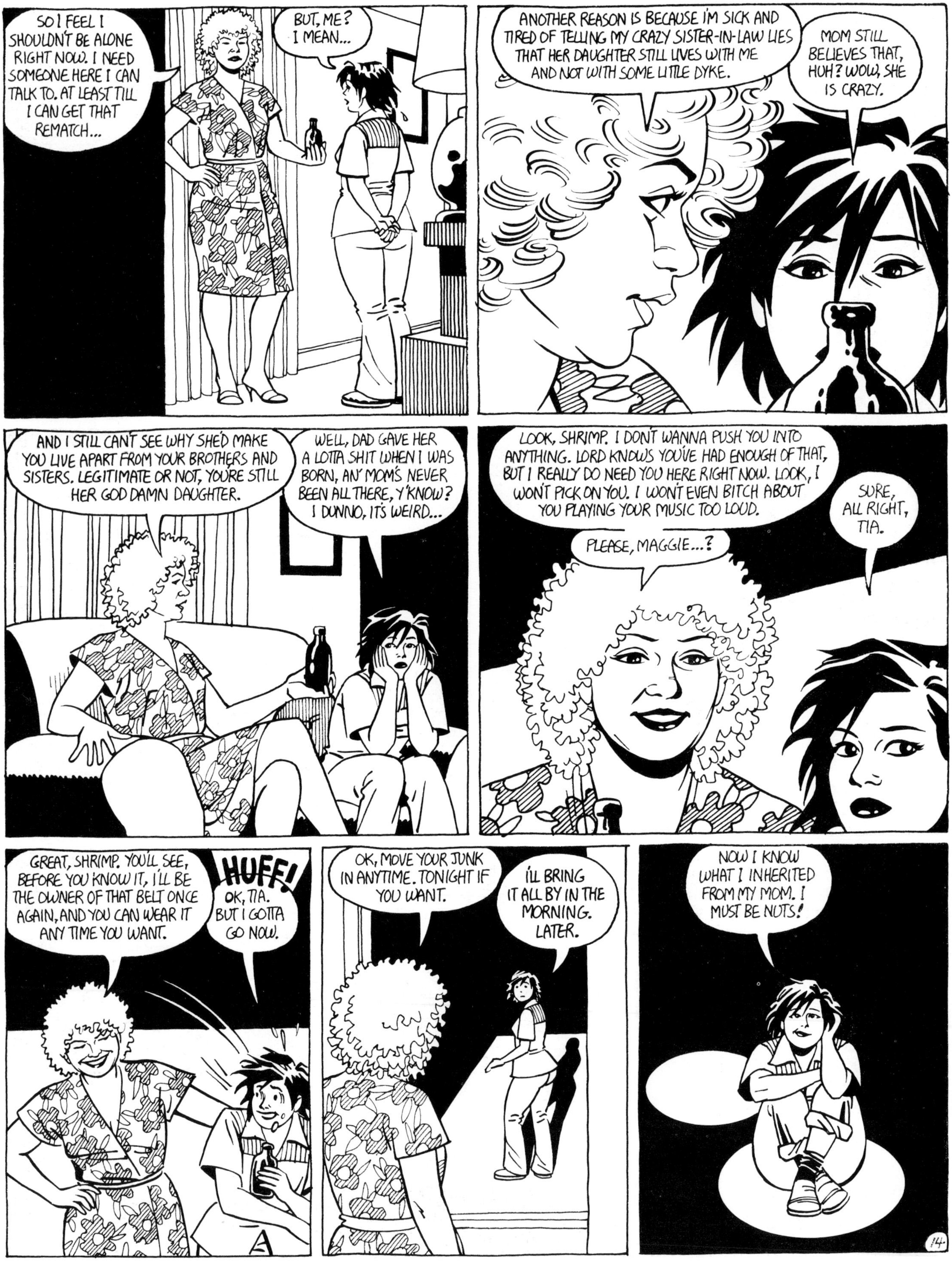
SO I FEEL I SHOULDN'T BE ALONE RIGHT NOW. I NEED SOMEONE HERE I CAN TALK TO. AT LEAST TILL I CAN GET THAT REMATCH...
BUT, ME? I MEAN...
ANOTHER REASON IS BECAUSE I'M SICK AND TIRED OF TELLING MY CRAZY SISTER-IN-LAW LIES THAT HER DAUGHTER STILL LIVES WITH ME AND NOT WITH SOME LITTLE DYKE.
MOM STILL BELIEVES THAT, HUH? WOW, SHE IS CRAZY.
AND I STILL CAN'T SEE WHY SHE'D MAKE YOU LIVE APART FROM YOUR BROTHERS AND SISTERS. LEGITIMATE OR NOT, YOU'RE STILL HER GOD DAMN DAUGHTER.
WELL, DAD GAVE HER A LOTTA SHIT WHEN I WAS BORN, AN' MOM'S NEVER BEEN ALL THERE, Y'KNOW? I DUNNO, IT'S WEIRD...
LOOK, SHRIMP. I DON'T WANNA PUSH YOU INTO ANYTHING. LORD KNOWS YOU'VE HAD ENOUGH OF THAT, BUT I REALLY DO NEED YOU HERE RIGHT NOW. LOOK, I WON'T PICK ON YOU. I WON'T EVEN BITCH ABOUT YOU PLAYING YOUR MUSIC TOO LOUD.
PLEASE, MAGGIE...?
SURE, ALL RIGHT, TIA.
GREAT, SHRIMP. YOU'LL SEE, BEFORE YOU KNOW IT, I'LL BE THE OWNER OF THAT BELT ONCE AGAIN, AND YOU CAN WEAR IT ANY TIME YOU WANT.
HUFF!
OK, TIA. BUT I GOTTA GO NOW.
OK, MOVE YOUR JUNK IN ANYTIME. TONIGHT IF YOU WANT.
I'LL BRING IT ALL BY IN THE MORNING. LATER.
NOW I KNOW WHAT I INHERITED FROM MY MOM. I MUST BE NUTS!
14

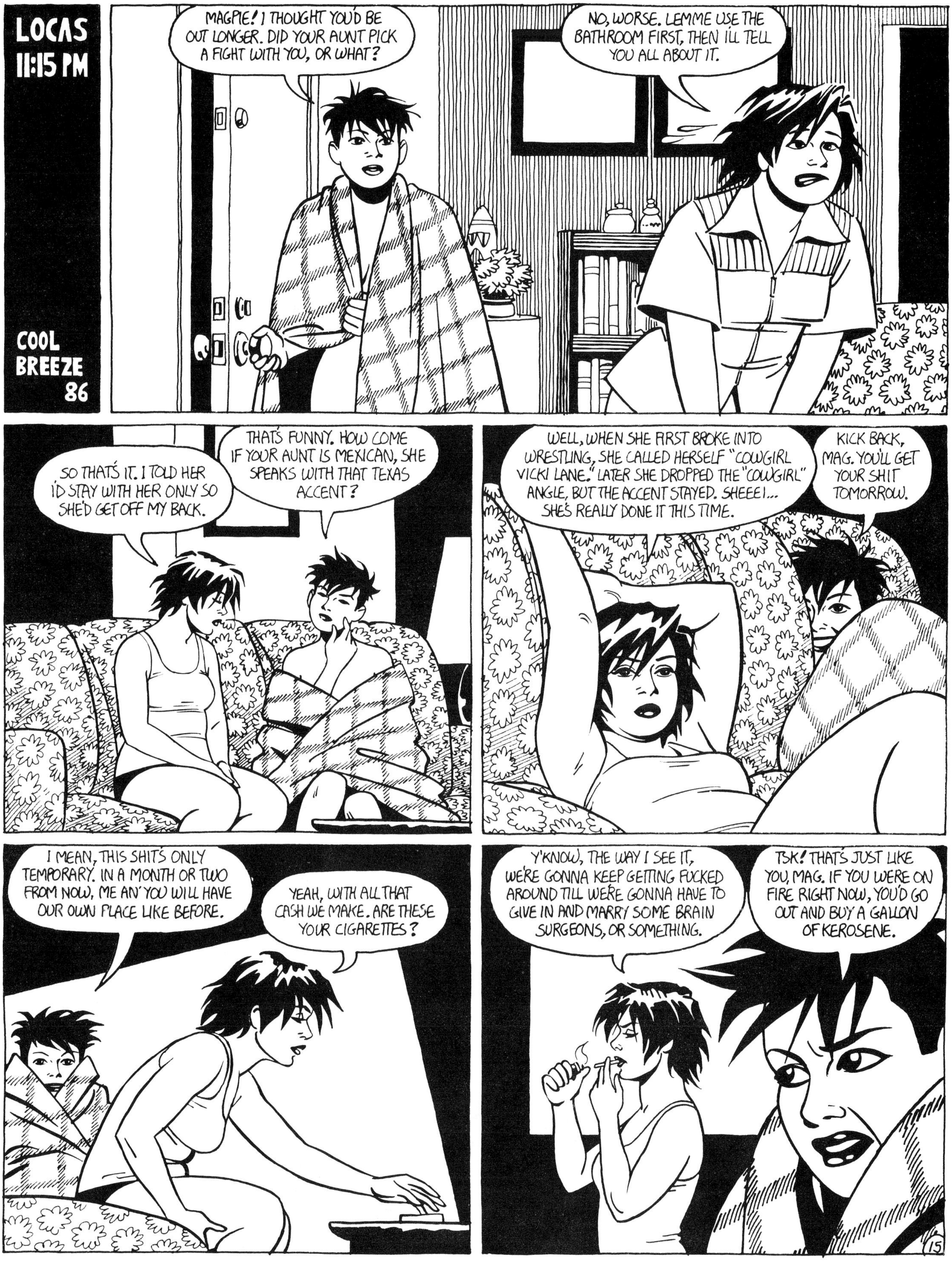
LOCAS
11:15 PM
COOL BREEZE 86
MAGPIE! I THOUGHT YOU'D BE OUT LONGER. DID YOUR AUNT PICK A FIGHT WITH YOU, OR WHAT?
NO, WORSE. LEMME USE THE BATHROOM FIRST, THEN I'LL TELL YOU ALL ABOUT IT.
SO THAT'S IT. I TOLD HER I'D STAY WITH HER ONLY SO SHE'D GET OFF MY BACK.
THAT'S FUNNY. HOW COME IF YOUR AUNT IS MEXICAN, SHE SPEAKS WITH THAT TEXAS ACCENT?
WELL, WHEN SHE FIRST BROKE INTO WRESTLING, SHE CALLED HERSELF "COWGIRL VICKI LANE." LATER SHE DROPPED THE "COWGIRL" ANGLE, BUT THE ACCENT STAYED. SHEEEI... SHE'S REALLY DONE IT THIS TIME.
KICK BACK, MAG. YOU'LL GET YOUR SHIT TOMORROW.
I MEAN, THIS SHIT'S ONLY TEMPORARY. IN A MONTH OR TWO FROM NOW, ME AN' YOU WILL HAVE OUR OWN PLACE LIKE BEFORE.
YEAH, WITH ALL THAT CASH WE MAKE. ARE THESE YOUR CIGARETTES?
Y'KNOW, THE WAY I SEE IT, WE'RE GONNA KEEP GETTING FUCKED AROUND TILL WE'RE GONNA HAVE TO GIVE IN AND MARRY SOME BRAIN SURGEONS, OR SOMETHING.
TSK! THAT'S JUST LIKE YOU, MAG. IF YOU WERE ON FIRE RIGHT NOW, YOU'D GO OUT AND BUY A GALLON OF KEROSENE.
15

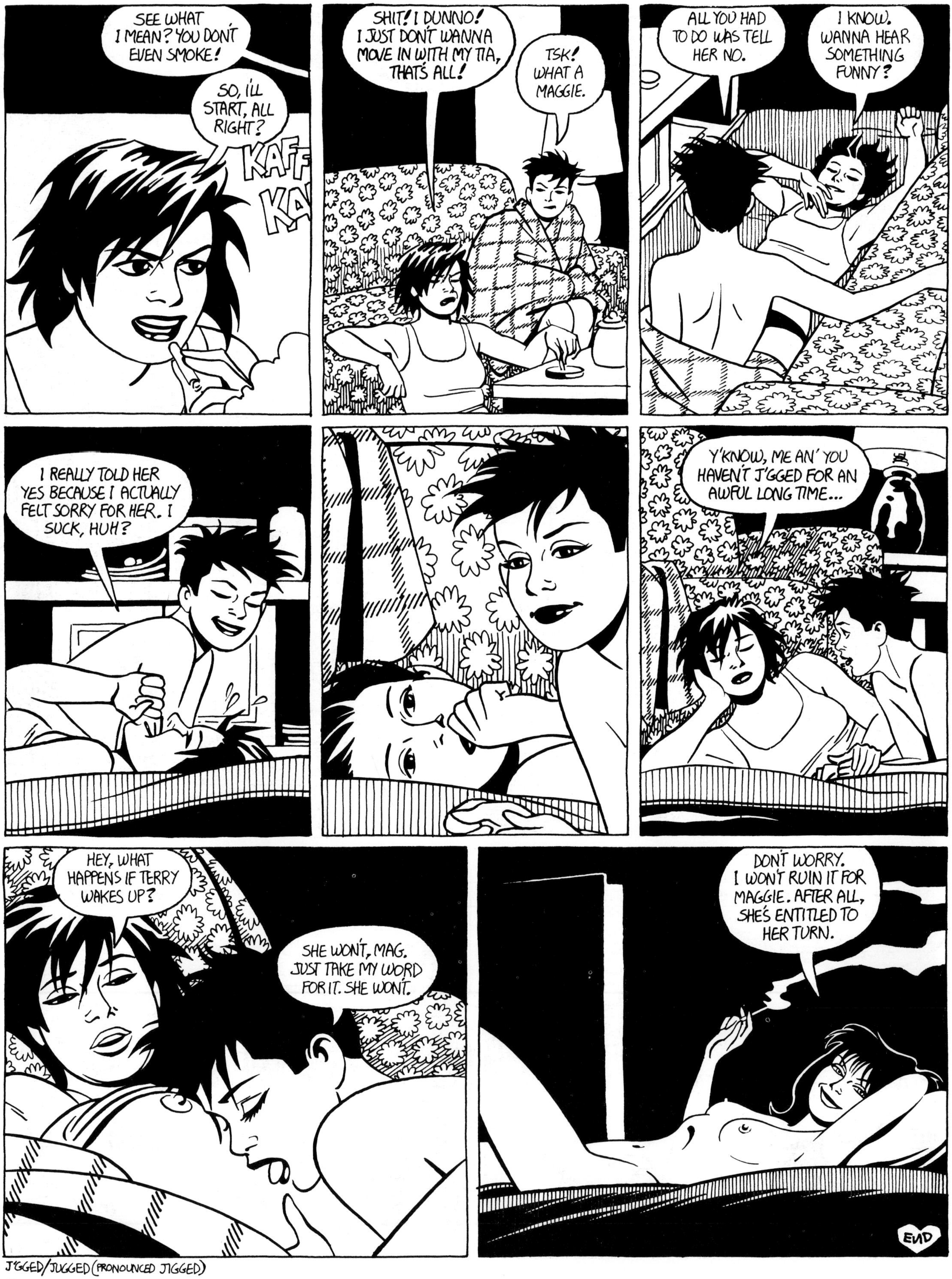
SEE WHAT I MEAN? YOU DON'T EVEN SMOKE!
SO, I'LL START, ALL RIGHT?
KAFF KA
SHIT! I DUNNO! I JUST DON'T WANNA MOVE IN WITH MY TIA, THAT'S ALL!
TSK! WHAT A MAGGIE.
ALL YOU HAD TO DO WAS TELL HER NO.
I KNOW. WANNA HEAR SOMETHING FUNNY?
I REALLY TOLD HER YES BECAUSE I ACTUALLY FELT SORRY FOR HER. I SUCK, HUH?
Y'KNOW, ME AN' YOU HAVEN'T J'GGED FOR AN AWFUL LONG TIME...
HEY, WHAT HAPPENS IF TERRY WAKES UP?
SHE WON'T, MAG. JUST TAKE MY WORD FOR IT. SHE WON'T.
DON'T WORRY. I WON'T RUIN IT FOR MAGGIE. AFTER ALL, SHE'S ENTITLED TO HER TURN.
END

J'GGED/JUGGED (PRONOUNCED JIGGED)

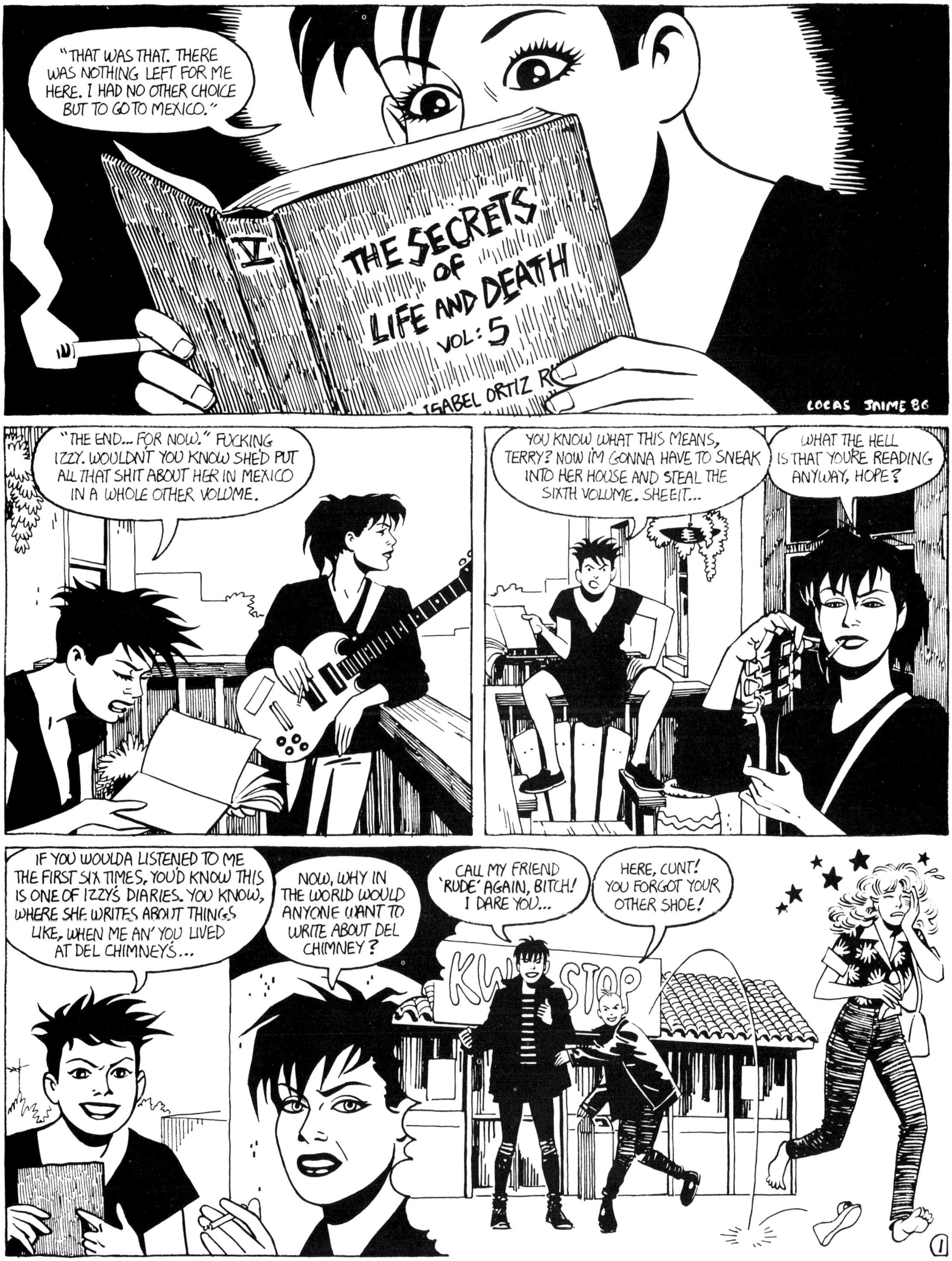
"THAT WAS THAT. THERE WAS NOTHING LEFT FOR ME HERE. I HAD NO OTHER CHOICE BUT TO GO TO MEXICO."
V
THE SECRETS OF LIFE AND DEATH VOL: 5
ISABEL ORTIZ R
LOCAS JAIME 86
"THE END... FOR NOW." FUCKING IZZY. WOULDN'T YOU KNOW SHE'D PUT ALL THAT SHIT ABOUT HER IN MEXICO IN A WHOLE OTHER VOLUME.
YOU KNOW WHAT THIS MEANS, TERRY? NOW I'M GONNA HAVE TO SNEAK INTO HER HOUSE AND STEAL THE SIXTH VOLUME. SHEEIT...
WHAT THE HELL IS THAT YOU'RE READING ANYWAY, HOPE?
IF YOU WOULDA LISTENED TO ME THE FIRST SIX TIMES, YOU'D KNOW THIS IS ONE OF IZZY'S DIARIES. YOU KNOW, WHERE SHE WRITES ABOUT THINGS LIKE, WHEN ME AN' YOU LIVED AT DEL CHIMNEY'S...
NOW, WHY IN THE WORLD WOULD ANYONE WANT TO WRITE ABOUT DEL CHIMNEY?
CALL MY FRIEND 'RUDE' AGAIN, BITCH! I DARE YOU...
HERE, CUNT! YOU FORGOT YOUR OTHER SHOE!
STOP
1

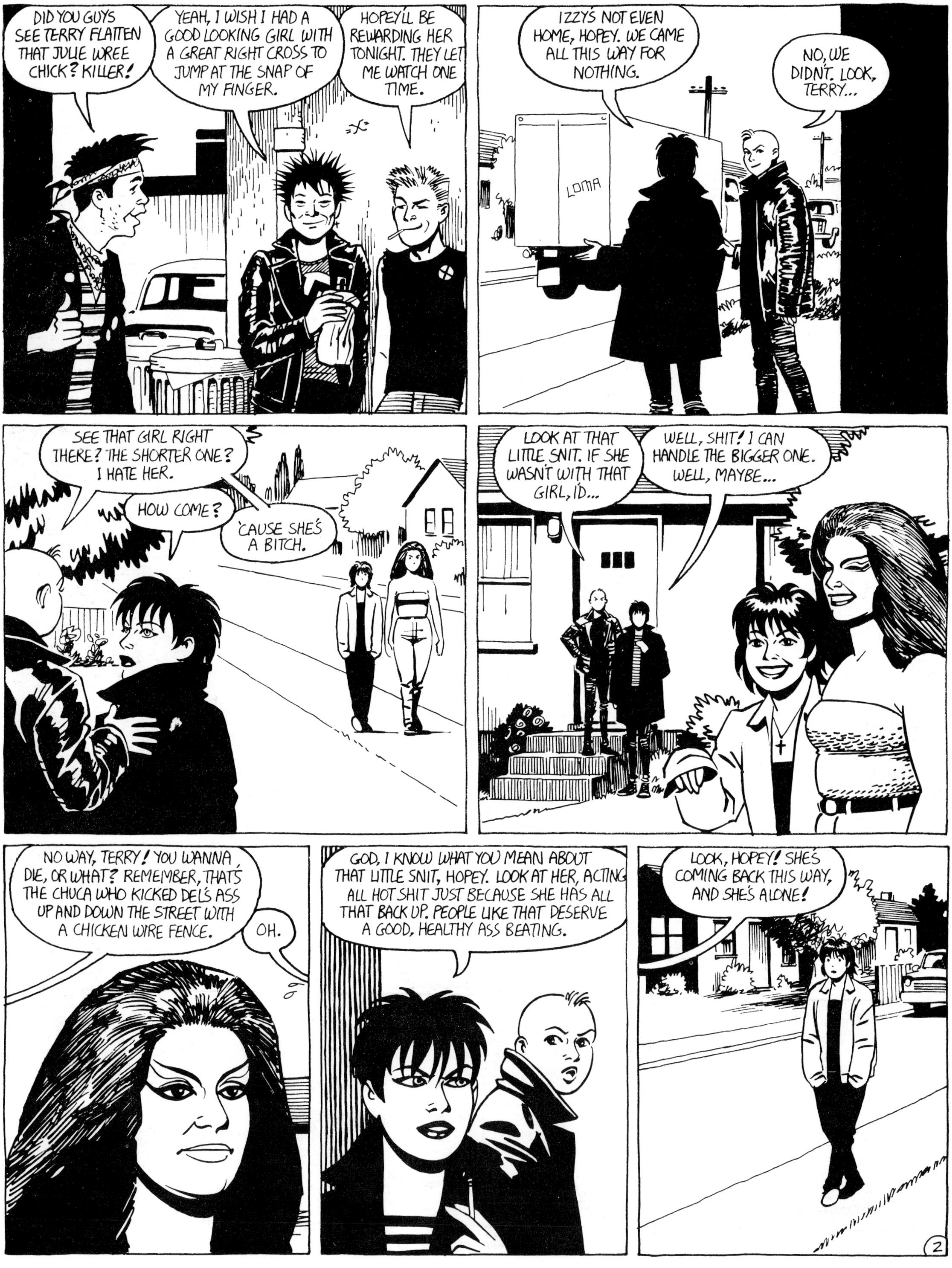

DID YOU GUYS SEE TERRY FLATTEN THAT JULIE WREE CHICK? KILLER!
YEAH, I WISH I HAD A GOOD LOOKING GIRL WITH A GREAT RIGHT CROSS TO JUMP AT THE SNAP OF MY FINGER.
HOPEY'LL BE REWARDING HER TONIGHT. THEY LET ME WATCH ONE TIME.
IZZY'S NOT EVEN HOME, HOPEY. WE CAME ALL THIS WAY FOR NOTHING.
NO, WE DIDN'T. LOOK, TERRY...
LOMA
SEE THAT GIRL RIGHT THERE? THE SHORTER ONE? I HATE HER.
HOW COME?
'CAUSE SHE'S A BITCH.
LOOK AT THAT LITTLE SNIT. IF SHE WASN'T WITH THAT GIRL, I'D...
WELL, SHIT! I CAN HANDLE THE BIGGER ONE. WELL, MAYBE...
NO WAY, TERRY! YOU WANNA DIE, OR WHAT? REMEMBER, THAT'S THE CHUCA WHO KICKED DEL'S ASS UP AND DOWN THE STREET WITH A CHICKEN WIRE FENCE.
OH.
GOD, I KNOW WHAT YOU MEAN ABOUT THAT LITTLE SNIT, HOPEY. LOOK AT HER, ACTING ALL HOT SHIT JUST BECAUSE SHE HAS ALL THAT BACK UP. PEOPLE LIKE THAT DESERVE A GOOD, HEALTHY ASS BEATING.
LOOK, HOPEY! SHE'S COMING BACK THIS WAY, AND SHE'S ALONE!
2

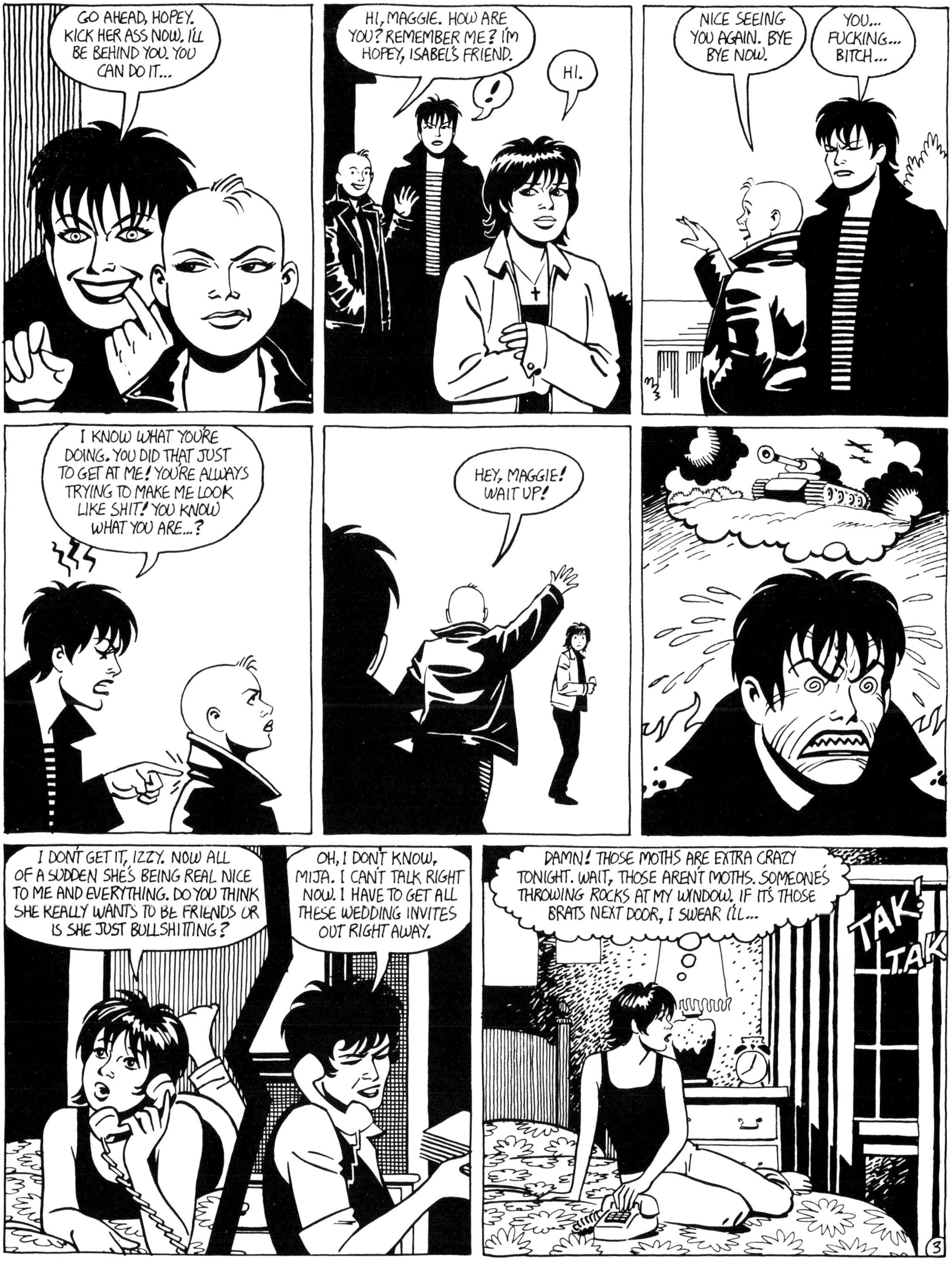
GO AHEAD, HOPEY. KICK HER ASS NOW. I'LL BE BEHIND YOU. YOU CAN DO IT...
HI, MAGGIE. HOW ARE YOU? REMEMBER ME? I'M HOPEY, ISABEL'S FRIEND.
!
HI.
NICE SEEING YOU AGAIN. BYE BYE NOW.
YOU... FUCKING... BITCH...
I KNOW WHAT YOU'RE DOING. YOU DID THAT JUST TO GET AT ME! YOU'RE ALWAYS TRYING TO MAKE ME LOOK LIKE SHIT! YOU KNOW WHAT YOU ARE...?
HEY, MAGGIE! WAIT UP!
I DON'T GET IT, IZZY. NOW ALL OF A SUDDEN SHE'S BEING REAL NICE TO ME AND EVERYTHING. DO YOU THINK SHE REALLY WANTS TO BE FRIENDS OR IS SHE JUST BULLSHITTING?
OH, I DON'T KNOW, MIJA. I CAN'T TALK RIGHT NOW. I HAVE TO GET ALL THESE WEDDING INVITES OUT RIGHT AWAY.
DAMN! THOSE MOTHS ARE EXTRA CRAZY TONIGHT. WAIT, THOSE AREN'T MOTHS. SOMEONE'S THROWING ROCKS AT MY WINDOW. IF IT'S THOSE BRATS NEXT DOOR, I SWEAR I'LL...
TAK! TAK
3

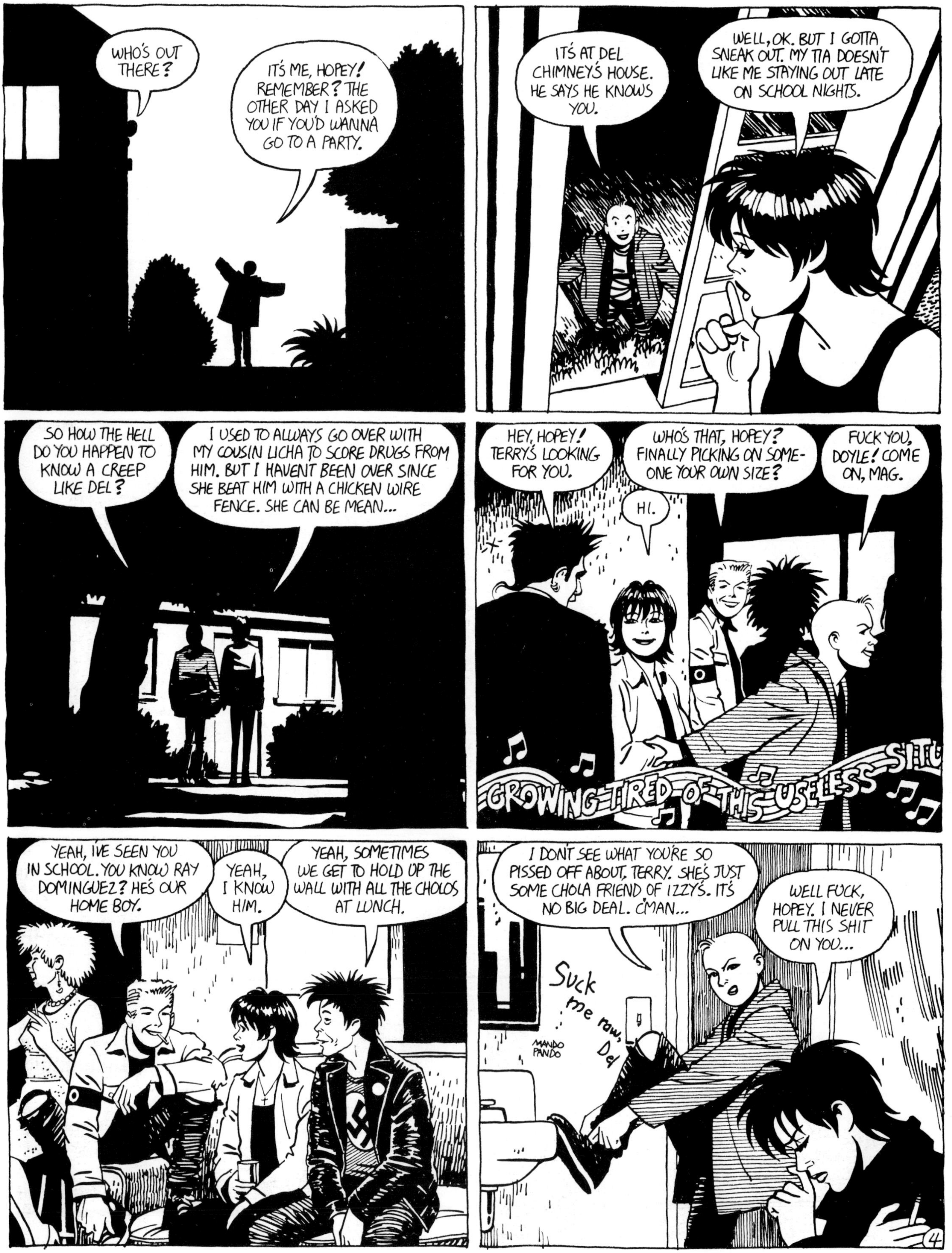
WHO'S OUT THERE?
IT'S ME, HOPEY! REMEMBER? THE OTHER DAY I ASKED YOU IF YOU'D WANNA GO TO A PARTY.
IT'S AT DEL CHIMNEY'S HOUSE. HE SAYS HE KNOWS YOU.
WELL, OK. BUT I GOTTA SNEAK OUT. MY TIA DOESN'T LIKE ME STAYING OUT LATE ON SCHOOL NIGHTS.
SO HOW THE HELL DO YOU HAPPEN TO KNOW A CREEP LIKE DEL?
I USED TO ALWAYS GO OVER WITH MY COUSIN LICHA TO SCORE DRUGS FROM HIM. BUT I HAVEN'T BEEN OVER SINCE SHE BEAT HIM WITH A CHICKEN WIRE FENCE. SHE CAN BE MEAN...
HEY, HOPEY! TERRY'S LOOKING FOR YOU.
HI.
WHO'S THAT, HOPEY? FINALLY PICKING ON SOMEONE YOUR OWN SIZE?
FUCK YOU, DOYLE! COME ON, MAG.
GROWING TIRED OF THIS USELESS SITU
YEAH, I'VE SEEN YOU IN SCHOOL. YOU KNOW RAY DOMINGUEZ? HE'S OUR HOME BOY.
YEAH, I KNOW HIM.
YEAH, SOMETIMES WE GET TO HOLD UP THE WALL WITH ALL THE CHOLOS AT LUNCH.
I DON'T SEE WHAT YOU'RE SO PISSED OFF ABOUT, TERRY. SHE'S JUST SOME CHOLA FRIEND OF IZZY'S. IT'S NO BIG DEAL. C'MAN...
WELL FUCK, HOPEY. I NEVER PULL THIS SHIT ON YOU...
Suck me raw, Del
MANDO PANDO
4

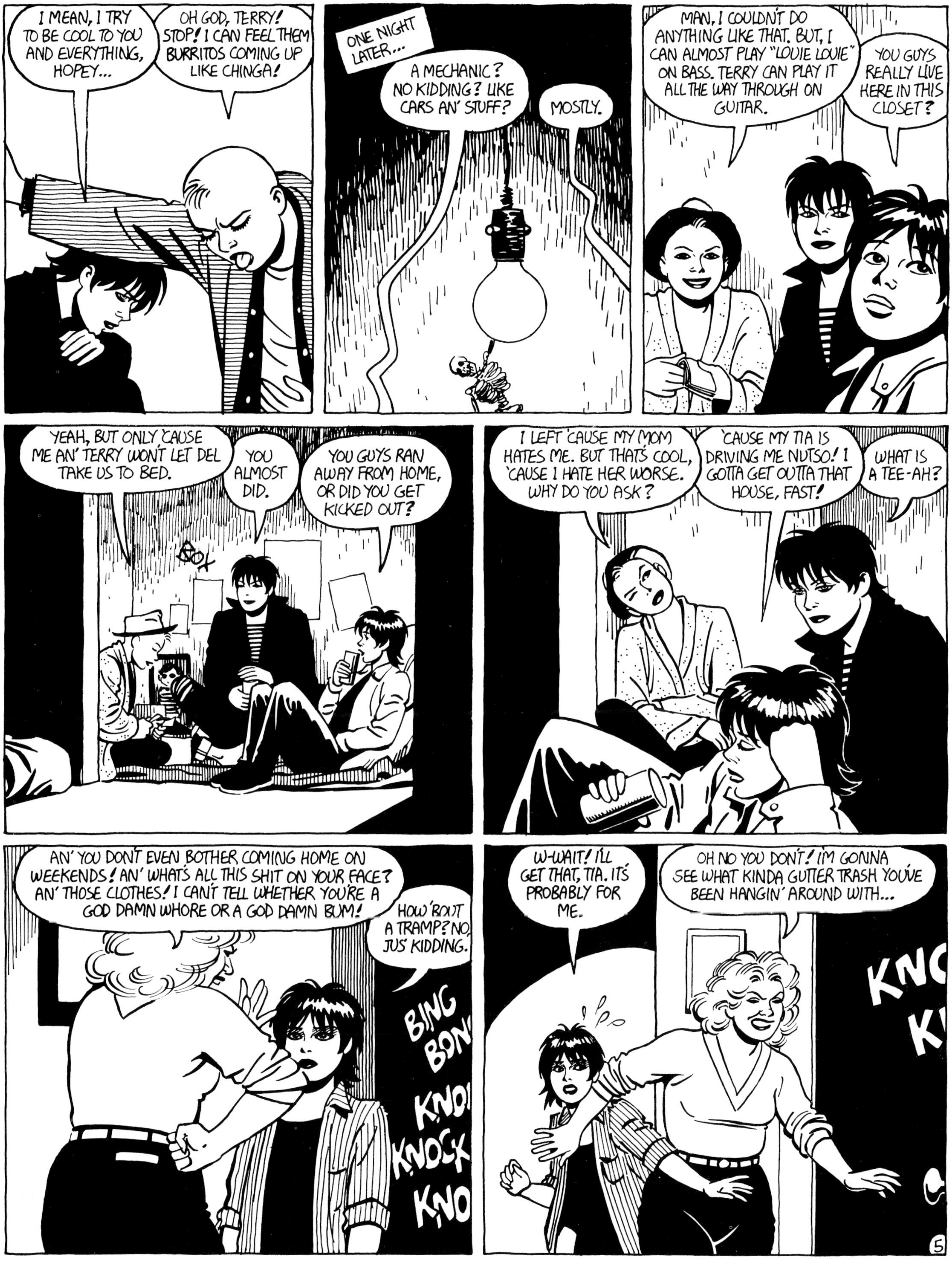
I MEAN, I TRY TO BE COOL TO YOU AND EVERYTHING, HOPEY...
OH GOD, TERRY! STOP! I CAN FEEL THEM BURRITOS COMING UP LIKE CHINGA!
ONE NIGHT LATER...
A MECHANIC? NO KIDDING? LIKE CARS AN' STUFF?
MOSTLY.
MAN, I COULDN'T DO ANYTHING LIKE THAT. BUT, I CAN ALMOST PLAY "LOUIE LOUIE" ON BASS. TERRY CAN PLAY IT ALL THE WAY THROUGH ON GUITAR.
YOU GUYS REALLY LIVE HERE IN THIS CLOSET?
YEAH, BUT ONLY 'CAUSE ME AN' TERRY WON'T LET DEL TAKE US TO BED.
YOU ALMOST DID.
YOU GUYS RAN AWAY FROM HOME, OR DID YOU GET KICKED OUT?
I LEFT 'CAUSE MY MOM HATES ME. BUT THAT'S COOL, 'CAUSE I HATE HER WORSE. WHY DO YOU ASK?
'CAUSE MY TIA IS DRIVING ME NUTSO! I GOTTA GET OUTTA THAT HOUSE, FAST!
WHAT IS A TEE-AH?
AN' YOU DON'T EVEN BOTHER COMING HOME ON WEEKENDS! AN' WHAT'S ALL THIS SHIT ON YOUR FACE? AN' THOSE CLOTHES! I CAN'T TELL WHETHER YOU'RE A GOD DAMN WHORE OR A GOD DAMN BUM!
HOW 'BOUT A TRAMP? NO, JUS' KIDDING.
BING BON
KNO
KNOCK
KNO
W-WAIT! I'LL GET THAT, TIA. IT'S PROBABLY FOR ME.
OH NO YOU DON'T! I'M GONNA SEE WHAT KINDA GUTTER TRASH YOU'VE BEEN HANGIN' AROUND WITH...
KNO
K
5

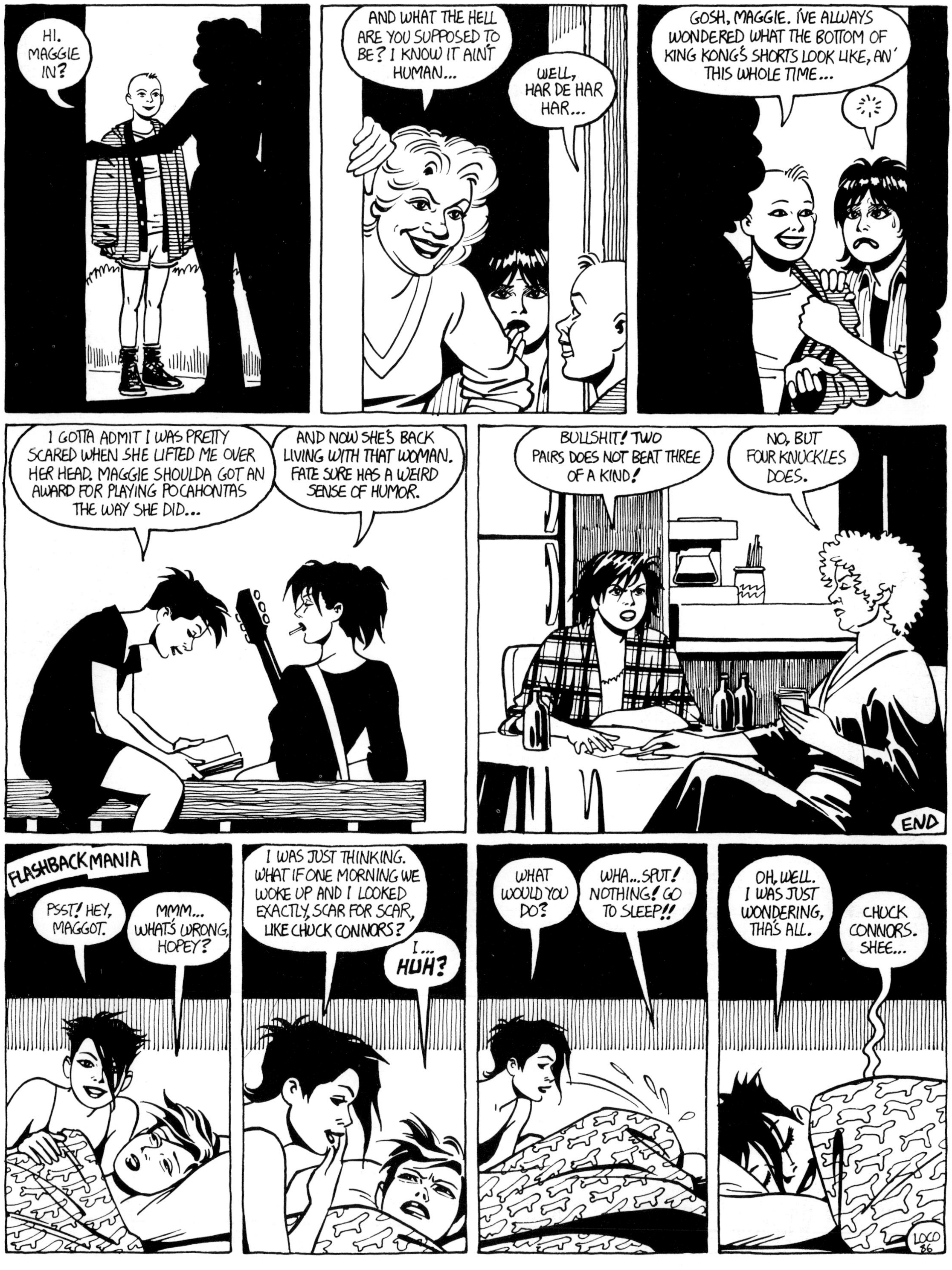
HI. MAGGIE IN?
AND WHAT THE HELL ARE YOU SUPPOSED TO BE? I KNOW IT AIN'T HUMAN...
WELL, HAR DE HAR HAR...
GOSH, MAGGIE. I'VE ALWAYS WONDERED WHAT THE BOTTOM OF KING KONG'S SHORTS LOOK LIKE, AN' THIS WHOLE TIME...
I GOTTA ADMIT I WAS PRETTY SCARED WHEN SHE LIFTED ME OVER HER HEAD. MAGGIE SHOULDA GOT AN AWARD FOR PLAYING POCAHONTAS THE WAY SHE DID...
AND NOW SHE'S BACK LIVING WITH THAT WOMAN. FATE SURE HAS A WEIRD SENSE OF HUMOR.
BULLSHIT! TWO PAIRS DOES NOT BEAT THREE OF A KIND!
NO, BUT FOUR KNUCKLES DOES.
END
FLASHBACK MANIA
PSST! HEY, MAGGOT.
MMM... WHAT'S WRONG, HOPEY?
I WAS JUST THINKING. WHAT IF ONE MORNING WE WOKE UP AND I LOOKED EXACTLY, SCAR FOR SCAR, LIKE CHUCK CONNORS?
I... HUH?
WHAT WOULD YOU DO?
WHA...SPUT! NOTHING! GO TO SLEEP!!
OH, WELL. I WAS JUST WONDERING, THA'S ALL.
CHUCK CONNORS. SHEE...
LOCO 86

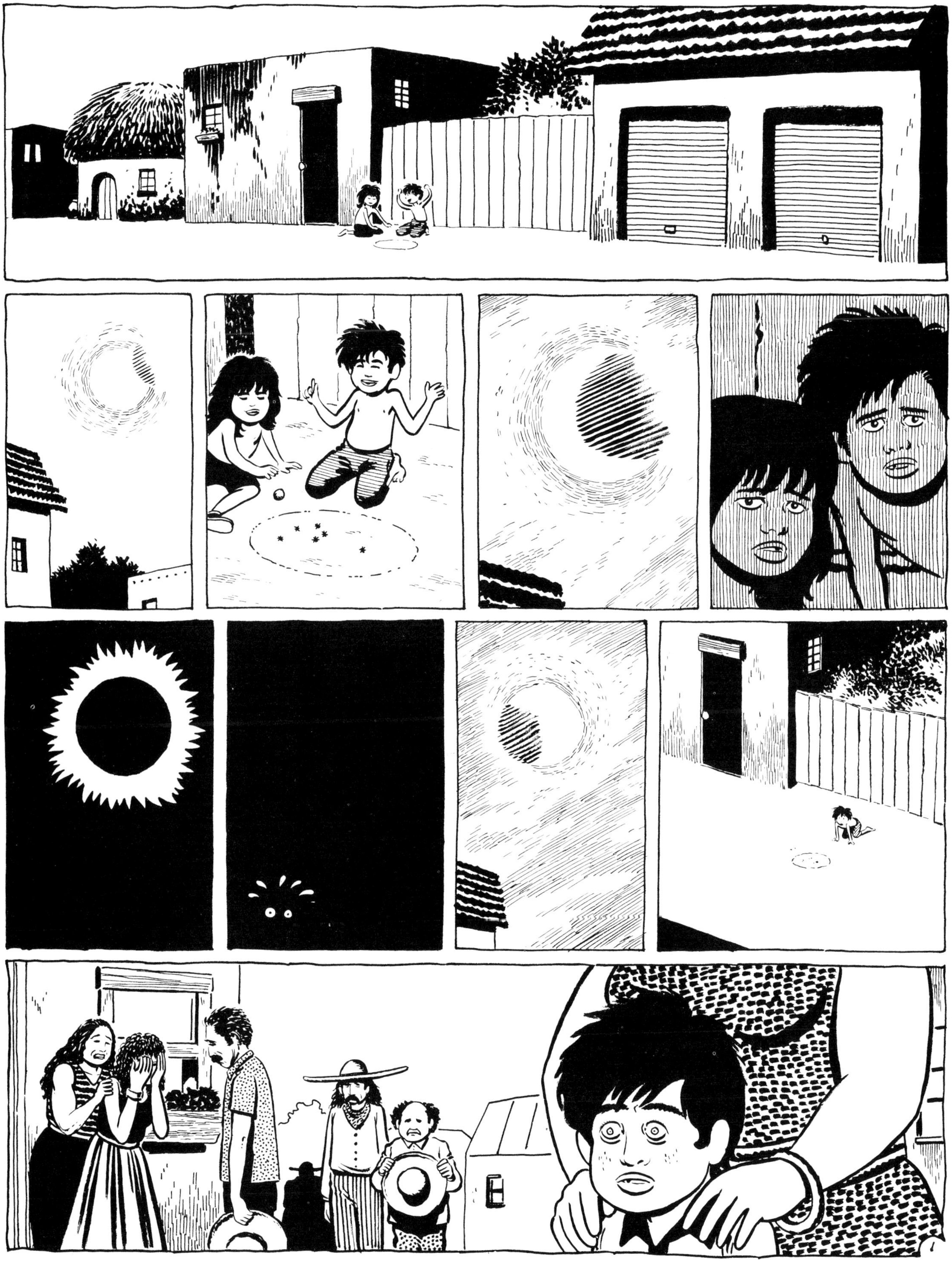

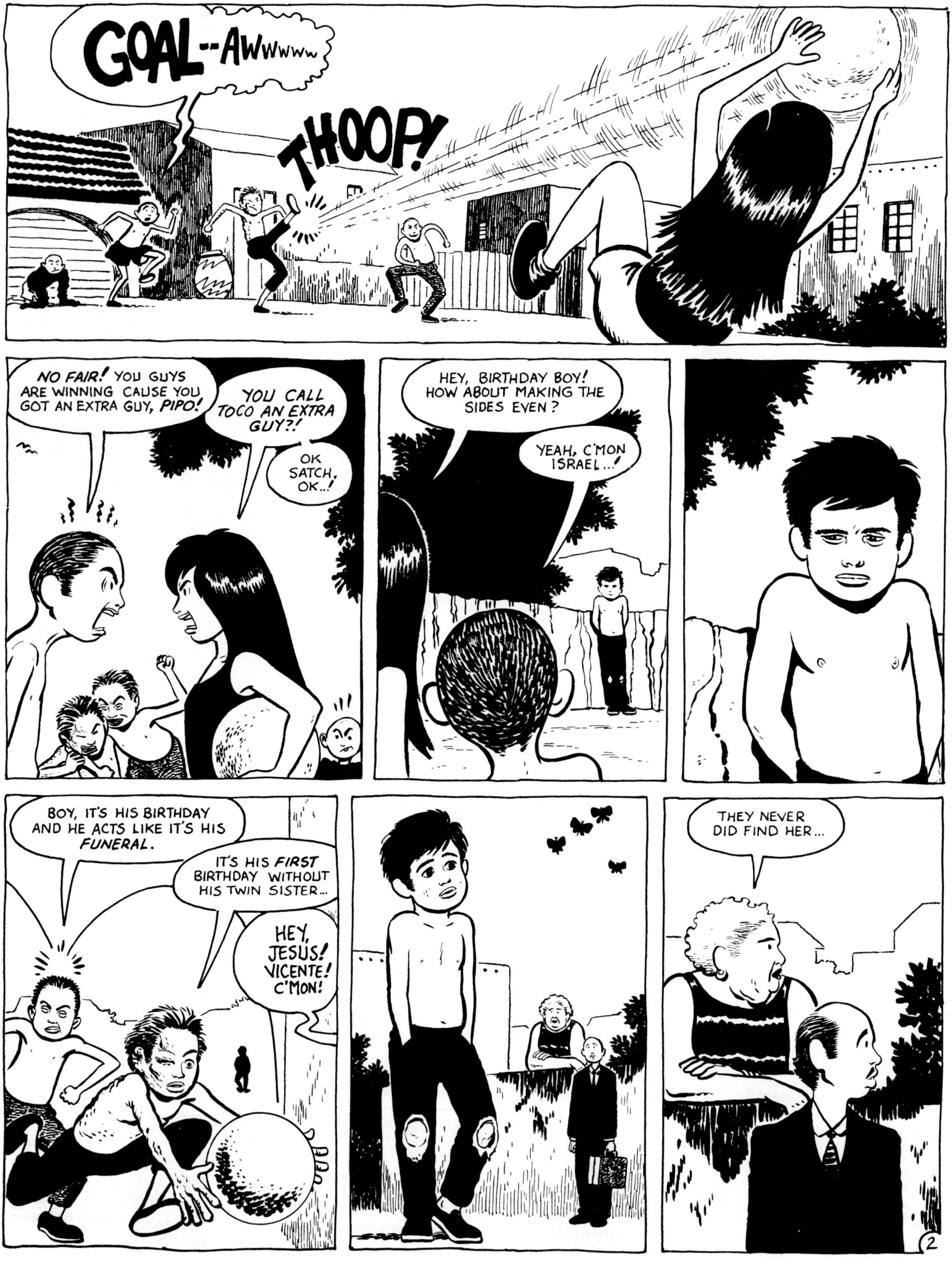
GOAL--AWWWWW
THOOP!
NO FAIR! YOU GUYS ARE WINNING CAUSE YOU GOT AN EXTRA GUY, PIPO!
YOU CALL TOCO AN EXTRA GUY?!
OK SATCH, OK...!
HEY, BIRTHDAY BOY! HOW ABOUT MAKING THE SIDES EVEN?
YEAH, C'MON ISRAEL...!
BOY, IT'S HIS BIRTHDAY AND HE ACTS LIKE IT'S HIS FUNERAL.
IT'S HIS FIRST BIRTHDAY WITHOUT HIS TWIN SISTER...
HEY, JESUS! VICENTE! C'MON!
THEY NEVER DID FIND HER...
2

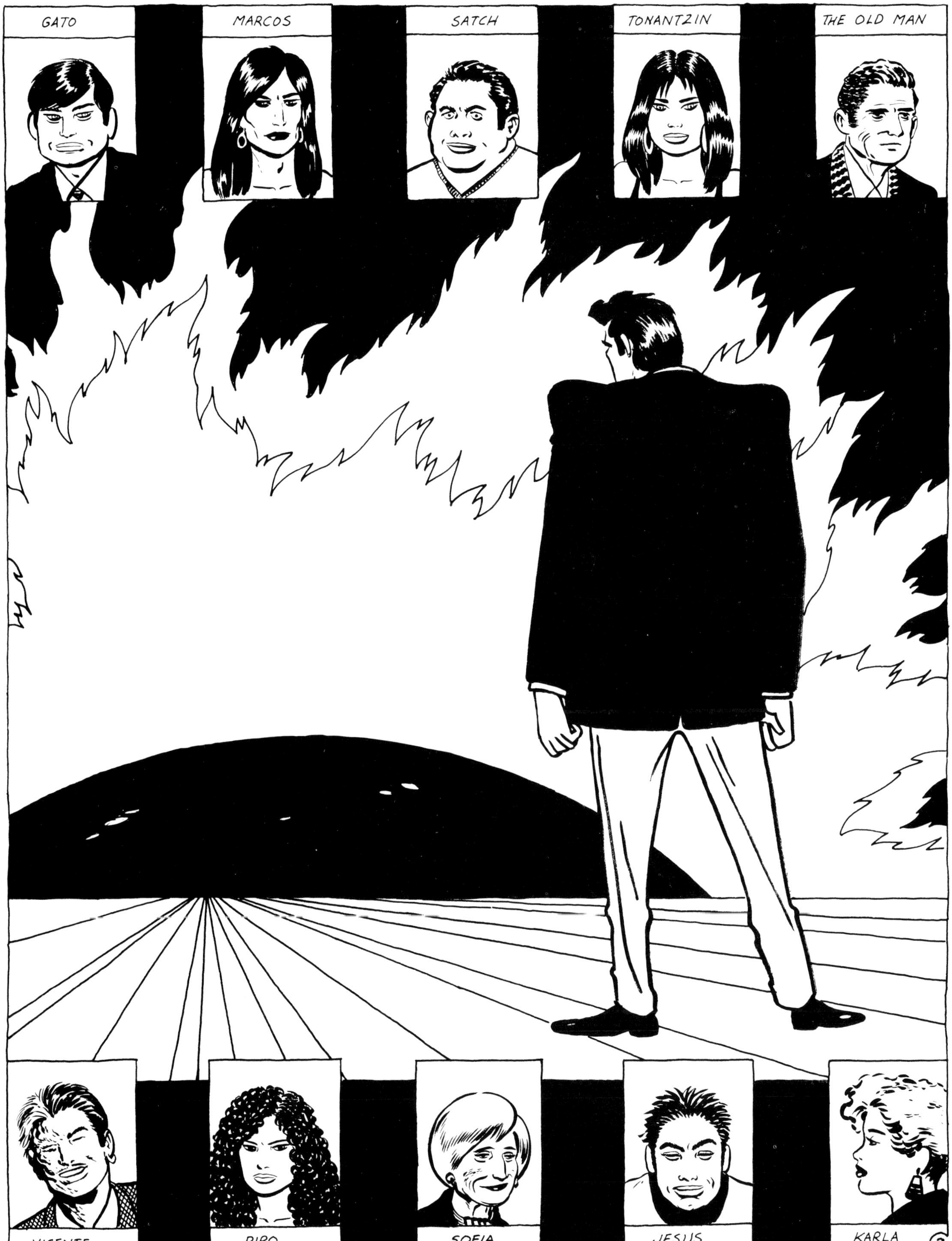
GATO
MARCOS
SATCH
TONANTZIN
THE OLD MAN
VICENTE
PIPO
SOFIA
JESUS
KARLA
3

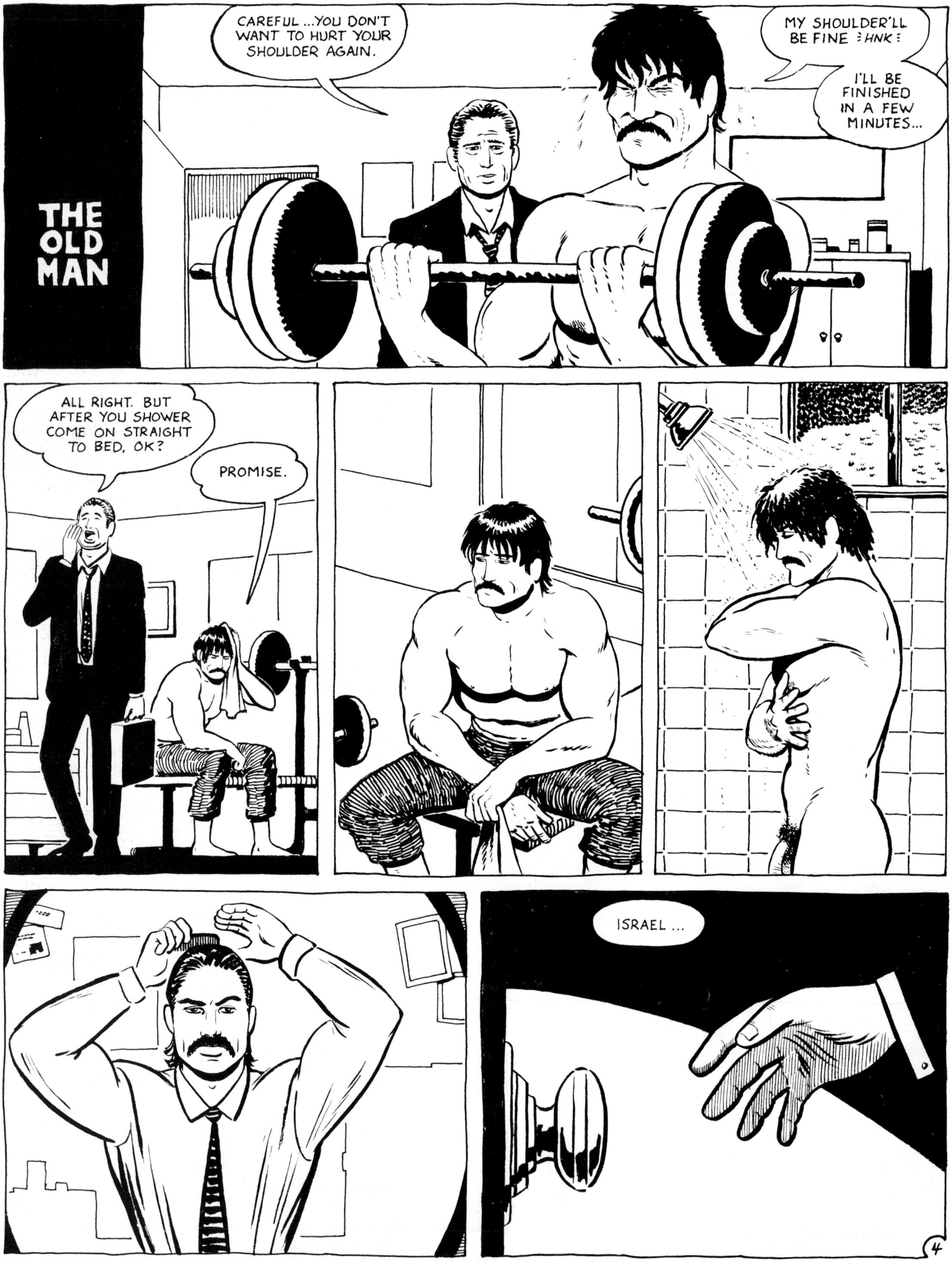
THE OLD MAN
CAREFUL ...YOU DON'T WANT TO HURT YOUR SHOULDER AGAIN.
MY SHOULDER'LL BE FINE ⁝HNK⁝
I'LL BE FINISHED IN A FEW MINUTES...
ALL RIGHT. BUT AFTER YOU SHOWER COME ON STRAIGHT TO BED, OK?
PROMISE.
ISRAEL ...
4

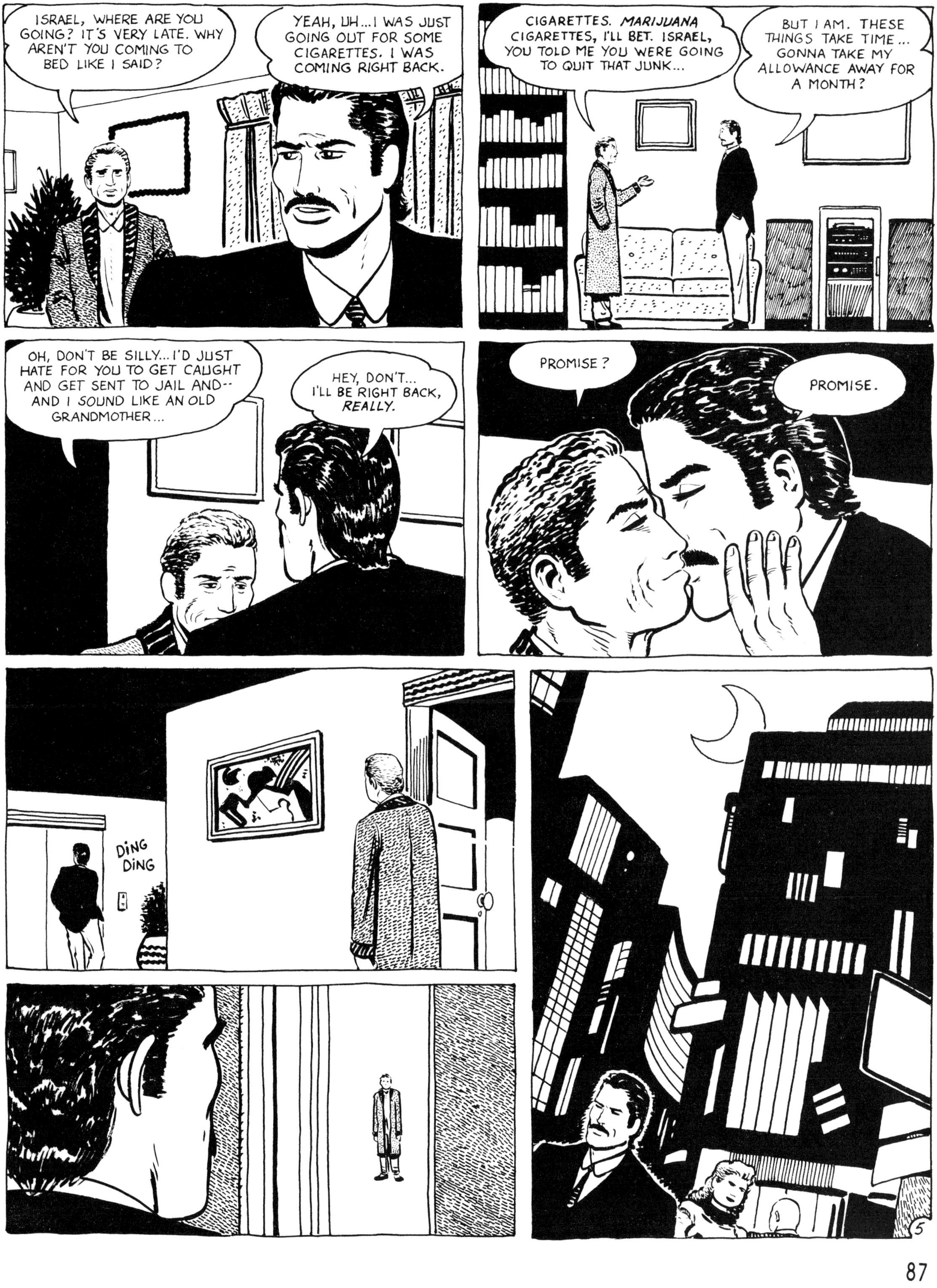
ISRAEL, WHERE ARE YOU GOING? IT'S VERY LATE. WHY AREN'T YOU COMING TO BED LIKE I SAID?
YEAH, UH... I WAS JUST GOING OUT FOR SOME CIGARETTES. I WAS COMING RIGHT BACK.
CIGARETTES. MARIJUANA CIGARETTES, I'LL BET. ISRAEL, YOU TOLD ME YOU WERE GOING TO QUIT THAT JUNK...
BUT I AM. THESE THINGS TAKE TIME... GONNA TAKE MY ALLOWANCE AWAY FOR A MONTH?
OH, DON'T BE SILLY... I'D JUST HATE FOR YOU TO GET CAUGHT AND GET SENT TO JAIL AND-- AND I SOUND LIKE AN OLD GRANDMOTHER...
HEY, DON'T... I'LL BE RIGHT BACK, REALLY.
PROMISE?
PROMISE.
DING DING
5

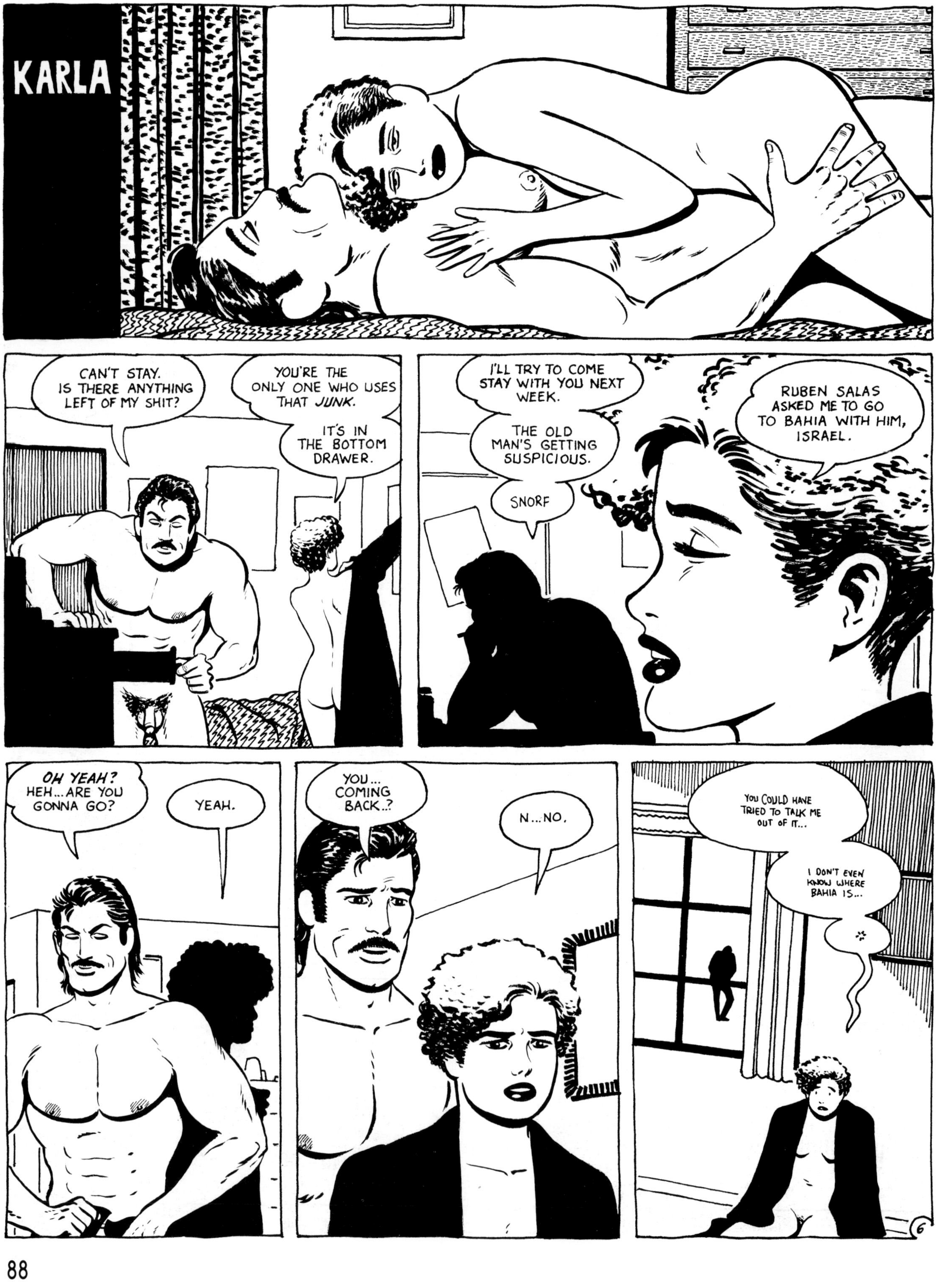
KARLA
CAN'T STAY. IS THERE ANYTHING LEFT OF MY SHIT?
YOU'RE THE ONLY ONE WHO USES THAT *JUNK*.
IT'S IN THE BOTTOM DRAWER.
I'LL TRY TO COME STAY WITH YOU NEXT WEEK.
THE OLD MAN'S GETTING SUSPICIOUS.
SNORF
RUBEN SALAS ASKED ME TO GO TO BAHIA WITH HIM, ISRAEL.
OH YEAH? HEH... ARE YOU GONNA GO?
YEAH.
YOU... COMING BACK..?
N... NO.
YOU COULD HAVE TRIED TO TALK ME OUT OF IT...
I DON'T EVEN KNOW WHERE BAHIA IS...

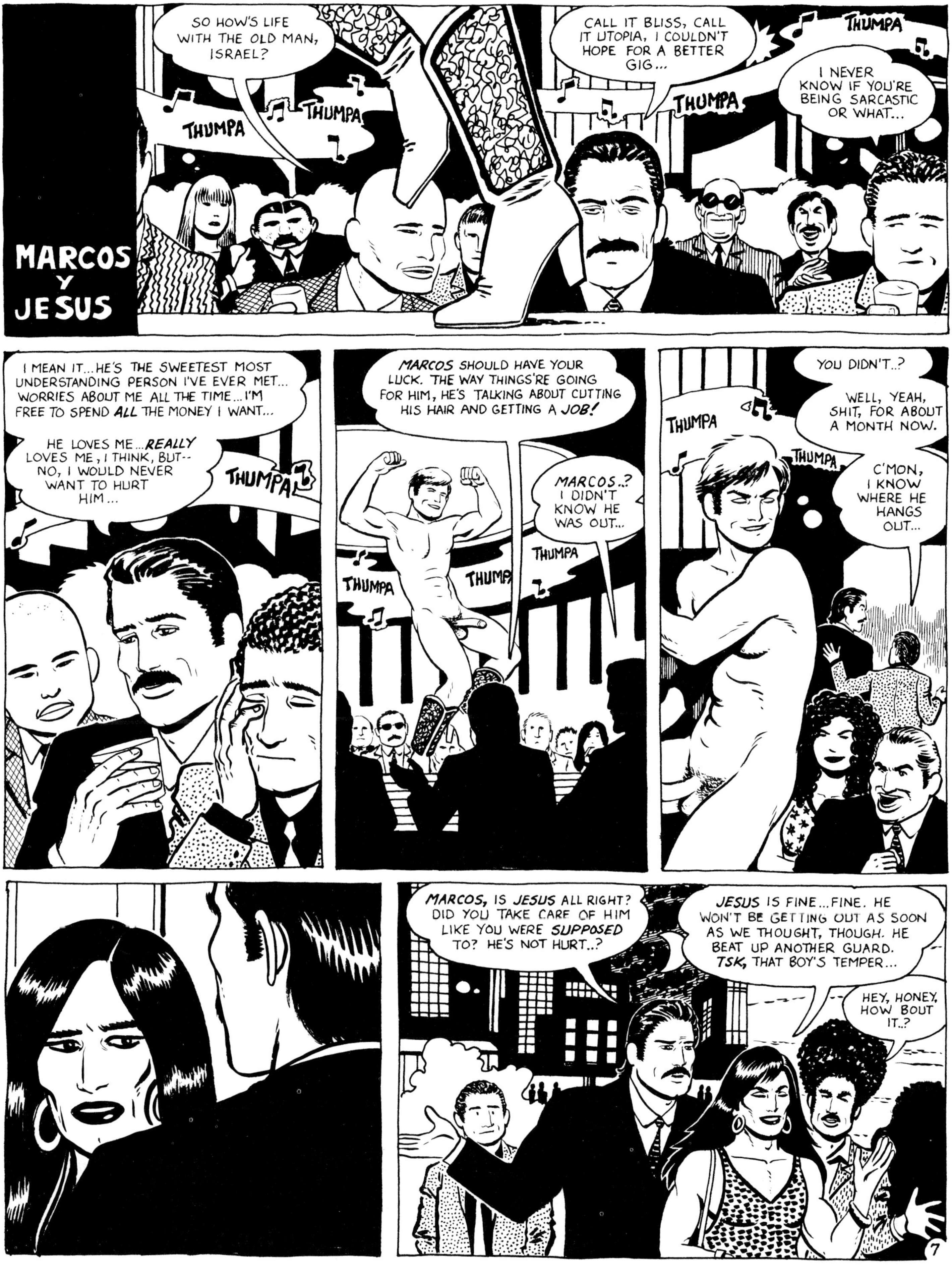
MARCOS Y JESUS
SO HOW'S LIFE WITH THE OLD MAN, ISRAEL?
THUMPA
THUMPA
CALL IT BLISS, CALL IT UTOPIA, I COULDN'T HOPE FOR A BETTER GIG...
THUMPA
THUMPA
I NEVER KNOW IF YOU'RE BEING SARCASTIC OR WHAT...
I MEAN IT... HE'S THE SWEETEST MOST UNDERSTANDING PERSON I'VE EVER MET... WORRIES ABOUT ME ALL THE TIME... I'M FREE TO SPEND ALL THE MONEY I WANT...
HE LOVES ME... REALLY LOVES ME, I THINK, BUT-- NO, I WOULD NEVER WANT TO HURT HIM...
THUMPA
MARCOS SHOULD HAVE YOUR LUCK. THE WAY THINGS'RE GOING FOR HIM, HE'S TALKING ABOUT CUTTING HIS HAIR AND GETTING A JOB!
MARCOS..? I DIDN'T KNOW HE WAS OUT...
THUMPA
THUMPA
THUMPA
YOU DIDN'T..?
WELL, YEAH, SHIT, FOR ABOUT A MONTH NOW.
THUMPA
THUMPA
C'MON, I KNOW WHERE HE HANGS OUT...
MARCOS, IS JESUS ALL RIGHT? DID YOU TAKE CARE OF HIM LIKE YOU WERE SUPPOSED TO? HE'S NOT HURT..?
JESUS IS FINE... FINE. HE WON'T BE GETTING OUT AS SOON AS WE THOUGHT, THOUGH. HE BEAT UP ANOTHER GUARD. TSK, THAT BOY'S TEMPER...
HEY, HONEY, HOW BOUT IT..?
7

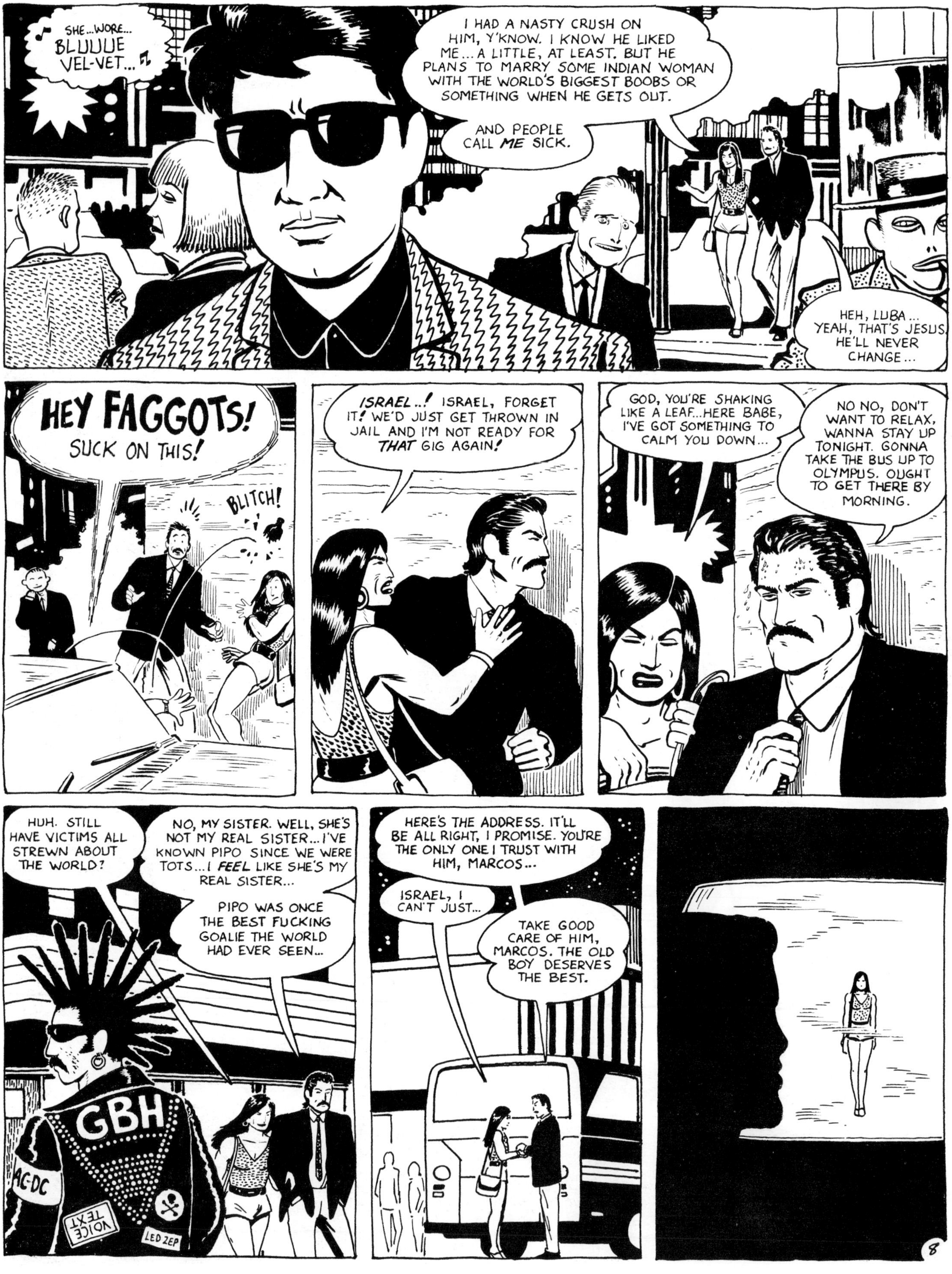
SHE...WORE... BLUUUE VEL-VET...
I HAD A NASTY CRUSH ON HIM, Y'KNOW. I KNOW HE LIKED ME... A LITTLE, AT LEAST. BUT HE PLANS TO MARRY SOME INDIAN WOMAN WITH THE WORLD'S BIGGEST BOOBS OR SOMETHING WHEN HE GETS OUT.
AND PEOPLE CALL ME SICK.
HEH, LUBA... YEAH, THAT'S JESUS. HE'LL NEVER CHANGE...
HEY FAGGOTS! SUCK ON THIS!
BLITCH!
ISRAEL..! ISRAEL, FORGET IT! WE'D JUST GET THROWN IN JAIL AND I'M NOT READY FOR THAT GIG AGAIN!
GOD, YOU'RE SHAKING LIKE A LEAF...HERE BABE, I'VE GOT SOMETHING TO CALM YOU DOWN...
NO NO, DON'T WANT TO RELAX, WANNA STAY UP TONIGHT. GONNA TAKE THE BUS UP TO OLYMPUS. OUGHT TO GET THERE BY MORNING.
HUH. STILL HAVE VICTIMS ALL STREWN ABOUT THE WORLD?
NO, MY SISTER. WELL, SHE'S NOT MY REAL SISTER... I'VE KNOWN PIPO SINCE WE WERE TOTS... I FEEL LIKE SHE'S MY REAL SISTER...
PIPO WAS ONCE THE BEST FUCKING GOALIE THE WORLD HAD EVER SEEN...
GBH
AC-DC
VOICE TEXT
LED ZEP
HERE'S THE ADDRESS. IT'LL BE ALL RIGHT, I PROMISE. YOU'RE THE ONLY ONE I TRUST WITH HIM, MARCOS...
ISRAEL, I CAN'T JUST...
TAKE GOOD CARE OF HIM, MARCOS. THE OLD BOY DESERVES THE BEST.
8

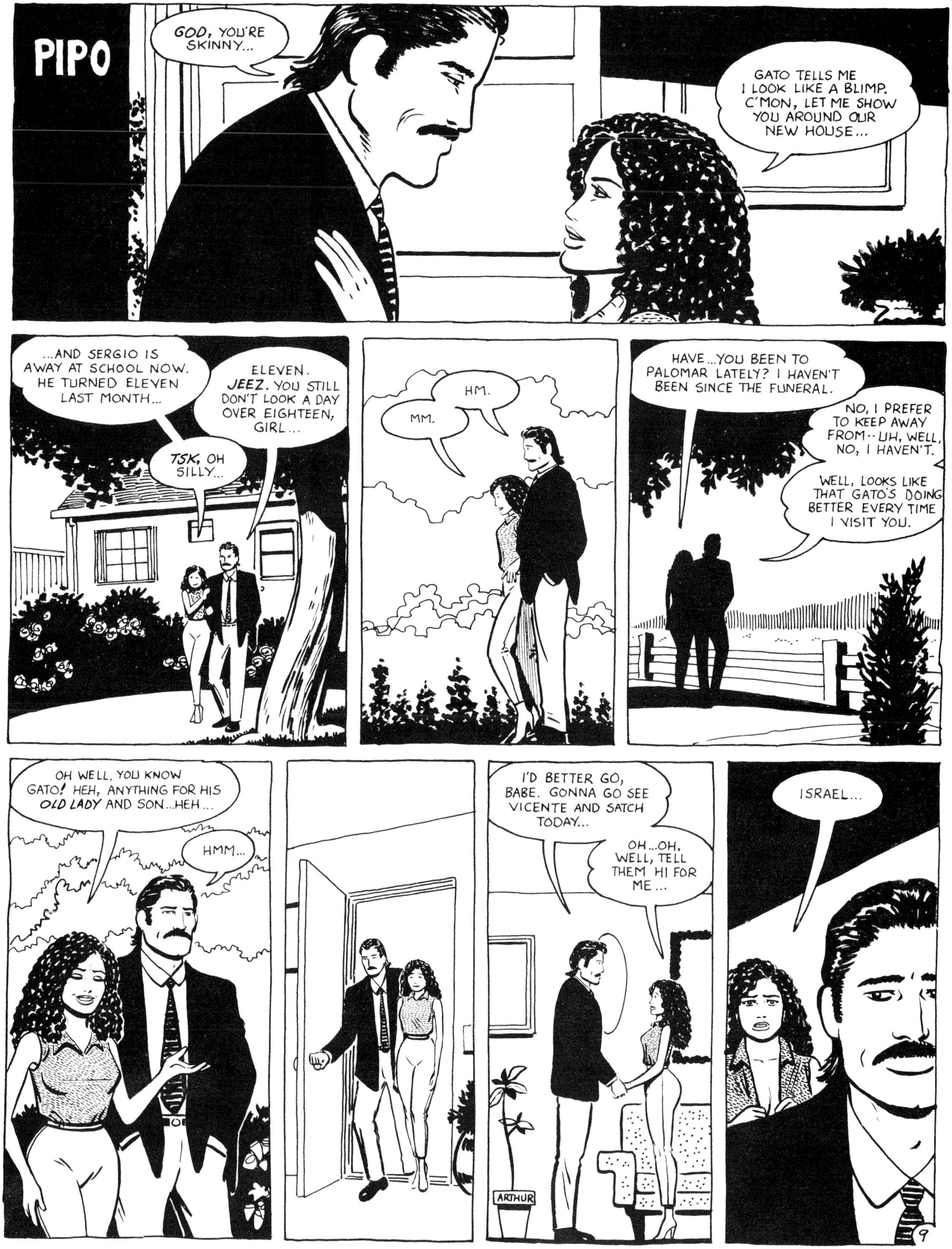
PIPO
GOD, YOU'RE SKINNY...
GATO TELLS ME I LOOK LIKE A BLIMP. C'MON, LET ME SHOW YOU AROUND OUR NEW HOUSE...
...AND SERGIO IS AWAY AT SCHOOL NOW. HE TURNED ELEVEN LAST MONTH...
ELEVEN. JEEZ. YOU STILL DON'T LOOK A DAY OVER EIGHTEEN, GIRL...
TSK, OH SILLY...
HM.
MM.
HAVE...YOU BEEN TO PALOMAR LATELY? I HAVEN'T BEEN SINCE THE FUNERAL.
NO, I PREFER TO KEEP AWAY FROM--UH, WELL, NO, I HAVEN'T.
WELL, LOOKS LIKE THAT GATO'S DOING BETTER EVERY TIME I VISIT YOU.
OH WELL, YOU KNOW GATO! HEH, ANYTHING FOR HIS OLD LADY AND SON...HEH...
HMM...
I'D BETTER GO, BABE. GONNA GO SEE VICENTE AND SATCH TODAY...
OH...OH, WELL, TELL THEM HI FOR ME...
ARTHUR
ISRAEL...
9

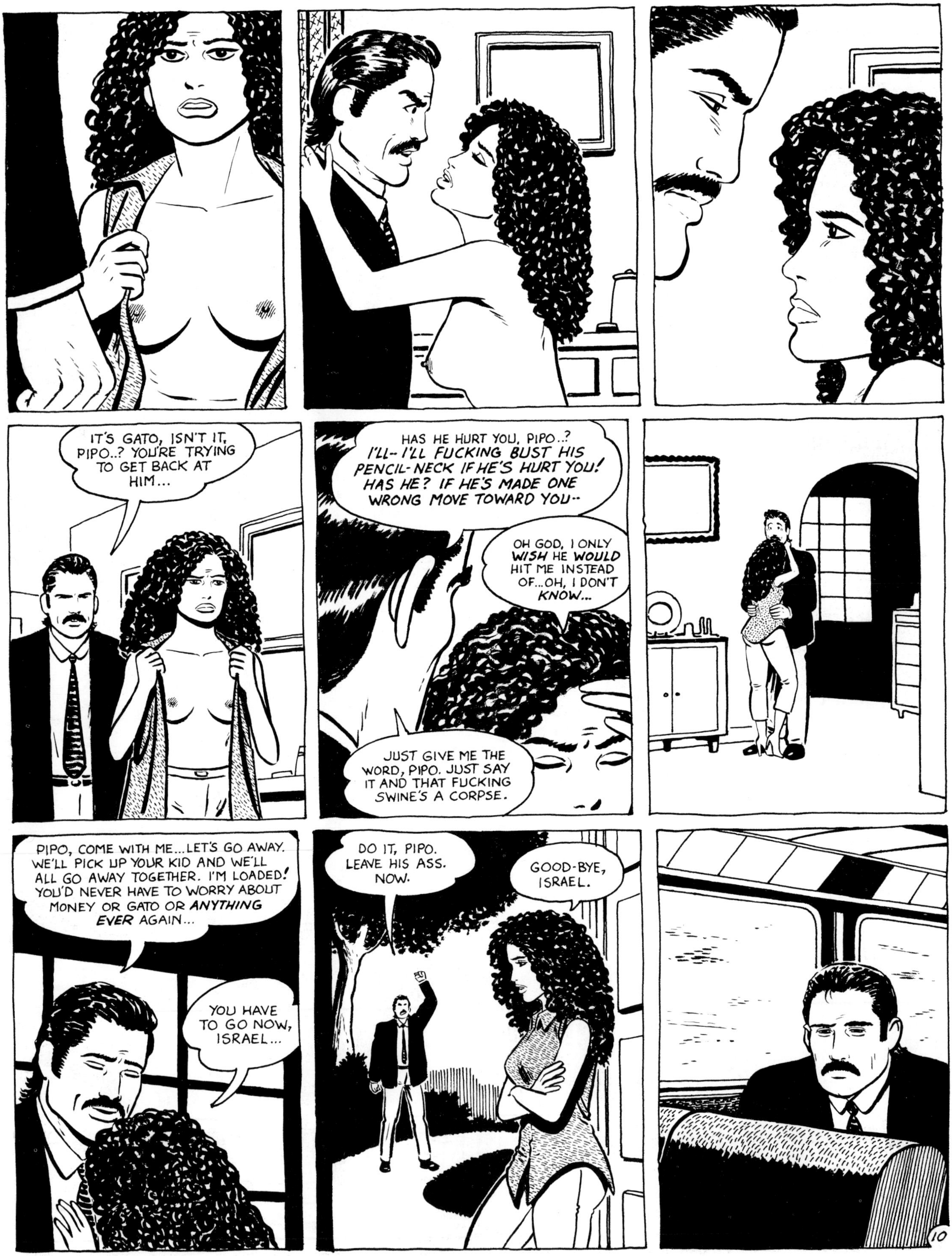
IT'S GATO, ISN'T IT, PIPO..? YOU'RE TRYING TO GET BACK AT HIM...
HAS HE HURT YOU, PIPO..? I'LL-- I'LL FUCKING BUST HIS PENCIL-NECK IF HE'S HURT YOU! HAS HE? IF HE'S MADE ONE WRONG MOVE TOWARD YOU--
OH GOD, I ONLY WISH HE WOULD HIT ME INSTEAD OF...OH, I DON'T KNOW...
JUST GIVE ME THE WORD, PIPO. JUST SAY IT AND THAT FUCKING SWINE'S A CORPSE.
PIPO, COME WITH ME...LET'S GO AWAY. WE'LL PICK UP YOUR KID AND WE'LL ALL GO AWAY TOGETHER. I'M LOADED! YOU'D NEVER HAVE TO WORRY ABOUT MONEY OR GATO OR ANYTHING EVER AGAIN...
YOU HAVE TO GO NOW, ISRAEL...
DO IT, PIPO. LEAVE HIS ASS. NOW.
GOOD-BYE, ISRAEL.
10

SATCH y VICENTE

I'M TELLING YOU, ISRAEL, VICENTE'S *GONE*. HE AND HIS BUDDY SATURNINO PULLED UP STAKES AND HEADED FOR THE STATES...

BUT WHY DIDN'T HE TELL ME. I COULD HAVE TRIED TALKING HIM OUT OF IT -- I COULD HAVE GONE WITH HIM...!

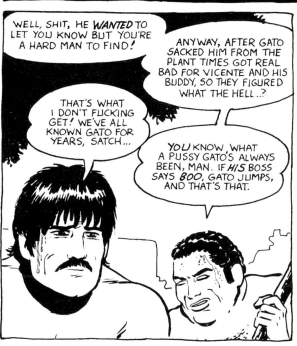

WELL, SHIT, HE *WANTED* TO LET YOU KNOW BUT YOU'RE A HARD MAN TO FIND!

ANYWAY, AFTER GATO SACKED HIM FROM THE PLANT TIMES GOT REAL BAD FOR VICENTE AND HIS BUDDY, SO THEY FIGURED WHAT THE HELL..?

THAT'S WHAT I DON'T FUCKING GET! WE'VE ALL KNOWN GATO FOR YEARS, SATCH...

YOU KNOW, WHAT A PUSSY GATO'S ALWAYS BEEN, MAN. IF *HIS* BOSS SAYS *BOO*, GATO JUMPS, AND THAT'S THAT.

YOU BOYS LOOK LIKE YOU BOTH COULD USE A COLD ONE.

OOH, YOU'RE A DREAM, MARTA.

THANKS, MART.

YEAH... FUCKIN' VICENTE...

GUESS I'M PRETTY LUCKY WITH WHAT I GOT... DON'T MAKE TOO MUCH MONEY, BUT I GOT A GOOD WIFE, GOOD KIDS, MY OWN HOME...

WELL, TAKE CARE THEN, ISRAEL... AND THANKS AGAIN FOR THE HELP. THIS WOULD HAVE TAKEN ME A WEEK TO DO BY MYSELF...

GLAD TO HELP OUT, SATCH. SAY BYE TO MARTA FOR ME...

OH. DID ISRAEL LEAVE ALREADY? I DIDN'T SEE HIM GO...

THE *HELL* YOU DIDN'T...

STARING AT HIM LIKE HE WAS A GODDAMN SIDE OF BEEF AND YOU HADN'T EATEN FOR A MONTH -- GET INSIDE!

WHONG

AAAA AAAAA-- I'LL POISON YOUR DINNER! I WILL!

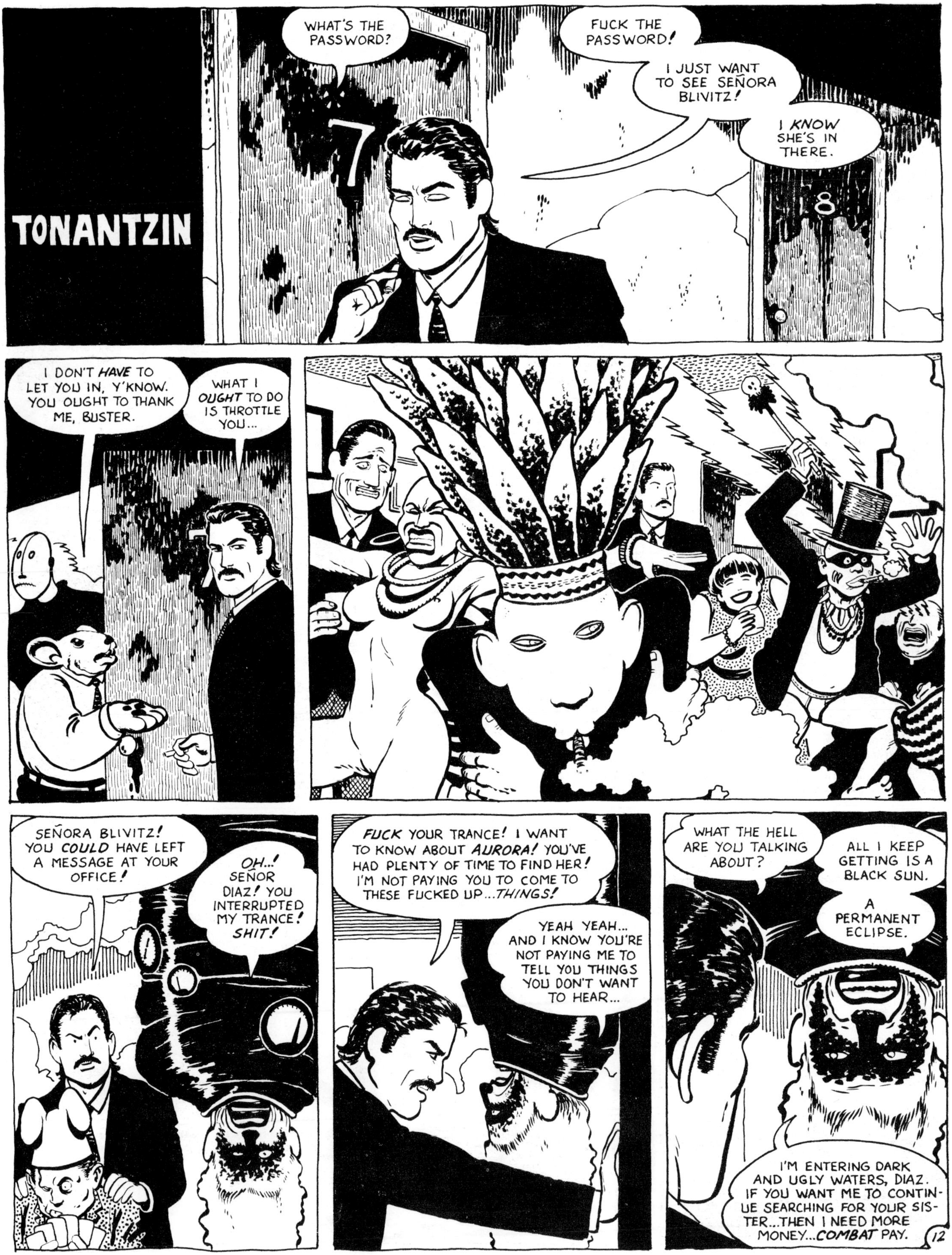

TONANTZIN
WHAT'S THE PASSWORD?
FUCK THE PASSWORD!
I JUST WANT TO SEE SEÑORA BLIVITZ!
I KNOW SHE'S IN THERE.
I DON'T HAVE TO LET YOU IN, Y'KNOW. YOU OUGHT TO THANK ME, BUSTER.
WHAT I OUGHT TO DO IS THROTTLE YOU...
SEÑORA BLIVITZ! YOU COULD HAVE LEFT A MESSAGE AT YOUR OFFICE!
OH...! SEÑOR DIAZ! YOU INTERRUPTED MY TRANCE! SHIT!
FUCK YOUR TRANCE! I WANT TO KNOW ABOUT AURORA! YOU'VE HAD PLENTY OF TIME TO FIND HER! I'M NOT PAYING YOU TO COME TO THESE FUCKED UP...THINGS!
YEAH YEAH... AND I KNOW YOU'RE NOT PAYING ME TO TELL YOU THINGS YOU DON'T WANT TO HEAR...
WHAT THE HELL ARE YOU TALKING ABOUT?
ALL I KEEP GETTING IS A BLACK SUN.
A PERMANENT ECLIPSE.
I'M ENTERING DARK AND UGLY WATERS, DIAZ. IF YOU WANT ME TO CONTINUE SEARCHING FOR YOUR SISTER...THEN I NEED MORE MONEY...COMBAT PAY.
12

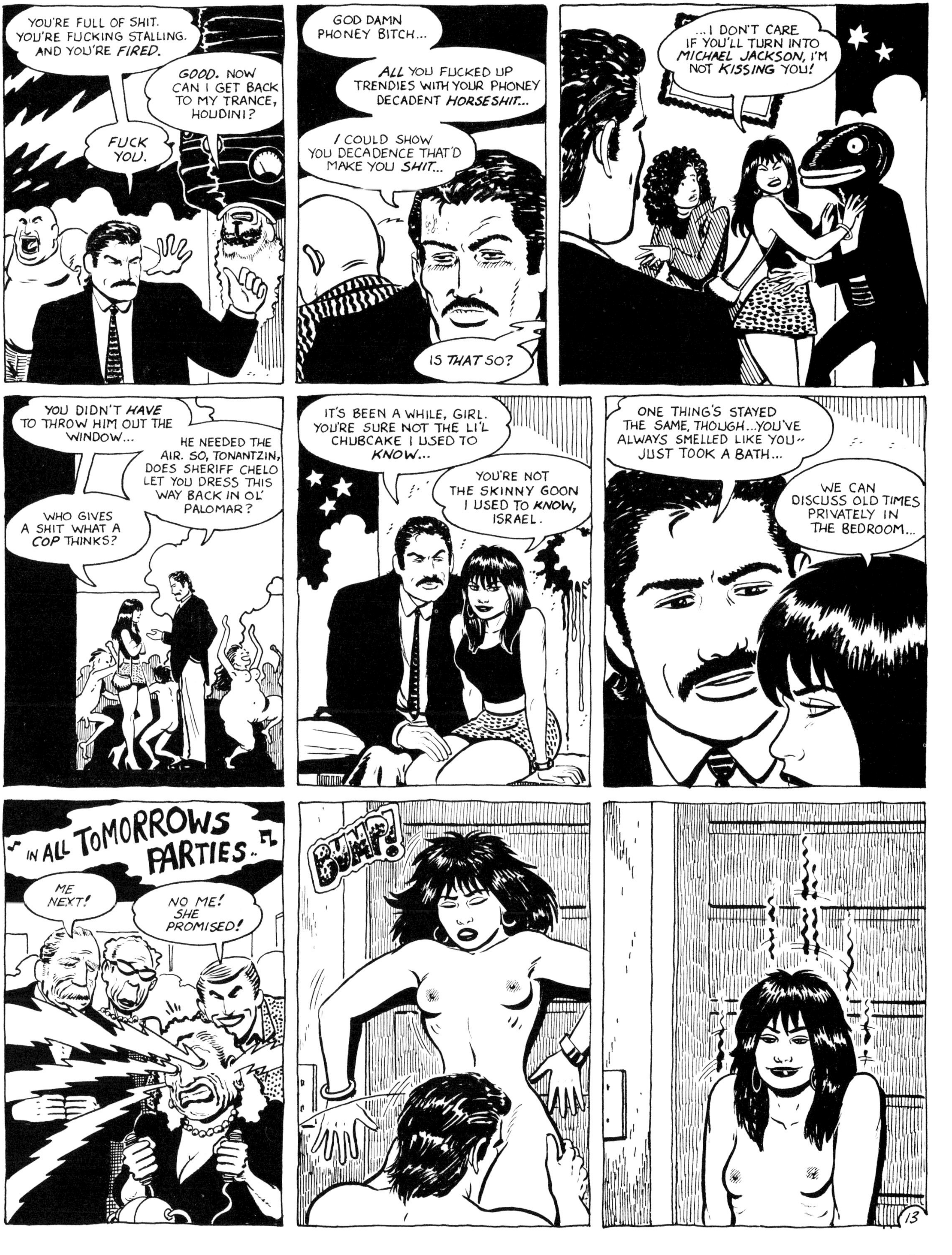
YOU'RE FULL OF SHIT. YOU'RE FUCKING STALLING. AND YOU'RE FIRED.
GOOD. NOW CAN I GET BACK TO MY TRANCE, HOUDINI?
FUCK YOU.
GOD DAMN PHONEY BITCH...
ALL YOU FUCKED UP TRENDIES WITH YOUR PHONEY DECADENT HORSESHIT...
I COULD SHOW YOU DECADENCE THAT'D MAKE YOU SHIT...
IS THAT SO?
...I DON'T CARE IF YOU'LL TURN INTO MICHAEL JACKSON, I'M NOT KISSING YOU!
YOU DIDN'T HAVE TO THROW HIM OUT THE WINDOW...
HE NEEDED THE AIR. SO, TONANTZIN, DOES SHERIFF CHELO LET YOU DRESS THIS WAY BACK IN OL' PALOMAR?
WHO GIVES A SHIT WHAT A COP THINKS?
IT'S BEEN A WHILE, GIRL. YOU'RE SURE NOT THE LI'L CHUBCAKE I USED TO KNOW...
YOU'RE NOT THE SKINNY GOON I USED TO KNOW, ISRAEL.
ONE THING'S STAYED THE SAME, THOUGH...YOU'VE ALWAYS SMELLED LIKE YOU" JUST TOOK A BATH...
WE CAN DISCUSS OLD TIMES PRIVATELY IN THE BEDROOM...
IN ALL TOMORROWS PARTIES..
ME NEXT!
NO ME! SHE PROMISED!
BUMP!
13

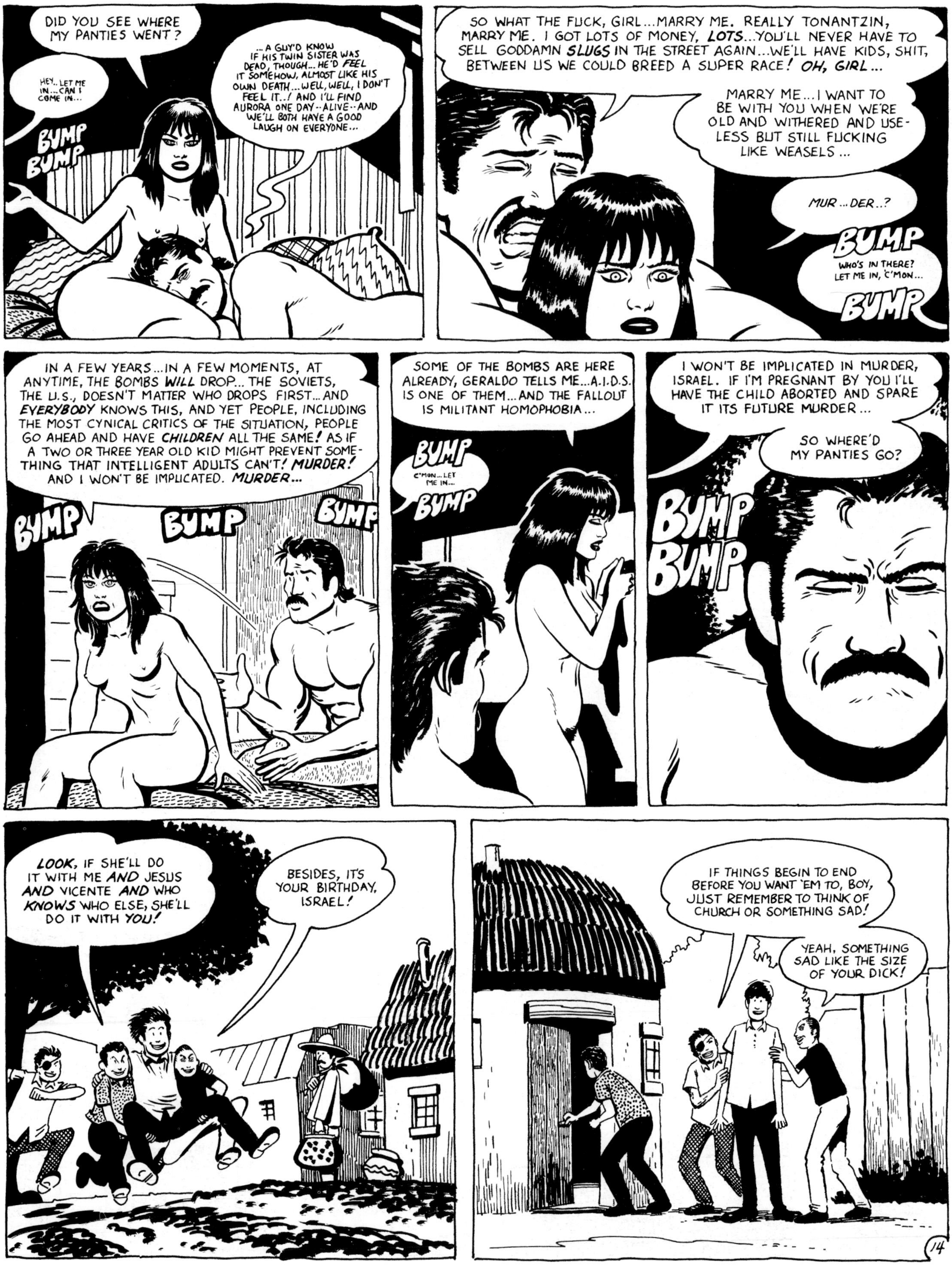

DID YOU SEE WHERE MY PANTIES WENT?
HEY.. LET ME IN... CAN I COME IN...
BUMP BUMP
... A GUY'D KNOW IF HIS TWIN SISTER WAS DEAD, THOUGH... HE'D FEEL IT SOMEHOW, ALMOST LIKE HIS OWN DEATH... WELL, WELL, I DON'T FEEL IT..! AND I'LL FIND AURORA ONE DAY -- ALIVE -- AND WE'LL BOTH HAVE A GOOD LAUGH ON EVERYONE...
SO WHAT THE FUCK, GIRL... MARRY ME. REALLY TONANTZIN, MARRY ME. I GOT LOTS OF MONEY, LOTS... YOU'LL NEVER HAVE TO SELL GODDAMN SLUGS IN THE STREET AGAIN... WE'LL HAVE KIDS, SHIT, BETWEEN US WE COULD BREED A SUPER RACE! OH, GIRL...
MARRY ME... I WANT TO BE WITH YOU WHEN WE'RE OLD AND WITHERED AND USELESS BUT STILL FUCKING LIKE WEASELS...
MUR... DER..?
BUMP
WHO'S IN THERE? LET ME IN, C'MON...
BUMP
IN A FEW YEARS... IN A FEW MOMENTS, AT ANYTIME, THE BOMBS WILL DROP... THE SOVIETS, THE U.S., DOESN'T MATTER WHO DROPS FIRST... AND EVERYBODY KNOWS THIS, AND YET PEOPLE, INCLUDING THE MOST CYNICAL CRITICS OF THE SITUATION, PEOPLE GO AHEAD AND HAVE CHILDREN ALL THE SAME! AS IF A TWO OR THREE YEAR OLD KID MIGHT PREVENT SOMETHING THAT INTELLIGENT ADULTS CAN'T! MURDER! AND I WON'T BE IMPLICATED. MURDER...
BUMP
BUMP
BUMP
SOME OF THE BOMBS ARE HERE ALREADY, GERALDO TELLS ME... A.I.D.S. IS ONE OF THEM... AND THE FALLOUT IS MILITANT HOMOPHOBIA...
BUMP
C'MON... LET ME IN...
BUMP
I WON'T BE IMPLICATED IN MURDER, ISRAEL. IF I'M PREGNANT BY YOU I'LL HAVE THE CHILD ABORTED AND SPARE IT ITS FUTURE MURDER...
SO WHERE'D MY PANTIES GO?
BUMP BUMP
LOOK, IF SHE'LL DO IT WITH ME AND JESUS AND VICENTE AND WHO KNOWS WHO ELSE, SHE'LL DO IT WITH YOU!
BESIDES, IT'S YOUR BIRTHDAY, ISRAEL!
IF THINGS BEGIN TO END BEFORE YOU WANT 'EM TO, BOY, JUST REMEMBER TO THINK OF CHURCH OR SOMETHING SAD!
YEAH, SOMETHING SAD LIKE THE SIZE OF YOUR DICK!
14

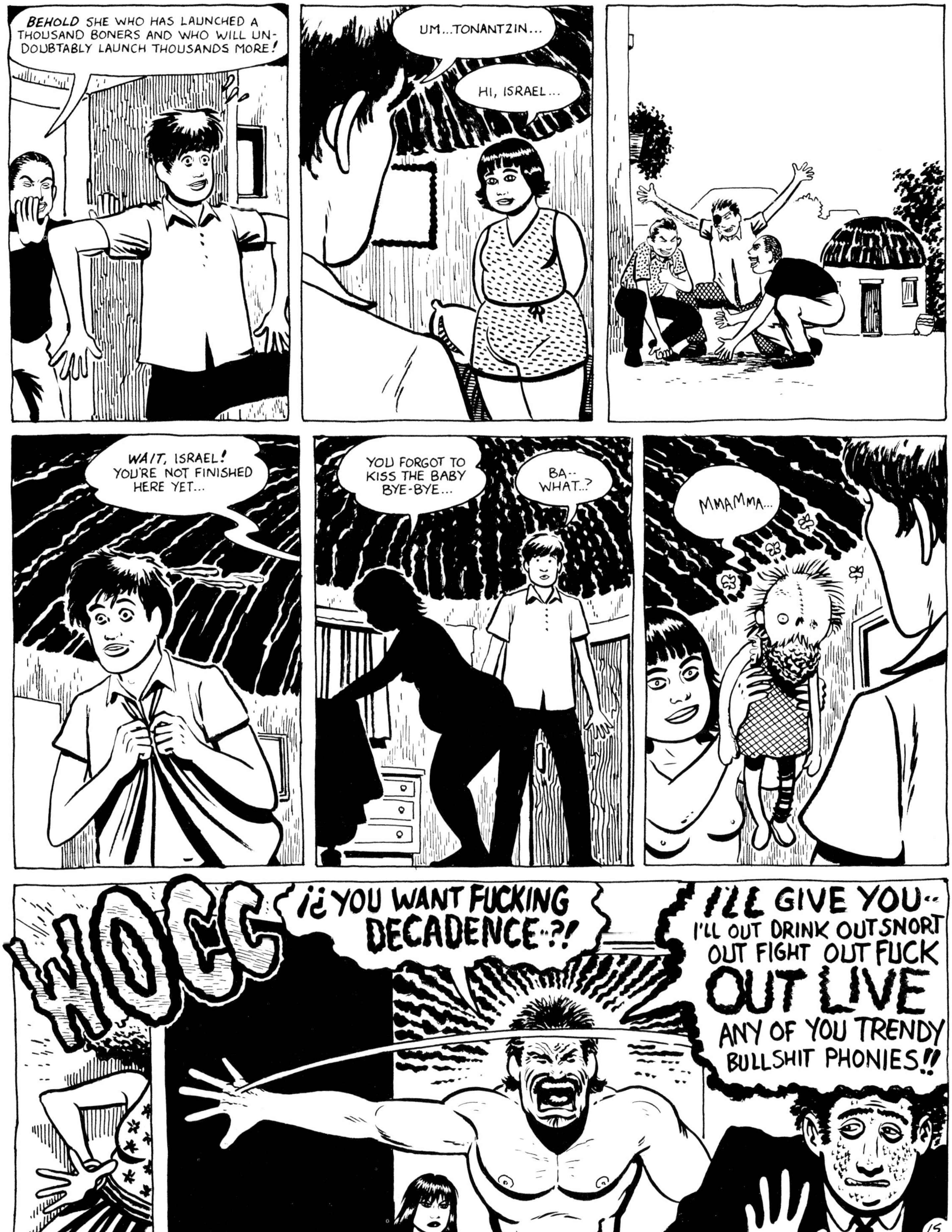
BEHOLD SHE WHO HAS LAUNCHED A THOUSAND BONERS AND WHO WILL UNDOUBTABLY LAUNCH THOUSANDS MORE!
UM...TONANTZIN...
HI, ISRAEL...
WAIT, ISRAEL! YOU'RE NOT FINISHED HERE YET...
YOU FORGOT TO KISS THE BABY BYE-BYE...
BA-- WHAT..?
MMAMMA...
WOCG
¡¿ YOU WANT FUCKING DECADENCE..?!
I'LL GIVE YOU.. I'LL OUT DRINK OUT SNORT OUT FIGHT OUT FUCK OUT LIVE ANY OF YOU TRENDY BULLSHIT PHONIES!!
15

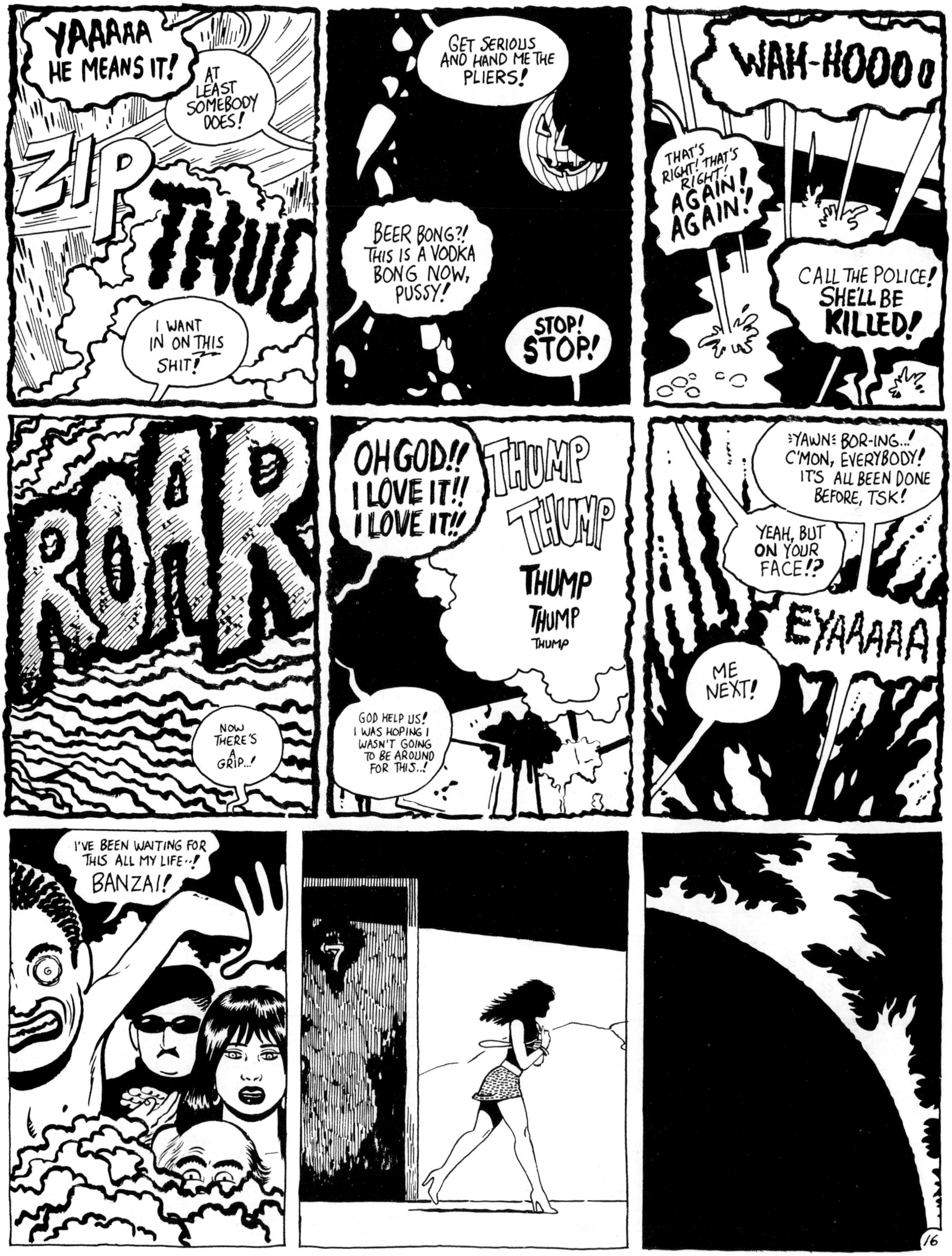
YAAAAA HE MEANS IT!
AT LEAST SOMEBODY DOES!
ZIP
THUD
I WANT IN ON THIS SHIT!
GET SERIOUS AND HAND ME THE PLIERS!
BEER BONG?! THIS IS A VODKA BONG NOW, PUSSY!
STOP! STOP!
WAH-HOOOO
THAT'S RIGHT! THAT'S RIGHT! AGAIN! AGAIN!
CALL THE POLICE! SHE'LL BE KILLED!
ROAR
NOW THERE'S A GRIP..!
OH GOD!! I LOVE IT!! I LOVE IT!!
THUMP THUMP THUMP THUMP THUMP
GOD HELP US! I WAS HOPING I WASN'T GOING TO BE AROUND FOR THIS..!
YAWN BOR-ING..! C'MON, EVERYBODY! IT'S ALL BEEN DONE BEFORE, TSK!
YEAH, BUT ON YOUR FACE!?
EYAAAAA
ME NEXT!
I'VE BEEN WAITING FOR THIS ALL MY LIFE..! BANZAI!
7
16

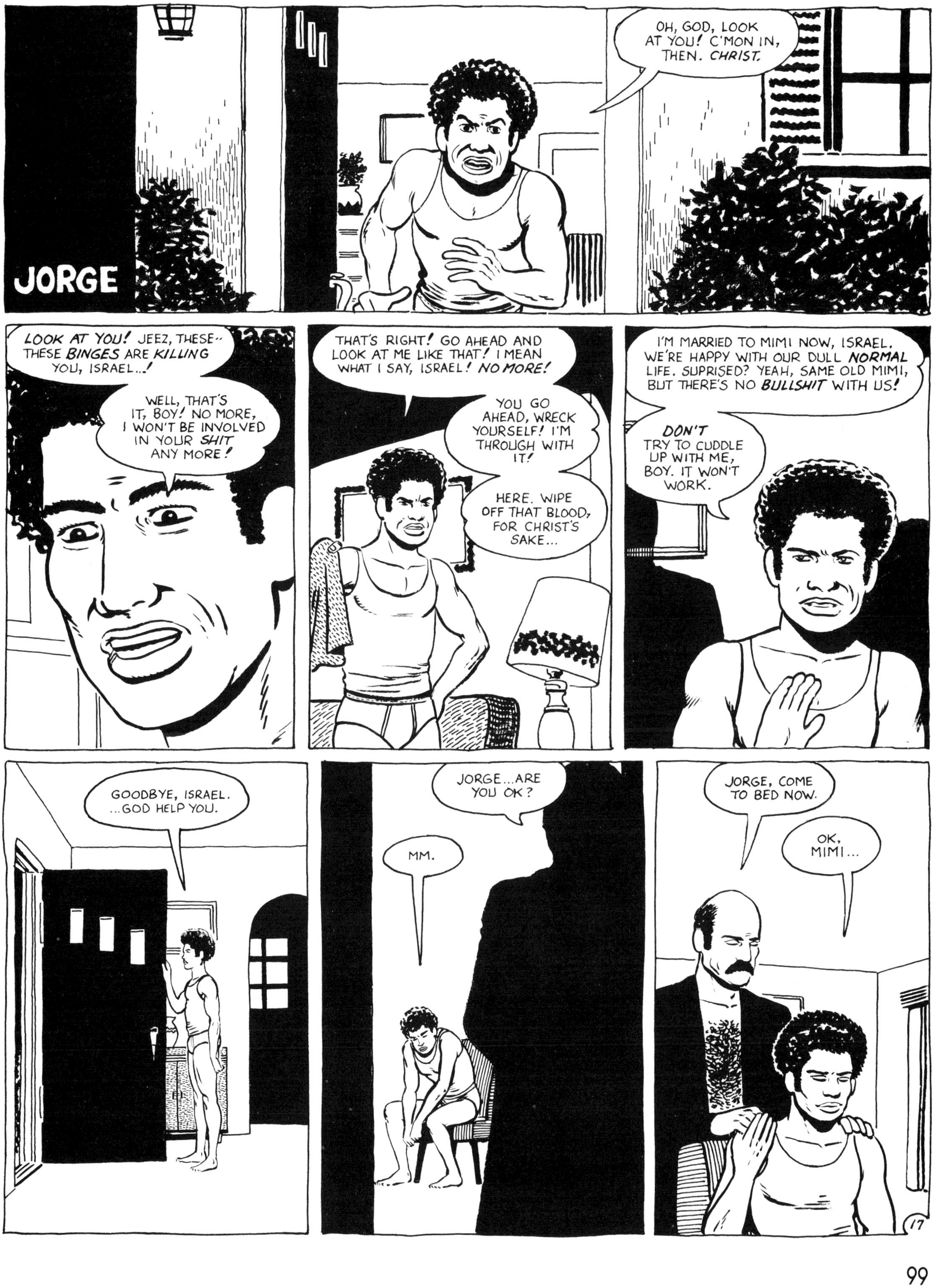
JORGE
OH, GOD, LOOK AT YOU! C'MON IN, THEN. CHRIST.
LOOK AT YOU! JEEZ, THESE-- THESE BINGES ARE KILLING YOU, ISRAEL...!
WELL, THAT'S IT, BOY! NO MORE, I WON'T BE INVOLVED IN YOUR SHIT ANY MORE!
THAT'S RIGHT! GO AHEAD AND LOOK AT ME LIKE THAT! I MEAN WHAT I SAY, ISRAEL! NO MORE!
YOU GO AHEAD, WRECK YOURSELF! I'M THROUGH WITH IT!
HERE. WIPE OFF THAT BLOOD, FOR CHRIST'S SAKE...
I'M MARRIED TO MIMI NOW, ISRAEL. WE'RE HAPPY WITH OUR DULL NORMAL LIFE. SUPRISED? YEAH, SAME OLD MIMI, BUT THERE'S NO BULLSHIT WITH US!
DON'T TRY TO CUDDLE UP WITH ME, BOY. IT WON'T WORK.
GOODBYE, ISRAEL. ...GOD HELP YOU.
JORGE...ARE YOU OK?
MM.
JORGE, COME TO BED NOW.
OK, MIMI...
17

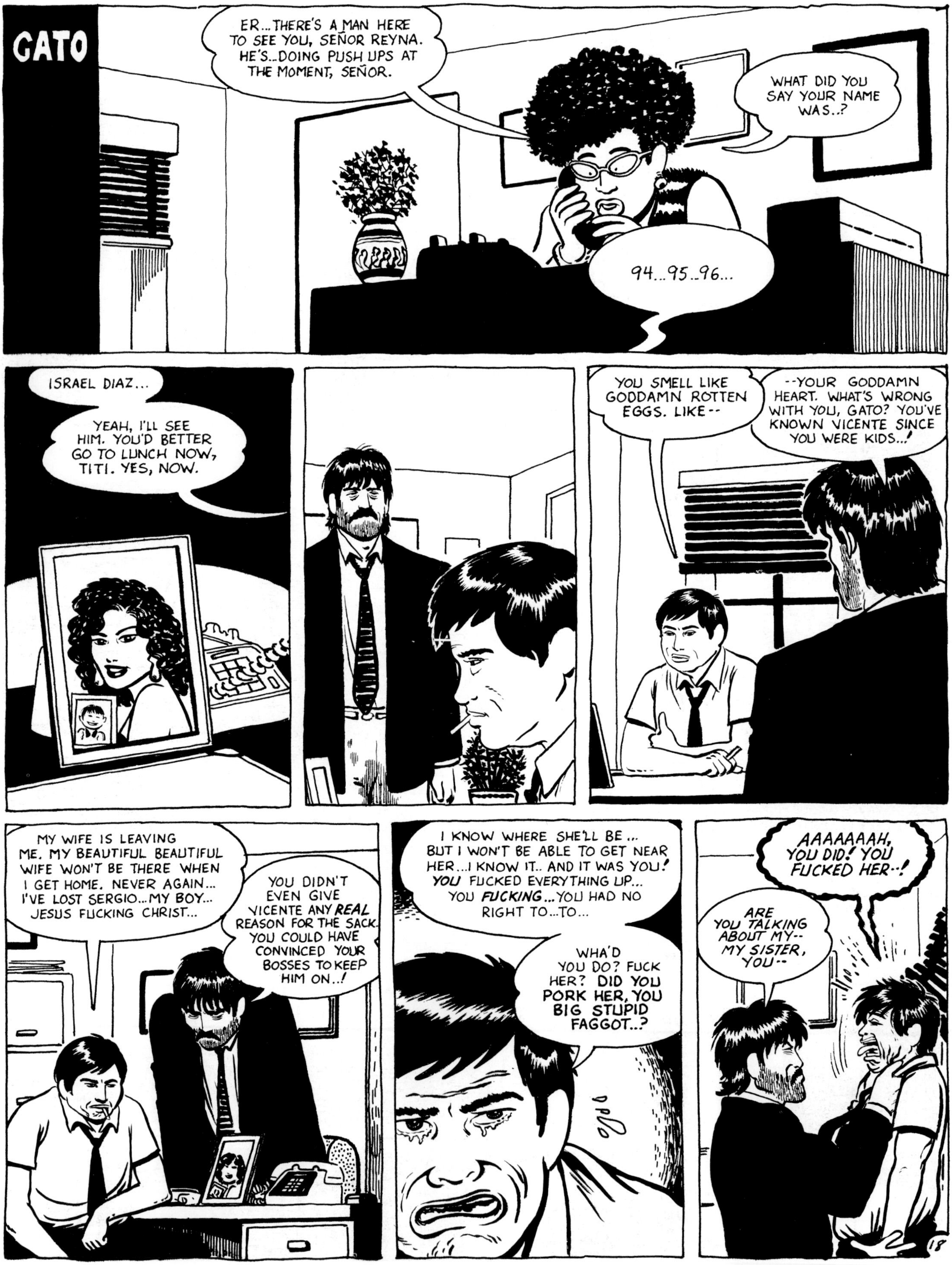
GATO
ER... THERE'S A MAN HERE TO SEE YOU, SEÑOR REYNA. HE'S...DOING PUSH UPS AT THE MOMENT, SEÑOR.
WHAT DID YOU SAY YOUR NAME WAS..?
94... 95.. 96...
ISRAEL DIAZ...
YEAH, I'LL SEE HIM. YOU'D BETTER GO TO LUNCH NOW, TITI. YES, NOW.
YOU SMELL LIKE GODDAMN ROTTEN EGGS. LIKE--
--YOUR GODDAMN HEART. WHAT'S WRONG WITH YOU, GATO? YOU'VE KNOWN VICENTE SINCE YOU WERE KIDS...!
MY WIFE IS LEAVING ME. MY BEAUTIFUL BEAUTIFUL WIFE WON'T BE THERE WHEN I GET HOME. NEVER AGAIN... I'VE LOST SERGIO... MY BOY... JESUS FUCKING CHRIST...
YOU DIDN'T EVEN GIVE VICENTE ANY REAL REASON FOR THE SACK. YOU COULD HAVE CONVINCED YOUR BOSSES TO KEEP HIM ON..!
I KNOW WHERE SHE'LL BE... BUT I WON'T BE ABLE TO GET NEAR HER... I KNOW IT.. AND IT WAS YOU! YOU FUCKED EVERYTHING UP... YOU FUCKING... YOU HAD NO RIGHT TO... TO...
WHA'D YOU DO? FUCK HER? DID YOU PORK HER, YOU BIG STUPID FAGGOT..?
AAAAAAAH, YOU DID! YOU FUCKED HER--!
ARE YOU TALKING ABOUT MY-- MY SISTER, YOU--
18

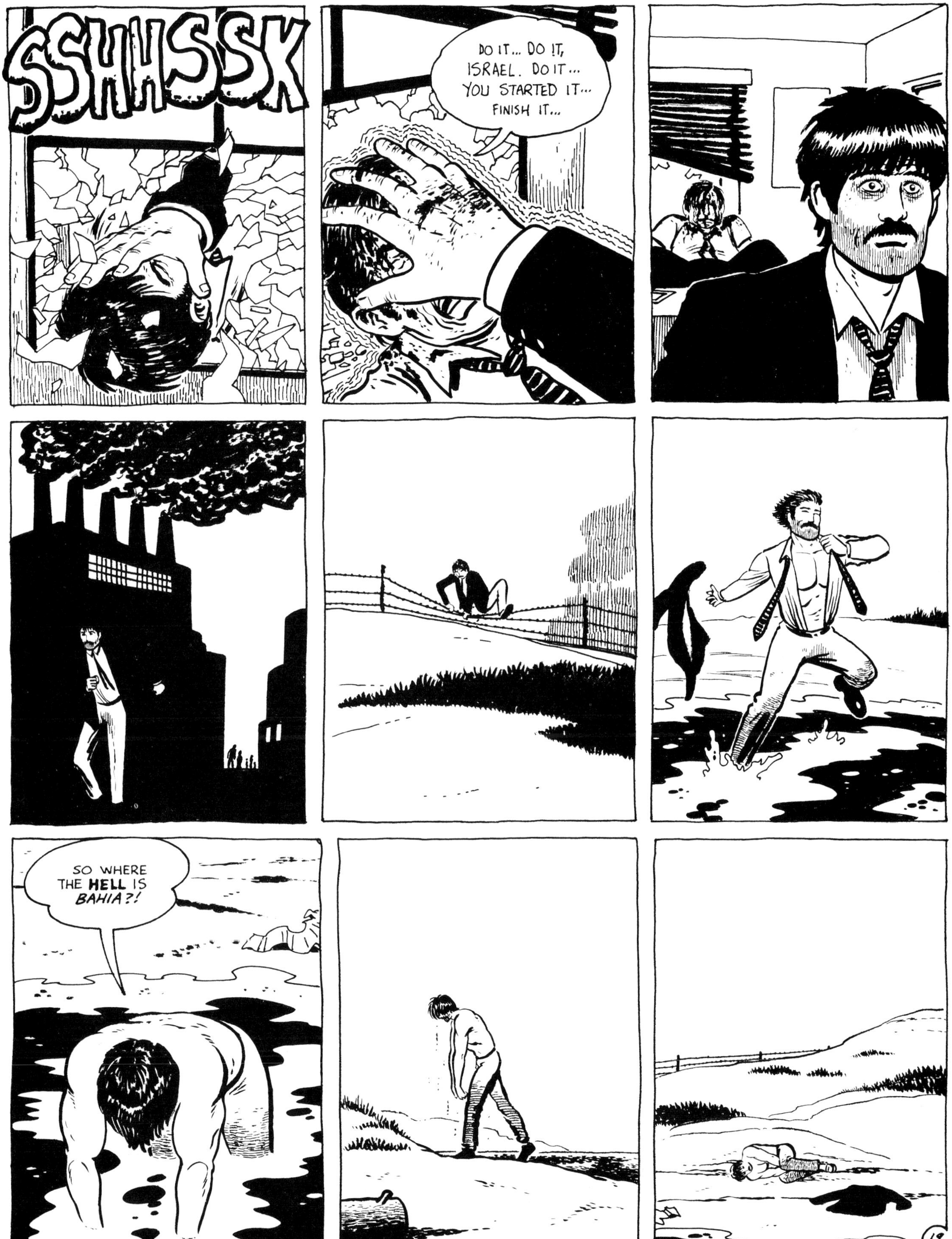
SSHHSSSK
DO IT... DO IT, ISRAEL. DO IT... YOU STARTED IT... FINISH IT...
SO WHERE THE **HELL** IS *BAHIA?!*
19

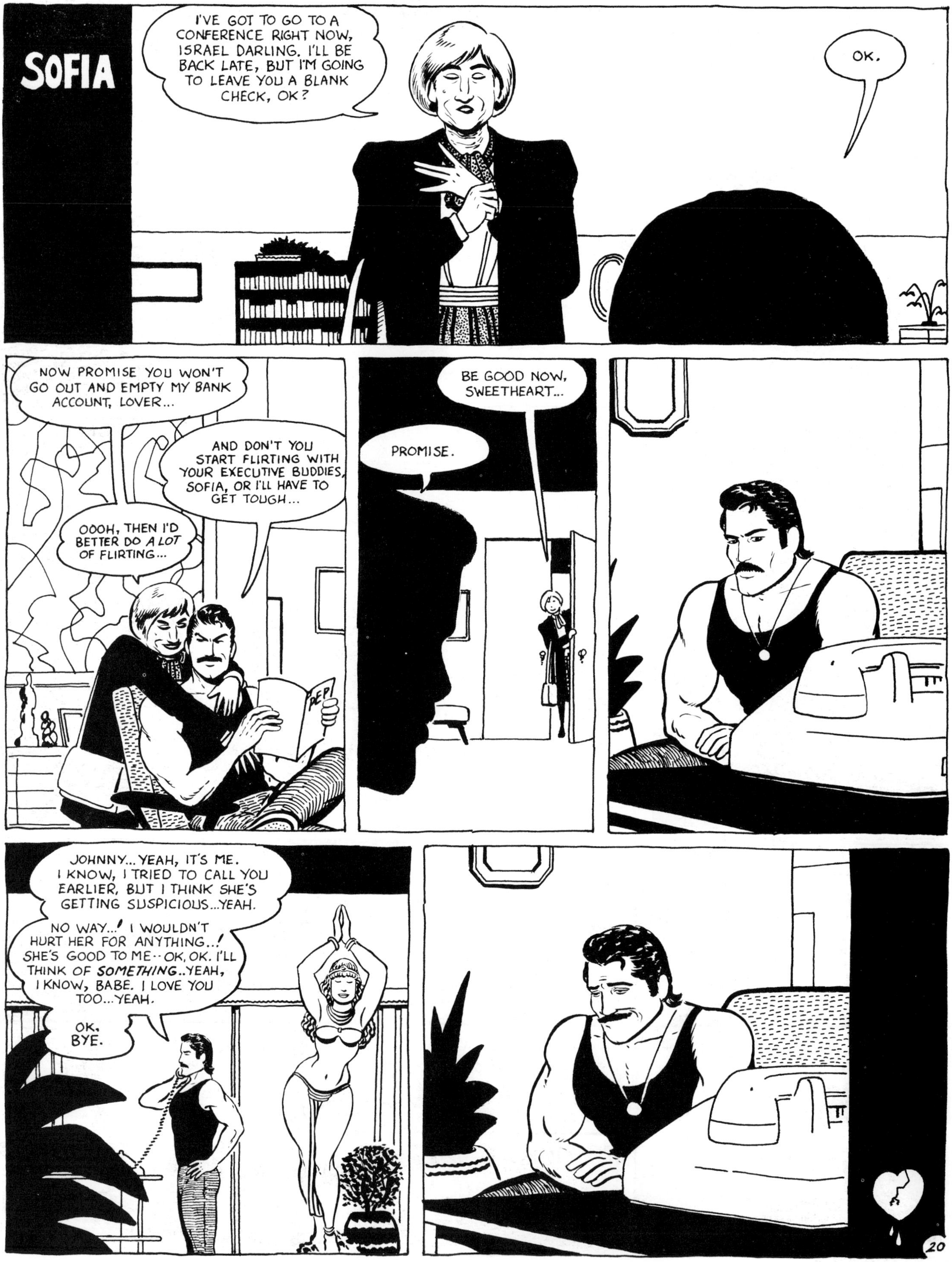
SOFIA
I'VE GOT TO GO TO A CONFERENCE RIGHT NOW, ISRAEL DARLING. I'LL BE BACK LATE, BUT I'M GOING TO LEAVE YOU A BLANK CHECK, OK?
OK.
NOW PROMISE YOU WON'T GO OUT AND EMPTY MY BANK ACCOUNT, LOVER...
AND DON'T YOU START FLIRTING WITH YOUR EXECUTIVE BUDDIES, SOFIA, OR I'LL HAVE TO GET TOUGH...
OOOH, THEN I'D BETTER DO *A LOT* OF FLIRTING...
PEP!
BE GOOD NOW, SWEETHEART...
PROMISE.
JOHNNY... YEAH, IT'S ME. I KNOW, I TRIED TO CALL YOU EARLIER, BUT I THINK SHE'S GETTING SUSPICIOUS... YEAH.
NO WAY...! I WOULDN'T HURT HER FOR ANYTHING...! SHE'S GOOD TO ME·· OK, OK. I'LL THINK OF *SOMETHING*.. YEAH, I KNOW, BABE. I LOVE YOU TOO... YEAH.
OK, BYE.
20

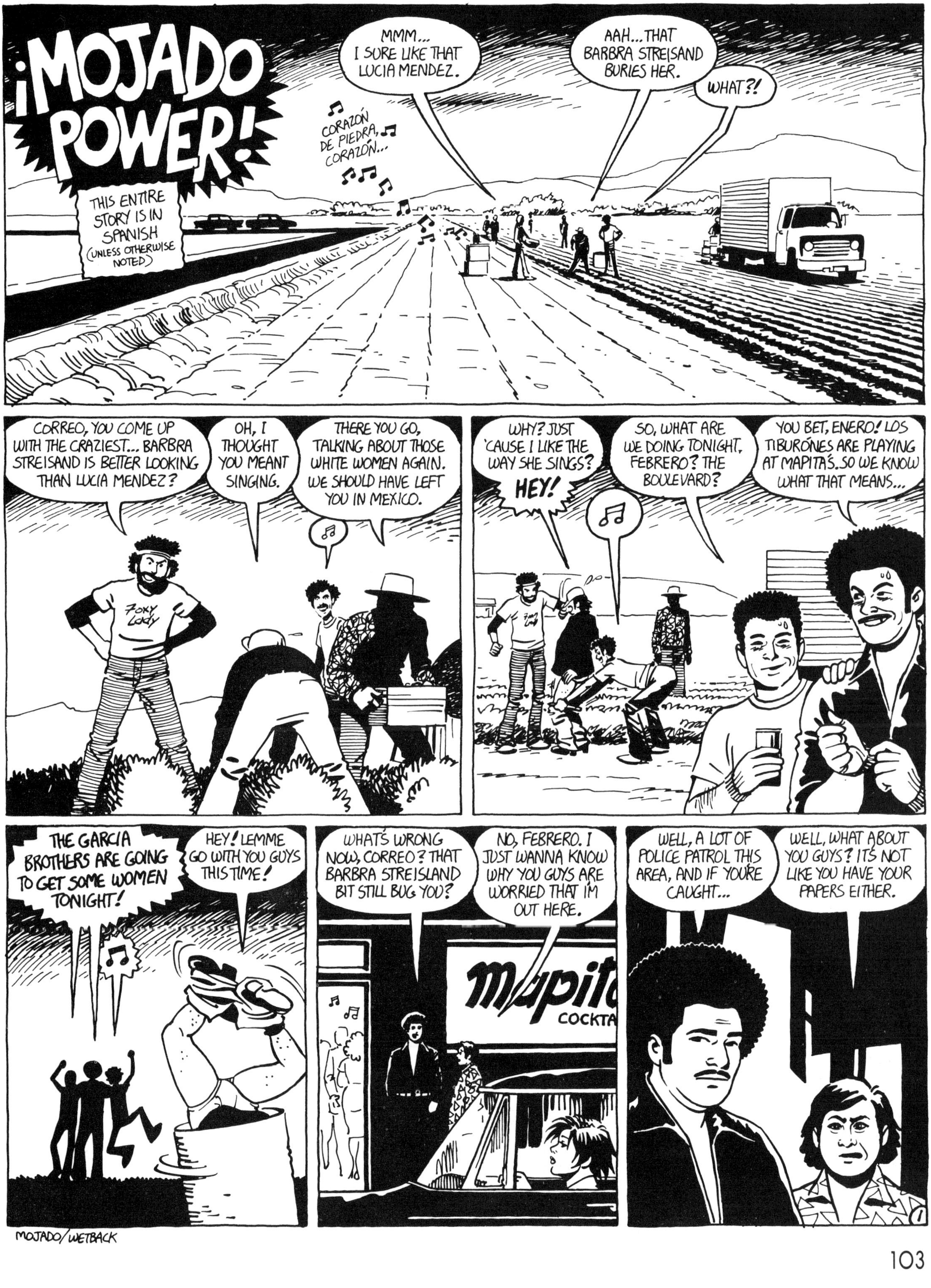

¡MOJADO POWER!
THIS ENTIRE STORY IS IN SPANISH (UNLESS OTHERWISE NOTED)
CORAZÓN DE PIEDRA, CORAZÓN...
MMM... I SURE LIKE THAT LUCIA MENDEZ.
AAH... THAT BARBRA STREISAND BURIES HER.
WHAT?!
CORREO, YOU COME UP WITH THE CRAZIEST... BARBRA STREISAND IS BETTER LOOKING THAN LUCIA MENDEZ?
OH, I THOUGHT YOU MEANT SINGING.
THERE YOU GO, TALKING ABOUT THOSE WHITE WOMEN AGAIN. WE SHOULD HAVE LEFT YOU IN MEXICO.
FOXY LADY
WHY? JUST 'CAUSE I LIKE THE WAY SHE SINGS?
HEY!
SO, WHAT ARE WE DOING TONIGHT, FEBRERO? THE BOULEVARD?
YOU BET, ENERO! LOS TIBURÓNES ARE PLAYING AT MAPITA'S. SO WE KNOW WHAT THAT MEANS...
THE GARCIA BROTHERS ARE GOING TO GET SOME WOMEN TONIGHT!
HEY! LEMME GO WITH YOU GUYS THIS TIME!
WHAT'S WRONG NOW, CORREO? THAT BARBRA STREISLAND BIT STILL BUG YOU?
NO, FEBRERO. I JUST WANNA KNOW WHY YOU GUYS ARE WORRIED THAT I'M OUT HERE.
MAPITA COCKTA
WELL, A LOT OF POLICE PATROL THIS AREA, AND IF YOU'RE CAUGHT...
WELL, WHAT ABOUT YOU GUYS? IT'S NOT LIKE YOU HAVE YOUR PAPERS EITHER.
1

MOJADO/WETBACK

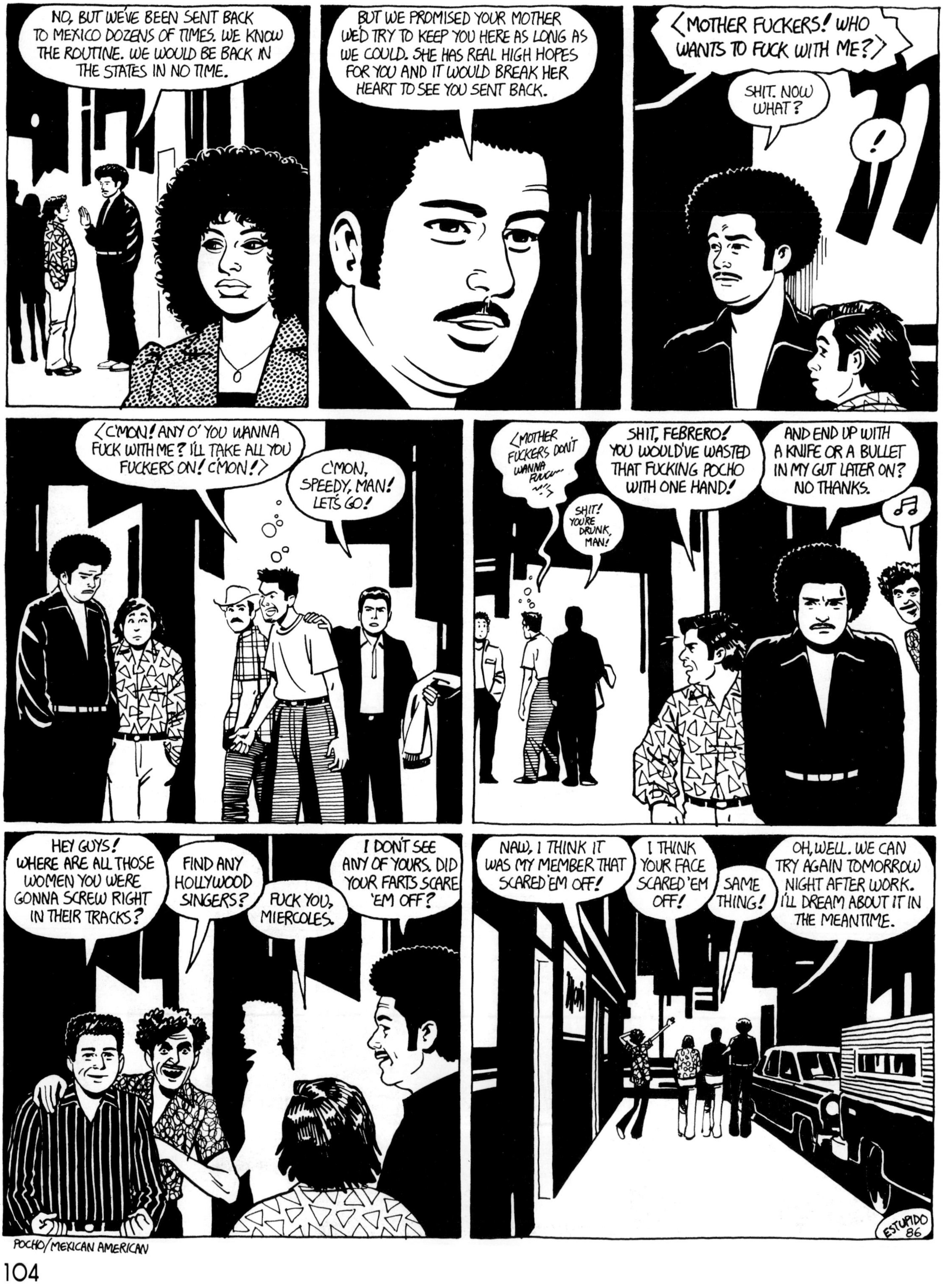
NO, BUT WE'VE BEEN SENT BACK TO MEXICO DOZENS OF TIMES. WE KNOW THE ROUTINE. WE WOULD BE BACK IN THE STATES IN NO TIME.
BUT WE PROMISED YOUR MOTHER WE'D TRY TO KEEP YOU HERE AS LONG AS WE COULD. SHE HAS REAL HIGH HOPES FOR YOU AND IT WOULD BREAK HER HEART TO SEE YOU SENT BACK.
<MOTHER FUCKERS! WHO WANTS TO FUCK WITH ME?>
SHIT. NOW WHAT?
!
<C'MON! ANY O' YOU WANNA FUCK WITH ME? I'LL TAKE ALL YOU FUCKERS ON! C'MON!>
C'MON, SPEEDY, MAN! LET'S GO!
<MOTHER FUCKERS DON'T WANNA FUCK...
SHIT! YOU'RE DRUNK, MAN!
SHIT, FEBRERO! YOU WOULD'VE WASTED THAT FUCKING POCHO WITH ONE HAND!
AND END UP WITH A KNIFE OR A BULLET IN MY GUT LATER ON? NO THANKS.
HEY GUYS! WHERE ARE ALL THOSE WOMEN YOU WERE GONNA SCREW RIGHT IN THEIR TRACKS?
FIND ANY HOLLYWOOD SINGERS?
FUCK YOU, MIERCOLES.
I DON'T SEE ANY OF YOURS. DID YOUR FARTS SCARE 'EM OFF?
NAW, I THINK IT WAS MY MEMBER THAT SCARED 'EM OFF!
I THINK YOUR FACE SCARED 'EM OFF!
SAME THING!
OH, WELL. WE CAN TRY AGAIN TOMORROW NIGHT AFTER WORK. I'LL DREAM ABOUT IT IN THE MEANTIME.
ESTUPIDO 86

POCHO/MEXICAN AMERICAN

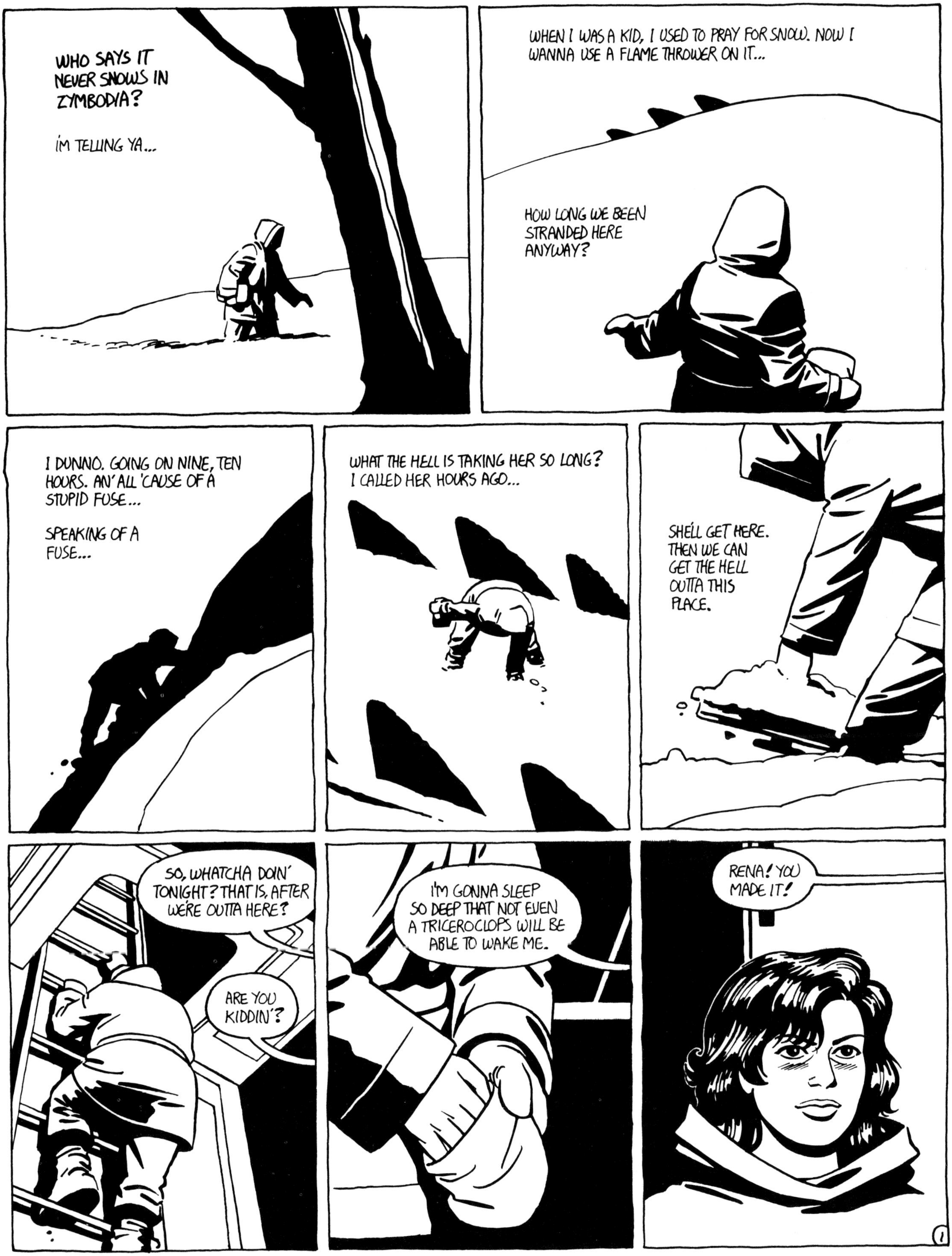
WHO SAYS IT NEVER SNOWS IN ZYMBODIA?
I'M TELLING YA...
WHEN I WAS A KID, I USED TO PRAY FOR SNOW. NOW I WANNA USE A FLAME THROWER ON IT...
HOW LONG WE BEEN STRANDED HERE ANYWAY?
I DUNNO. GOING ON NINE, TEN HOURS. AN' ALL 'CAUSE OF A STUPID FUSE...
SPEAKING OF A FUSE...
WHAT THE HELL IS TAKING HER SO LONG? I CALLED HER HOURS AGO...
SHE'LL GET HERE. THEN WE CAN GET THE HELL OUTTA THIS PLACE.
SO, WHATCHA DOIN' TONIGHT? THAT IS, AFTER WE'RE OUTTA HERE?
ARE YOU KIDDIN'?
I'M GONNA SLEEP SO DEEP THAT NOT EVEN A TRICEROCLOPS WILL BE ABLE TO WAKE ME.
RENA! YOU MADE IT!
1

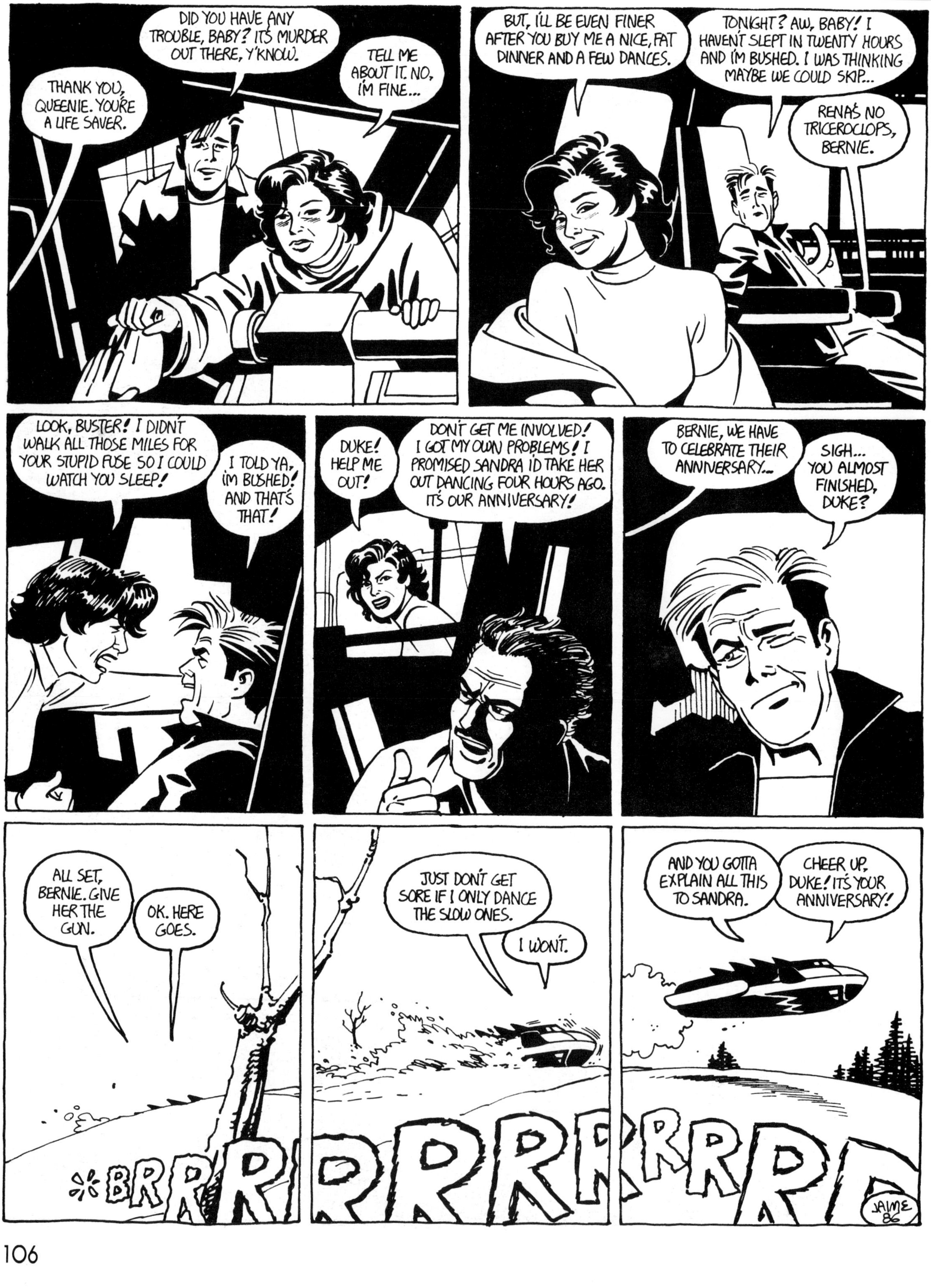
THANK YOU, QUEENIE. YOU'RE A LIFE SAVER.
DID YOU HAVE ANY TROUBLE, BABY? IT'S MURDER OUT THERE, Y'KNOW.
TELL ME ABOUT IT. NO, I'M FINE...
BUT, I'LL BE EVEN FINER AFTER YOU BUY ME A NICE, FAT DINNER AND A FEW DANCES.
TONIGHT? AW, BABY! I HAVEN'T SLEPT IN TWENTY HOURS AND I'M BUSHED. I WAS THINKING MAYBE WE COULD SKIP...
RENA'S NO TRICEROCLOPS, BERNIE.
LOOK, BUSTER! I DIDN'T WALK ALL THOSE MILES FOR YOUR STUPID FUSE SO I COULD WATCH YOU SLEEP!
I TOLD YA, I'M BUSHED! AND THAT'S THAT!
DUKE! HELP ME OUT!
DON'T GET ME INVOLVED! I GOT MY OWN PROBLEMS! I PROMISED SANDRA I'D TAKE HER OUT DANCING FOUR HOURS AGO. IT'S OUR ANNIVERSARY!
BERNIE, WE HAVE TO CELEBRATE THEIR ANNIVERSARY...
SIGH... YOU ALMOST FINISHED, DUKE?
ALL SET, BERNIE. GIVE HER THE GUN.
OK. HERE GOES.
JUST DON'T GET SORE IF I ONLY DANCE THE SLOW ONES.
I WON'T.
AND YOU GOTTA EXPLAIN ALL THIS TO SANDRA.
CHEER UP, DUKE! IT'S YOUR ANNIVERSARY!
BRRRRRRRRRRRRRRR
JAIME 86

ROCKET RHODES

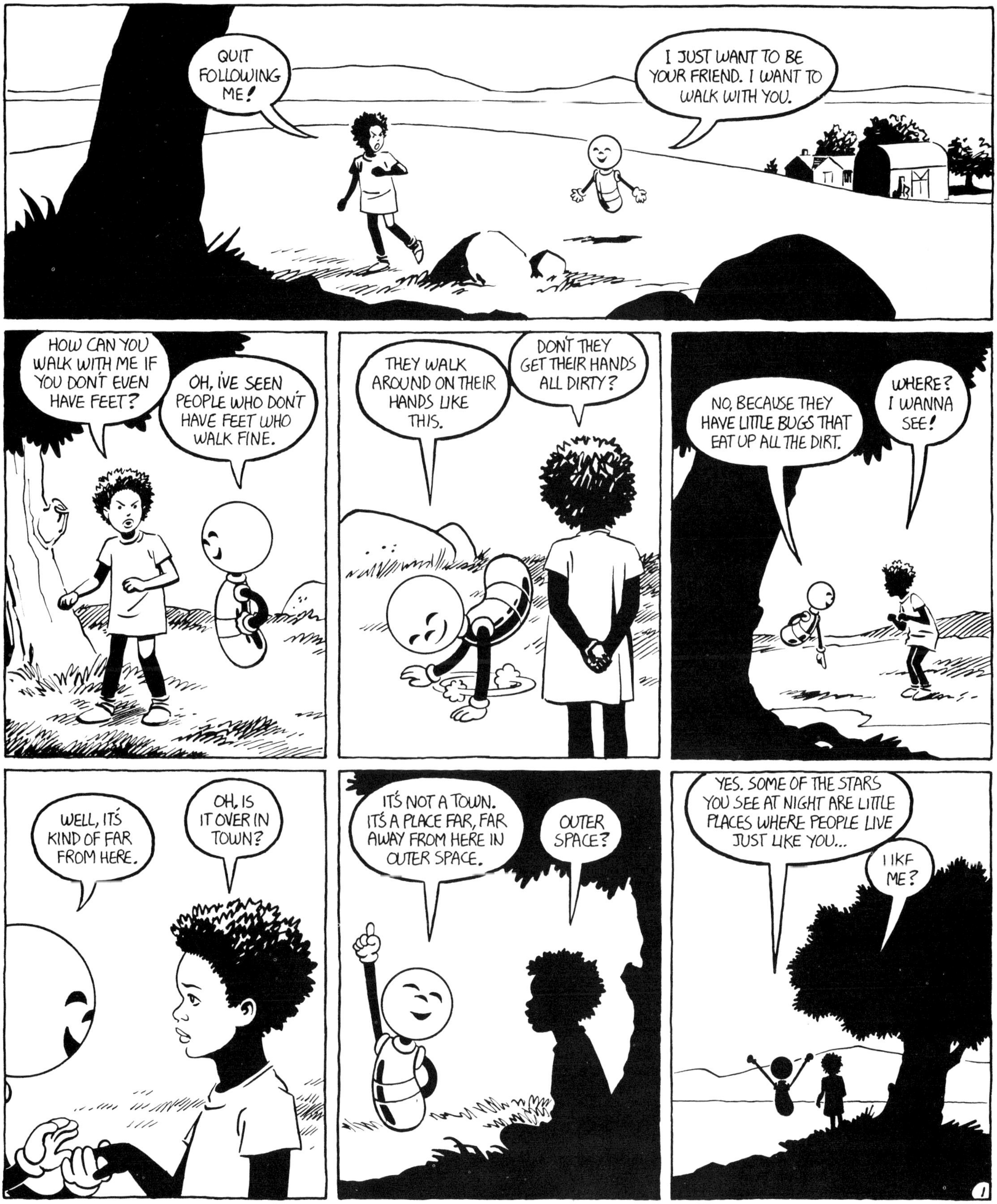
QUIT FOLLOWING ME!
I JUST WANT TO BE YOUR FRIEND. I WANT TO WALK WITH YOU.
HOW CAN YOU WALK WITH ME IF YOU DON'T EVEN HAVE FEET?
OH, I'VE SEEN PEOPLE WHO DON'T HAVE FEET WHO WALK FINE.
THEY WALK AROUND ON THEIR HANDS LIKE THIS.
DON'T THEY GET THEIR HANDS ALL DIRTY?
NO, BECAUSE THEY HAVE LITTLE BUGS THAT EAT UP ALL THE DIRT.
WHERE? I WANNA SEE!
WELL, IT'S KIND OF FAR FROM HERE.
OH, IS IT OVER IN TOWN?
IT'S NOT A TOWN. IT'S A PLACE FAR, FAR AWAY FROM HERE IN OUTER SPACE.
OUTER SPACE?
YES. SOME OF THE STARS YOU SEE AT NIGHT ARE LITTLE PLACES WHERE PEOPLE LIVE JUST LIKE YOU...
LIKE ME?
1

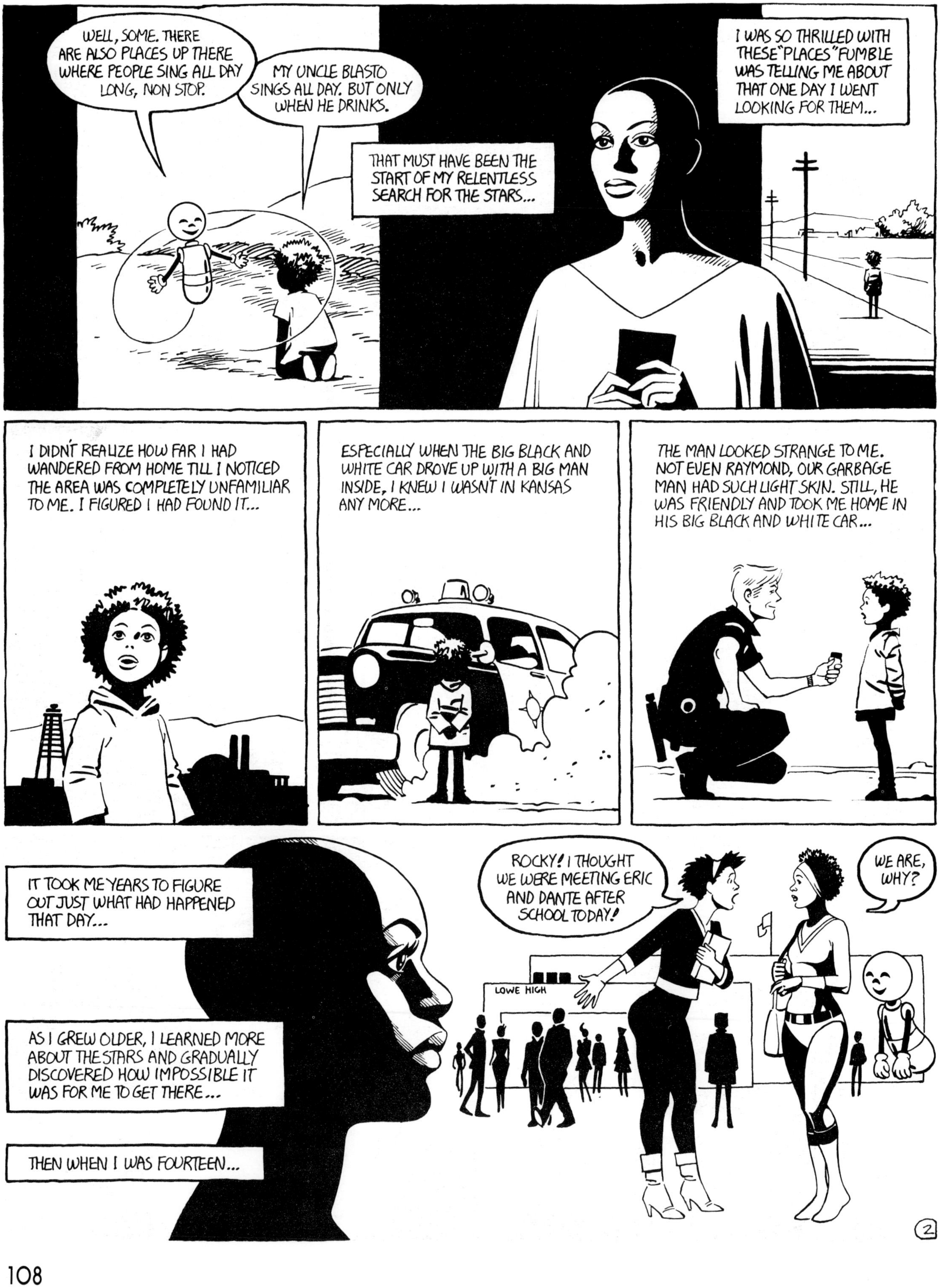
WELL, SOME. THERE ARE ALSO PLACES UP THERE WHERE PEOPLE SING ALL DAY LONG, NON STOP.
MY UNCLE BLASTO SINGS ALL DAY. BUT ONLY WHEN HE DRINKS.
THAT MUST HAVE BEEN THE START OF MY RELENTLESS SEARCH FOR THE STARS...
I WAS SO THRILLED WITH THESE "PLACES" FUMBLE WAS TELLING ME ABOUT THAT ONE DAY I WENT LOOKING FOR THEM...
I DIDN'T REALIZE HOW FAR I HAD WANDERED FROM HOME TILL I NOTICED THE AREA WAS COMPLETELY UNFAMILIAR TO ME. I FIGURED I HAD FOUND IT...
ESPECIALLY WHEN THE BIG BLACK AND WHITE CAR DROVE UP WITH A BIG MAN INSIDE, I KNEW I WASN'T IN KANSAS ANY MORE...
THE MAN LOOKED STRANGE TO ME. NOT EVEN RAYMOND, OUR GARBAGE MAN HAD SUCH LIGHT SKIN. STILL, HE WAS FRIENDLY AND TOOK ME HOME IN HIS BIG BLACK AND WHITE CAR...
IT TOOK ME YEARS TO FIGURE OUT JUST WHAT HAD HAPPENED THAT DAY...
AS I GREW OLDER, I LEARNED MORE ABOUT THE STARS AND GRADUALLY DISCOVERED HOW IMPOSSIBLE IT WAS FOR ME TO GET THERE...
THEN WHEN I WAS FOURTEEN...
ROCKY! I THOUGHT WE WERE MEETING ERIC AND DANTE AFTER SCHOOL TODAY!
WE ARE, WHY?
LOWE HIGH
2

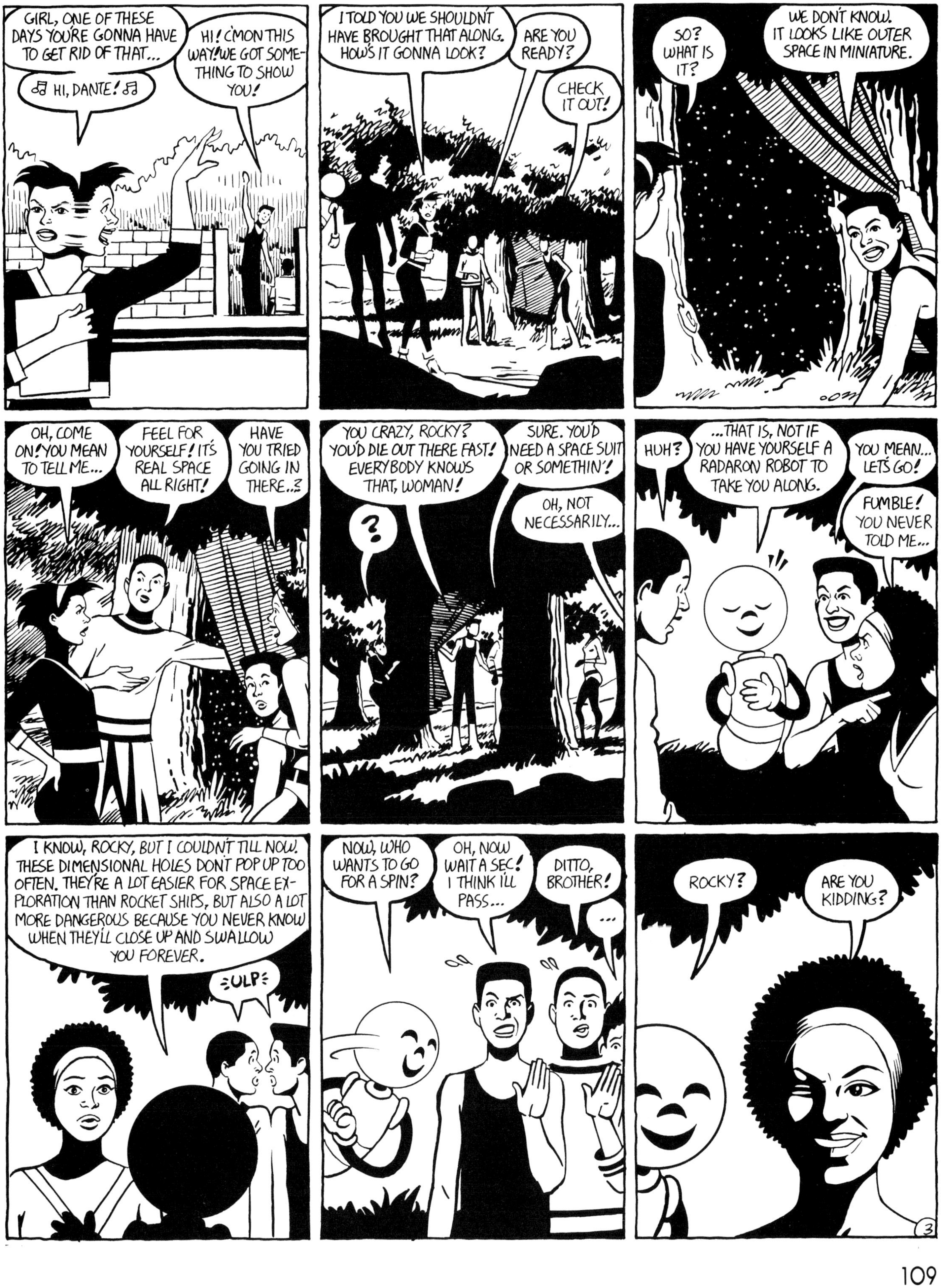

GIRL, ONE OF THESE DAYS YOU'RE GONNA HAVE TO GET RID OF THAT...
♫ HI, DANTE! ♫
HI! C'MON THIS WAY! WE GOT SOMETHING TO SHOW YOU!
I TOLD YOU WE SHOULDN'T HAVE BROUGHT THAT ALONG. HOW'S IT GONNA LOOK?
ARE YOU READY?
CHECK IT OUT!
SO? WHAT IS IT?
WE DON'T KNOW. IT LOOKS LIKE OUTER SPACE IN MINIATURE.
OH, COME ON! YOU MEAN TO TELL ME...
FEEL FOR YOURSELF! IT'S REAL SPACE ALL RIGHT!
HAVE YOU TRIED GOING IN THERE..?
YOU CRAZY, ROCKY? YOU'D DIE OUT THERE FAST! EVERYBODY KNOWS THAT, WOMAN!
SURE. YOU'D NEED A SPACE SUIT OR SOMETHIN'!
?
OH, NOT NECESSARILY...
HUH?
...THAT IS, NOT IF YOU HAVE YOURSELF A RADARON ROBOT TO TAKE YOU ALONG.
YOU MEAN... LET'S GO!
FUMBLE! YOU NEVER TOLD ME...
I KNOW, ROCKY, BUT I COULDN'T TILL NOW. THESE DIMENSIONAL HOLES DON'T POP UP TOO OFTEN. THEY'RE A LOT EASIER FOR SPACE EXPLORATION THAN ROCKET SHIPS, BUT ALSO A LOT MORE DANGEROUS BECAUSE YOU NEVER KNOW WHEN THEY'LL CLOSE UP AND SWALLOW YOU FOREVER.
ULP
NOW, WHO WANTS TO GO FOR A SPIN?
OH, NOW WAIT A SEC! I THINK I'LL PASS...
DITTO, BROTHER!
...
ROCKY?
ARE YOU KIDDING?
3

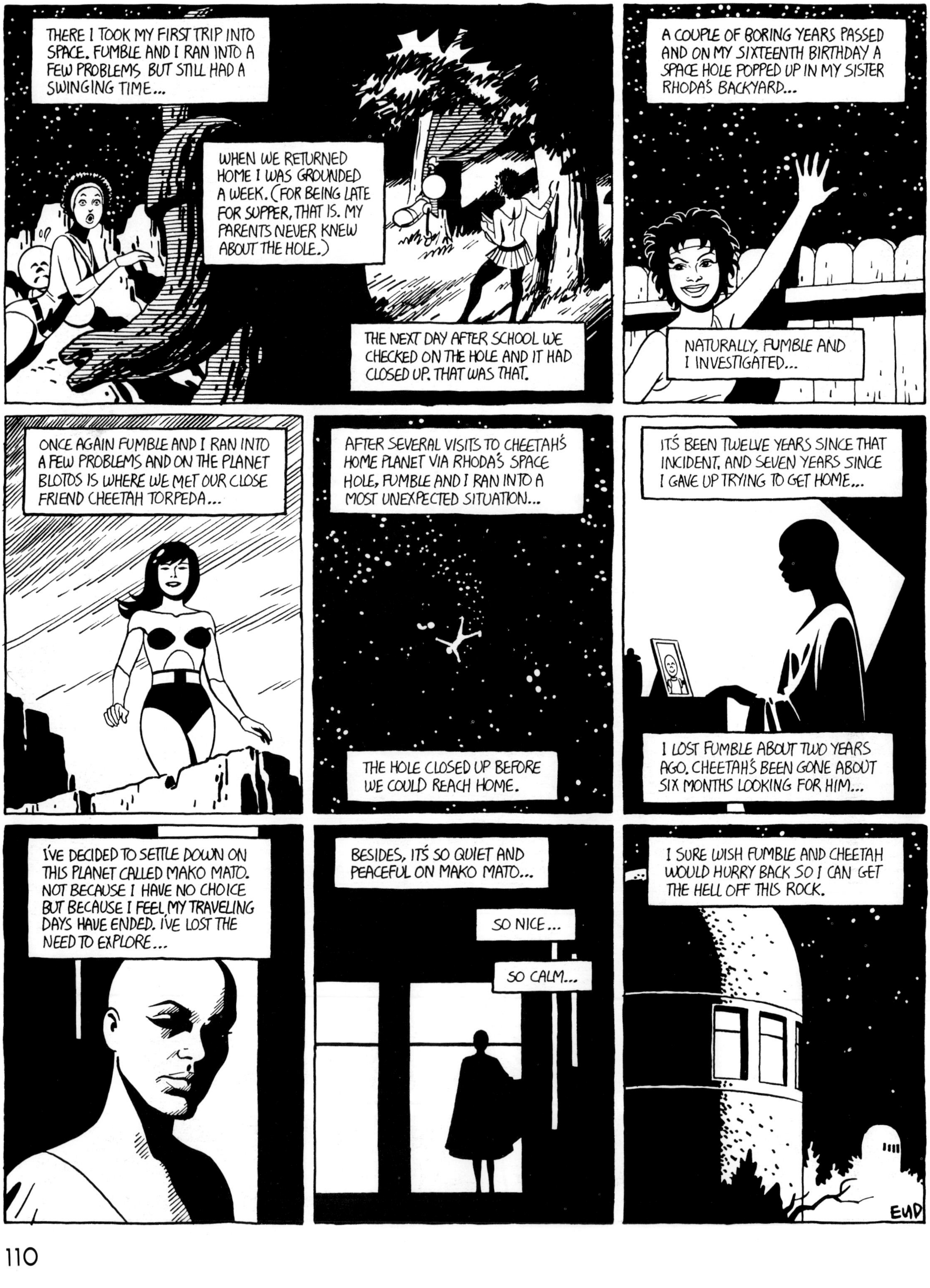
THERE I TOOK MY FIRST TRIP INTO SPACE. FUMBLE AND I RAN INTO A FEW PROBLEMS BUT STILL HAD A SWINGING TIME...
WHEN WE RETURNED HOME I WAS GROUNDED A WEEK. (FOR BEING LATE FOR SUPPER, THAT IS. MY PARENTS NEVER KNEW ABOUT THE HOLE.)
THE NEXT DAY AFTER SCHOOL WE CHECKED ON THE HOLE AND IT HAD CLOSED UP. THAT WAS THAT.
A COUPLE OF BORING YEARS PASSED AND ON MY SIXTEENTH BIRTHDAY A SPACE HOLE POPPED UP IN MY SISTER RHODA'S BACKYARD...
NATURALLY, FUMBLE AND I INVESTIGATED...
ONCE AGAIN FUMBLE AND I RAN INTO A FEW PROBLEMS AND ON THE PLANET BLOTOS IS WHERE WE MET OUR CLOSE FRIEND CHEETAH TORPEDA...
AFTER SEVERAL VISITS TO CHEETAH'S HOME PLANET VIA RHODA'S SPACE HOLE, FUMBLE AND I RAN INTO A MOST UNEXPECTED SITUATION...
THE HOLE CLOSED UP BEFORE WE COULD REACH HOME.
IT'S BEEN TWELVE YEARS SINCE THAT INCIDENT, AND SEVEN YEARS SINCE I GAVE UP TRYING TO GET HOME...
I LOST FUMBLE ABOUT TWO YEARS AGO. CHEETAH'S BEEN GONE ABOUT SIX MONTHS LOOKING FOR HIM...
I'VE DECIDED TO SETTLE DOWN ON THIS PLANET CALLED MAKO MATO. NOT BECAUSE I HAVE NO CHOICE BUT BECAUSE I FEEL MY TRAVELING DAYS HAVE ENDED. I'VE LOST THE NEED TO EXPLORE...
BESIDES, IT'S SO QUIET AND PEACEFUL ON MAKO MATO...
SO NICE...
SO CALM...
I SURE WISH FUMBLE AND CHEETAH WOULD HURRY BACK SO I CAN GET THE HELL OFF THIS ROCK.
END

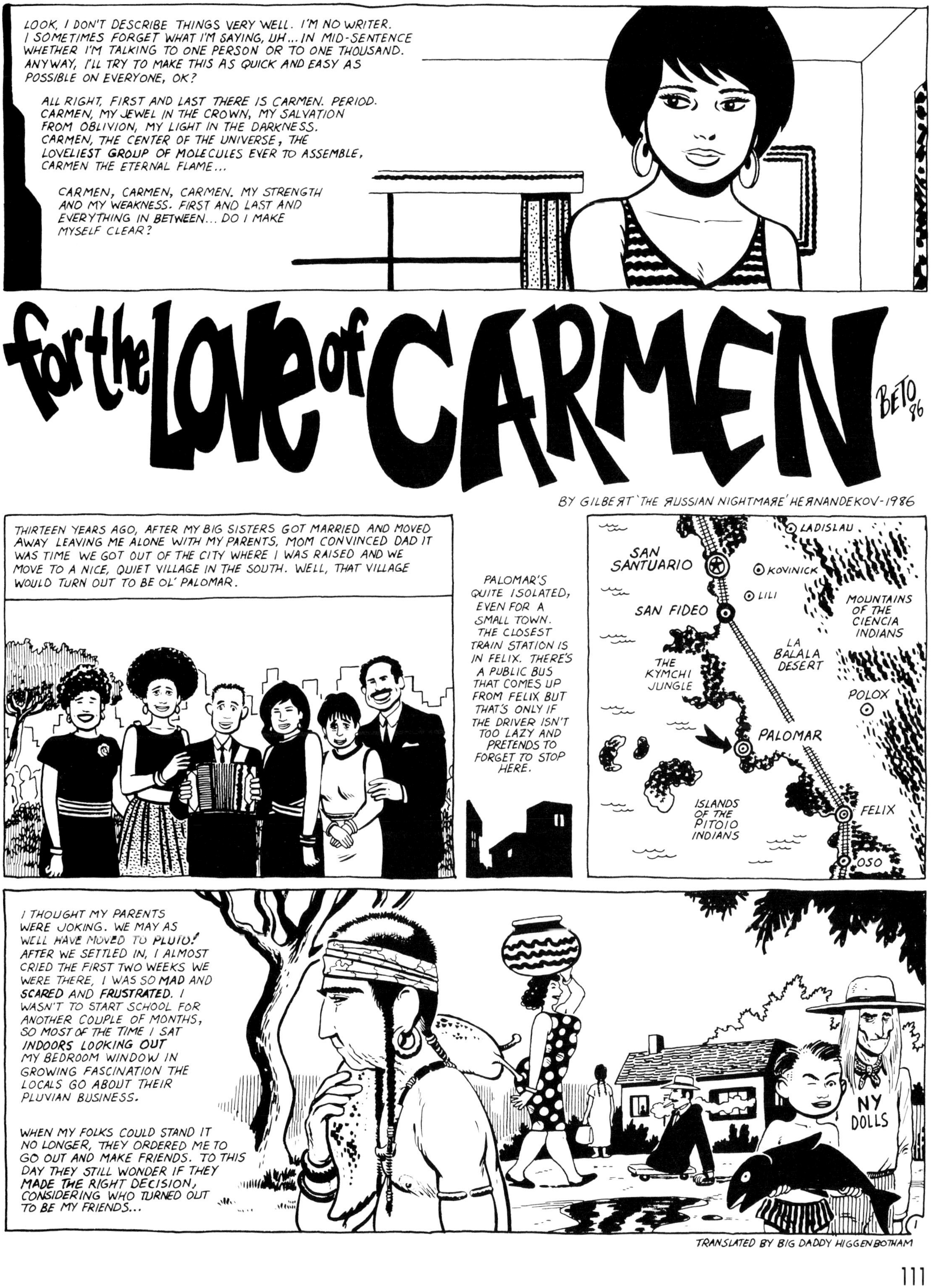
LOOK, I DON'T DESCRIBE THINGS VERY WELL. I'M NO WRITER. I SOMETIMES FORGET WHAT I'M SAYING, UH... IN MID-SENTENCE WHETHER I'M TALKING TO ONE PERSON OR TO ONE THOUSAND. ANYWAY, I'LL TRY TO MAKE THIS AS QUICK AND EASY AS POSSIBLE ON EVERYONE, OK?
ALL RIGHT, FIRST AND LAST THERE IS CARMEN. PERIOD. CARMEN, MY JEWEL IN THE CROWN, MY SALVATION FROM OBLIVION, MY LIGHT IN THE DARKNESS. CARMEN, THE CENTER OF THE UNIVERSE, THE LOVELIEST GROUP OF MOLECULES EVER TO ASSEMBLE, CARMEN THE ETERNAL FLAME...
CARMEN, CARMEN, CARMEN. MY STRENGTH AND MY WEAKNESS. FIRST AND LAST AND EVERYTHING IN BETWEEN... DO I MAKE MYSELF CLEAR?
for the LOVE of CARMEN
BETO 86
BY GILBERT 'THE RUSSIAN NIGHTMARE' HERNANDEKOV-1986
THIRTEEN YEARS AGO, AFTER MY BIG SISTERS GOT MARRIED AND MOVED AWAY LEAVING ME ALONE WITH MY PARENTS, MOM CONVINCED DAD IT WAS TIME WE GOT OUT OF THE CITY WHERE I WAS RAISED AND WE MOVE TO A NICE, QUIET VILLAGE IN THE SOUTH. WELL, THAT VILLAGE WOULD TURN OUT TO BE OL' PALOMAR.
PALOMAR'S QUITE ISOLATED, EVEN FOR A SMALL TOWN. THE CLOSEST TRAIN STATION IS IN FELIX. THERE'S A PUBLIC BUS THAT COMES UP FROM FELIX BUT THAT'S ONLY IF THE DRIVER ISN'T TOO LAZY AND PRETENDS TO FORGET TO STOP HERE.
LADISLAU
SAN SANTUARIO
KOVINICK
LILI
SAN FIDEO
MOUNTAINS OF THE CIENCIA INDIANS
LA BALALA DESERT
THE KYMCHI JUNGLE
POLOX
PALOMAR
ISLANDS OF THE PITOIO INDIANS
FELIX
OSO
I THOUGHT MY PARENTS WERE JOKING. WE MAY AS WELL HAVE MOVED TO PLUTO! AFTER WE SETTLED IN, I ALMOST CRIED THE FIRST TWO WEEKS WE WERE THERE, I WAS SO MAD AND SCARED AND FRUSTRATED. I WASN'T TO START SCHOOL FOR ANOTHER COUPLE OF MONTHS, SO MOST OF THE TIME I SAT INDOORS LOOKING OUT MY BEDROOM WINDOW IN GROWING FASCINATION THE LOCALS GO ABOUT THEIR PLUVIAN BUSINESS.
WHEN MY FOLKS COULD STAND IT NO LONGER, THEY ORDERED ME TO GO OUT AND MAKE FRIENDS. TO THIS DAY THEY STILL WONDER IF THEY MADE THE RIGHT DECISION, CONSIDERING WHO TURNED OUT TO BE MY FRIENDS...
NY DOLLS
1
TRANSLATED BY BIG DADDY HIGGENBOTHAM

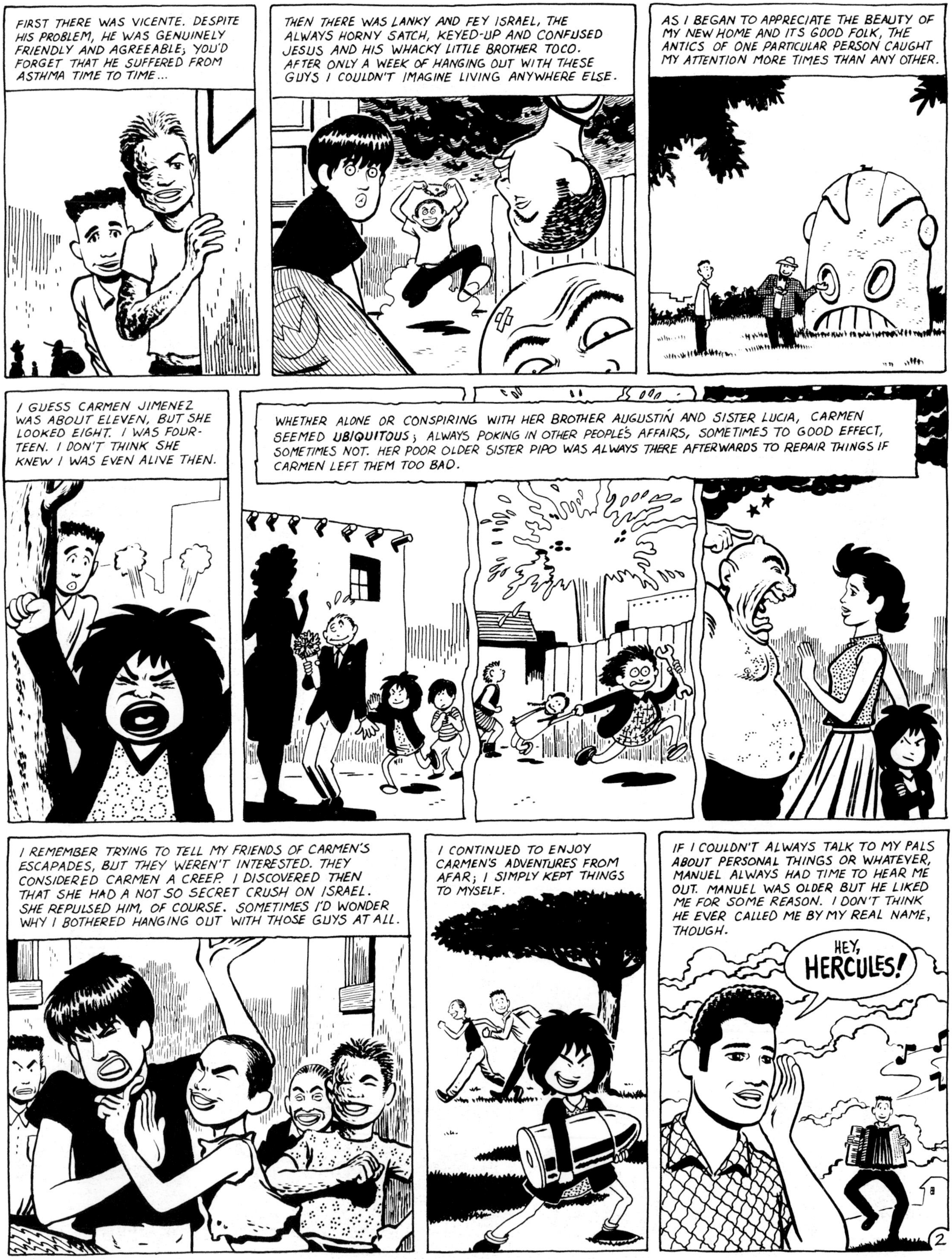
FIRST THERE WAS VICENTE. DESPITE HIS PROBLEM, HE WAS GENUINELY FRIENDLY AND AGREEABLE; YOU'D FORGET THAT HE SUFFERED FROM ASTHMA TIME TO TIME...
THEN THERE WAS LANKY AND FEY ISRAEL, THE ALWAYS HORNY SATCH, KEYED-UP AND CONFUSED JESUS AND HIS WHACKY LITTLE BROTHER TOCO. AFTER ONLY A WEEK OF HANGING OUT WITH THESE GUYS I COULDN'T IMAGINE LIVING ANYWHERE ELSE.
AS I BEGAN TO APPRECIATE THE BEAUTY OF MY NEW HOME AND ITS GOOD FOLK, THE ANTICS OF ONE PARTICULAR PERSON CAUGHT MY ATTENTION MORE TIMES THAN ANY OTHER.
I GUESS CARMEN JIMENEZ WAS ABOUT ELEVEN, BUT SHE LOOKED EIGHT. I WAS FOURTEEN. I DON'T THINK SHE KNEW I WAS EVEN ALIVE THEN.
WHETHER ALONE OR CONSPIRING WITH HER BROTHER AUGUSTÍN AND SISTER LUCIA, CARMEN SEEMED **UBIQUITOUS**; ALWAYS POKING IN OTHER PEOPLE'S AFFAIRS, SOMETIMES TO GOOD EFFECT, SOMETIMES NOT. HER POOR OLDER SISTER PIPO WAS ALWAYS THERE AFTERWARDS TO REPAIR THINGS IF CARMEN LEFT THEM TOO BAD.
I REMEMBER TRYING TO TELL MY FRIENDS OF CARMEN'S ESCAPADES, BUT THEY WEREN'T INTERESTED. THEY CONSIDERED CARMEN A CREEP. I DISCOVERED THEN THAT SHE HAD A NOT SO SECRET CRUSH ON ISRAEL. SHE REPULSED HIM, OF COURSE. SOMETIMES I'D WONDER WHY I BOTHERED HANGING OUT WITH THOSE GUYS AT ALL.
I CONTINUED TO ENJOY CARMEN'S ADVENTURES FROM AFAR; I SIMPLY KEPT THINGS TO MYSELF.
IF I COULDN'T ALWAYS TALK TO MY PALS ABOUT PERSONAL THINGS OR WHATEVER, MANUEL ALWAYS HAD TIME TO HEAR ME OUT. MANUEL WAS OLDER BUT HE LIKED ME FOR SOME REASON. I DON'T THINK HE EVER CALLED ME BY MY REAL NAME, THOUGH.
HEY, HERCULES!
2

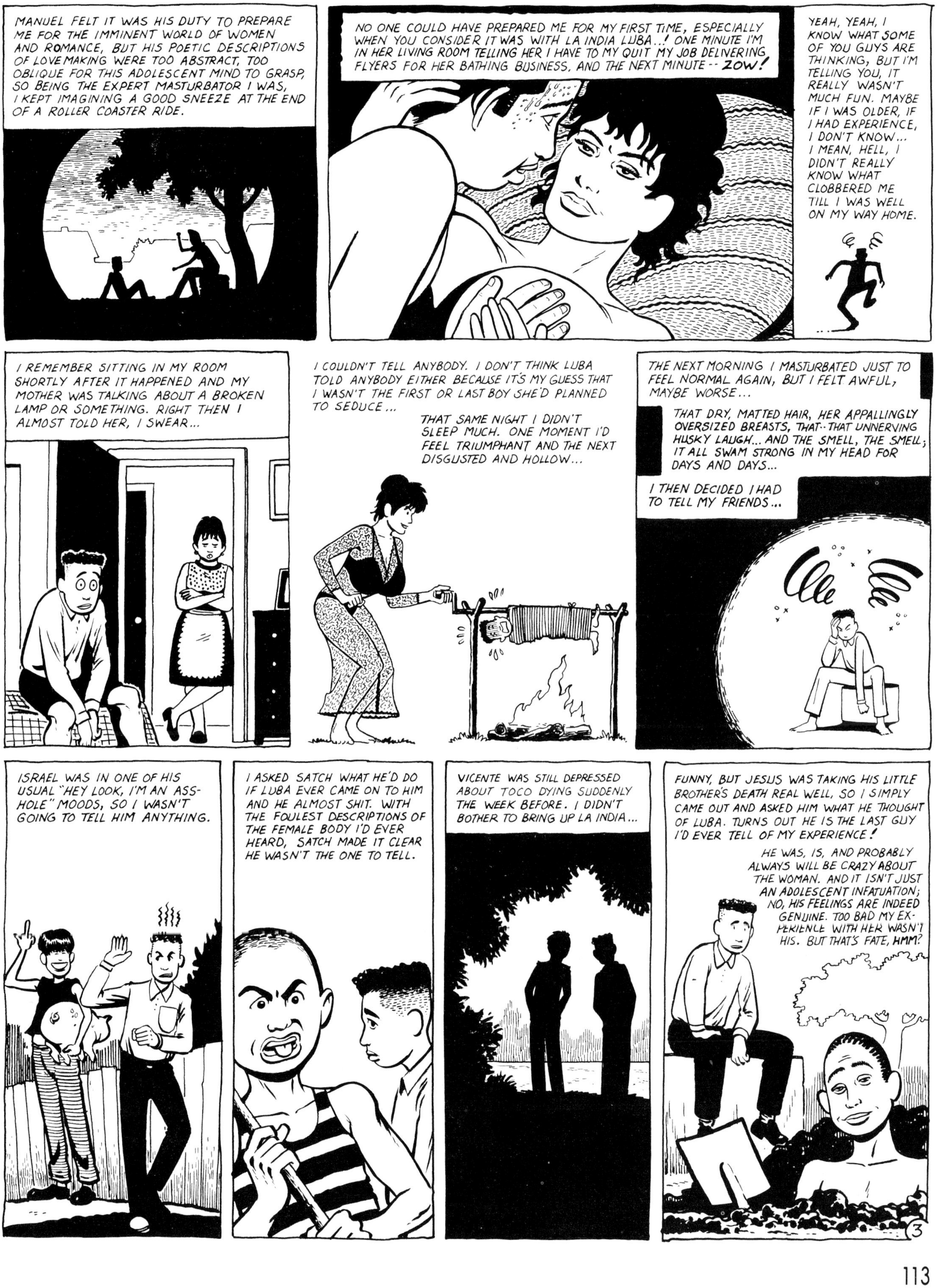

MANUEL FELT IT WAS HIS DUTY TO PREPARE ME FOR THE IMMINENT WORLD OF WOMEN AND ROMANCE, BUT HIS POETIC DESCRIPTIONS OF LOVE MAKING WERE TOO ABSTRACT, TOO OBLIQUE FOR THIS ADOLESCENT MIND TO GRASP, SO BEING THE EXPERT MASTURBATOR I WAS, I KEPT IMAGINING A GOOD SNEEZE AT THE END OF A ROLLER COASTER RIDE.
NO ONE COULD HAVE PREPARED ME FOR MY FIRST TIME, ESPECIALLY WHEN YOU CONSIDER IT WAS WITH LA INDIA LUBA..! ONE MINUTE I'M IN HER LIVING ROOM TELLING HER I HAVE TO MY QUIT MY JOB DELIVERING FLYERS FOR HER BATHING BUSINESS, AND THE NEXT MINUTE -- ZOW!
YEAH, YEAH, I KNOW WHAT SOME OF YOU GUYS ARE THINKING, BUT I'M TELLING YOU, IT REALLY WASN'T MUCH FUN. MAYBE IF I WAS OLDER, IF I HAD EXPERIENCE, I DON'T KNOW... I MEAN, HELL, I DIDN'T REALLY KNOW WHAT CLOBBERED ME TILL I WAS WELL ON MY WAY HOME.
I REMEMBER SITTING IN MY ROOM SHORTLY AFTER IT HAPPENED AND MY MOTHER WAS TALKING ABOUT A BROKEN LAMP OR SOMETHING. RIGHT THEN I ALMOST TOLD HER, I SWEAR...
I COULDN'T TELL ANYBODY. I DON'T THINK LUBA TOLD ANYBODY EITHER BECAUSE IT'S MY GUESS THAT I WASN'T THE FIRST OR LAST BOY SHE'D PLANNED TO SEDUCE...
THAT SAME NIGHT I DIDN'T SLEEP MUCH. ONE MOMENT I'D FEEL TRIUMPHANT AND THE NEXT DISGUSTED AND HOLLOW...
THE NEXT MORNING I MASTURBATED JUST TO FEEL NORMAL AGAIN, BUT I FELT AWFUL, MAYBE WORSE...
THAT DRY, MATTED HAIR, HER APPALLINGLY OVERSIZED BREASTS, THAT··THAT UNNERVING HUSKY LAUGH... AND THE SMELL, THE SMELL; IT ALL SWAM STRONG IN MY HEAD FOR DAYS AND DAYS...
I THEN DECIDED I HAD TO TELL MY FRIENDS...
ISRAEL WAS IN ONE OF HIS USUAL "HEY LOOK, I'M AN ASS-HOLE" MOODS, SO I WASN'T GOING TO TELL HIM ANYTHING.
I ASKED SATCH WHAT HE'D DO IF LUBA EVER CAME ON TO HIM AND HE ALMOST SHIT. WITH THE FOULEST DESCRIPTIONS OF THE FEMALE BODY I'D EVER HEARD, SATCH MADE IT CLEAR HE WASN'T THE ONE TO TELL.
VICENTE WAS STILL DEPRESSED ABOUT TOCO DYING SUDDENLY THE WEEK BEFORE. I DIDN'T BOTHER TO BRING UP LA INDIA...
FUNNY, BUT JESUS WAS TAKING HIS LITTLE BROTHER'S DEATH REAL WELL, SO I SIMPLY CAME OUT AND ASKED HIM WHAT HE THOUGHT OF LUBA. TURNS OUT HE IS THE LAST GUY I'D EVER TELL OF MY EXPERIENCE!
HE WAS, IS, AND PROBABLY ALWAYS WILL BE CRAZY ABOUT THE WOMAN. AND IT ISN'T JUST AN ADOLESCENT INFATUATION; NO, HIS FEELINGS ARE INDEED GENUINE. TOO BAD MY EX-PERIENCE WITH HER WASN'T HIS. BUT THAT'S FATE, HMM?
3

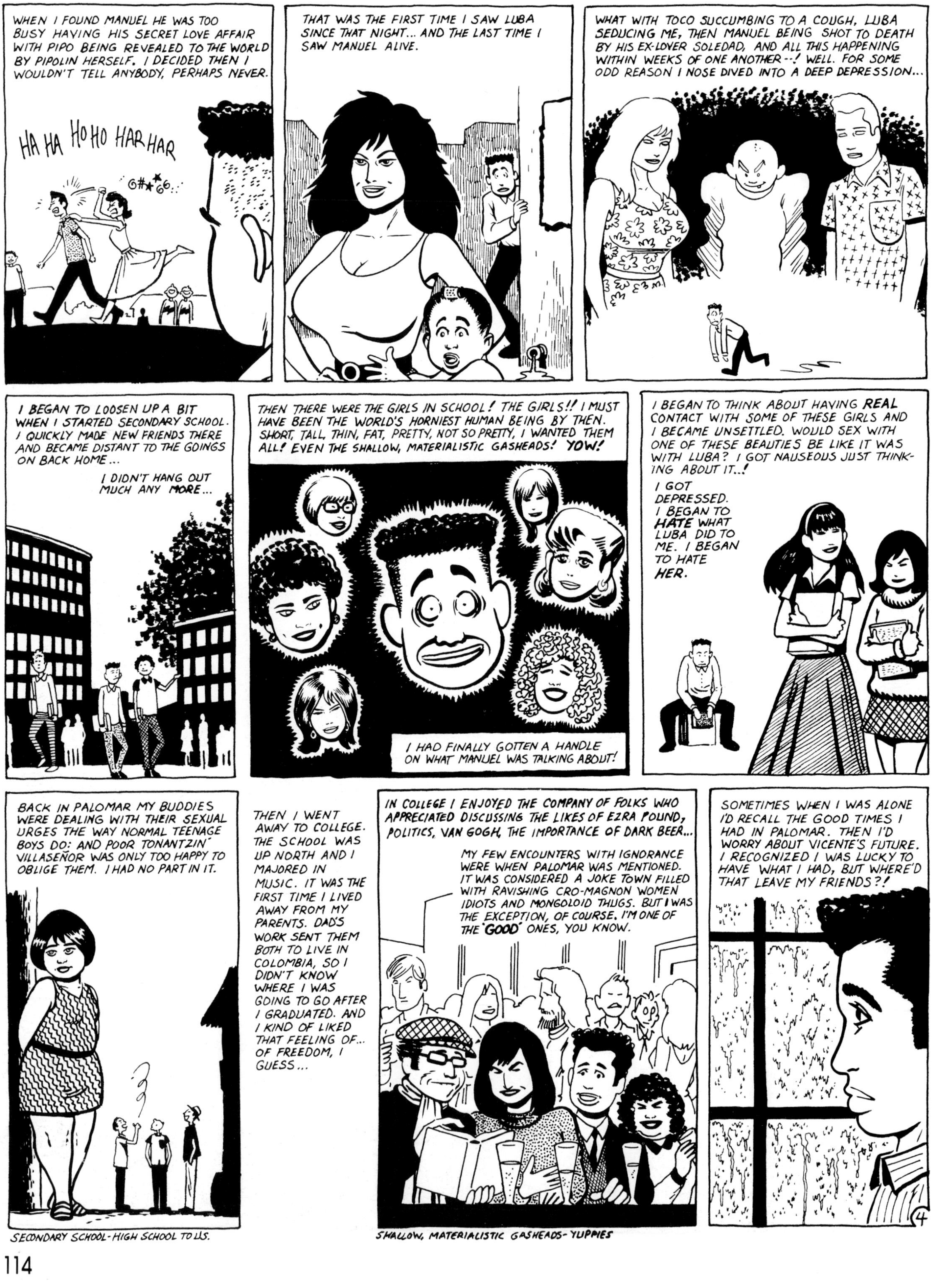
WHEN I FOUND MANUEL HE WAS TOO BUSY HAVING HIS SECRET LOVE AFFAIR WITH PIPO BEING REVEALED TO THE WORLD BY PIPOLIN HERSELF. I DECIDED THEN I WOULDN'T TELL ANYBODY, PERHAPS NEVER.
HA HA HO HO HAR HAR
THAT WAS THE FIRST TIME I SAW LUBA SINCE THAT NIGHT... AND THE LAST TIME I SAW MANUEL ALIVE.
WHAT WITH TOCO SUCCUMBING TO A COUGH, LUBA SEDUCING ME, THEN MANUEL BEING SHOT TO DEATH BY HIS EX-LOVER SOLEDAD, AND ALL THIS HAPPENING WITHIN WEEKS OF ONE ANOTHER --! WELL. FOR SOME ODD REASON I NOSE DIVED INTO A DEEP DEPRESSION...
I BEGAN TO LOOSEN UP A BIT WHEN I STARTED SECONDARY SCHOOL. I QUICKLY MADE NEW FRIENDS THERE AND BECAME DISTANT TO THE GOINGS ON BACK HOME...
I DIDN'T HANG OUT MUCH ANY MORE...
THEN THERE WERE THE GIRLS IN SCHOOL! THE GIRLS!! I MUST HAVE BEEN THE WORLD'S HORNIEST HUMAN BEING BY THEN. SHORT, TALL, THIN, FAT, PRETTY, NOT SO PRETTY, I WANTED THEM ALL! EVEN THE SHALLOW, MATERIALISTIC GASHEADS! YOW!
I HAD FINALLY GOTTEN A HANDLE ON WHAT MANUEL WAS TALKING ABOUT!
I BEGAN TO THINK ABOUT HAVING REAL CONTACT WITH SOME OF THESE GIRLS AND I BECAME UNSETTLED. WOULD SEX WITH ONE OF THESE BEAUTIES BE LIKE IT WAS WITH LUBA? I GOT NAUSEOUS JUST THINKING ABOUT IT...!
I GOT DEPRESSED. I BEGAN TO HATE WHAT LUBA DID TO ME. I BEGAN TO HATE HER.
BACK IN PALOMAR MY BUDDIES WERE DEALING WITH THEIR SEXUAL URGES THE WAY NORMAL TEENAGE BOYS DO: AND POOR TONANTZIN VILLASEÑOR WAS ONLY TOO HAPPY TO OBLIGE THEM. I HAD NO PART IN IT.
SECONDARY SCHOOL-HIGH SCHOOL TO US.
THEN I WENT AWAY TO COLLEGE. THE SCHOOL WAS UP NORTH AND I MAJORED IN MUSIC. IT WAS THE FIRST TIME I LIVED AWAY FROM MY PARENTS. DAD'S WORK SENT THEM BOTH TO LIVE IN COLOMBIA, SO I DIDN'T KNOW WHERE I WAS GOING TO GO AFTER I GRADUATED. AND I KIND OF LIKED THAT FEELING OF... OF FREEDOM, I GUESS...
IN COLLEGE I ENJOYED THE COMPANY OF FOLKS WHO APPRECIATED DISCUSSING THE LIKES OF EZRA POUND, POLITICS, VAN GOGH, THE IMPORTANCE OF DARK BEER...
MY FEW ENCOUNTERS WITH IGNORANCE WERE WHEN PALOMAR WAS MENTIONED. IT WAS CONSIDERED A JOKE TOWN FILLED WITH RAVISHING CRO-MAGNON WOMEN IDIOTS AND MONGOLOID THUGS. BUT I WAS THE EXCEPTION, OF COURSE. I'M ONE OF THE 'GOOD' ONES, YOU KNOW.
SHALLOW, MATERIALISTIC GASHEADS-YUPPIES
SOMETIMES WHEN I WAS ALONE I'D RECALL THE GOOD TIMES I HAD IN PALOMAR. THEN I'D WORRY ABOUT VICENTE'S FUTURE. I RECOGNIZED I WAS LUCKY TO HAVE WHAT I HAD, BUT WHERE'D THAT LEAVE MY FRIENDS?!
4

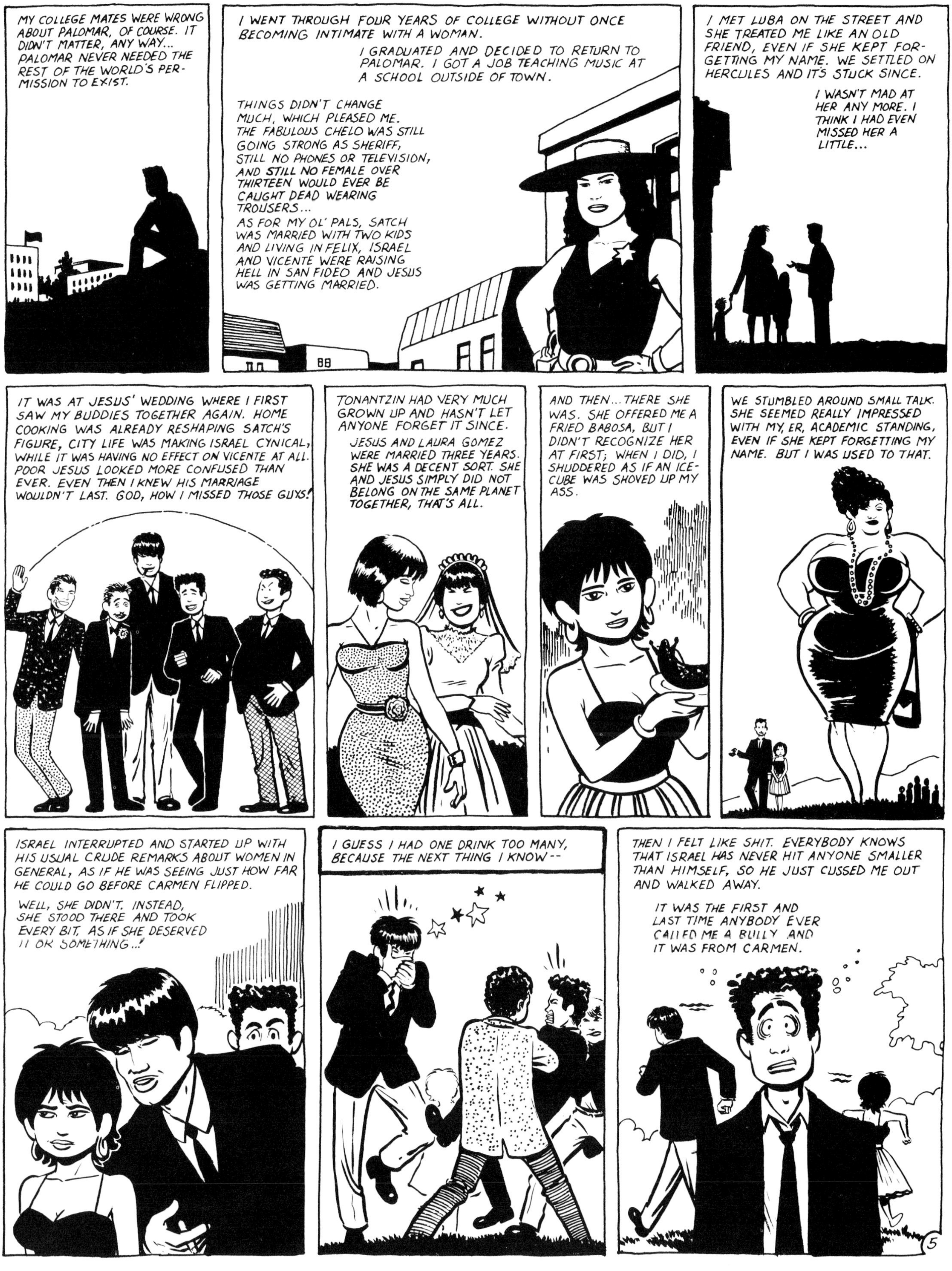
MY COLLEGE MATES WERE WRONG ABOUT PALOMAR, OF COURSE. IT DIDN'T MATTER, ANY WAY... PALOMAR NEVER NEEDED THE REST OF THE WORLD'S PERMISSION TO EXIST.
I WENT THROUGH FOUR YEARS OF COLLEGE WITHOUT ONCE BECOMING INTIMATE WITH A WOMAN.
I GRADUATED AND DECIDED TO RETURN TO PALOMAR. I GOT A JOB TEACHING MUSIC AT A SCHOOL OUTSIDE OF TOWN.
THINGS DIDN'T CHANGE MUCH, WHICH PLEASED ME. THE FABULOUS CHELO WAS STILL GOING STRONG AS SHERIFF, STILL NO PHONES OR TELEVISION, AND STILL NO FEMALE OVER THIRTEEN WOULD EVER BE CAUGHT DEAD WEARING TROUSERS...
AS FOR MY OL' PALS, SATCH WAS MARRIED WITH TWO KIDS AND LIVING IN FELIX, ISRAEL AND VICENTE WERE RAISING HELL IN SAN FIDEO AND JESUS WAS GETTING MARRIED.
I MET LUBA ON THE STREET AND SHE TREATED ME LIKE AN OLD FRIEND, EVEN IF SHE KEPT FORGETTING MY NAME. WE SETTLED ON HERCULES AND IT'S STUCK SINCE.
I WASN'T MAD AT HER ANY MORE. I THINK I HAD EVEN MISSED HER A LITTLE...
IT WAS AT JESUS' WEDDING WHERE I FIRST SAW MY BUDDIES TOGETHER AGAIN. HOME COOKING WAS ALREADY RESHAPING SATCH'S FIGURE, CITY LIFE WAS MAKING ISRAEL CYNICAL, WHILE IT WAS HAVING NO EFFECT ON VICENTE AT ALL. POOR JESUS LOOKED MORE CONFUSED THAN EVER. EVEN THEN I KNEW HIS MARRIAGE WOULDN'T LAST. GOD, HOW I MISSED THOSE GUYS!
TONANTZIN HAD VERY MUCH GROWN UP AND HASN'T LET ANYONE FORGET IT SINCE.
JESUS AND LAURA GOMEZ WERE MARRIED THREE YEARS. SHE WAS A DECENT SORT. SHE AND JESUS SIMPLY DID NOT BELONG ON THE SAME PLANET TOGETHER, THAT'S ALL.
AND THEN... THERE SHE WAS. SHE OFFERED ME A FRIED BABOSA, BUT I DIDN'T RECOGNIZE HER AT FIRST; WHEN I DID, I SHUDDERED AS IF AN ICE-CUBE WAS SHOVED UP MY ASS.
WE STUMBLED AROUND SMALL TALK. SHE SEEMED REALLY IMPRESSED WITH MY, ER, ACADEMIC STANDING, EVEN IF SHE KEPT FORGETTING MY NAME. BUT I WAS USED TO THAT.
ISRAEL INTERRUPTED AND STARTED UP WITH HIS USUAL CRUDE REMARKS ABOUT WOMEN IN GENERAL, AS IF HE WAS SEEING JUST HOW FAR HE COULD GO BEFORE CARMEN FLIPPED.
WELL, SHE DIDN'T. INSTEAD, SHE STOOD THERE AND TOOK EVERY BIT, AS IF SHE DESERVED IT OR SOMETHING...!
I GUESS I HAD ONE DRINK TOO MANY, BECAUSE THE NEXT THING I KNOW--
THEN I FELT LIKE SHIT. EVERYBODY KNOWS THAT ISRAEL HAS NEVER HIT ANYONE SMALLER THAN HIMSELF, SO HE JUST CUSSED ME OUT AND WALKED AWAY.
IT WAS THE FIRST AND LAST TIME ANYBODY EVER CALLED ME A BULLY AND IT WAS FROM CARMEN.
5

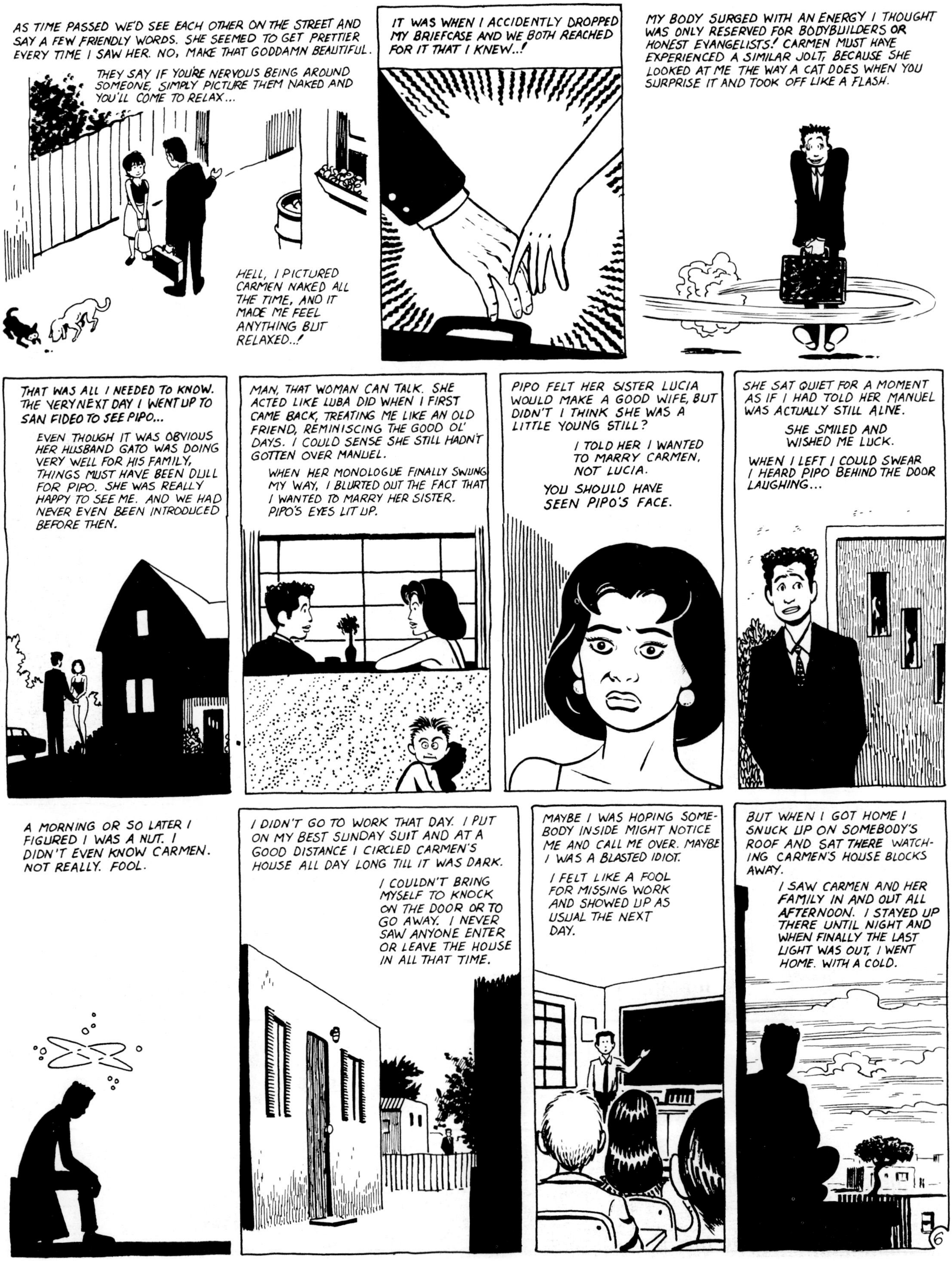
AS TIME PASSED WE'D SEE EACH OTHER ON THE STREET AND SAY A FEW FRIENDLY WORDS. SHE SEEMED TO GET PRETTIER EVERY TIME I SAW HER. NO, MAKE THAT GODDAMN BEAUTIFUL.
THEY SAY IF YOU'RE NERVOUS BEING AROUND SOMEONE, SIMPLY PICTURE THEM NAKED AND YOU'LL COME TO RELAX...
HELL, I PICTURED CARMEN NAKED ALL THE TIME, AND IT MADE ME FEEL ANYTHING BUT RELAXED..!
IT WAS WHEN I ACCIDENTLY DROPPED MY BRIEFCASE AND WE BOTH REACHED FOR IT THAT I KNEW..!
MY BODY SURGED WITH AN ENERGY I THOUGHT WAS ONLY RESERVED FOR BODYBUILDERS OR HONEST EVANGELISTS! CARMEN MUST HAVE EXPERIENCED A SIMILAR JOLT, BECAUSE SHE LOOKED AT ME THE WAY A CAT DOES WHEN YOU SURPRISE IT AND TOOK OFF LIKE A FLASH.
THAT WAS ALL I NEEDED TO KNOW. THE VERY NEXT DAY I WENT UP TO SAN FIDEO TO SEE PIPO...
EVEN THOUGH IT WAS OBVIOUS HER HUSBAND GATO WAS DOING VERY WELL FOR HIS FAMILY, THINGS MUST HAVE BEEN DULL FOR PIPO. SHE WAS REALLY HAPPY TO SEE ME. AND WE HAD NEVER EVEN BEEN INTRODUCED BEFORE THEN.
MAN, THAT WOMAN CAN TALK. SHE ACTED LIKE LUBA DID WHEN I FIRST CAME BACK, TREATING ME LIKE AN OLD FRIEND, REMINISCING THE GOOD OL' DAYS. I COULD SENSE SHE STILL HADN'T GOTTEN OVER MANUEL.
WHEN HER MONOLOGUE FINALLY SWUNG MY WAY, I BLURTED OUT THE FACT THAT I WANTED TO MARRY HER SISTER. PIPO'S EYES LIT UP.
PIPO FELT HER SISTER LUCIA WOULD MAKE A GOOD WIFE, BUT DIDN'T I THINK SHE WAS A LITTLE YOUNG STILL?
I TOLD HER I WANTED TO MARRY CARMEN, NOT LUCIA.
YOU SHOULD HAVE SEEN PIPO'S FACE.
SHE SAT QUIET FOR A MOMENT AS IF I HAD TOLD HER MANUEL WAS ACTUALLY STILL ALIVE.
SHE SMILED AND WISHED ME LUCK.
WHEN I LEFT I COULD SWEAR I HEARD PIPO BEHIND THE DOOR LAUGHING...
A MORNING OR SO LATER I FIGURED I WAS A NUT. I DIDN'T EVEN KNOW CARMEN. NOT REALLY. FOOL.
I DIDN'T GO TO WORK THAT DAY. I PUT ON MY BEST SUNDAY SUIT AND AT A GOOD DISTANCE I CIRCLED CARMEN'S HOUSE ALL DAY LONG TILL IT WAS DARK.
I COULDN'T BRING MYSELF TO KNOCK ON THE DOOR OR TO GO AWAY. I NEVER SAW ANYONE ENTER OR LEAVE THE HOUSE IN ALL THAT TIME.
MAYBE I WAS HOPING SOMEBODY INSIDE MIGHT NOTICE ME AND CALL ME OVER. MAYBE I WAS A BLASTED IDIOT.
I FELT LIKE A FOOL FOR MISSING WORK AND SHOWED UP AS USUAL THE NEXT DAY.
BUT WHEN I GOT HOME I SNUCK UP ON SOMEBODY'S ROOF AND SAT THERE WATCHING CARMEN'S HOUSE BLOCKS AWAY.
I SAW CARMEN AND HER FAMILY IN AND OUT ALL AFTERNOON. I STAYED UP THERE UNTIL NIGHT AND WHEN FINALLY THE LAST LIGHT WAS OUT, I WENT HOME. WITH A COLD.
6

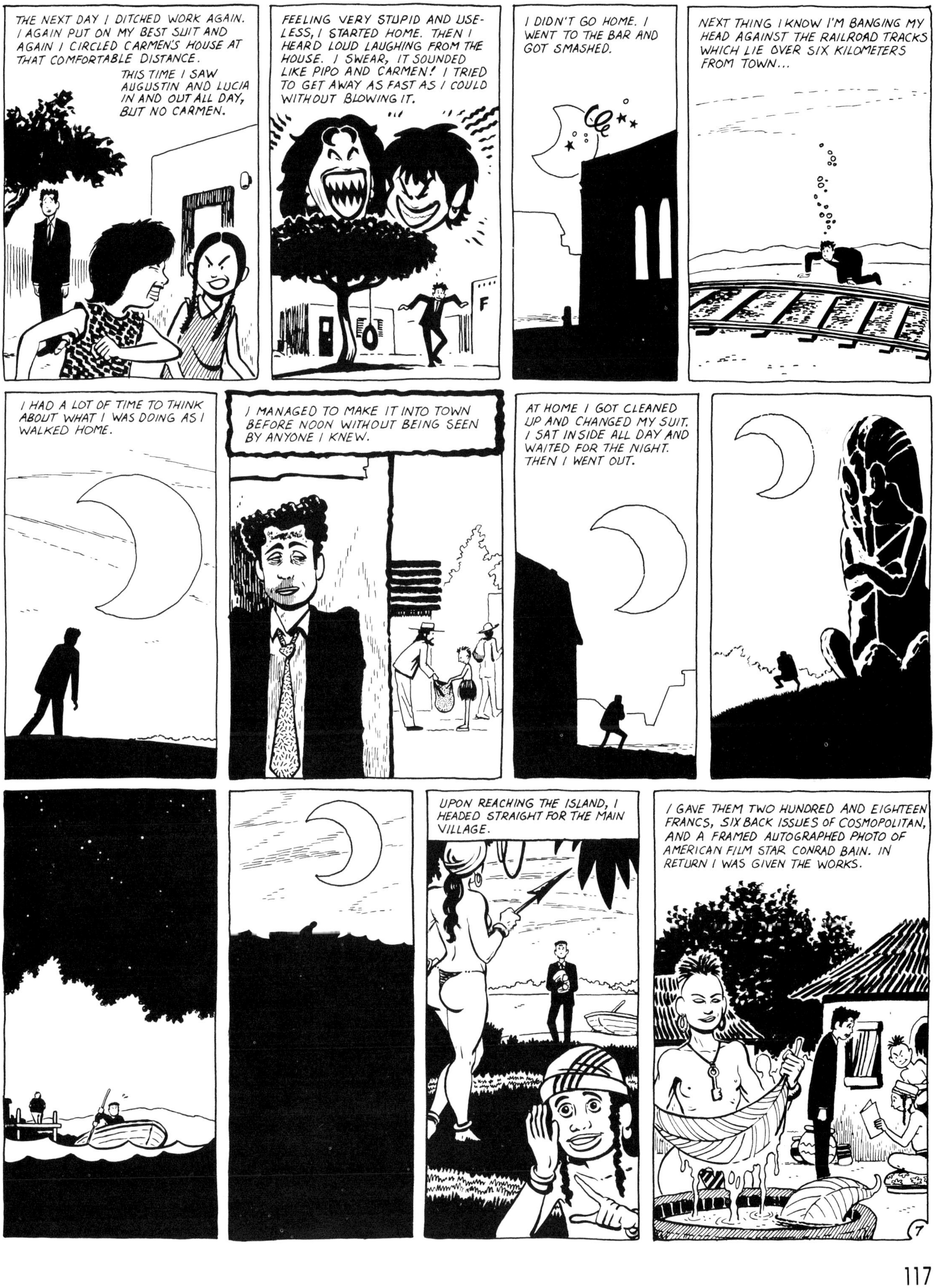

THE NEXT DAY I DITCHED WORK AGAIN. I AGAIN PUT ON MY BEST SUIT AND AGAIN I CIRCLED CARMEN'S HOUSE AT THAT COMFORTABLE DISTANCE.
THIS TIME I SAW AUGUSTIN AND LUCIA IN AND OUT ALL DAY, BUT NO CARMEN.
FEELING VERY STUPID AND USELESS, I STARTED HOME. THEN I HEARD LOUD LAUGHING FROM THE HOUSE. I SWEAR, IT SOUNDED LIKE PIPO AND CARMEN! I TRIED TO GET AWAY AS FAST AS I COULD WITHOUT BLOWING IT.
F
I DIDN'T GO HOME. I WENT TO THE BAR AND GOT SMASHED.
NEXT THING I KNOW I'M BANGING MY HEAD AGAINST THE RAILROAD TRACKS WHICH LIE OVER SIX KILOMETERS FROM TOWN...
I HAD A LOT OF TIME TO THINK ABOUT WHAT I WAS DOING AS I WALKED HOME.
I MANAGED TO MAKE IT INTO TOWN BEFORE NOON WITHOUT BEING SEEN BY ANYONE I KNEW.
AT HOME I GOT CLEANED UP AND CHANGED MY SUIT. I SAT INSIDE ALL DAY AND WAITED FOR THE NIGHT. THEN I WENT OUT.
UPON REACHING THE ISLAND, I HEADED STRAIGHT FOR THE MAIN VILLAGE.
I GAVE THEM TWO HUNDRED AND EIGHTEEN FRANCS, SIX BACK ISSUES OF COSMOPOLITAN, AND A FRAMED AUTOGRAPHED PHOTO OF AMERICAN FILM STAR CONRAD BAIN. IN RETURN I WAS GIVEN THE WORKS.
7

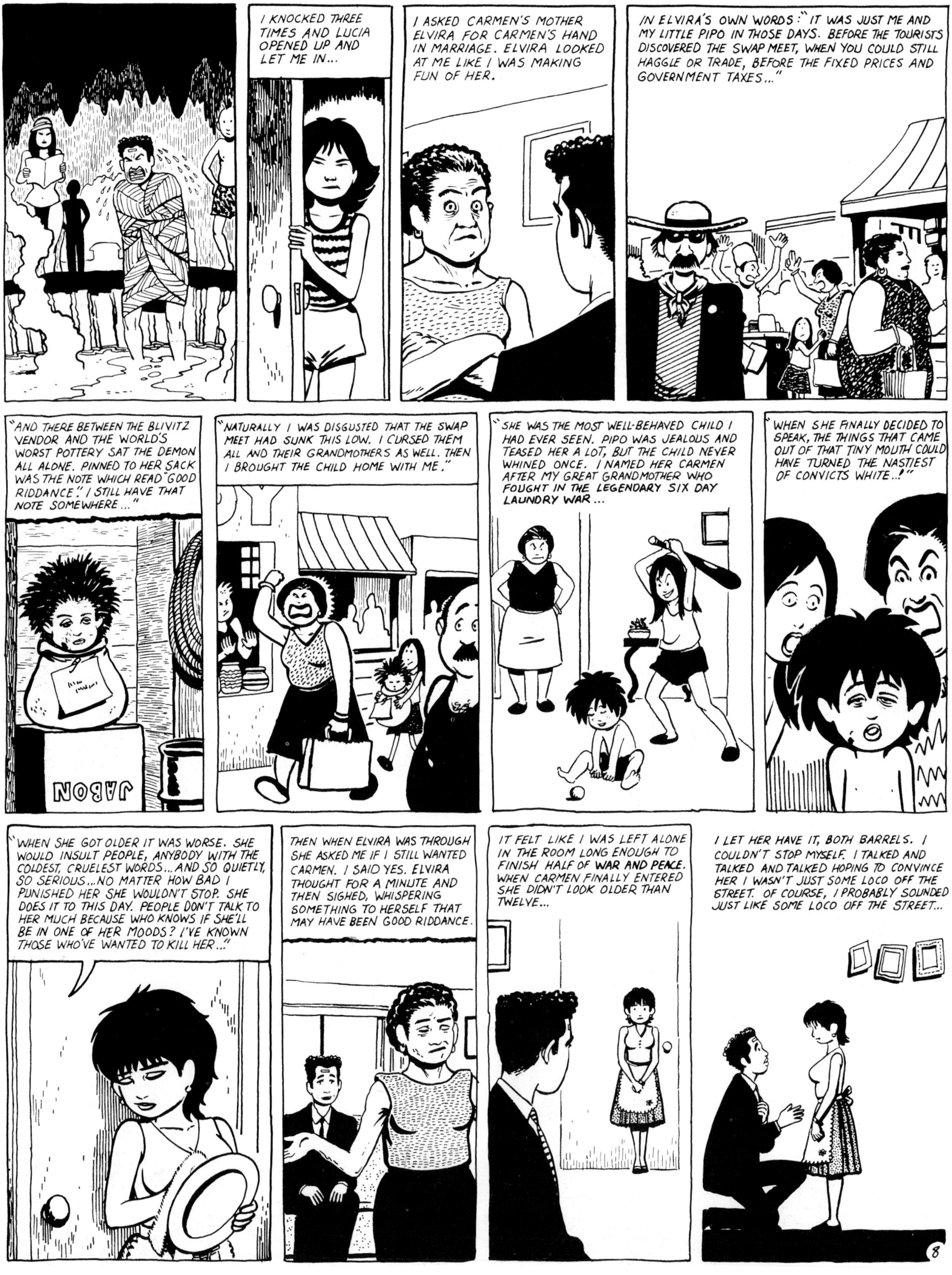
I KNOCKED THREE TIMES AND LUCIA OPENED UP AND LET ME IN...
I ASKED CARMEN'S MOTHER ELVIRA FOR CARMEN'S HAND IN MARRIAGE. ELVIRA LOOKED AT ME LIKE I WAS MAKING FUN OF HER.
IN ELVIRA'S OWN WORDS: "IT WAS JUST ME AND MY LITTLE PIPO IN THOSE DAYS. BEFORE THE TOURISTS DISCOVERED THE SWAP MEET, WHEN YOU COULD STILL HAGGLE OR TRADE, BEFORE THE FIXED PRICES AND GOVERNMENT TAXES..."
"AND THERE BETWEEN THE BLIVITZ VENDOR AND THE WORLD'S WORST POTTERY SAT THE DEMON ALL ALONE. PINNED TO HER SACK WAS THE NOTE WHICH READ "GOOD RIDDANCE." I STILL HAVE THAT NOTE SOMEWHERE..."
JABON
"NATURALLY I WAS DISGUSTED THAT THE SWAP MEET HAD SUNK THIS LOW. I CURSED THEM ALL AND THEIR GRANDMOTHERS AS WELL. THEN I BROUGHT THE CHILD HOME WITH ME."
"SHE WAS THE MOST WELL-BEHAVED CHILD I HAD EVER SEEN. PIPO WAS JEALOUS AND TEASED HER A LOT, BUT THE CHILD NEVER WHINED ONCE. I NAMED HER CARMEN AFTER MY GREAT GRANDMOTHER WHO FOUGHT IN THE LEGENDARY SIX DAY LAUNDRY WAR...
"WHEN SHE FINALLY DECIDED TO SPEAK, THE THINGS THAT CAME OUT OF THAT TINY MOUTH COULD HAVE TURNED THE NASTIEST OF CONVICTS WHITE..!"
"WHEN SHE GOT OLDER IT WAS WORSE. SHE WOULD INSULT PEOPLE, ANYBODY WITH THE COLDEST, CRUELEST WORDS...AND SO QUIETLY, SO SERIOUS...NO MATTER HOW BAD I PUNISHED HER SHE WOULDN'T STOP. SHE DOES IT TO THIS DAY. PEOPLE DON'T TALK TO HER MUCH BECAUSE WHO KNOWS IF SHE'LL BE IN ONE OF HER MOODS? I'VE KNOWN THOSE WHO'VE WANTED TO KILL HER..."
THEN WHEN ELVIRA WAS THROUGH SHE ASKED ME IF I STILL WANTED CARMEN. I SAID YES. ELVIRA THOUGHT FOR A MINUTE AND THEN SIGHED, WHISPERING SOMETHING TO HERSELF THAT MAY HAVE BEEN GOOD RIDDANCE.
IT FELT LIKE I WAS LEFT ALONE IN THE ROOM LONG ENOUGH TO FINISH HALF OF WAR AND PEACE. WHEN CARMEN FINALLY ENTERED SHE DIDN'T LOOK OLDER THAN TWELVE...
I LET HER HAVE IT, BOTH BARRELS. I COULDN'T STOP MYSELF. I TALKED AND TALKED AND TALKED HOPING TO CONVINCE HER I WASN'T JUST SOME LOCO OFF THE STREET. OF COURSE, I PROBABLY SOUNDED JUST LIKE SOME LOCO OFF THE STREET...
8

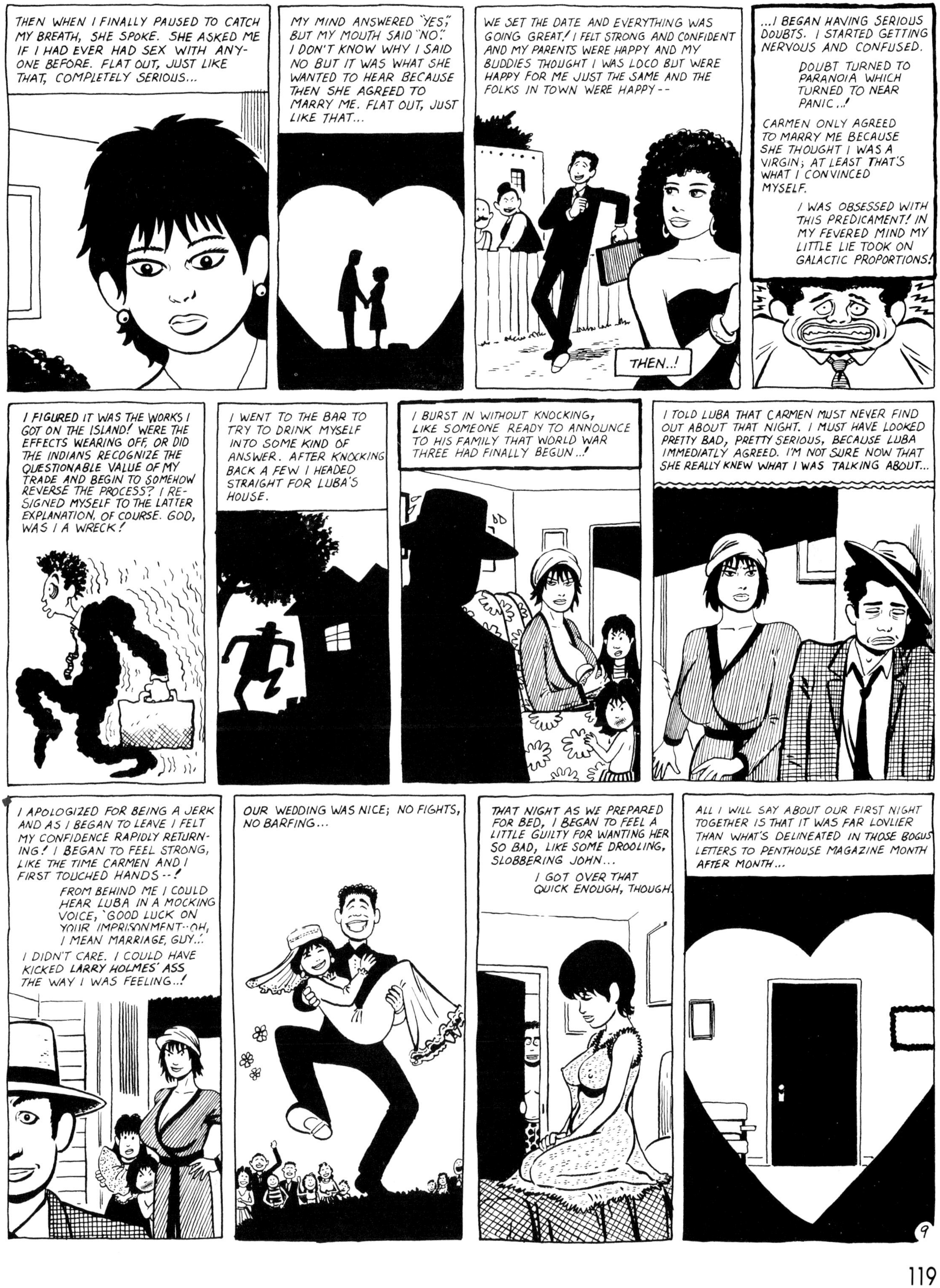
THEN WHEN I FINALLY PAUSED TO CATCH MY BREATH, SHE SPOKE. SHE ASKED ME IF I HAD EVER HAD SEX WITH ANYONE BEFORE. FLAT OUT, JUST LIKE THAT, COMPLETELY SERIOUS...
MY MIND ANSWERED "YES," BUT MY MOUTH SAID "NO." I DON'T KNOW WHY I SAID NO BUT IT WAS WHAT SHE WANTED TO HEAR BECAUSE THEN SHE AGREED TO MARRY ME. FLAT OUT, JUST LIKE THAT...
WE SET THE DATE AND EVERYTHING WAS GOING GREAT! I FELT STRONG AND CONFIDENT AND MY PARENTS WERE HAPPY AND MY BUDDIES THOUGHT I WAS LOCO BUT WERE HAPPY FOR ME JUST THE SAME AND THE FOLKS IN TOWN WERE HAPPY --
THEN..!
...I BEGAN HAVING SERIOUS DOUBTS. I STARTED GETTING NERVOUS AND CONFUSED.
DOUBT TURNED TO PARANOIA WHICH TURNED TO NEAR PANIC...!
CARMEN ONLY AGREED TO MARRY ME BECAUSE SHE THOUGHT I WAS A VIRGIN; AT LEAST THAT'S WHAT I CONVINCED MYSELF.
I WAS OBSESSED WITH THIS PREDICAMENT! IN MY FEVERED MIND MY LITTLE LIE TOOK ON GALACTIC PROPORTIONS!
I FIGURED IT WAS THE WORKS I GOT ON THE ISLAND! WERE THE EFFECTS WEARING OFF, OR DID THE INDIANS RECOGNIZE THE QUESTIONABLE VALUE OF MY TRADE AND BEGIN TO SOMEHOW REVERSE THE PROCESS? I RESIGNED MYSELF TO THE LATTER EXPLANATION, OF COURSE. GOD, WAS I A WRECK!
I WENT TO THE BAR TO TRY TO DRINK MYSELF INTO SOME KIND OF ANSWER. AFTER KNOCKING BACK A FEW I HEADED STRAIGHT FOR LUBA'S HOUSE.
I BURST IN WITHOUT KNOCKING, LIKE SOMEONE READY TO ANNOUNCE TO HIS FAMILY THAT WORLD WAR THREE HAD FINALLY BEGUN...!
I TOLD LUBA THAT CARMEN MUST NEVER FIND OUT ABOUT THAT NIGHT. I MUST HAVE LOOKED PRETTY BAD, PRETTY SERIOUS, BECAUSE LUBA IMMEDIATLY AGREED. I'M NOT SURE NOW THAT SHE REALLY KNEW WHAT I WAS TALKING ABOUT...
I APOLOGIZED FOR BEING A JERK AND AS I BEGAN TO LEAVE I FELT MY CONFIDENCE RAPIDLY RETURNING! I BEGAN TO FEEL STRONG, LIKE THE TIME CARMEN AND I FIRST TOUCHED HANDS --!
FROM BEHIND ME I COULD HEAR LUBA IN A MOCKING VOICE, 'GOOD LUCK ON YOUR IMPRISONMENT--OH, I MEAN MARRIAGE, GUY...'
I DIDN'T CARE. I COULD HAVE KICKED LARRY HOLMES' ASS THE WAY I WAS FEELING...!
OUR WEDDING WAS NICE; NO FIGHTS, NO BARFING...
THAT NIGHT AS WE PREPARED FOR BED, I BEGAN TO FEEL A LITTLE GUILTY FOR WANTING HER SO BAD, LIKE SOME DROOLING, SLOBBERING JOHN...
I GOT OVER THAT QUICK ENOUGH, THOUGH.
ALL I WILL SAY ABOUT OUR FIRST NIGHT TOGETHER IS THAT IT WAS FAR LOVLIER THAN WHAT'S DELINEATED IN THOSE BOGUS LETTERS TO PENTHOUSE MAGAZINE MONTH AFTER MONTH...
9

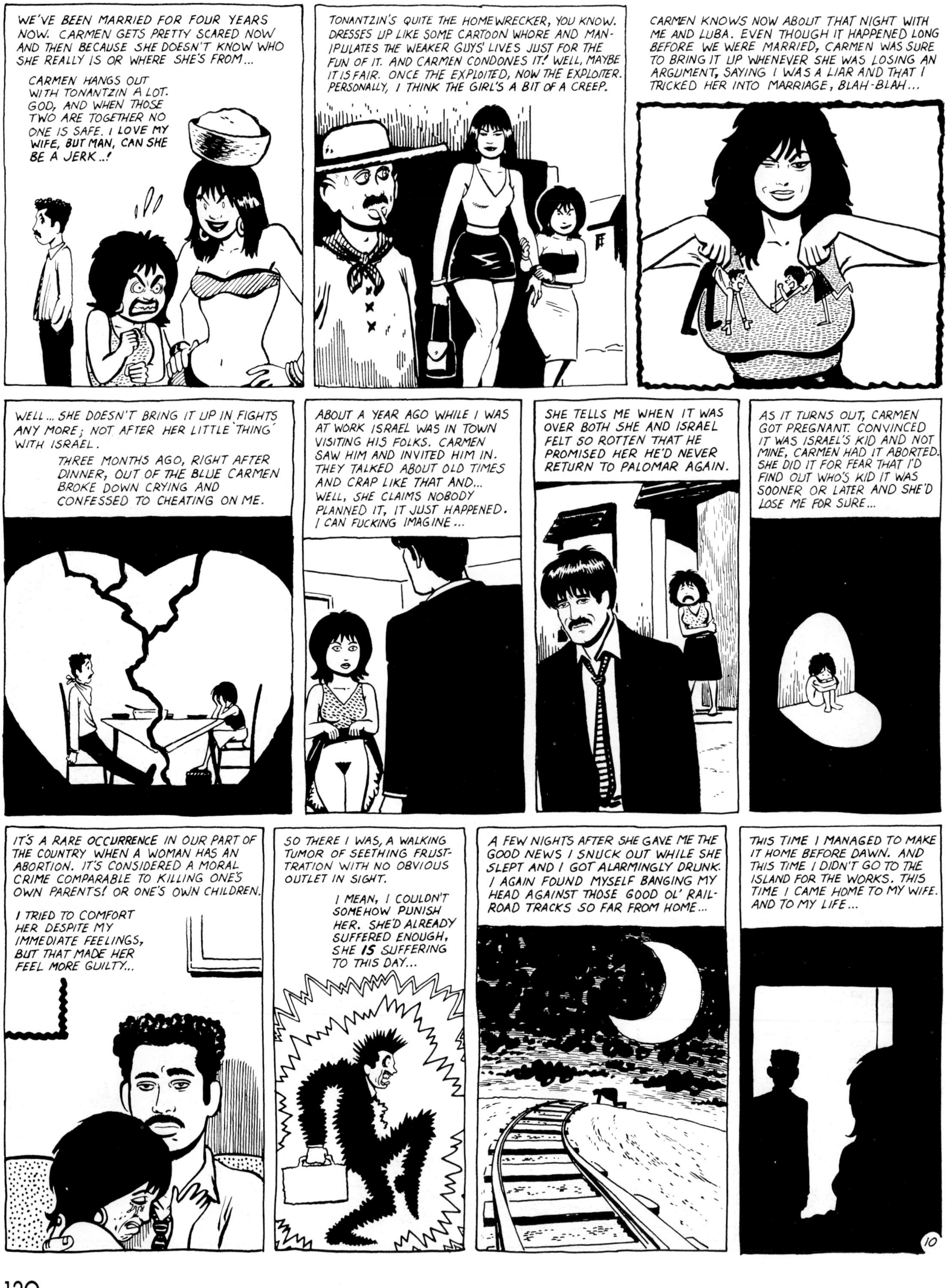
WE'VE BEEN MARRIED FOR FOUR YEARS NOW. CARMEN GETS PRETTY SCARED NOW AND THEN BECAUSE SHE DOESN'T KNOW WHO SHE REALLY IS OR WHERE SHE'S FROM...
CARMEN HANGS OUT WITH TONANTZIN A LOT. GOD, AND WHEN THOSE TWO ARE TOGETHER NO ONE IS SAFE. I LOVE MY WIFE, BUT MAN, CAN SHE BE A JERK..!
TONANTZIN'S QUITE THE HOMEWRECKER, YOU KNOW. DRESSES UP LIKE SOME CARTOON WHORE AND MANIPULATES THE WEAKER GUYS' LIVES JUST FOR THE FUN OF IT. AND CARMEN CONDONES IT! WELL, MAYBE IT IS FAIR. ONCE THE EXPLOITED, NOW THE EXPLOITER. PERSONALLY, I THINK THE GIRL'S A BIT OF A CREEP.
CARMEN KNOWS NOW ABOUT THAT NIGHT WITH ME AND LUBA. EVEN THOUGH IT HAPPENED LONG BEFORE WE WERE MARRIED, CARMEN WAS SURE TO BRING IT UP WHENEVER SHE WAS LOSING AN ARGUMENT, SAYING I WAS A LIAR AND THAT I TRICKED HER INTO MARRIAGE, BLAH-BLAH...
WELL... SHE DOESN'T BRING IT UP IN FIGHTS ANY MORE; NOT AFTER HER LITTLE 'THING' WITH ISRAEL.
THREE MONTHS AGO, RIGHT AFTER DINNER, OUT OF THE BLUE CARMEN BROKE DOWN CRYING AND CONFESSED TO CHEATING ON ME.
ABOUT A YEAR AGO WHILE I WAS AT WORK ISRAEL WAS IN TOWN VISITING HIS FOLKS. CARMEN SAW HIM AND INVITED HIM IN. THEY TALKED ABOUT OLD TIMES AND CRAP LIKE THAT AND... WELL, SHE CLAIMS NOBODY PLANNED IT, IT JUST HAPPENED. I CAN FUCKING IMAGINE...
SHE TELLS ME WHEN IT WAS OVER BOTH SHE AND ISRAEL FELT SO ROTTEN THAT HE PROMISED HER HE'D NEVER RETURN TO PALOMAR AGAIN.
AS IT TURNS OUT, CARMEN GOT PREGNANT. CONVINCED IT WAS ISRAEL'S KID AND NOT MINE, CARMEN HAD IT ABORTED. SHE DID IT FOR FEAR THAT I'D FIND OUT WHO'S KID IT WAS SOONER OR LATER AND SHE'D LOSE ME FOR SURE...
IT'S A RARE OCCURRENCE IN OUR PART OF THE COUNTRY WHEN A WOMAN HAS AN ABORTION. IT'S CONSIDERED A MORAL CRIME COMPARABLE TO KILLING ONE'S OWN PARENTS! OR ONE'S OWN CHILDREN.
I TRIED TO COMFORT HER DESPITE MY IMMEDIATE FEELINGS, BUT THAT MADE HER FEEL MORE GUILTY...
SO THERE I WAS, A WALKING TUMOR OF SEETHING FRUSTRATION WITH NO OBVIOUS OUTLET IN SIGHT.
I MEAN, I COULDN'T SOMEHOW PUNISH HER. SHE'D ALREADY SUFFERED ENOUGH, SHE IS SUFFERING TO THIS DAY...
A FEW NIGHTS AFTER SHE GAVE ME THE GOOD NEWS I SNUCK OUT WHILE SHE SLEPT AND I GOT ALARMINGLY DRUNK. I AGAIN FOUND MYSELF BANGING MY HEAD AGAINST THOSE GOOD OL' RAILROAD TRACKS SO FAR FROM HOME...
THIS TIME I MANAGED TO MAKE IT HOME BEFORE DAWN. AND THIS TIME I DIDN'T GO TO THE ISLAND FOR THE WORKS. THIS TIME I CAME HOME TO MY WIFE. AND TO MY LIFE...
10

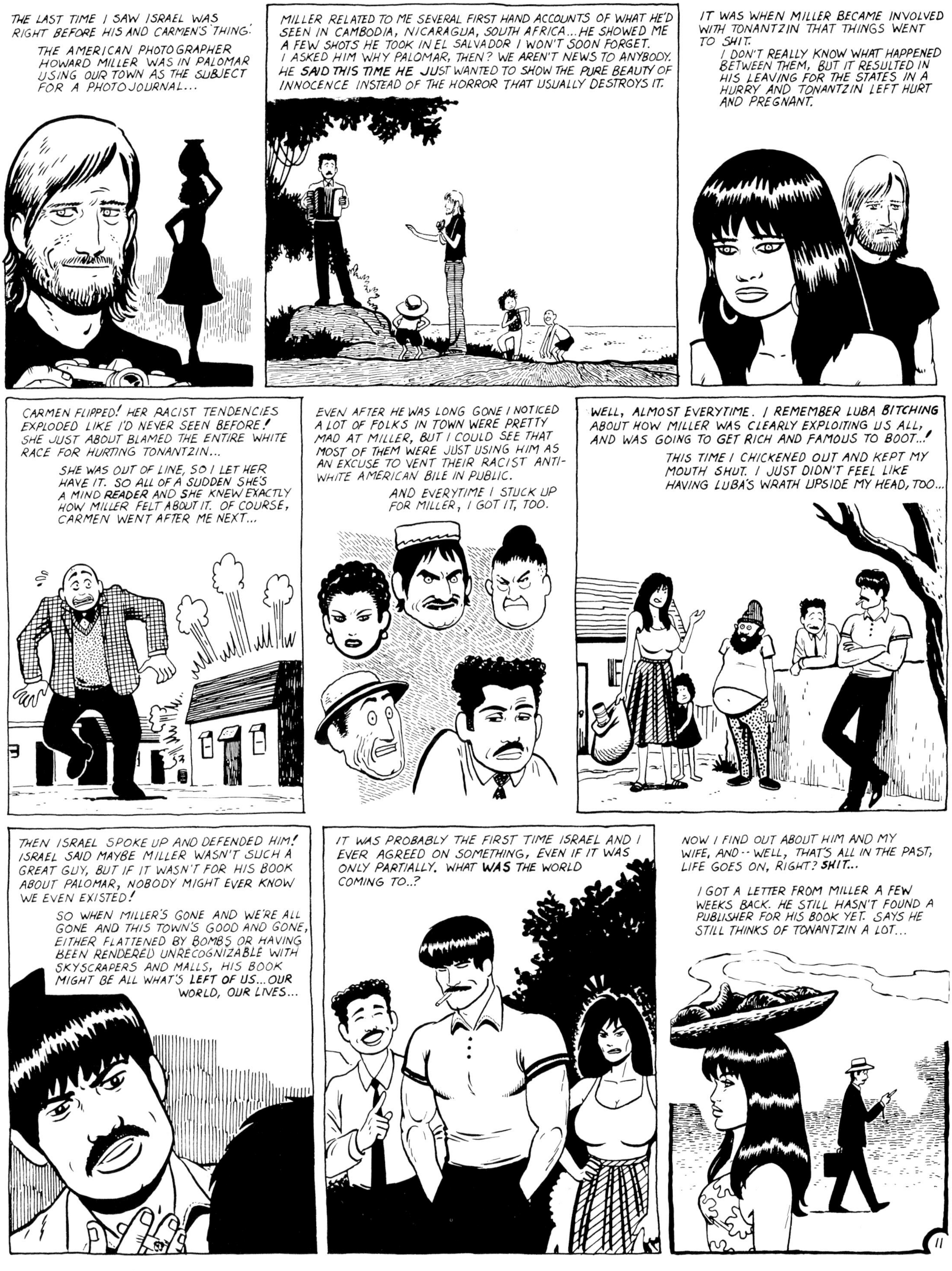
THE LAST TIME I SAW ISRAEL WAS RIGHT BEFORE HIS AND CARMEN'S THING.
THE AMERICAN PHOTOGRAPHER HOWARD MILLER WAS IN PALOMAR USING OUR TOWN AS THE SUBJECT FOR A PHOTOJOURNAL...
MILLER RELATED TO ME SEVERAL FIRST HAND ACCOUNTS OF WHAT HE'D SEEN IN CAMBODIA, NICARAGUA, SOUTH AFRICA... HE SHOWED ME A FEW SHOTS HE TOOK IN EL SALVADOR I WON'T SOON FORGET. I ASKED HIM WHY PALOMAR, THEN? WE AREN'T NEWS TO ANYBODY. HE SAID THIS TIME HE JUST WANTED TO SHOW THE PURE BEAUTY OF INNOCENCE INSTEAD OF THE HORROR THAT USUALLY DESTROYS IT.
IT WAS WHEN MILLER BECAME INVOLVED WITH TONANTZIN THAT THINGS WENT TO SHIT.
I DON'T REALLY KNOW WHAT HAPPENED BETWEEN THEM, BUT IT RESULTED IN HIS LEAVING FOR THE STATES IN A HURRY AND TONANTZIN LEFT HURT AND PREGNANT.
CARMEN FLIPPED! HER RACIST TENDENCIES EXPLODED LIKE I'D NEVER SEEN BEFORE! SHE JUST ABOUT BLAMED THE ENTIRE WHITE RACE FOR HURTING TONANTZIN...
SHE WAS OUT OF LINE, SO I LET HER HAVE IT. SO ALL OF A SUDDEN SHE'S A MIND READER AND SHE KNEW EXACTLY HOW MILLER FELT ABOUT IT. OF COURSE, CARMEN WENT AFTER ME NEXT...
EVEN AFTER HE WAS LONG GONE I NOTICED A LOT OF FOLKS IN TOWN WERE PRETTY MAD AT MILLER, BUT I COULD SEE THAT MOST OF THEM WERE JUST USING HIM AS AN EXCUSE TO VENT THEIR RACIST ANTI-WHITE AMERICAN BILE IN PUBLIC.
AND EVERYTIME I STUCK UP FOR MILLER, I GOT IT, TOO.
WELL, ALMOST EVERYTIME. I REMEMBER LUBA BITCHING ABOUT HOW MILLER WAS CLEARLY EXPLOITING US ALL, AND WAS GOING TO GET RICH AND FAMOUS TO BOOT...!
THIS TIME I CHICKENED OUT AND KEPT MY MOUTH SHUT. I JUST DIDN'T FEEL LIKE HAVING LUBA'S WRATH UPSIDE MY HEAD, TOO...
THEN ISRAEL SPOKE UP AND DEFENDED HIM! ISRAEL SAID MAYBE MILLER WASN'T SUCH A GREAT GUY, BUT IF IT WASN'T FOR HIS BOOK ABOUT PALOMAR, NOBODY MIGHT EVER KNOW WE EVEN EXISTED!
SO WHEN MILLER'S GONE AND WE'RE ALL GONE AND THIS TOWN'S GOOD AND GONE, EITHER FLATTENED BY BOMBS OR HAVING BEEN RENDERED UNRECOGNIZABLE WITH SKYSCRAPERS AND MALLS, HIS BOOK MIGHT BE ALL WHAT'S LEFT OF US... OUR WORLD, OUR LIVES...
IT WAS PROBABLY THE FIRST TIME ISRAEL AND I EVER AGREED ON SOMETHING, EVEN IF IT WAS ONLY PARTIALLY. WHAT WAS THE WORLD COMING TO..?
NOW I FIND OUT ABOUT HIM AND MY WIFE, AND -- WELL, THAT'S ALL IN THE PAST, LIFE GOES ON, RIGHT? SHIT...
I GOT A LETTER FROM MILLER A FEW WEEKS BACK. HE STILL HASN'T FOUND A PUBLISHER FOR HIS BOOK YET. SAYS HE STILL THINKS OF TONANTZIN A LOT...
11

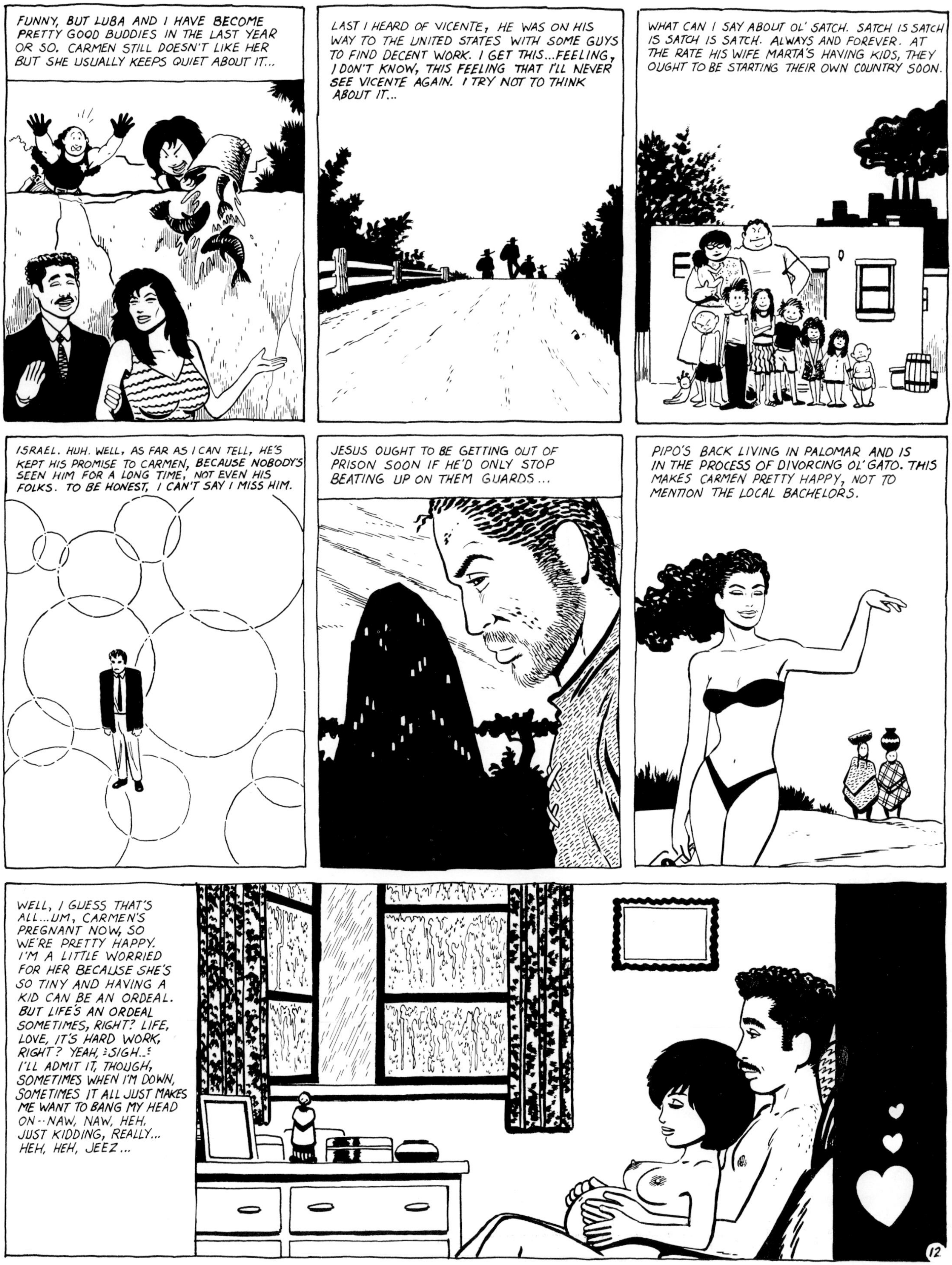
FUNNY, BUT LUBA AND I HAVE BECOME PRETTY GOOD BUDDIES IN THE LAST YEAR OR SO. CARMEN STILL DOESN'T LIKE HER BUT SHE USUALLY KEEPS QUIET ABOUT IT...
LAST I HEARD OF VICENTE, HE WAS ON HIS WAY TO THE UNITED STATES WITH SOME GUYS TO FIND DECENT WORK. I GET THIS...FEELING, I DON'T KNOW, THIS FEELING THAT I'LL NEVER SEE VICENTE AGAIN. I TRY NOT TO THINK ABOUT IT...
WHAT CAN I SAY ABOUT OL' SATCH. SATCH IS SATCH IS SATCH IS SATCH. ALWAYS AND FOREVER. AT THE RATE HIS WIFE MARTA'S HAVING KIDS, THEY OUGHT TO BE STARTING THEIR OWN COUNTRY SOON.
ISRAEL. HUH. WELL, AS FAR AS I CAN TELL, HE'S KEPT HIS PROMISE TO CARMEN, BECAUSE NOBODY'S SEEN HIM FOR A LONG TIME, NOT EVEN HIS FOLKS. TO BE HONEST, I CAN'T SAY I MISS HIM.
JESUS OUGHT TO BE GETTING OUT OF PRISON SOON IF HE'D ONLY STOP BEATING UP ON THEM GUARDS...
PIPO'S BACK LIVING IN PALOMAR AND IS IN THE PROCESS OF DIVORCING OL' GATO. THIS MAKES CARMEN PRETTY HAPPY, NOT TO MENTION THE LOCAL BACHELORS.
WELL, I GUESS THAT'S ALL...UM, CARMEN'S PREGNANT NOW, SO WE'RE PRETTY HAPPY. I'M A LITTLE WORRIED FOR HER BECAUSE SHE'S SO TINY AND HAVING A KID CAN BE AN ORDEAL. BUT LIFE'S AN ORDEAL SOMETIMES, RIGHT? LIFE, LOVE, IT'S HARD WORK, RIGHT? YEAH, ≡SIGH..≡ I'LL ADMIT IT, THOUGH, SOMETIMES WHEN I'M DOWN, SOMETIMES IT ALL JUST MAKES ME WANT TO BANG MY HEAD ON--NAW, NAW, HEH, JUST KIDDING, REALLY... HEH, HEH, JEEZ...
12

cover gal

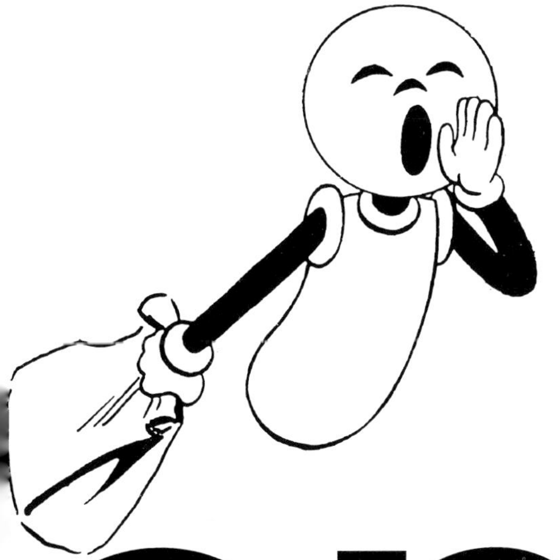

ery

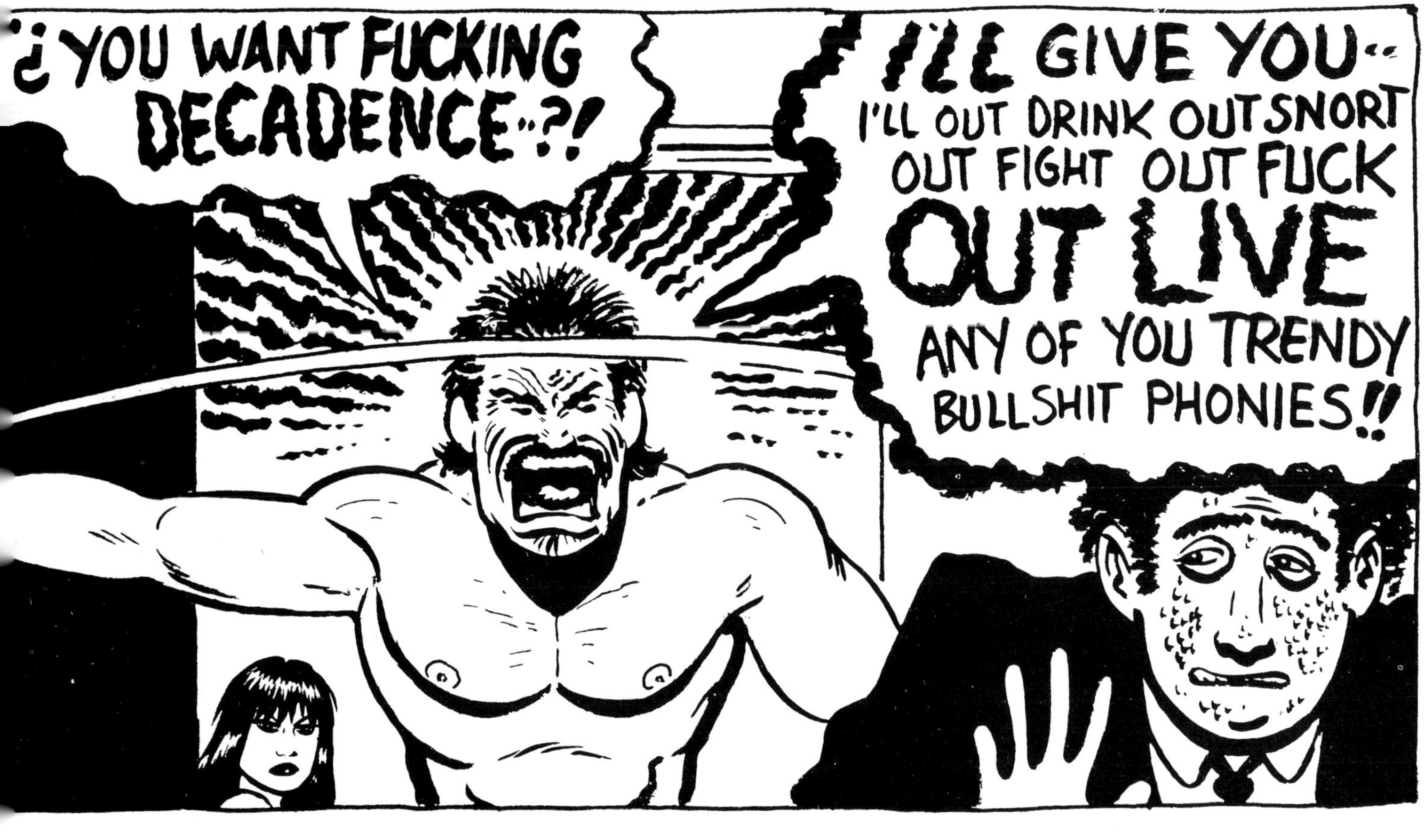
¿YOU WANT FUCKING DECADENCE..?!
I'LL GIVE YOU.. I'LL OUT DRINK OUT SNORT OUT FIGHT OUT FUCK OUT LIVE ANY OF YOU TRENDY BULLSHIT PHONIES!!

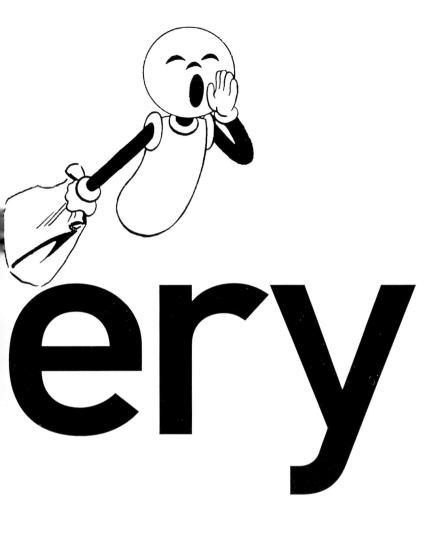

Love and Rockets

Recommended for mature readers

No. 17 ■ $2.25
$3.15 in Canada

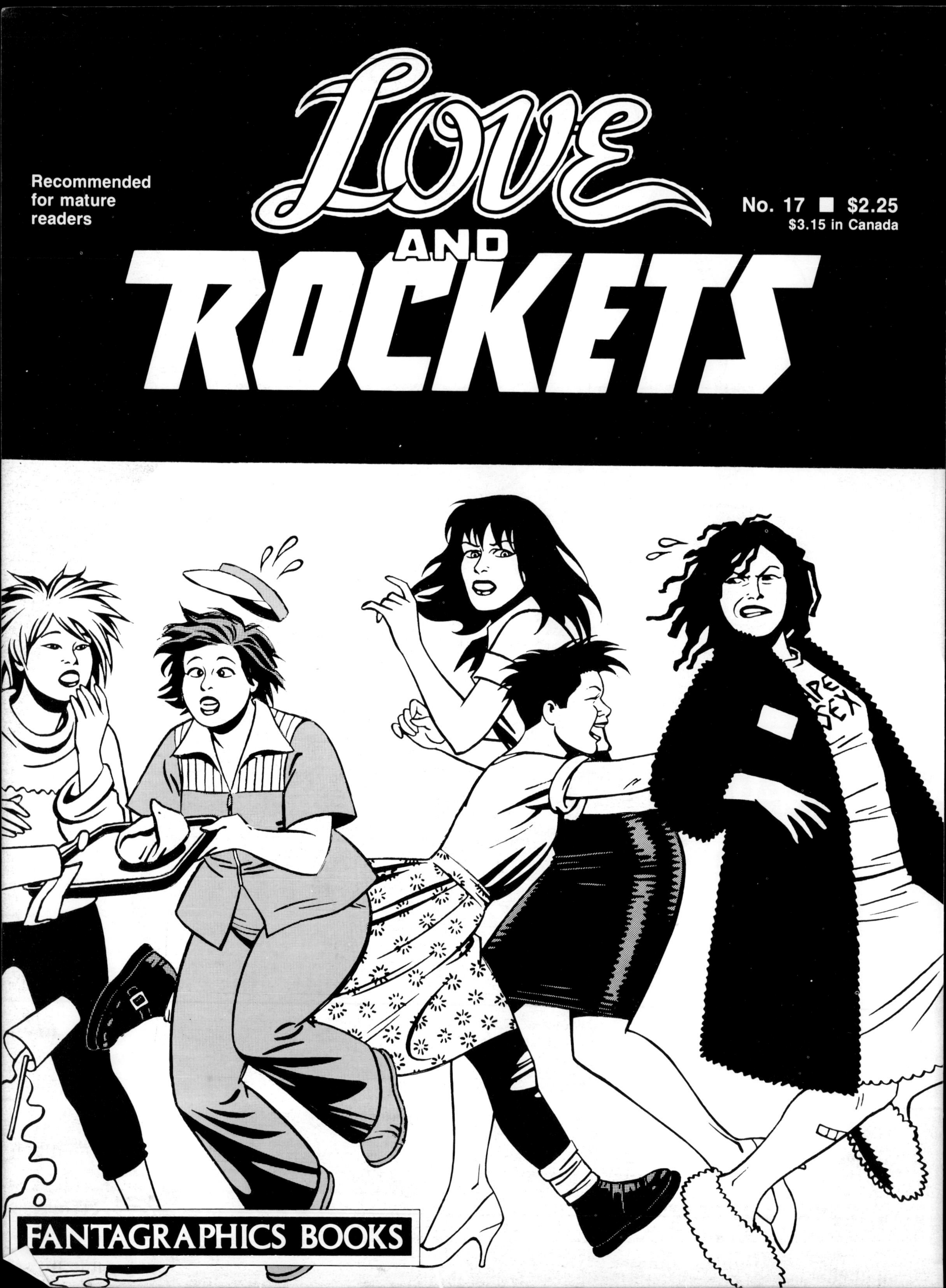

FANTAGRAPHICS BOOKS

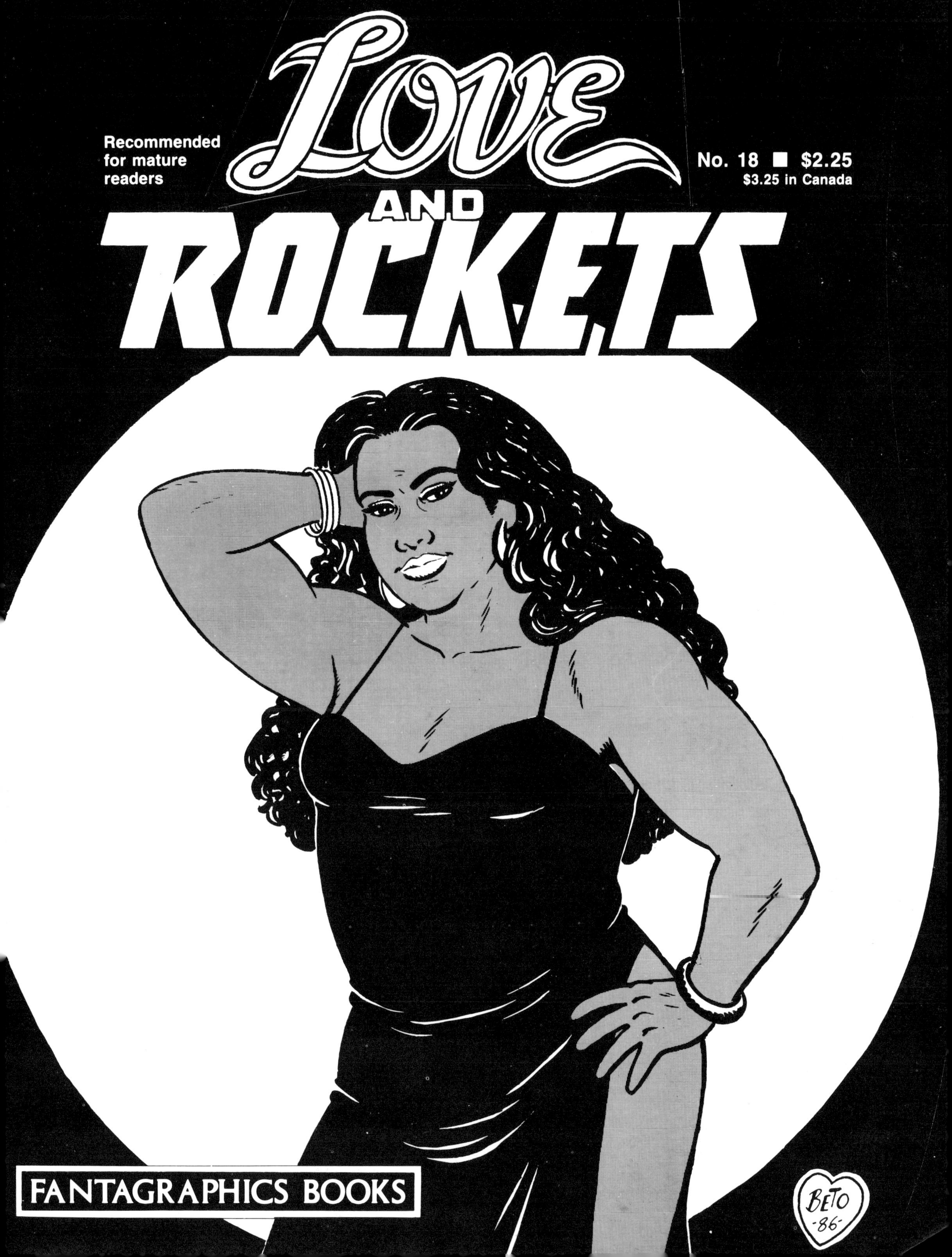
Recommended for mature readers
LOVE AND ROCKETS
No. 18 ■ $2.25
$3.25 in Canada
FANTAGRAPHICS BOOKS
BETO -86-

No. 19 ■$2.25
$3.15 in Canada

LOVE AND ROCKETS

Recommended for mature readers

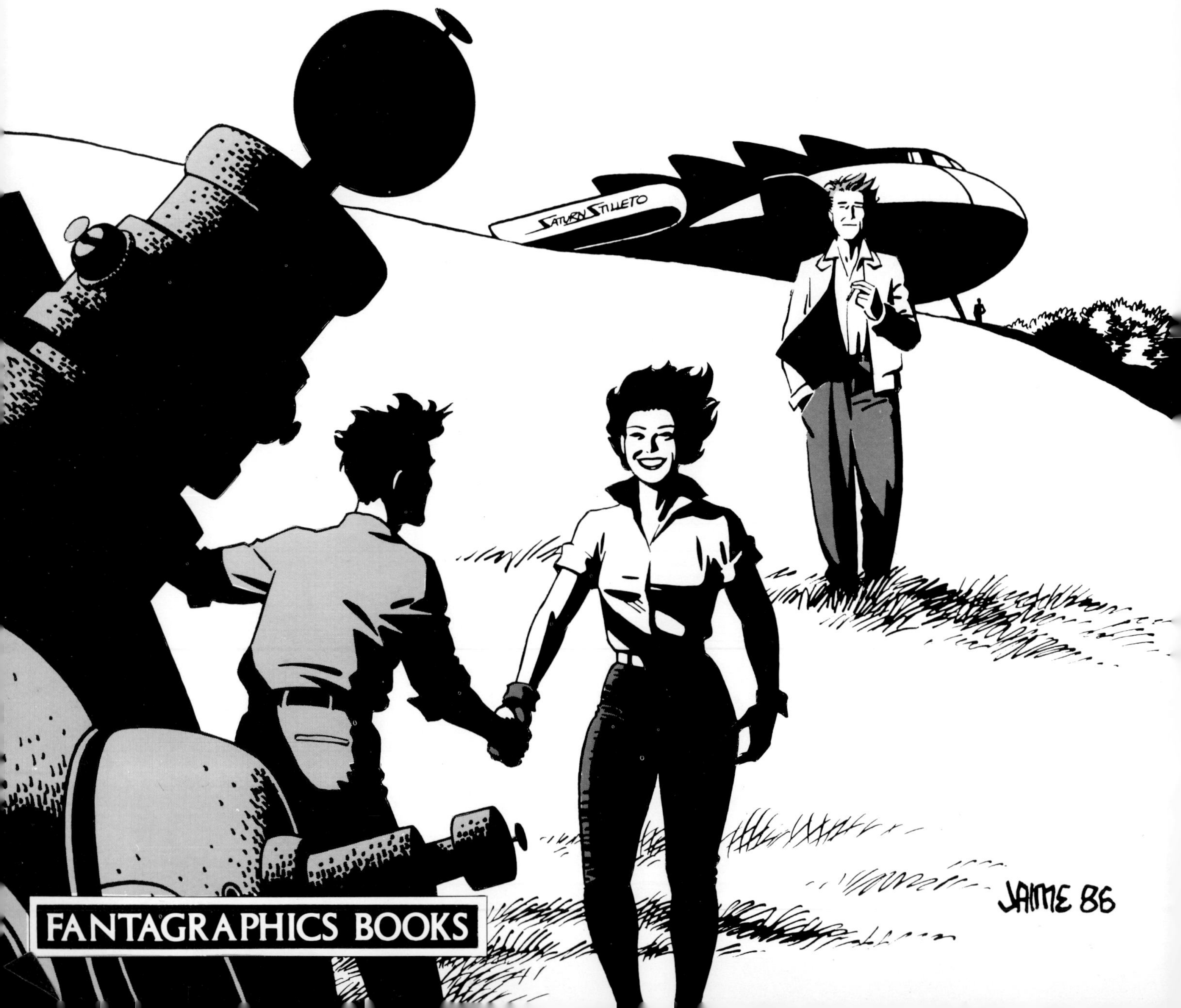
SATURN STILLETO
JAIME 86

FANTAGRAPHICS BOOKS

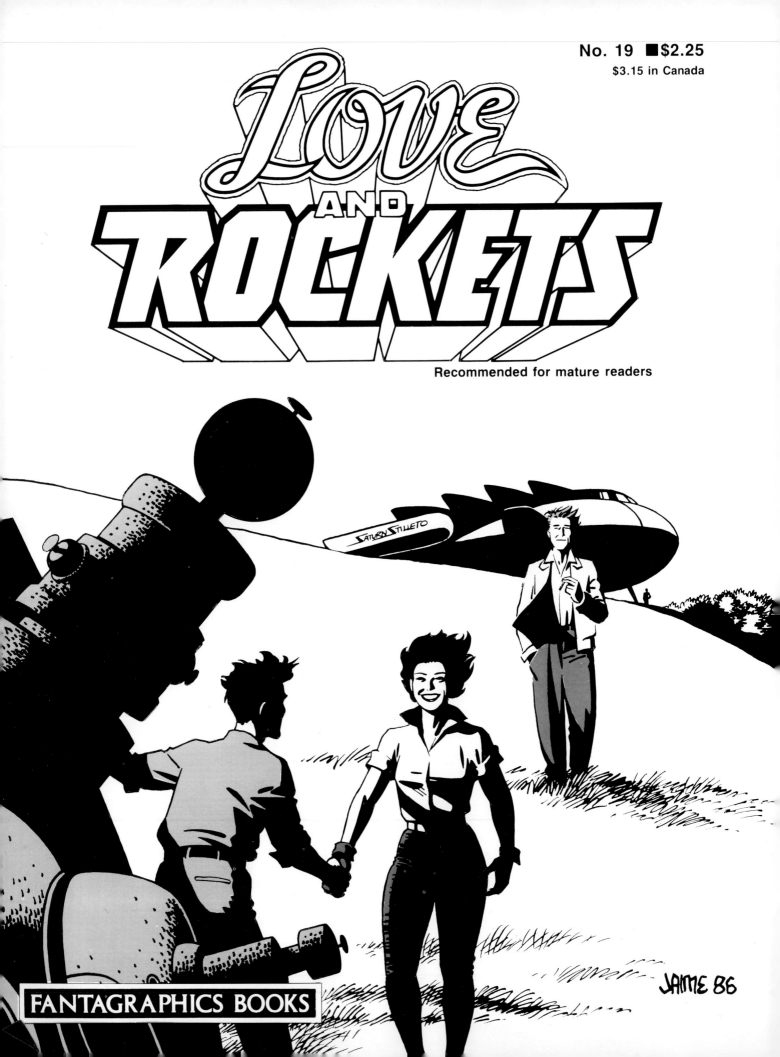

Also available from
Fantagraphics Books:

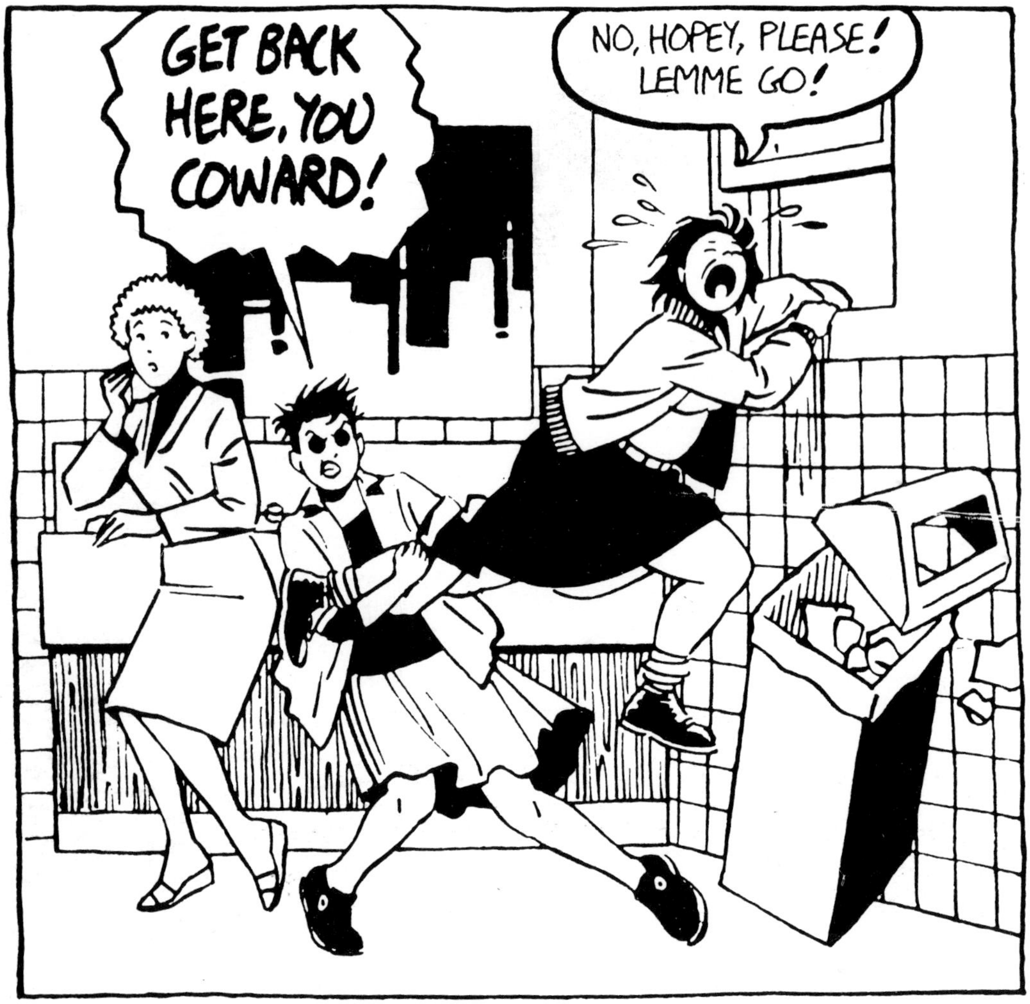

GET BACK HERE, YOU COWARD!
NO, HOPEY, PLEASE! LEMME GO!

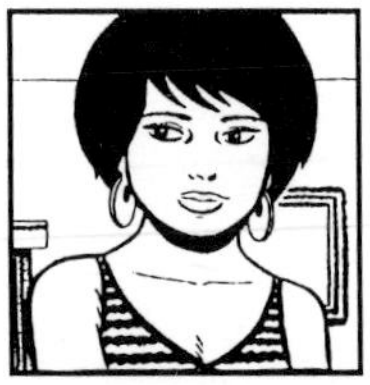